PHILANTHROPY AND THE CONSTRUCTION OF VICTORIAN WOMEN'S CITIZENSHIP

Philanthropy and the Construction of Victorian Women's Citizenship

Lady Frederick Cavendish and Miss Emma Cons

ANDREA GEDDES POOLE

UNIVERSITY OF TORONTO PRESS
Toronto Buffalo London

Toronto Buffalo London
www.utppublishing.com

ISBN 978-1-4426-4231-7

Library and Archives Canada Cataloguing in Publication

Geddes Poole, Andrea, 1959–, author
Philanthropy and the construction of Victorian women's citizenship : Lady Frederick Cavendish and Miss Emma Cons / Andrea Geddes Poole.

Includes bibliographical references and index.
ISBN 978-1-4426-4231-7 (bound)

1. Cavendish, Lucy Caroline Lyttelton, Lady, 1841–1925. 2. Cons, Emma, 1838–1912. 3. Women in charitable work – Great Britain – History – 19th century. 4. Women – Great Britain – Social conditions – 19th century. 5. Citizenship – Social aspects – Great Britain – History – 19th century. 6. Social reformers – Great Britain – Biography. 7. Women philanthropists – Great Britain – Biography. I. Title.

HV541.G43 2014 361.7092'52094209034 C2013-906039-1

This book has been published with the help of a grant from the Canadian Federation for the Humanities and Social Sciences, through the Awards to Scholarly Publications Program, using funds provided by the Social Sciences and Humanities Research Council of Canada.

University of Toronto Press acknowledges the financial assistance to its publishing program of the Canada Council for the Arts and the Ontario Arts Council.

Canada Council for the Arts
Conseil des Arts du Canada

University of Toronto Press acknowledges the financial support of the Government of Canada through the Canada Book Fund for its publishing activities.

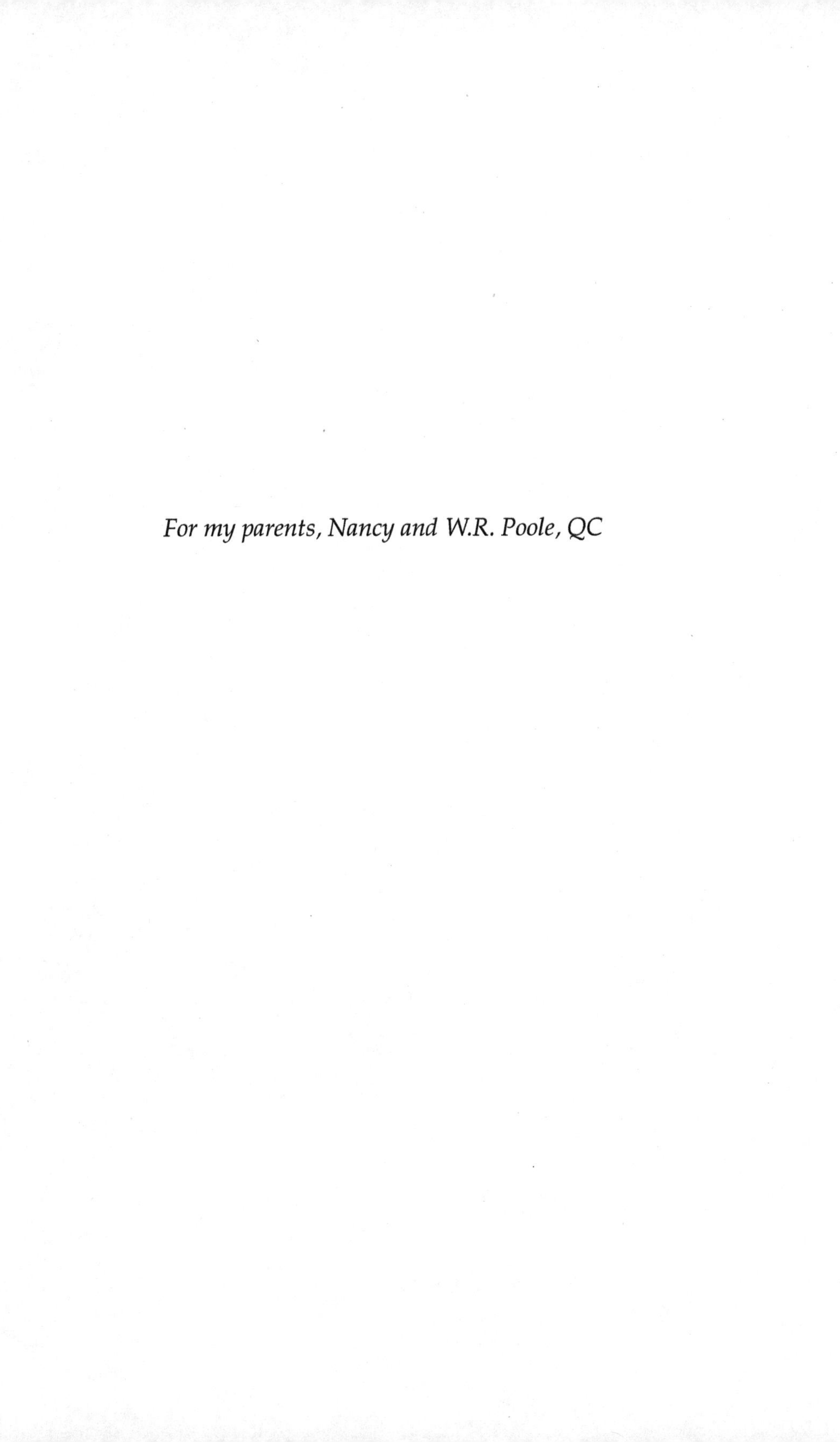

For my parents, Nancy and W.R. Poole, QC

Contents

Illustrations

Acknowledgments

There are many persons who have contributed to the building of this book. First I should like to thank Neville Masterman for allowing me to use his mother's unpublished biography of her godmother, Lucy Cavendish. In the same way I should also like to thank Viscount Cobham for his kind permission to use parts of the Lyttelton family correspondence and for his kind hospitality at Hagley.

I should particularly like to thank the Social Sciences and Humanities Research Council of Canada for the grant which allowed me to travel to and from the UK to conduct the research for this book.

An earlier version of chapter 5 appeared as "Citizens of Morley College" in the *Journal of British Studies* 50, no. 4 (October 2011): 840–62.

The staff of the White Ribbon Association were most helpful in granting me access to the archives of the British Women's Temperance Society. In the same way the staff at the library at Lambeth Palace were unfailingly helpful, as were the archivists at the Theatre Collection at the University of Bristol, the Centre for Kentish Studies, Lucy Cavendish College Cambridge, the London School of Economics, and the University of Birmingham.

As always, many helpful comments have smoothed some of the rougher stages of this manuscript. Frank Prochaska and Peter Mandler were particularly astute and constructive in asking pertinent questions and challenging certain assumptions I made as this manuscript found its feet. Richard Ratzlaff at the University of Toronto Press was exceedingly helpful and supportive.

Finally, I should like to thank my husband, Michael Robinson, without whose unflagging support this book simply would not have seen the light of day. I should like to single out for special commendation my daughter, Caroline Laurier Geddes Poole. Wise, generous, and forgiving in ways that stand beyond her thirteen years, she continually lifted my spirits when they flagged and lent me her instinctive sense of mature proportion.

PHILANTHROPY AND THE CONSTRUCTION OF VICTORIAN WOMEN'S CITIZENSHIP

Introduction

In 1893 the philanthropist Baroness Angela Burdett-Coutts assembled a comprehensive report calculating the extent and the variety of British women's work in charitable endeavours. One of the conclusions she reached was that well over half a million women in Britain were "occupied continuously and more or less professionally" working with charities and that more than twenty thousand were able to financially support themselves by such work.[1] Beyond that lay the thousands of other women who worked for pay with charities on a part-time basis and beyond even them stood the hundreds of thousands – if not millions – of women who volunteered their time on a regular basis. This was a mighty army of women. Charitable work was a boon to Victorian women in many ways. Socially sanctioned, even encouraged, philanthropy was an honourable field in which women could exercise their altruistic inclinations and simultaneously create a life and identity outside the home. Through their work with charitable organizations, women acquired organizational training and increased their sense of purpose and confidence in their administrative abilities; these skills and attitudes were often deployed to secure future, broader engagement in the public sphere.[2]

But philanthropy did a great deal more than teach Victorian women leadership skills or provide them with an occupation apart from their domestic obligations. Philanthropic work, particularly in cities and large towns, was usually conducted by volunteer committees, often very influential ones. These committees, societies, and associations were often highly structured, sometimes developing from particular campaigns into permanent local, and sometimes national, organizations. One noteworthy aspect of the philanthropic world of the last third of the nineteenth century is the presence of many of the same persons working with different organizations, creating a series of interlocking Venn diagrams of overlapping committee membership. The lives of two women deeply involved in many different philanthropic causes – Lucy Cavendish and Emma Cons – provide us with a pair of particularly illustrative case studies showing the network of connections based on philanthropic allegiance, built regardless of sex or class, which so typified the late Victorian world of philanthropy. These two women's stories, however, give us more; they also help us better understand not only how the horizons for Victorian women expanded through their philanthropic work but also how broader societal perceptions of their capacities grew.

In the ordinary course of events, it would have been unlikely that the Hon. Lucy (Lady Frederick) Cavendish would ever have met Miss Emma Cons socially, as they moved in very different circles. Lucy Cavendish was connected to the great and powerful of the Victorian world by both birth and marriage. She was born in 1841 into the landed aristocracy; her father was the fourth Lord Lyttelton and she grew up at the bucolic family seat of Hagley Hall in Worcestershire.[3] Lucy's maternal aunt was married to the political giant William Ewart Gladstone and the two families were close; the Lyttelton children spent a great deal of time at the Gladstones' country seat of Hawarden. But there were many other connections to the world of influence and privilege. Lucy's grandmother was a daughter of the Earl Spencer. As a young woman Lucy Lyttelton had been a maid of honour to Queen Victoria. At twenty-three she married Lord Frederick Cavendish, a younger son of the Duke of Devonshire. One of her brothers became the first Master of Selwyn College, Cambridge, another became chief of the General Staff, yet another was appointed colonial secretary. Her sister married the Bishop of Winchester. Her dear friend Beatrice Lascelles married Frederick Temple, successively Bishop of Exeter and London and, finally, Archbishop of Canterbury. By the time Lucy Cavendish was forty, the year her husband was named chief secretary for Ireland, she occupied a position in the very epicentre of a world of power and influence. Her husband's murder, in Dublin's Phoenix Park shortly after his arrival in 1882 to take up his new position, did not diminish Lucy's position. As a friend commented in her diary after tea with Lucy Cavendish fourteen years later: "she lives from her relationships so at the centre of things."[4]

Emma Cons's life was quite different. Her father, Frederick, was a well-respected crafter of ivory keys and piano cases, and she was born in 1838 and brought up in the centre of London. She had a distinctly artistic bent but, having to earn a living, she worked first as an engraver of watch cases and subsequently as a painter of stained glass – a good one, whose work was much esteemed and encouraged by the art critic and social reformer John Ruskin. It was his recommendation that resulted in her being commissioned to work on the restoration of the windows of Merton College's chapel. She was also, however, seriously interested in social reform and worked with Octavia Hill, first as a rent collector (a paid one, not a volunteer, for she needed to support herself) and later as a manager of Hill's housing projects organized for the working poor. Emma Cons's life until she was well into her forties, while utterly respectable, was not the least bit glamorous, nor did her circle of connections encompass many wealthy or influential friends.

Nevertheless, the affinities between Emma Cons and Lucy Cavendish were in many ways far greater and more binding than were their differences. It is true that Emma virtually lived for art. An artist herself, she saw colour as a divine creation and could not pass a wall without wanting to decorate it in some way.[5] Lucy did not have much time for art; her drawing room, ornamented with distinctly bad copies in oil of famous pictures, "was the ugliest in London," and though she lived within a five-minute walk of the National Gallery, she set foot in it exactly once.[6] Emma was a dedicated suffragist whereas Lucy thought women were not "up to" a parliamentary vote.[7] And yet, as the *Old Vic Magazine* put it at Lucy Cavendish's death, "when she stood shoulder to shoulder with Emma Cons in putting up the good fight," these two women were, in a thousand ways, two sides of single, philanthropic, and public-spirited coin.[8] This book uses the lives of these two women to cast light on the way Victorian women were able to negotiate different paths of public service, often transcending barriers of both class and gender. Their lives also serve as complicating and complementary stories, representative in many ways and utterly idiosyncratic in others. These women, originating from very different points on the English social landscape, came together time and again between 1880 and 1912 to establish or further many good causes. Together, they established a theatre as a locally popular hub of culture (and as a reasonable alternative to the pub) in a grimy and dismal working-class neighbourhood of South London; they both fought for women's right to serve on county councils; together they founded Lambeth's Morley College as a place where both working men and women could transcend educational class barriers, not simply train to be better workers. They also had philanthropic – and in Emma Cons's case, political – careers independently of each other. But this study attempts to do more than simply explore two interesting and productively intersecting lives. It uses the careers of Lucy Cavendish and Emma Cons and certain of the organizations with which they worked as examples of how women could grow through their philanthropic work and how they were able to organize, deploy, and steer circles of influential supporters to address the needs of the poor and helpless. Time and again, as one campaign would reach maturity, many of the same men and women would form into a new association to address a different cause. This study, as it examines many of the organizations and campaigns which Lucy Cavendish and Emma Cons either established or involved themselves in, also shows how late Victorian women were able to use philanthropic enterprises to affect the broader debate on public policy, and, in the process, construct new identities as citizens.

Scholarship on Victorian women's philanthropic activity has sparked a lively discussion among historians as to whether Victorian women were able to rise to leadership roles within charities. Some argue that women were able to play prominent roles both in specific charities and in broader philanthropic campaigns.[9] Others view women's work in charities as being entirely subordinated to that of men or see women as able to assume leadership positions only when entirely committed to careers in philanthropies of their own construction, in the manner of, for example, Octavia Hill.[10] The philanthropic careers of Lucy Cavendish and Emma Cons go directly to this debate. Each, in its own way, is an excellent example of how women could acquire both skills and confidence through philanthropic work and grow into positions of authority both in national campaigns and within organizations of their own founding. Lucy Cavendish was, from an early age, active in the sort of charity work expected of women of her class. In her twenties she visited various charitable institutions for the poor and the infirm with her aunt, Mrs (Catherine) Gladstone. Lucy helped her brother-in-law, John Talbot, MP for Kent West, who had established a local penitentiary laundry for young girls reclaimed from prostitution. She became a workhouse lady visitor. And through her work she grew. A shy, self-effacing young woman when she began to accompany her aunt on visitations, by her forties Lucy Cavendish was chairing meetings and negotiating staff salaries and was much in demand as a speaker on various causes, often making two speeches a day, in different counties. By her early sixties, her reputation as a leader in philanthropy preceded her.

Emma Cons's philanthropic career took a similar trajectory. As a young woman she managed several of Octavia Hill's properties as a live-in general manager, organizing the maintenance, enrolling volunteer workers, and keeping the accounts. Most important, she learned how to cultivate and deploy the wealthy and influential men and women who were seriously interested in addressing the problems of the urban poor. By the time she turned forty-one, in 1879, she had gathered unto herself a circle of supporters of her own and had focused her attention on South London. She established the South London Dwellings Company, buying properties in Lambeth which she transformed into model worker housing according to her own vision. Emma Cons observed that the working poor of Lambeth had virtually no entertainment other than the pub. When in 1881 the lease came up on the disreputable and shabby Royal Victoria Theatre in the Waterloo Road, she and the group of supporters she had organized established a charitable trust to lease it and turn the old theatre into a "temperance coffee music hall" providing first-rate entertainment: the Royal Victoria Coffee Music Hall. It was here that the two women met when the recently widowed Lucy Cavendish became one of the first governors of the "Old Vic." When Emma Cons decided to expand the Old Vic's Friday night "penny science lectures" into proper classes, run out of the rehearsal rooms, Lucy Cavendish helped her develop what became, in 1889, Morley College for Working Men and Women (named after the wealthy philanthropist Samuel Morley, a great supporter of Emma Cons's enterprises). Morley College was devoted to giving the working men and women of Lambeth a proper education: not more technical skills, but history, literature, science, politics, art, music, the classics – all the liberal arts. For the next thirty years, while Lucy effectively led the boards of governors of the Old Vic and Morley College, Emma served as the managing director. When, at the age of fifty-two, she was asked to stand for election as London's first woman alderman, it was her experience and expertise in working with the poor that was both proffered and unhesitatingly accepted as her qualification.

The philanthropic careers of these women were broad as well as deep. Examining the variety of organizations and charities with which they worked opens for critical examination new causes, campaigns, and endeavours beyond care for the poor. Lucy Cavendish, in addition to her work with young prostitutes or with the Old Vic and Morley College, was a pioneer of women's education, taking her father's seat on the Girls Public Day School Trust and serving as president of the

Yorkshire Ladies Council of Education. For her understanding of the issues surrounding women and education and as a result of her service thereto, she was the first woman placed on a Royal Commission (the 1894 Bryce Commission on Education) and the first person awarded a doctorate *honoris causa* by the University of Leeds. It is for these reasons also that Lucy Cavendish College at Cambridge University (established to give mature women an opportunity at a university education) was named for her.

Similarly, Emma Cons ran more than the Old Vic and Morley College; the South London Dwellings Company, which she ran from her offices in Surrey Lodge, provided model housing for approximately one thousand of the working poor of Lambeth.[11] She helped found the Swanley Horticultural College for Women and a home for "simple-minded" girls at Bodmin. She was the first woman to sit as an alderman on London's first County Council, in 1889. Both women were also deeply committed to temperance and supported the Church of England Temperance Society's Women's Union, each holding a belief that alcohol was a pernicious element in the lives of the working poor. Both were adamant that women were vital to local government and both served on the executive of the Women's Local Government Society. Simply measuring the scope of the work of these two women extends into many corners of late Victorian life. Examining the careers of Lucy Cavendish and Emma Cons not only shows how women of their day were able to command national charities, or how they could refashion charity into public service, but also highlights how important was the mutual support of the interconnected networks of women and men, engaged in different philanthropic endeavours but willing to reach across and, once more, be enlisted to further yet another good cause.

This study is situated within a rich context of studies and debates addressing questions concerning philanthropy and nineteenth-century women from a variety of perspectives. It also fills important gaps in the literature. Insufficient attention has been paid to the lives of these two women. The most detailed account of Emma Cons's life is contained in the small biographical sketch affectionately and uncritically written by her niece, Lilian Baylis, and is included as a separate coda in the history of the Old Vic written by the actress, dramatist, and suffragette Cicely Hamilton, *The Old Vic* (1926). Cons also has a solid entry in the Dictionary of National Biography and is featured in Elizabeth Schafer's 2006 biography of Lilian Baylis; her political work is mentioned in the accounts of the first women on the London County Council by Patricia

Hollis, *Ladies Elect* (1987), and in Jonathan Schneer's "Politics and Feminism" (1991).[12] The numerous histories of the Old Vic are useful but generally lack context and do not focus much on the temperance, managerial, and generally non-artistic aspects of the theatre between 1880 and 1914. George Rowell's *The Old Vic Theatre: A History* (1993) is by far the most analytical and comprehensive, particularly on the early years.[13] The institutional history of Morley College, Denis Richards's *Offspring of the Vic: A History of Morley College* (1958), includes a good general account of what is known of Cons's life, but neither Richards, Rowell, Hamilton, nor those historians who examine Cons's political life show the whole woman or speak to the great drivers of her life: temperance and her philanthropic work outside the context of the Old Vic or Morley College.[14]

Even less attention has been paid to Lucy Cavendish, although she does share an entry in the Dictionary of National Biography with her husband. This, however, mentions only that she was involved in philanthropic work without providing any detail. The same is true of *Lord Lyttelton's Daughters*, a work by Sheila Fletcher on the early years of Lucy and her sisters.[15] This book is largely based on Lucy Cavendish's diaries and, unfortunately, trails off after Lord Frederick's assassination in 1882, the very point at which his widow ventured out into the world of good works. A similar perspective affects *The Lytteltons: A Family Chronicle of the Nineteenth Century* (1975), a biography of the Lyttelton family written by a relative, Betty Askwith.[16] Although a more thorough biography of Lucy Cavendish was written in the 1950s by her niece, namesake, and goddaughter, Lucy Masterman, it was never published and remains in the archives of Lucy Cavendish College, Cambridge. Clearly, although some attention has been paid to these two women, many of the most interesting and revealing aspects of their lives have been overlooked.

A vigorous, continuing debate among historians concerns the extent to which Victorian (and to a lesser extent, Edwardian) women embraced or acquiesced in a gendered separation of society into separate spheres. One school of thought established a view of middle-class Victorian families during the industrializing first half of the nineteenth century as increasingly taking up a cult of domesticity, encapsulated in the bifurcating of society into private (women's) and public (men's) spheres.[17] This view of how nineteenth-century men and women organized their world, although attuned to the irregular and frequently ill-defined borders between the spheres and the exceptions and contradictions of complicated lives, nonetheless established the idea that the dominant discourse of nineteenth-century social structure, certainly for the middle class, lay in a binary of separate spheres.[18] However, the idea of Victorian women acquiescing in their confinement to a domestic life and to their exclusion from a public sphere has been aggressively challenged.[19] The lives and work of Lucy Cavendish and Emma Cons show two women from very different parts of British society who firmly and publicly took positions on matters of policy, gathering supporters as they went. Moreover, we can see, in the campaigning work of their women colleagues, connected to each other through various interlinked philanthropic organizations, more broadly seated evidence that women of the mid- and late nineteenth century, even without votes, were active elements in the Victorian public sphere.

But the issue of separate spheres has further complexities. Elaine Chalus, Amanda Foreman, and Linda Colley, among others, have argued that late eighteenth-century aristocratic women asserted and retained a presence in public, political life which did not necessarily contract after the Napoleonic wars. K.D. Reynolds similarly maintains that for aristocratic women, public political life was quite lively well into the nineteenth century.[20] Reynolds argues that, mid-nineteenth century, there may well have been separate spheres for middle-class women (who lacked the standing to create independent lives for themselves – hence the attractions of charity work, which could respectably, even virtuously, draw them out of their domesticity), however, for their aristocratic counterparts, who had their own authority and who often acted as political agents in their own right, their homes were far from private spaces cut off from public life. Indeed, Reynolds asserts, the public sphere often intruded directly into the very drawing rooms of aristocratic women. We can see exactly this pattern not only in the life of Lucy Cavendish but also in the activities of her aristocratic colleagues in her various charitable activities. Since there has been little work on aristocratic women who undertook philanthropy in an urban setting (away from bounty for their rural tenants), Lucy Cavendish's endeavours, apart from her work with Emma Cons, show how one aristocratic woman functioned in an urban environment, how she viewed her authority, understood her ability to navigate society, and saw public and private spheres, and further our sense of her view (and society's view) of her proper place in the world.

Women's philanthropic activities also contributed directly towards creating, by the 1880s, a distinct women's public sphere. Within it, women could engage with other women about public policy regarding health and welfare, the optimum kind of education for girls or for adult women, suffrage, and professional opportunities for women. A separate women's public sphere, however, did not bar women from contributing to the broader Victorian deliberation on the obligations of the state versus the obligations of the individual. Through this network of philanthropic organizations, women advertised for volunteers and organized, lobbied, and agitated for recognition, funding, and change. Women, particularly civically engaged women, might not have been able to vote for their members of Parliament, but they could assemble petitions, write letters to the editor, address MPs' committees, royal commissions, and journalists, and speak on public platforms; in all the ways men attempted to move the discussion of social reform forwards, so too did this army of philanthropic women. In other words, women involved in the business of social welfare staked out their own territory of engagement in shaping public policy through the efflorescence, in the latter third of the nineteenth century, of charities, many of which were founded, directed, and staffed entirely by women. The speeches, writings, and philanthropic activities of Lucy Cavendish and Emma Cons and the campaigns undertaken by the organizations with which they were affiliated show women speaking to women about how to affect matters of significant public policy.

The progression of thought about the citizenship of British women during this period has also evolved into a rich discussion. Jane Rendall, in her examination of the alliances British women forged with radical/liberal political men as a strategy towards inclusion within the Second Reform Bill, observed that citizenship in late Victorian and Edwardian Britain was a deeply gendered matter.[21] Both Rendall and Anna Clark, in her discussion of the impact of successive Reform Acts, see a solidifying of citizenship as a male preserve over the course of the nineteenth century – a capacity synonymous with voting rights.[22] Conversely, Julia Parker has examined how Arnold Toynbee, T.H. Green, John Ruskin, William Morris, and R.H. Tawney all, in their writings, linked citizenship to public service, a view increasingly embraced by a variety of women.[23] A Victorian understanding of citizenship, borrowed from the ancient Greek tradition of a civic republic and emphasizing the virtues of participation in the public sphere, served as the ideal foundation for both Emma's and Lucy's growing sense of the connection between their philanthropic work and their citizenship.[24] Certainly militant suffragettes instinctively made the connection between citizenship and public service – an understanding embraced by a broader segment of the female population, increasingly conscious of their place as citizens during and after the First World War.[25] But Lucy Cavendish and Emma Cons saw themselves as citizens decades before that. Emma, a fierce proponent of votes for women, was speaking very clearly about her citizenly obligations and duties and her right to vote in the early 1880s. But this association was also made by women who were not suffragettes. Lucy did not support parliamentary votes for women, yet by 1885 she clearly saw herself as a citizen.[26] This study thus amplifies prior inquiries concerning women's citizenship and public duty not only by explicitly linking them to the equally fruitful line of scholarship concerned with nineteenth-century women's charitable works but also by showing how the development of these two women's understanding of their citizenship reflects the self-perception of Victorian women, linked through public service, changing over the latter third of the century.

But, as with the question of aristocratic women and the public sphere, this study looks at change rather than continuity in perceptions from the mid-nineteenth to the early twentieth century. Linda Colley, in discussing Hannah More and the women who boycotted sugar in the campaign against the slave trade, observed how women acquired standing to publicly engage on issues of national importance not by asserting their rights as citizens but by invoking moral outrage and conscience as a natural outgrowth of their nature and their sphere: "angels of the nation" as well as angels in the house.[27] This book shows how women restyled this mantle of maternalist moral superiority into a broader sense of female civic consciousness, public service, and citizenship. It will also argue that, following Barbara Bodichon and John Stuart Mill's attempt to include women in the Second Reform Act of 1867, the idea of women as citizens did not languish.[28] Consciously by some, unconsciously by others, the idea of women as citizens was nurtured over the next forty years exactly through women's charitable works. Lucy Cavendish's and Emma Cons's perceptions and works can serve as tangible examples of the connection these two women – and others – made between the worlds of citizenship and philanthropy.

Victorian philanthropy was not all soup kitchens and settlement missions in the East End. The interest of some Victorian philanthropists and social reformers in bringing art and beauty to poorer quarters has received excellent but very focused attention and has also aroused some interesting debates. Ian Fletcher, examining the Kyrle Society for the Diffusion of Beauty among the People, coined the telling phrase "missionary aestheticism" to describe those middle-class reformers who, following the dictates of Ruskin and Morris, went forth into the East End to bring art and beauty to the poor.[29] But Fletcher saw these "missionary aesthetes" less as representative and more as an idiosyncratic fringe group, a view that has been contested by Diana Maltz in her study, *British Aestheticism and the Urban Working Classes 1870–1900* (2006), and Ruth Livesey in *Socialism, Sex and the Culture of Aestheticism* (2006).[30] Maltz's study examines not only the Kyrle Society but also the art exhibitions of the middle-class aesthetic reformers Canon Samuel Barnett and his wife, Henrietta, at Toynbee Hall, extending her work to address the often dubious working-class recipients of all this cultural missionary work.[31] The efforts of Lucy Cavendish, Emma Cons, and the other shareholders of the Coffee Music-Halls Company at the Old Vic to bring great opera to South London's workers show a different side to "missionary aestheticism." We can see, in their work at the Old Vic, aspects of the belief among Victorian social reformers that the redemptive powers of beauty, music, and high culture could lift such men as E.M. Forster's character, the clerk Leonard Bast, into a more fully realized life.[32] But, by focusing not only on reactions of the working poor of Lambeth and Southwark to the introduction of opera into their neighbourhood, but also on how Lucy Cavendish and Emma Cons saw their audiences, we can also see how and why the theatre that became known as the "People's Opera House" and the good works of Canon Barnett at Toynbee Hall were as far apart as chalk and cheese.

This book addresses our two case studies and the networked world of Victorian philanthropy from several different perspectives. The first chapter sets out the framework of Lucy Cavendish's career, examining the philanthropic and political life of one aristocratic Victorian woman at mid-century, asking whether the extent and focus of her involvement in public life was representative of aristocratic women of this period or idiosyncratic. By examining the three Anglican organizations with which Lucy Cavendish involved herself, the second chapter shows how elite and middle-class women were able to organize themselves into circles of mutual assistance, to establish organizations within the Church of England, demonstrating their own variety of citizenly involvement in the greater question of social welfare. This second chapter also shows how elite Anglican women could use societies already extant within the Anglican Church to find their own voice and even, somewhat subversively, assert their own authority from within a hierarchical and patriarchal organization. Focusing on Lucy Cavendish's political and philanthropic life, these first two chapters also pose the question of whether the idea of "separate spheres" applies to aristocratic Victorian women at all.

The third chapter, focusing on Emma Cons's life, examines conduits through which working-class women were able to become part of the Victorian women's army of philanthropy and shows how women – whether part of the elite or not – were able to inject themselves into the broader public debate and affect public policy. This chapter also specifically examines the homosocial aspects of the philanthropic grouping of women Emma Cons established between the model worker housing of the Surrey Buildings and the Royal Victoria Hall – home to both the Old Vic and Morley College – as all three operations were entirely administered and run by women. The chapter on Cons's life shows how a woman from an upper working-class background was able to use her expertise and knowledge to create both a circle of influence and a base of authority.

The fourth chapter addresses the programming of the Old Vic, examining how, although the Coffee Music-Halls Company that Emma Cons formed about her may have initially sought to use opera as a means of simply distracting the working men and women of South London from drink, they soon happily found opera to be the most consistently popular item on the playbill. This chapter also contrasts the welcoming reactions of the Lambeth audience with the almost hostile reception often given concerts organized by Canon and Mrs Samuel Barnett at Toynbee Hall in London's East End. The fifth chapter focuses on Morley College, showing how its curriculum was expressly designed to create citizens, not better-trained workers, asking whether this curriculum was a form of assimilation or emancipation. This work also intends to point to a new way of looking at the space of the Old Vic. It was not simply a Victorian theatre, or even a lecture-hall or classroom. The space that Lucy Cavendish and Emma Cons carved out at the corner of Lambeth's Waterloo Road and the New Cut was one where questions of who could gain access to elite culture, what made for the best society, and the utility of cultural capital were tested and where new configurations of citizenship could be tried. In their South Bank endeavours, two middle-aged Victorian women waged a revolutionary campaign from within the very heart of Victorian respectability. Whether or not they were wholly conscious of what they were doing, Lucy Cavendish and Emma Cons's work was nothing short of subversive.

The sixth and final chapter examines Cons's career as London's first woman alderman and argues that a broader shift in perceptions took place in the latter third of the nineteenth century, replacing women's charity as "a Christian duty" with women's philanthropy as a display of their citizenship. In all these chapters we see not only the work of the two women who stand as illustrative case studies but also the shifting formation and re-coalescence of committees of philanthropically minded men and women who repeatedly found themselves sitting across the committee table from the same men and women, attempting to address the plight of the poor, attacking problems from different angles. The careers of Emma Cons and Lucy Cavendish serve both as a point of departure and as a frame of reference for the broader picture of Victorian women's charitable work.

1 Lucy Cavendish

In early December 1863, Lucy Lyttelton, then twenty-two, spent the weekend at Chatsworth, the principal country house of the Duke of Devonshire. Late Friday night she recorded in her diary: "At dinner I got into an argument with Lord Frederick Cavendish on the Church, which excited and interested me."[1] It must have been an interesting conversation for both parties: a week later, as Lord Frederick had been invited by Lucy's aunt, Catherine Gladstone, to spend the weekend at Hawarden, the two young persons continued to discuss "Church questions."[2] Four months later, they were engaged. So were brought together the two great passions of Lucy's life: the Church of England and Lord Frederick Cavendish. It would make sense then that, twenty-four years later, utterly bereft after her husband's murder, Lucy would find solace and purpose through both the Anglican Church and continuing the philanthropic work she and her husband had so often shared.

Taken as a whole, the rich philanthropic career of Lady Frederick Cavendish – indeed, the narrative of her life itself – is a rich vein of material. Through its account we can learn much about how charitably minded Victorian men and women organized themselves to promote various philanthropic causes, for in some ways her life was quite representative and in others, much less so. First of all, Lucy Cavendish's career vividly illustrates the overlapping and intersecting circles of committees, societies, and associations that made up the philanthropic world of late Victorian and Edwardian England. Second, her story is useful because, although there is good consensus on the charitable patterns of elite women who, when based in the country, would personally see to their own tenants, there has simply been less attention paid to how aristocratic Victorian women spent their philanthropic time when in London. Both K.D. Reynolds and Kathryn Gleadle have suggested that by the middle of the nineteenth century the aristocratic pattern of visiting and personal contact employed by titled women on their estates had been adopted by urban middle-class women who worked with the metropolitan poor.[3] But Reynolds's work on aristocratic urban women has also led her to the conclusion that, when resident in London, they moved away from that rural model of personal philanthropy; they did not engage with the poor of London. Reynolds maintains that aristocratic urban women tended to involve themselves in the management of structured charities, which permitted them to stay at a distance, using their organizational skills and networks of contacts to solicit support and build fundraising events, such as bazaars and charity balls. This, Reynolds maintains, was the case in the early years of the nineteenth century and did not change much; even after 1880, Reynolds sees aristocratic women in London as heading committees, organizing bazaars, administering, and delegating duties, but not visiting the poor.[4]

This model may have typified the majority of urban aristocratic women, but it was not the case with Lucy Cavendish, nor was it the rule among many of her aristocratic women friends. For one, she had an "invariable rule against patronizing bazaars," even turning down a plea from her sister Lavinia for an organization they both vigorously supported, the Church of England Temperance Society.[5] With some philanthropic endeavours, for example the Royal Victoria Hall or the Mental After-Care Association, Lucy Cavendish was indeed involved in committee work, soliciting funds, delegating, and administering. But with most of her philanthropies, particularly those connected to the Anglican Church, she and many of the aristocratic women with whom she worked took a much more immediate and hands-on approach with London's poor.

This was not uncommon. Extrapolating from the clutch of women who worked with Lucy Cavendish, we can see that aristocratic women often combined the two approaches, both administering charities and directly involving themselves with London's poor. In this way they were able to link their particular familiarity with visiting to their networks of social contacts, cobbling together a unique and very practical corpus of expertise for London charities. Often the needs of a particular charity would dictate what approach would be adopted. When Lucy Cavendish worked with the Ladies Diocesan Association and the Parochial Mission Women Society, she visited workhouses and families in the East End; when she worked with the Church of England Temperance Society's Women's Union, she served on committees and made speeches. Thus, the trajectory of her philanthropic career can serve as an instructive example of just how women used the options expanding for them in the latter half of the nineteenth century.[6]

Lucy Cavendish's life can also give us a useful study of the political lives of aristocratic women in mid-Victorian Britain. A number of distinguished historians have engaged in much vigorous discussion concerning whether women's involvement in politics faded over the course of the first half of the nineteenth century, withdrawing from a late eighteenth-century zenith. One school of thought sees a wave of domesticity rising during the early nineteenth century, extinguishing political activity among women as they retreated into dominion over a private sphere.[7] Others maintain that whereas a Victorian society of separate spheres might well apply to the middle classes, aristocratic women maintained their political involvement well into the nineteenth century.[8] K.D. Reynolds, again, looking specifically at aristocratic women of the middle and late Victorian period, punctures of the notion of a hard and fast wall between a private sphere of serene (and largely female) domesticity and an entirely separate, boisterous (and male) public sphere of debate and disputation, arguing that the drawing rooms of aristocratic women remained places where policy and high politics were routinely discussed; the public sphere intruded into their private space.[9] Lucy – and Frederick – Cavendish's unhesitating and automatic assumption regarding Lucy's active involvement in her husband's political life mirrored in many ways the assumptions made a generation earlier by her mother's great friend, the Hon. Caroline Talbot, quite politically engaged at the time of the Great Reform Act of 1832. In sum, Lucy Cavendish's social, political, and philanthropic career opens many doors on the lives of aristocratic Victorian women. Examining her work broadens our understanding of aristocratic women's mode of urban philanthropy, illustrates the intersecting circles that women constructed to accomplish their philanthropic goals, and also shows the continuing political engagement of elite Victorian women.

Early Life

Lucy Cavendish occupied a position at the centre of public life from a young age. Lucy Lyttelton's early life at her family's rural estate was idyllic. Her parents were George, fourth Baron Lyttelton, and Mary Glynne, daughter of Sir Stephen Glynne of Hawarden, Flintshire,

Wales. George Lyttelton and Mary Glynne had been married in a double ceremony in 1839, together with Mary's sister Catherine and her fiancé, William Ewart Gladstone. Lucy was the second of twelve children and only sixteen when her mother died in 1857, leaving twelve children between the ages of seventeen and seven months.[10] As she lay dying, Lady Lyttelton had individual conversations with each of her children; she asked each of the elder ones to take particular care of one of their younger siblings. Lucy was specifically charged with taking care of the baby, Alfred, seven months old at the time of their mother's death. Thereafter, Lucy Lyttelton's life largely centred on working with her sister Meriel (only a year older) to organize the Hagley Hall household and caring for her baby brother. Lucy was also occupied with keeping up the spirits of her father, who habitually tended towards melancholy and who was devastated at the loss of his wife. Given these claims on Lucy's time, and the absence of a mother, it is impressive that her diary for her early years also includes more than the occasional mention of local charity work – as Lucy put it, "walking parochially." Moreover, the two eldest Lyttelton girls were obliged to run the household on economical lines as Lord Lyttelton's income was not great. The Lyttelton land holdings were only about 1,000 acres and the income therefrom was only about £1,000 a year; in addition there was a certain amount of debt to finance.[11] Lucy had once, when they were younger, chided her sister Meriel on her losing her slate: "Remember, Papa and Mamma are not rich."[12] Lucy noted in her diary the day, when she was seventeen, that the "great Rubens" was taken down from the walls of the billiard room to be valued and later sold for £500.[13]

Lucy Lyttelton's life as a girl was not much different from that of other girls of the landed aristocracy, alternating between Hagley Hall and country house visiting. Her education had been spotty: she and her two sisters and much younger brothers had been served by a succession of governesses, some of whom were effective, most of whom were not. Her accomplishments, as she left the schoolroom, were significantly fewer than those of most aristocratic girls her age. She was fluent in Italian and French, but knew no German or Latin and certainly no Greek. She had no training in art whatsoever; she enjoyed music, but could not read it and played no instruments. But she had a lively mind and loved to read. Ishbel Marjoribanks remembered her as "the embodiment of brightness and attraction, taking the keenest interest in every side of life."[14] She also recalled that, on one country house visit, Lucy discovered that Ishbel was not permitted to read novels and persuaded Ishbel's mother to allow the two girls to read *Pride and Prejudice* together.

"A new world opened to me from those days," Lady Aberdeen recalled years later, "and I can never be grateful enough for her friendship."[15]

Lucy Lyttelton was an ardent Anglican and her faith was a great joy in her life. Even as a grown woman, the recollection of her Confirmation was "a sacred and precious memory to me, almost beyond anything else."[16] She came by her enthusiasm honestly, for her father, the fourth Lord Lyttelton (1817–1876), was a great churchman. But Lord Lyttelton did not support the Church of England merely as part of the duties commensurate with his place in society. Although Hugh McLeod rightly maintains that many elite figures of Victorian society saw the established church as "an essential part of the social order within which they held privileged positions, and which they felt a duty to uphold," this was not the case with Lord Lyttelton.[17] His faith was a heartfelt expression of a pure conviction in the rightness of the Anglican doctrine. Lord Lyttelton did not simply troop his family to church on Sundays as an example to his tenants, he taught Sunday school and would frequently, on weekdays, after a day of hunting, slip an overcoat over his hunting pinks and, fresh from the field, attend the daily evening service at the Hagley Church, his spurs clanking up the aisle.[18]

Like that of her father, Lucy Lyttelton's religious faith had its roots and foundation in the great Evangelical upswell of the early nineteenth century. The Church of England's Evangelical movement was a response to a variety of challenges. The emergence from within the Anglican Church of the Wesley brothers and Methodism's very personal notion of salvation through faith created an attractive alternative that proved to be particularly popular among the British working class, who also responded welcomingly to the emphasis on the equality of souls. The perceived laxity of eighteenth-century society in general and of the Anglican clergy in particular (who often appeared to be content to administer services but disinclined to maintain regular parochial duties) inspired those who sought to instil within the Church of England a greater sense of personal responsibility and rectitude. Similarly, the foothold which English Jacobinism had found at the turn of the eighteenth century within working-class Methodist congregations spurred forward a sense of combined spiritual and social urgency. All these vexations that beset the Anglican Church in the early nineteenth century coalesced to produce an evangelical call for Anglican renewal.[19]

But neither Lucy nor her father was Evangelical. Although she would instinctively adopt the evangelical idea of parochial work – and in particular, work with the poor – both Lord Lyttelton and his daughter firmly believed in the church at its highest. Surpliced choirs, chanting, vestments, and the Eastward position were all elements of the Anglican service of which both Lytteltons heartily approved, and both saw the High Church Tractarians and Edward Pusey as the bulwark of all that was best in the Church of England.[20] In May of 1862, Lucy recorded in her diary how the vestry of the local Hagley Church had "CONSENTED UNANIMOUSLY AND JOYFULLY TO THE CHOIR'S SURPLICES!!!" later describing how she and her father both "went wild with excitement over the *surpliced future*."[21] Religion was an important part of Lucy Lyttelton's upbringing and a High Church was her expression of choice.

By 1863, Lucy Lyttelton was twenty-two and had been "out" and enjoyed two London seasons when she received an invitation to become a maid of honour to Queen Victoria.[22] Although this was a position restricted to those whose grandfathers, at least, had been peers, the offer was largely the result of Lucy's paternal grandmother having been governess to Queen Victoria's children from 1842 to 1850 and affectionately known to the children as "Laddle."[23] Although Lucy was quite nervous about performing public duties, she was giddy about earning her first money and thus, as she put it, "relieving Father of an extra burden," as the position paid an annual stipend of £400.[24]

Lucy Lyttelton, shy by nature, found her public court duties stressful. Her arrival at court was noted in the diary of Louisa Bowater, daughter of General Bowater, former equerry to William IV: "In the morning Miss Lyttelton arrived for almost her first waiting. She was as shy as possible, so remembering what my own feelings were, I went to try and make friends, and thought her very nice. We all dined together in the Queen's dining-room. Anything half so stiff you never knew! Princess Louise, myself and Miss Lyttelton enacted the three different degrees of comparison – shy, shyer, shyest."[25]

Louisa Bowater, apart from the young princesses, was the only other young woman at court, and her diaries give a good sense of the impression made by the young Lucy Lyttelton: "Miss Lyttelton and I started some squabbles, and shall, I foresee, differ on most subjects. She is deeply religious, and has a strong orthodox bias and some prejudices, combined with lots of good sense and a dash of intolerance. I like her very much; she is so pretty and pleasing, and decidedly clever, although she neither plays, nor draws, nor speaks German."[26] Unfortunately, as Lucy Lyttelton recorded in her diary only days later, "poor Miss Bowater heard of her cousin's death and went away in great trouble, thus interrupting the early growth between us of a very promising friendship: indeed I miss her much as the only companion among all these elderly people."[27] Lucy Lyttelton would herself only be at court for a few more months, as she became engaged to Lord Frederick Cavendish in April of 1864 and married him two months later.[28]

It was a true love match and the two were devoted to one another. As a newlywed, Lucy recorded in her diary after four months of marriage, "My first separation from my Fred, who went up to London ... for 1 night for a Furness railway meeting. He has only been gone 6 hours and yet I miss him grievously!"[29] When in the country, the newlyweds would stay at one of the Duke of Devonshire's many houses: Chatsworth, Hardwicke, Bolton, or, their favourite, Holker, in Cumbria, where Lord Frederick had principally been raised. But the young couple soon settled in London, as Lord Frederick intended to go into Parliament, and Lucy viewed prospective houses in Westminster with one of the Duke of Devonshire's seven housekeepers. They quickly decided on 21 Carlton House Terrace, usefully located across the street from the Gladstones, and the Duke purchased it for them. Lord Frederick Cavendish was elected as a Liberal member of Parliament for the West Riding of Yorkshire (Northern Division) at the next election and Lucy now entered the world of being a political wife. Her days were occupied in attendance at the debates in the House of Commons, from behind the grille of the Ladies Gallery, and charitable activities to which she now turned in earnest.

Committees for Soup Kitchens and Workhouses

Almost immediately after her marriage, Lucy Cavendish began charitable work in a way very typical for young women of her class, joining her aunt Catherine Gladstone as a lady visitor to the Saint Luke's Home for Epileptic and Incurable Women, recently established by Louisa Twining. Louisa Twining was also responsible for Lucy's joining the visiting committee of the Soho House of Charity, a lodging and advising institution founded on the principles of self-help; as they put it: "directing persons away from pauperism."[30] She also frequently assisted at a soup kitchen set up in Westminster by her late mother's great friend, the Hon. Caroline Talbot, a woman who was also one of the closest friends of Lucy's aunt Catherine Gladstone.[31] The widow of the Hon. John Chetwynd-Talbot, KC, and the daughter of Lord Wharncliffe, Caroline Talbot was a compelling figure of authority and rectitude. Her son Edward once described her as "a woman of very great reserve and of concentrated rather than expansive affections."[32] She certainly thoroughly intimidated both the Lyttelton and Gladstone children in their youths.[33] But Lucy, as a young matron, became closely involved with several of Mrs Talbot's philanthropic endeavours. One, the Parochial Mission Women Society, which Mrs Talbot had established in 1865 to organize working-class women as parish visitors, was affiliated with the Anglican Church, but was independently operated and funded.[34] Here Lucy Cavendish became a "supplemental lady," supervising the work in particular parishes. Mrs Talbot evidently ran the Parochial Mission Women Society in a most efficient manner: Lucy Cavendish was "greatly struck with the way business was done without waste of words or irrelevancy or red tape."[35] Similarly, Mrs Talbot's Westminster soup kitchen was run very much along the lines of classic Victorian political economy, eschewing charity *per se* as having a deforming effect on the poor since it inculcated a culture of dependence; the prevalent ethos was rather to encourage thrift and self-help. As Lucy noted in her diary, "poor people (not beggars) are given tickets, on showing which and paying a sum not exceeding 2*d* they get good meat, soup, beef-tea, or pudding of at least twice the value of what they pay."[36] Lucy immediately enlisted her husband as treasurer of the soup kitchen.

This soup kitchen gave Lucy her first encounter with profound squalor and it affected her deeply. She noted in her diary on 2 March 1866: "a poor tiny whose mother came this morning for a beef-tea ticket; and whose little year of life seemed to have been all suffering, cold and starvation. I have been thinking of it revived by the good beef tea; but it is terrible to know that I only see glimpses of the deep, wide misery all round us and can hardly do any good."[37] During these early years of her marriage, Lucy also began to work with a Church of England organization, the Ladies Diocesan Association, which had been established in 1864 by the Bishop of London and his wife to enlist women from wealthier parishes who wished to volunteer in needier parts of London, mostly in workhouses but also in women's charity hospitals and girls' homes.[38] Lucy was assigned to the St Anne's Workhouse, Limehouse, and occasionally to the workhouses of St George's-in-the-East and of her own parish, St Martin's-in-the-Fields. Lucy did not take her duties lightly and she stuck with the work; she clearly found it satisfying:

> At the poor dinner was pretty bright-eyed little pussy-girl of five, whose remains of dinner I carried home for her, for fear she'd come to grief with the plate. She showed me the way, trotting fearlessly along down a squalid street and court, up to the top of a wretched house. On the last landing, a

> door opened and out peeped another darling little girl. This was "home" and I went in. Father and mother, 4 children and a baby were in the tiny place; the little things all pretty and chubby but the parents pinched and starved looking. It was a tidy room, considering and I felt ashamed of myself, coming back to this big house where there is not even one little baby to take up room.[39]

Lucy Cavendish's efforts often collided incongruously with the glamour of an elite life. For example, a diary entry for 10 March 1865 begins full of good works in Limehouse:

> Mr. Rousel mentioned a terrible case of a struggling curate, so poor at best that he could not have a fire in his house, or eat meat for days together; and now with his large family in the scarlet fever. Meriel Bathurst (who came for the first time), my Meriel, Mrs. Talbot, Agnes and I agreed to send him a hamper among us; and M. and I got the things after luncheon; *viz.* tea, arrowroot, tapioca, sago, grapes, concentrated beef tea, currant jelly, ½ a dozen of port wine, and a bottle of brandy. The 2 latter items we found it rather blowing (daunting) to order...[40]

But the same diary entry concludes the day with a return to a world infinitely distant from that of poor curates: "We dined at Lady Cowper's and had to go afterwards to a ball at Marlborough House where the Princess of Wales looked lovely. I saw my dear Princess Helena (but not to speak to), also Princess Louise and many Court friends. I wore all the diamonds on my head for the first time."[41]

Lucy Cavendish's diary in the early years of her marriage gives a clear indication that she started her charitable work with great enthusiasm, both for the sense of useful occupation it gave her and for the camaraderie among other philanthropic aristocratic ladies of her acquaintance. She clearly liked being part of a contingent with purpose: "I went to London House with a brigade of Associated Ladies.[42] Charlotte Spencer came for the first time and was immediately pounced upon by the Parochial Mission Women Lady manageress to be a Supplemental Lady. Miss Twining, who has the *workhouseums* shut herself up with Atie P. [one of Lucy's other aunts] and others and burst forth into schemes for improving pauper sick arrangements."[43] Lucy did a fair amount of pouncing herself. Ishbel Marjoribanks recalled how Lucy made "a surprise descent on my father in his library at Brook House one day, and dragged out of him permission for me to act in the capacity of what was termed her 'supplemental' in caring for the families of a district in Limehouse."[44]

1 Lucy Cavendish. From a portrait by George Richmond, RA, painted about the time of her marriage.

But although Lucy Cavendish's initial philanthropic motivations may have been unremarkable, within a few years her work with the poor of London's East End gave her more than sociability with like-minded ladies and even more than a pleasing sense of being useful. She did not shrink from what she saw in her workhouses and she grasped the fact that she and her companions were often the only safety net that existed for poor women. After five years working in the East End, she made another entry in her diary: "A poor dressmaker to whom I gave some old clothes on Tuesday, having reason to believe her story true, came, overcome with gratitude to-night to say that she had got work the very day after. Such a contrast, in the decent clothes and with a brightened face, to the poor, ragged, starved tramp who tottered into the room on Tuesday, crying helplessly and yet giving me the impression of respectability. I keep thanking God over and over for letting me do this."[45]

Thus, as a young woman in her twenties and early thirties, Lucy Cavendish was learning much about the state of London's poor and much about herself in relation to them. She was also learning from her work, particularly her work with Mrs. Talbot's Parochial Mission Women Society and her Westminster soup kitchen. Moreover, she was beginning to understand more about the power of philanthropic committees and how one would encounter many of the same men and women again and again, in different associations' committees and societies, enlisted in different causes. Seeing how peoples' experiences from different campaigns could be shared, Lucy saw the importance of contacts as well as expertise. She began to gain experience in fundraising for charities and learning how attitudes among the wealthy could differ widely. With some appeals, she was successful. In response to one appeal to her brother-in-law, she received a cheque for £100 with £50 of it earmarked for the Soho House of Charity, £25 for the Parochial Mission Women, and £25 for her to dispose of as she saw fit. ("Wrote him an intoxicated thank-you," she wrote in her diary).[46] With others, appeals would fall on deaf ears: "We dined at the Loyd Lindsays – I sat next to Lord Overstone, who put me in a rage by crowing over his sagacity in snubbing begging letters. He is *choked-up* with money and has a monomania against all charities."[47]

Political Life

At the same time she was beginning her work at the Limehouse workhouse, Lucy was also starting to become more immediately involved in the politics of the day. As a young woman, her political consciousness had been somewhat unformed and certainly she had divided loyalties: when twenty, she had debated in her diary whether she was, like her father, a Conservative or a Liberal like her uncle Gladstone. Having listened in the House of Commons to both her uncle and Disraeli debate the merits of the 1861 budget, she still failed to reach a conclusion.[48] But after her marriage to Lord Frederick Cavendish (Whig by inheritance, Liberal by personal inclination), as with many of the political wives studied by Pat Jalland in *Women, Marriage and Politics 1860–1914* (1986), Lucy closed the door on her father's Toryism and unhesitatingly embraced her husband's politics.[49] That was made easier as Lord Frederick Cavendish, scion of one of the great Whig families of England, now became something of a protégé of Gladstone's.

For women of Lucy Cavendish's circle, and political wives in particular, politics was a constant presence. This was much as it had been for some time. Elaine Chalus, Amanda Foreman, Linda Colley, Dror Wahrman, and others have described the involvement in political life of aristocratic women in the later eighteenth century. Georgiana, Duchess of Devonshire (the sister of Lucy's great-grandfather and her husband's great-aunt), is frequently held up as an exemplar of the politically active eighteenth-century aristocratic woman.[50] But it is a matter of debate whether women's political participation constricted in the early decades of the nineteenth century. Three short extracts from the diaries of Mrs Talbot, as a young political wife, suggest a vibrant and continuing involvement of aristocratic women in political life early in the nineteenth century:

February 10th, 1831

Went to Lady Grey's party – much talk about the new taxes announced in the House of Commons this evening – immense disapprobation of that of the transfer of funded property.

February 21st, 1831

Went to Lady Lansdowne's and Lady Salisbury's parties in the evening; the committee on the Civil list has recommended reductions in all the official and household salaries.

March 2nd, 1831

Everybody is *consterné*. Even many Whigs and Reformers are frightened like the rest of us at the sweeping extent of the plan. The general opinion is that it will certainly not be carried but if it is what will follow? Lord F. Leveson spoke very well last night against it. Went to the dowager Lady Salisbury's in the evening. Nothing but reform talked of and little but one expression of dismay from people of all opinion and of execration at the Duke of Wellington's obstinacy which has brought us to this. The debate is adjourned again, many young members have been speaking tonight.[51]

There is an even more active debate among historians as to whether women were able to hold on to political power and influence of their own after the Great Reform Act of 1832.[52] Some see a continuity of aristocratic women's influence through the nineteenth century by way of political wives' salons and drawing-room caucusing.[53] Others see women possessing little actual power to affect an agenda of policy.[54] Certainly, judging from her correspondence with her husband, Mrs Talbot's interest in and understanding of the political debates and personages of the day remained acute through the 1830s and 1840s. But after his death in 1852, her interests became less overtly political and more focused on philanthropy. Lucy Cavendish's discussion of political events and concerns in her diaries from the 1860s through the early 1880s closely resemble Mrs Talbot's of thirty and forty years previous. To Lucy Cavendish, politics and discussions of policy were something which took place at her dining-room table, in her drawing room, in her garden. Indeed, after Gladstone gave up his London residence at 11 Carlton House Terrace (across the street from Lucy at no. 21) in 1875, he would frequently use his niece's house as his London headquarters, freely receiving visitors and advisers there. Whether she wielded much influence over her husband's political life, however, is not clear from her papers. But Lucy embraced this life; she did not stay in London during her husband's campaigns; she worked the hustings with him and his committee, "up to the ears" in electioneering.[55] Nor was she reticent about sitting on display to the crowd on public platforms, in public squares or packed halls, as can be seen from her diary during the 1880 election:

Fred made a fine speech and Sir Matthew [Wilson, Bt., the other Liberal candidate, for Yorkshire West Riding] was in the midst of his, pegging

> away with his usual spirit when I became aware of an ecstatic whisper going 'round the platform – "Gladstone's in! Gladstone's in!" By some magic the multitude found out in a minute, there arose an immense cheer like a roar of many waters. It was minutes before they could stop and hear the numbers and the short telegram was interrupted again and again by renewed outbursts. In the midst of the shouting, I wrote off a telegram in Frederick's name, dictated by Mr. Stansfeld: "6,000 Yorkshiremen at Halifax Liberal meeting have received news of your victory with enthusiasm such as no living man has ever seen the like."[56]

Working the campaign trail with her husband had been pointedly suggested by one of his political advisers, who had rather surprised her with the assumption not only that she was *au courant* with the political debates with which her husband was involved but also that she would likely function as a kind of right hand.[57] As with many of her aristocratic contemporaries who were married to politicians, Lucy seemed to move between the political and the domestic life with the same ease as had their great-grandmothers. Now with her husband and his brother, Lord Hartington, both in the House with her uncle, Lucy Cavendish paid closer attention to the minutiae of politics and seemed to delight in developing critical political faculties of her own, as can be seen from the commentary from her diary concerning the debates over a stillborn Second Reform Bill (proposed by the Liberals, torpedoed by Disraeli, the division caused the fall of the Liberal government).

> The Conservatives have been and gone and done it to-day! for they have been supporting a proposal for an educational franchise versus the modest Government rental one for no other conceivable purpose than to defeat Government: if they had divided and won they would have had to come in pledged to a franchise that points straight to universal suffrage! Bright is not such a Radical! His ideal being household suffrage; and he made a conservative speech opposing this. I suppose Uncle Wm. is wanting in tact; for there is treason through the camp; and the oddest fermentations and combinations of parties against him.[58]

These political senses became further cultivated and Lucy and her husband moved closer to the centre of political life when Lord Frederick Cavendish, after seven years as a backbencher, became Gladstone's private secretary in 1872. Lucy was now in the thick of politics. In the aftermath of the 1880 election when it was not immediately clear whether

her brother-in-law, Lord Frederick's elder brother Hartington, or her uncle Gladstone would be called to form a Liberal government, both her aunt Catherine and her cousin Mary Gladstone were quick to ask Lucy to suggest, either directly or through Lord Frederick, that Hartington step aside in favour of Gladstone.[59] It is unlikely that this was a novel idea to Hartington, who made it clear that he thought Gladstone the obvious, even inevitable, prime minister.

But it was not only Lord Frederick Cavendish's opinions which Gladstone sought. Gladstone increasingly valued Lucy's own judgment. He spoke frankly and openly with her, and his diaries are peppered with notes of their discussions on political questions: 24 December 1873, "Conversation with Lucy Cavendish on Hartington's prospects"; 11 June 1887, "Retrospective conversation with Lucy C. on political incidents"; 8 August 1888, "Gave my manuscript to Lucy. Her judgment is worth having."[60] Lucy's diaries show us the other side of the same coin: "June 17, 1870, Mrs. Talbot came to see me and we went across to see Lavinia's [wedding] presents at No. 11. Hearing my voice in the hall, who should call me into his study but the Prime Minister! To ask me what I thought of the Government proceedings last night about the Education Bill. Things have been going very *ticklishly* with it lately."[61] Notwithstanding the fact that she had been raised in a household best described as high Anglican and higher Tory, Lucy Cavendish's commitment to her husband's and her uncle's politics had become quite solid. But her political senses were being sharpened at exactly the same time as was her understanding of the crippling poverty experienced by the very poor. For example, the same day she read to a workhouse of oakum-picking women, she went on to the House to listen with distinct interest to the debate on the Second Reform Bill.

> *This is my never to be forgotten day* ... Went to the House afterwards, quite on the chance; and had the immense luck of hearing the famous Mr. J.S. Mill make a most perfect speech in favour of the Franchise Bill. In spite of the cry-down humour the Tories are in, it was striking to have this small-voiced philosopher listened to with the greatest possible attention and respect; and indeed the speech was irresistibly fair, profound, and trenchant. Three or 4 times he made a dead pause of more than a minute, but only to produce some new, cogent argument armed at all points and perfectly expressed; though he was keenly satirical once or twice, the whole tone of his speech was gentle and temperate to a degree. The Opposition held their tongues as if bewitched! He followed Sir Bulwer Lytton

> who made a slashing, clever speech. I found myself a good deal struck and moved, coming straight out of one of the depths of misery and pauperism, to hear the claims of the people so grandly brought forward: those "dumb" thousands, as Bright called them, among whom there must be so many feeling, as none of us can feel, for all this degradation; and voiceless in the nation whom they might help to rouse to the most noble of battles.[62]

This burgeoning liberal identity did not lessen. She carefully noted with approval in her diary her uncle's saying to her, in October, 1876, "When have the upper 10,000 ever led the attack in the cause of humanity? Their heads are always full of class interests and the main chance."[63] Whether through her work with the soup kitchens or her exposure to Liberal politics, Lucy Cavendish had become more liberal in her attitudes.

Lord Frederick Cavendish's views had been decidedly liberal from a young age. He was much impressed with the views of the Christian Socialist the Rev. F.D. Maurice and, early in their marriage, persuaded his more skeptical wife to join him at services where Maurice would give his sermons. Maurice and the Christian Socialists held a good deal of influence in the latter third of the nineteenth century among those of liberal inclinations. Gladstone, too, was much taken with Maurice, regarding him as "a man nothing short of 'spiritual splendour.'"[64] If Lucy initially gravitated, on her own, away from her Tory upbringing and towards the views of her husband and uncle, her experiences with the Parochial Mission Women Society and the Ladies Diocesan Association only drew her more steadily in that liberal direction.

By this point Lucy had also clearly emerged from her earlier shyness. She had always had an exuberant and somewhat unconventional personality, which, growing up in the country with eight brothers, her parents and a succession of lackadaisical governesses had not hampered. She was remarkably frank. But at the same time she was usually careful, when in public, not to let her high spirits run away with her. She did not always succeed. On one occasion, at a large house party at Chatsworth, her sister-in-law put her in charge of finding out what the guests would like to do after luncheon. She did this by calling out to the guests en masse: "Hands up those who would like to drive!"[65] Whether gaining confidence in her own abilities through working with various charitable organizations or working with her husband's campaigns, by the early 1880s Lucy Cavendish could no longer be described as shy.

The Starting of a Philanthropic Career

It was at this point in her life that Lucy Cavendish encountered another admirer of F.D. Maurice, Emma Cons. The two women had first met in 1880 when Lucy accompanied her husband to the second meeting of the committee that was organizing shareholders for what would become the Coffee Music-Halls Company. This company, run on not-for-profit lines, had been established by Cons and a number of temperance reformers to assume the lease of the disreputable Royal Victoria Theatre, located in a working-class neighbourhood south of the Thames. The timing was propitious; the Royal Victoria Theatre in Lambeth was now dark and its lease and licence would soon be up for auction.[66] Situated in the rather grim Waterloo Road at the corner of the even more dismal New Cut, the once-dignified Cobourg Theatre had declined with the surrounding neighbourhood. The mid-century extension of the London and Southwestern Railway, which cut through Southwark and Lambeth, ending at its new Waterloo terminus, lessened the value of neighbouring properties. New tenants, many of whom worked on the railways, moved into the neighbourhood. The Cobourg, now renamed the Royal Victoria Palace Theatre, was sold and quickly sold again, rapidly passing through a succession of various proprietors who changed the playbill to attract the new inhabitants. The management of the theatre was infinitely more concerned with the lucrative sale of alcohol and much less attentive to what on-stage attractions drew paying customers. In the decade preceding the theatre's going dark, melodramas "of the deepest dye and coarsest texture" became the staple commodity of the "Old Vic."[67] The objective of the Coffee Music-Halls Company was to extinguish the Vic as a source of alcohol and to provide the working poor of Lambeth and Southwark with some – any – alternative form of entertainment to that offered by the area's ubiquitous public houses.

The establishment of the Coffee Music-Halls Company was part of the resurgence, in the mid-1870s, of temperance as an important issue affecting the state of the nation. Many, in the last third of the nineteenth century, saw alcohol abuse, particularly among the working classes of Britain, as the most crucial problem facing the nation. This problem affected not only the nation's health but its ability to work. For example, Seebohm Rowntree, in a famous survey, estimated that in York 28 per cent of the workforce lived in "secondary poverty" owing to the unwise nutritional allocation of their wages, far too much of which was spent on drink. Workers' wages were so low, he explicitly noted, that even if well spent, such income would have been able to provide for "merely physical efficiency," not robust health.[68] In short, alcohol was sapping those who could least afford it. Temperance was thus a crusade about national productivity as well as moral control. It was also a cause embraced and promoted by all classes. Working-class affiliation with the temperance cause speaks to sobriety as an aspect of the growing appeal of self-improvement and upward mobility. Temperance organizations similarly offered opportunities for cross-class collaboration in what was seen as a national reclamation project. Thus, when Lucy Cavendish began to work more closely with Emma Cons at the Royal Victoria Hall, she was already attuned to the issue of drink as a destructive force.

At this point, Lucy had not yet become an advocate of temperance. Years later she confessed:

> At the onset of my acquaintance with the Victoria Hall, I ventured to suggest that it, under strict limitations, might be advisable to turn an honest penny on the premises by the sale of wholesome beer. I was, however, entirely bowled over by Miss Cons' reply. She said that, in the first place, such a plan would sweep away all her teetotal supporters. Secondly, if any drink was going on the premises, she could never depend on keeping sober employees. And thirdly, that no moderate sale of beer would ever float any concern; it would have to be diligently touted all through the Hall and everywhere all night to make it a paying thing. I immediately hauled down my colours and never suggested it again.[69]

Although, at this early stage of her involvement with the Royal Victoria Hall, the temperance aspect of the Old Vic was evidently not as vital to Lucy Cavendish as it would later become, it was the cause that later became of primary importance to her. The ill effects of drinking had been in her mind at least since the mid-1870s when she made a note in her diary regarding the death in childbirth of the young Lady Anne Buller: "I wish that doctors would investigate the causes of the terrible delicacy of the 'upper 10,000' women in childbirth: my own small bit of experience makes me wonder if wine-drinking – which I don't think used to be so regular a thing among women formerly as it is now – has to do with it."[70] Shortly after beginning her work with Emma Cons on the Royal Victoria Hall, Lucy joined the newly formed Women's Union of the Church of England Temperance Society (CETS). By 1887 she would become one of the Union's vice-presidents, travelling the country making speeches on temperance and the evils of drink. Her niece and god-daughter, Lucy Masterman, in her biography of her aunt, speculated that Lucy Cavendish's conversion to temperance might have come through the influence of Rosalind, the adamantly teetotal Countess of Carlisle, one-time president of the British Women's Temperance Association.[71] This is unlikely; the devout and conservative Anglican Lucy had much affection but little respect for the judgment of the radical Unitarian Rosalind (and much sympathy for her Howard in-laws). In an 11 October 1880 entry in her diary, Lucy described Rosalind, newly installed at Castle Howard, as a "hopelessly incongruous creature,"[72] going on to note (6 December 1880) that "the descriptions of Rosalind's manners and customs at Castle Howard make one despair of her ever knowing how to be gentle, humble or considerate; and yet she *is* kind and affectionate."[73] In an 1885 letter to her sister Meriel, Lucy described the atmosphere at Castle Howard brought in by Rosalind as the "noisy Radical rattle of the newest and crudest description, and the sight of six boys being brought up no how … and worst of it all, their being both professed Unitarians – the whole a grievous pain … unspeakably incongruous and painful to the old Howards."[74] Lucy had joined the Women's Union through her friend Beatrice Temple, wife of Frederick Temple, Archbishop of Canterbury (and vigorous leader of the CETS).[75] Joining the Women's Union had not made much impact; Lucy was initially a rather desultory supporter of temperance. But by the middle of the 1880s, after a few years of working with Emma Cons at the Royal Victoria Hall, she had become more aware of the destructive aspects of alcohol, and by 1890 she was quite active in speaking publicly in furtherance of temperance. It is likely that this progress was the result of Emma Cons's influence. Emma was a persuasive temperance advocate of long standing, and her condemnation of the effects of alcohol on the lives of the families in her courts was steely and inflexible and came from a solid base of knowledge.

Alcoholism was a problem which Lucy Cavendish increasingly saw affecting all classes. Addressing the Women's Union of the Church of England Temperance Society at the Duke of Westminster's Grosvenor House in 1882, the Bishop of London spoke of his work among the laundresses of Notting Hill, a group he referred to as a large class of inebriates. A few days later he received a letter from a titled lady he described as being "from a noble family" – almost certainly Lucy Cavendish – who had been present and who now remonstrated with him. She wrote that during his speech she "could scarcely restrain herself from coming to the platform and protesting against the inference that might be drawn from my words, that this intemperance was the vice of working-class women only. She then went on to give me a detailed list of women in her own rank of life giving everything but their names[;] there were fifteen of them, whom she had known, and known well, and who, although the world either knew nothing of it or had only the faintest suspicion of, it had first embittered the lives of themselves and their nearest relations ... some had literally died of drink."[76]

Alcohol abuse among elite women was a cause that Lucy Cavendish saw as a real but hidden problem. In October 1892 at that year's Church Congress, she read her paper in which she made explicit that alcoholism was not a problem which beset the working class alone. She spoke frankly of middle-class and upper-class women who favoured "nips" and "pick-me-ups" during stressful seasons, who had a "white cup" instead of tea at five o'clock, who closed the day with a "B&S" (brandy-and-soda) or "a mysterious something hot at bed-time," observing quite frankly to her audience that drink was almost as much of a problem among elite women as it was among working women. The newspapers and periodicals of the day leapt on this with ill-disguised appetite: "Lady Frederick Cavendish, in her paper on 'Temperance as it affects women of the upper and middle classes' has thrown a bomb-shell into the camp of society."[77] Lucy Cavendish had become persuaded that alcohol was a pernicious influence and one that she increasingly saw as affecting society as a whole, regardless of class or sex.

Lucy Cavendish was fussy about the causes to which she would give her name, let alone her time, yet she was willing to travel far to make speeches on "the Drink," as can be seen from a letter to her sister from 17 November 1890: "2 Drink speeches at Leeds and 2 at Hagley ... prize-giving at Portsmouth and Dover on Friday, a drink speech that B. Temple has let me in for. You'll think I am a regular stumper, but I get off anything that has nothing to hook itself onto."[78] That said, Lucy was far from didactic on the subject of alcohol. There was a distinct divide at that time between those who advocated temperance and those who were teetotallers, and Lucy saw herself very much on one side of the battle. As she put it during an 1896 address to the women of the CETS, urging them to redouble their efforts for temperance, "are we to leave all the effort to teetotallers?"[79] She served wine to her guests. She arranged for champagne to be served at her niece Margaret's wedding at Penshurst.[80] Her niece and goddaughter Lucy Masterman recalled that, at a dinner party, around the third spoonful of soup, Lucy Cavendish announced, "there's alcohol in that soup," and, taking another spoonful, added "and how dreadfully good it is."[81]

Lucy Cavendish began to give more than the prestige of her name and useful counsel to the Royal Victoria Hall. She enlisted her father, Lord Lyttelton, as chairman of the first Friday night "penny science lectures" at the Hall. She invoked her old connection with the royal family. She persuaded Princess Frederica of Hanover (daughter of the Queen's first cousin, George) to attend performances. She had the Marquess of Lorne open a Morley College picture exhibition. She convinced the Prince and Princess of Wales to come for a special "Irish night." The *Daily News* reported the next day that the royal couple seemed to be "much amused at the free and easy style of the pit" as the young men in the front row listened to Madame Liebhart sing "The Harp That Once through Tara's Hall" in their shirt-sleeves with their elbows propped on the stage's apron.[82] Lucy was assiduous in persuading her titled friends, such as the Earl and Countess Brownlow and the Earl and Countess of Pembroke, to become patrons of the Royal Victoria Hall. Her old friend Princess Helena was carefully cultivated to become a mainstay for the Hall and year after year could be regularly depended upon to open seasons, cut ribbons, take a box, and bring people to performances.[83] The imprimatur of the royal family and the patronage of so many titled personages gave the Royal Victoria Hall prestige and publicity. On 4 December 1885, when the Prince and Princess Henry of Battenberg (the Queen's youngest daughter) attended a gala ballad concert, the *Morning Post* mentioned every single royal and noble name attached to the Hall as patrons and made particular note of the fact that the Queen herself was the patron of the concert.[84] The Annual Report of the Royal Victoria Hall for 1884 stated with satisfaction that "£1,000 was raised, thanks in great part to Lady Frederick Cavendish, who exerted herself with much success to win new friends to the cause."[85]

Lucy Cavendish and Emma Cons worked together on a variety of other charities in addition to the Royal Victoria Hall, and it is not known whether they both spontaneously were drawn to a particular cause or whether the one recruited the other. Lucy agreed to join the Board (and in 1892 gave the address at the Annual Meeting) of the Drury Lane girls' hostel that Emma had established years earlier. Lucy likely recruited Emma for Friends of Armenia, an association associated with the Gladstones; Lucy became president, Emma travelled to Cyprus to set up a silk-weaving concern to assist Armenian women refugees to get back on their feet.[86] It is likely that Emma Cons drew Lucy Cavendish into the establishment of an organization devoted to facilitating "the readmission of female convalescents from lunatic asylums into social and domestic life."[87] Emma Cons was the first layperson invited to be part of the Mental After-Care Association, which was founded in June of 1879 by the Rev. Dr Henry Hawkins, the chaplain of the Colney Hatch mental asylum, together with a handful of "mental physicians" and clergymen, including the brothers Dr Harrington Tuke and Dr Hack Tuke. Her involvement was logical, as the residents of the tenement courts she administered were frequently in and out of mental asylums. The Rev. Hawkins observed in his initial address to the founding group that these were particularly fragile persons. "For some who have relatives or friends, the transition from a spacious asylum ward with its comforts and even refinements to a close musty room in some crowded court would be the reverse of salutary."[88] Not only would the reintegration of these women into society inevitably involve the tenement court manager, but Emma Cons's expertise with the mentally fragile women in her courts would also be invaluable to the Association. Lucy Cavendish had become involved, within a few months of the Association's founding, hosting a luncheon for the group at her house and enlisting her friends as supporters. Together with her sisters Meriel and Lavinia, Mrs Gladstone and Louisa Twining, the Earl and Countess of Meath and the Earl of Shaftesbury, these were many of the same men and women who also formed the foundational bedrock for the Royal Victoria Hall.

But care for the mentally disordered who had recently been deinstitutionalized would have been a cause that Lucy Cavendish would have embraced as naturally as had Emma Cons, though for different reasons. In 1876, Lucy's father had committed suicide, breaking away from his valet and throwing himself over the banister of the staircase of their London townhouse in Cromwell Road onto the marble floor beneath, fracturing his skull and dying without recovering consciousness. Lord Lyttelton frequently fell into what the family termed "father's wretched blues," although they were usually short-lived.[89] However, in April of 1876 he was still in deep mourning for his youngest daughter, Mary, who had died of typhoid thirteen months previous. Indeed, at the time of his death, he was being looked after by a valet-attendant, recently retained and instructed to keep a close watch on Lord Lyttelton, precisely to prevent him killing himself. His older children, in conjunction with his second wife, Sybella, had had serious family discussions about whether to have him committed to a private asylum.[90] Lucy Cavendish thus brought a specific perspective to the Mental After-Care Association.

Thus, by 1882, Lucy Cavendish had extended her philanthropic activities from those involving strictly Church of England organizations (the Parochial Mission Women Society and the Ladies Diocesan Association) to include the cause of the mentally ill, temperance, and the Royal Victoria Hall. In her particular involvement with these causes and organizations, we see hands-on involvement as well as organizational, administrative, and committee work where direct contact was delegated to others. It was to these organizations that she would turn in the following year when her husband was stabbed to death by a group of Irish nationalists known as the "Invincibles" in Dublin's Phoenix Park, shortly after Gladstone had appointed him chief secretary for Ireland.[91]

Widowhood

When Lord Frederick Cavendish was murdered, his wife was forty-one. Lucy Cavendish's uncle Gladstone, responsible for sending Lord Frederick out to Dublin, instinctively sought to frame his death as a Christ-like sacrifice that would be the catalyst for an end to the troubles in Ireland. The first words out of Gladstone's mouth to his niece, when he and her sister Meriel hurried to the Cavendish house late on the night of 6 May to break the news to Lucy, were "Father, forgive them for they know not what they do. Be assured it will not be in vain." This was an construal onto which Lucy Cavendish latched immediately: "across all my agony there fell a bright ray of hope, and I saw in a vision, Ireland at peace, and my darling's life-blood accepted as a sacrifice for Christ's sake, to help to bring this to pass." Her cousin, Mary Gladstone, heard the next day the same message from Lucy as she attended Sunday services: "Pray that what Uncle W says may come true, the saving of Ireland thro' the sacrifice of Freddy's innocent blood."[92] She remained remarkably dignified through the ordeal of the semi-public funeral; as Sir Edward Hamilton, Gladstone's principal private secretary, noted in his diary: "Lady Frederick is behaving as the personification of courage and goodness combined. She is more than marvellous."[93] This notion of her husband's assassination as a form of blood-sacrifice was one to which Lucy Cavendish would repeatedly return for comfort.

The British's public's reaction was different. Unused to political assassinations (it had been exactly seventy years since Spencer Perceval's murder), the British public reacted with a kind of ghoulish, fascinated horror. Newspaper reports of Lord Frederick Cavendish's death streamed in through the weekend: "Terrible News from Ireland," "Lord Frederick Cavendish Foully Murdered." The *Glasgow Herald*, having detailed every possible description of the murder, the victim, and the murderers, then fell back, for a fresh angle, to "Breaking the news to Lady Cavendish." The *Daily News* gave reports of the effect the news had on the continent and in New York. The town of Barrow immediately resolved to erect a statue to Lord Frederick's memory. Poems *in memoriam* sprang up in numerous serious periodicals, but also in *Punch* and even in French in the *Journal du Grande Monde*.[94] The *Pall Mall Gazette*'s report of Gladstone's speech to the House of Commons concerning the death of Lord Frederick Cavendish was typical of the exaggerated tone: "Since the night when Chatham sank back in his place in 1778 there has probably been no more solemn episode, no more painful or pathetic episode in parliamentary history than the impressive function in the House of Commons yesterday afternoon."[95] But the press and the public took their tone directly from Gladstone, who had spoken of a crime "unparalleled in our history, unparalleled for the blackness of the crime which has been committed, unparalleled I fully believe, for the horror which it had excited in the entire population of the United Kingdom." Notwithstanding the hyperbole, Lord Frederick Cavendish was a genuinely admired man and much esteemed by his parliamentary colleagues; the funeral at Chatsworth was attended by thirty thousand persons, including half the House of Commons, who journeyed up by special train to the adjacent town of Edensor, where Lord Frederick would be buried.

There was no opportunity for Lucy Cavendish to experience her husband's death privately – her loss was immediately appropriated as a public and national one. Her grief became public property, suitable for comment. For example, the periodical *Court and High Life* did not see it as too intrusive, less than a month after her husband's murder, to feature a story describing the mien of the widow coping with her recent loss: "The bereaved lady supports her terrible affliction with a spirit of the greatest fortitude and with a self-denying courage which few mourners may attain although all may emulate."[96] Lord Frederick and his murder even became the subject of a wax-work exhibit in Madame Tussaud's Chamber of Horrors.[97] The only way for her to be able to cope with a private loss made so maddeningly public was to embrace the construction of her dead husband as a martyr.

Shortly after her husband's death Lucy wrote to her cousin John, the Earl Spencer and lord lieutenant of Ireland, who had been resident in

Dublin at the time of the murder. She was still focused on the idea of a Christ-like sacrifice.

> I should be very glad if there can be any means of letting it be known in Ireland, so as to have some good effect, that I would never grudge the sacrifice of my darling's life if only it leads to the putting down of the frightful spirit of evil in the land. He would never have grudged it if he could have hoped that his death would do more than his life. There does seem some hope of this, and you are doing all you can to keep down that dreadful danger of "panic and blind vengeance."[98]

Receiving varied deputations shortly after receiving her letter, Spencer read it out to them, and its tone of sacrifice and forgiveness quickly became widely known. Writing to her cousin that month, Mary Gladstone remarked on "the immense impression made by your letter in Ireland. At Connemara the priest read it out in the service (in his sermon, I suppose) and the whole congregation fell on their knees."[99] Indeed, the public construal of Lord Frederick Cavendish as a martyr for the cause of Home Rule was continually reinforced. A year after his death, Lucy's cousin Stephen Gladstone, the rector of Hawarden, preached a sermon, "A Life Given for Ireland," on the occasion of the dedication of a memorial stained-glass window in St James church in Barrow-in-Furness, taking as its subject the parable of the Good Samaritan. Here the idea of a martyr's sacrifice was made explicit: "Oh Irish hearts, he died for you as well as by the hands of cruel men amongst you. Oh English hearts he died for the wicked tyranny, the awful selfishness, the bloody cruelty of many of your forefathers. Let both countries be conscience-stricken with a common shame and sorrow."[100] A second stained-glass window had been commissioned by members of the House of Commons for the church of St Margaret's, Westminster, and at its installation ceremony, 22 July 1883, the sermon on the subject of the window – scenes from the life of Christ from the Garden to the entombment – referred explicitly to the idea of Christ-like sacrifice.[101] A number of historians have examined the Victorian approach to death and mourning, and this framework was not unusual in a culture as steeped in religion as mid-nineteenth-century Britain.[102] But it was a comfort for Lucy Cavendish to see her husband's death as a potentially constructive sacrifice and it was a perspective to which she clung for the rest of her life.[103] It also cemented her position in the world. From then on, she was Britain's other public widow.

Lucy Cavendish never fully recovered from the death of her husband. Her life was financially secure, since her father-in-law, the Duke of Devonshire, had given her, on her husband's death, a life-interest in the house in Carlton House Terrace and an annual income of £1,500. But emotionally she moved from intense grief into dull depression. Nine months after her husband's murder, when the newspapers were full of reports from the trial of the Phoenix Park conspirators, she wrote to her husband's brother Edward, Lord Hartington: "my sorrow is too changeless and the sad, sad picture in my mind too constant for the disclosures to be to me what people call 'reopening the wound.' *Never, never is it closed!* and the very greatness of any grief saves me from the new pain and shock which others feel. But I am beginning to feel the prolonged strain as if the aching spot was day after day being pressed."[104] A year later she wrote to her sister Meriel, "You can't think how heavy life is to bear, not from unbearableness but from the utter vanishing of all my old mainspring of joy and delight."[105] She stopped keeping her regular diary, although from time to time, she would reproach herself and make an attempt to start anew. On 25 January 1885, for example, she wrote: "I don't know if I shall ever force myself into regular journal-keeping again – I have let the year all slip by – my grief is become a thing of long, long habit ... But the changeless thing is the grey endless atmosphere that seems always to surround me."[106] Even as an older woman, she dreaded receiving visitors or even telephone messages late in the evening, as she "couldn't stand sudden shocks."[107]

She contemplated joining an Anglican sisterhood, but was dissuaded by her brothers and sisters.[108] She did, however, and for the first time, go on a retreat, something she had often wished to do but had previously put off, not wanting to leave her husband for any stretch of time. St Mary's Penitentiary (not a jail, but a residence for those who were "penitent") was the "magdalen" residence for the reform and reclamation of juvenile prostitutes that Lucy's brother-in-law (and Caroline Talbot's son) John Talbot, member of Parliament for Kent West, had established shortly after he married Lucy's sister Meriel in 1860. Located at Stone, near Dartford in Kent, the same county as the Talbot home of Falconhurst, this institution featured, as many "penitentiaries" did, a laundry that attempted not only to take young prostitutes off the streets but also to provide them with marketable skills as laundresses, the idea being that this was a skill that was unlikely to lose its utility; people would always have laundry.[109] The penitentiary was affiliated with the old Saxon church of St Mary's, Stone, and thus it could now offer Lucy Cavendish both a religious retreat and a useful place to spend time in mourning.

This was also particularly useful in that she could also avoid the trial of public speculation in the periodicals *Man about Town*, the *Country Gentleman*, and *Vanity Fair* that she would soon have a new husband. About a year after Lord Frederick Cavendish's death it was rumoured that she would marry the country squire Meysey Bolton Clive, JP, whose wife, Lucy's friend the former Lady Katherine Feilding, had recently died.[110] Sir Edward Hamilton referred to this as "the most monstrous of all social papers' monstrosities."[111] But Lucy was not left without family, comfort, or support after her husband's murder; her brother Neville, who was between military postings and had been lodging with the Cavendishes at the time of Lord Frederick's murder, stayed on at Carlton House Terrace until his marriage to Katharine Wortley in 1883. Their brother Alfred also moved in with them almost immediately after the funeral and he stayed until his marriage to Laura Tennant in 1885.

Unlike the widow of Balmoral, who virtually cloistered herself after the death of Prince Albert, Lucy soon turned outwards, finding consolation in altruistic activity. Gladstone noted in his diaries, almost a year after her husband's death, how impressed he was with how his niece filled her life with philanthropic occupation: "What an edifying picture in all her words and work."[112] Her husband's death also gave Lucy an impetus to re-create her life as one devoted to public service. Whether from a need to fill an emptiness, a desire to keep busy, or a new maturity of vision, she threw herself into philanthropic enterprises before her period of mourning was officially over. Years later, consoling a young cousin who had recently lost her own husband, Lucy advised her that one must "make your happiness out of the happiness of others. It is not the same happiness; but it *is* happiness."[113] The consolation of a purpose-driven life sustained her and provides further insight into what motivated so much of her philanthropic works in what was, so clearly, the other half of her life. Writing to her aunt, Mrs Gladstone, sixteen years after her husband's murder, Lucy showed a conscious connection between her widowhood and her need to be useful: "when I used to feel that most heart-breaking of all feelings, that I had nobody but myself to think of or to plan for, in some ways it is 100 times easier to help people than to be helped."[114]

Educational Philanthropy

In the summer of 1884, eighteen months after her husband's murder, Lucy was approached about the possibility of becoming the Mistress of Girton College, Cambridge. It was not a position which was of interest to her, for a number of reasons. First, she was somewhat self-conscious about what she and her sisters had termed their "slip-sloppy" education.[115] As she wrote to her cousin Mary Gladstone, although she was "most immensely grattered and flattified" by the offer and although she acknowledged that she had "some strong points that would come in well," her "hopeless unfitness on several grounds made the whole thing seem only a joke."[116] Her sister Lavinia Talbot wrote to Mary about Lucy's immediate decision to decline the offer: "She does not entertain the idea for an instant ... I should say she would not be specially qualified for any of the main demands on a lady Principal ... one may say why do these competent women think of her, if she is not qualified; but they have, so she says, seen her only on committees where she shines, and know of her as a beautiful, saintly character ... She thought it ludicrously out of the question from the outset."[117] But there was a second and, at the time, a more important reason to decline the offer of Girton: her bereavement was still very fresh to her and, since she had gone through the utterly public death of her husband, deliberately putting herself into a public position, not congenial at the best of times, would have been torturous. Lucy made her views clear in a letter to her cousin: "I cannot see why, because my sorrow came upon me in that tremendous way, I should conclude that I am called to be dragged up prominent mountain tops. Dear Freddy would wish me rather to be useful in quiet, natural ways."[118]

This offer regarding the Mistresship of Girton, however, was not as lacking in foundation as Lucy made out to her sister and cousin. She had taken over her father's seat on the Girls Public Day School Trust in 1874, very shortly after its founding.[119] She had shown no reticence about expressing her own views in meetings; writing to her father in 1874, she argued, "I don't think there is any truth in Sir J. Kay Shuttleworth's notion that headmistresses can never reach equal excellence with headmasters because the latter have huge salaries and the prospect of bishoprics to encourage them. I am very sure that such motives are not necessary to produce efficiency in our headmistresses. Already it looks as if what we offer secures the best possible applicants. And tho' I do believe that we must suffer for many years to come from want of long and continued experience, I should have imagined we were more likely to improve our race of headmistresses by showing full confidence in them and giving them ample liberty than by cramping their powers."[120] She took the Girls Public Day School Trust seriously, as she did girls' education generally. When first married to Lord Frederick Cavendish she had been asked to serve on the executive council of the Yorkshire Ladies Council of Education, and, since her husband's constituency included Leeds, this seemed a good organization with which to concern herself. After her husband's death she became more seriously involved, becoming Council president, assiduous in her leadership and her commitment to girls' education.[121] In an early address to the Council, she observed that perhaps the most "far-reaching result" of the 1870 Education Act was the "recognition of the fact that girls' brains differed little in degree from those of boys and that their health gained, rather than lost by plenty of hard work."[122] Her commitment to the Council – which was thought of as a model of such institutions – remained strong.[123] Although Lucy Cavendish did not wish even the pallid public life that would have come with being Mistress of Girton, that did not mean she did not take the educating of girls and women seriously.

Lucy Cavendish made her feelings on the importance of women's education very clear when she made a fundraising speech at the Royal Victoria Hall on 15 May 1888, expressly on the importance of the admission of women to Morley College. Unfortunately, four days after her speech at the Hall, her life received a second bereavement in the death of her nephew Christopher of meningitis at the age of twenty-one months.[124] For her brother Alfred this was a particularly bitter blow. His marriage to Laura Tennant had been happy but cruelly short-lived; after only eleven months she died in childbirth, leaving the one child, Christopher. Although Laura Tennant's sister, Charty, and her husband moved into Alfred Lyttelton's Brook Street house in order to help him raise the baby, they stayed only until August of 1887; thereafter Lucy Cavendish took their place. Since she had, in many ways, become responsible at the age of sixteen for mothering Alfred Lyttelton after their own mother had died giving birth to him, so again taking care of Alfred and now his son Christopher was profoundly satisfying for Lucy. He was evidently a delightful child, "intelligent, merry" and filled with laughter. Lucy wrote in her diary that he "became the joy of my heart, it seems such a blessing to be called upon for mothers love in my second sad life for a little fellow so nearly my own." At his death, Lucy recorded in her diary that the sudden loss of her young nephew was "a deeper sorrow to me than I thought I was still capable of."[125] Neither she nor her brother Alfred could bear to stay in the Brook Street house. It was sold and Lucy returned to her house at 21 Carlton Terrace. After this devastating second bereavement, she determined upon a change of scenery and in September 1889 she and her brother Spencer went to South Africa to visit their brother Albert, a clergyman in Kimberley. They did not return to England for a year.

By this stage, Lucy Cavendish's name brought more than aristocratic lustre to a committee. She was known for a corpus of administrative experience. While she was in Africa, the Committee for Promoting the Return of Women as County Councillors spontaneously sent a resolution to the leadership of the recently victorious Progressives, who had secured a firm majority on the first elections for London's County Council. The Committee reminded the Progressive caucus, in strong terms, of the women rate-payers who had supported them and suggested that they nominate two women as aldermen. Emma Cons was the sole successful nominee, but Lucy Cavendish was the other name put forward.[126]

Governing the Old Vic

In the two years since her husband's murder, Lucy Cavendish had become increasingly involved with the setting up of the newly reclaimed Royal Victoria Hall. She solicited Queen Victoria's daughter Princess Helena (Princess Christian of Schleswig-Holstein), whom she knew from her days as a maid of honour to the Queen and who was one of the princesses who so fondly remembered Lucy's grandmother, Lady Lyttelton, as her governess. Princess Helena now happily became the Hall's patroness, opening exhibitions and attending opening nights. When Emma Cons initiated a fundraising drive to purchase the freehold of the Royal Victoria Hall, it was Lucy Cavendish who coordinated the logistics of this successful appeal with the Duke of Westminster, and who led the lists of donations with a gift of £1,000. When the successful campaign was concluded, she accepted a seat as one of the trustee governors for the new Royal Victoria Hall.

Lucy Cavendish was consistent in her attention to the Royal Victoria Hall. As its Friday night "penny scientific lectures" grew into Morley College for Working Men and Women, conducted out of the spare rehearsal rooms at the back of the theatre, she served on the College's Board of Trustees in addition to the Board of Governors of the Royal Victoria Hall. She gave money, every year writing a cheque as part of a scheme on the part of the Hall's supporters, to cancel any deficit.[127] She gave in service, pulling friends in high places, on one occasion personally soliciting the Admiralty to see if Robert Falcon Scott would give one of the scientific lectures. In that she was unsuccessful, but she managed to persuade Ernest Shackleton to lecture on "An Antarctic Winter."[128] Members of court were regularly persuaded to attend the Hall: Princess Frederica and Princess Beatrice dutifully came almost every year. The Prince and Princess of Wales were once again brought to the Hall, this time to attend the opening of the Hall's 1897 season. Lucy Cavendish had cannily employed the Prince of Wales's sister Princess Helena as her agent. In triumph, Lucy wrote to Emma Cons:

> Dear Miss Cons,
>
> There now! Don't I deserve 2/6 commission at least! Mind you obey HRH and write *yourself* to *her* in the autumn. No doubt it's a thing you have done before; but in case you have not, I will just inform you that one uses one's best pen, begins "Madam," says "Your Royal Highness" (full length!) instead of you; only its better to say "you" once in a way rather than repeat that unwieldy business too often, and ends "I am, Madam, HRH's most humble servant, but *full length* of course. *I* always seal a royal letter but I daresay this is now old fashioned.[129]

The sensitive diplomacy suggesting how Emma Cons might navigate royal protocol shows a certain degree of familiarity, if not affection, between the two women. It is a tone which, interestingly, marks the fragments of both sides of their correspondence that have survived. Lucy might well be comfortable writing in a familiar tone to Emma, but, given Lucy's social prominence, it is a mark of genuine friendship that Emma felt no compunction in writing so bluntly and so frankly in return, as can be seen from a postscript to a letter (dated 30 January 1904) to Lucy regarding one of her fellow governors, the new Duke of Westminster: "Can you do anything more to induce that horrid young Duke to take the Chair? He seems so different to the dear late Duke. Shall I write officially to our Governing Body reminding him that he is our President?"[130]

Absentee chairmen and trustees who allowed their names to adorn the Hall's letterhead but did little else were a particular irritation to Lucy Cavendish, as were inadequate governors. She was, herself, punctilious about attendance at executive committee meetings and so could be somewhat intolerant of other governors' failings. In a letter briefing her sister Lavinia, about to come onto the board, Lucy was explicit: "The Old Vic Chairman was Harris – he has resigned and it's a good thing for he is getting rather crusty and stupid."[131] She was consistent in her in frustration: "the present lot on the Governing Body are really just logs as to forking out money or putting their backs into things: they think they have squared all the circles when they tell you with a smack that money is wanted for everything."[132] The minutes of the Executive Committee for 1915 contain an explicit message that Lucy Cavendish wished spelt out to her fellow governors:

> Lady Frederick Cavendish presents her compliments. She has observed with regret that many of the Council are only nominal members and she would point out how very much it is to be desired that *every* member whether by annual subscription or by interesting friends or by taking a box on Concert nights should back up and encourage the excellent popular entertainments for which the "Vic" has gained such a well-deserved reputation ...[133]

Lucy Cavendish was an invaluable member of the board, for she knew what was expected and what was needed from governors. She purchased rugs and furniture for Morley College's common room and forwarded her copies of *Punch* to the same destination when she had finished with them.[134] Emma Cons had her revise the fundraising appeal for the Hall when all other attempts proved inadequate. "You see that we cannot get on without you and must again trouble you. None of us have the gifts of language or feeling as you have and we cannot draft an appeal, alas ... we all beg you to pull them to pieces or write anything you prefer. Mr. Harris says that he will sign anything that you will. There's confidence in you!!!."[135] Lucy would also suggest and find new blood, bringing on, for example, among others, Rhoda Legge (the musically inclined granddaughter of the Earl of Dartmouth), a governor who actually attended board meetings.[136] In fact, Lucy actually functioned as *de facto* head of the governing bodies of both Morley College and the Royal Victoria Hall, a state of affairs which, between them, both she and Emma Cons openly acknowledged. As Emma put it: "As you are our *real* President, others are only figureheads, which unfortunately, we must have, in the present."[137] Meetings were scheduled around Lucy Cavendish's availability: "As you know it is *most important* to have *you* at our governing body meeting, so that it is you who must settle the day, time and place. We can meet at the Hall or the College on either day, but shall we get you? I regret having to bother you but you are so important!"[138] "Please choose any date *you* think best as we *must fit* into your convenience as we cannot have this meeting without you; with the Princess or without HRH, *we must have you!!!*"[139] Her attendance governed the dates of board meetings. This was not simply the window-dressing of a socially lustrous name; when Emma Cons and Caroline Martineau needed someone to conduct negotiations with the staff at Morley College on salaries, it was Lucy Cavendish, of all the trustee governors, who was given this task.[140]

Suffrage

Lucy Cavendish was also deeply affiliated to the Liberal party and had an insider's position in the midst of Liberal politics both through her uncle and her husband. Her aunt Catherine Gladstone served as president of the Women's Liberal Federation and her cousin Helen Gladstone sat with Emma Cons on the Federation's executive.[141] But Lucy would not become active in the Women's Liberal Federation; she would not join her friends and relations on the executive. In a letter to the Liberal activist Lady Hayter, Lucy explained it was simply a matter of Home Rule. Her views and those of her late husband on this matter differed from those of both her father-in-law, the old Duke of Devonshire, and her brother-in-law Hartington, who had led a number of Liberal MPs away from Gladstone's Home Rule policy in 1886 and towards the Conservative benches to sit as Liberal Unionists. Since her husband's death, her father-in-law, but particularly her brother-in-law, had been protective and caring. "They have all been kinder and more generous to me than I can ever say, and the love between us has been unaltered. The best I can do is to avoid parading our differences in public, – a thing to which most certainly no duty calls me. Until (which Heaven avert!) I get the Franchise, I feel I may put these strong private reasons for abstention from political action in the first place."[142]

In spite of her many liberal attitudes and notwithstanding her Liberal political involvements, Lucy Cavendish's views on women in politics were conservative; she did not support women's suffrage. She had been brought up to these views. Her father, Lord Lyttelton (notwithstanding his agitations for better schools for girls), similarly did not support women's suffrage. Her uncle Gladstone was well known to abhor votes for women.[143] When, in 1867, the question of extending a broader franchise to women on the same basis as men arose during the debate over the Second Reform Bill, Lucy, then twenty-six, had specific opinions. She noted in her diary at the beginning of the year: "the subject of female suffrage (odious and ridiculous notion as it is) is actually now beginning to be spoken of without laughter as if it was an open question. – I trust we are not coming to that."[144] Her ideas did not change much as she matured and acquired broader experience.[145] Perhaps because she was averse to changing a system that seemed to her to function well, perhaps because she thought men's education better prepared them for weighing the questions of the day, Lucy Cavendish did not support giving women a parliamentary vote.

Thus we find the apparent conundrum that in the spring of 1889, shortly after heartily applauding her colleague Emma Cons's election by the new county councillors as the only woman alderman of the newly created London County Council, Lucy Cavendish lent her name to Mary (Mrs Humphry) Ward and Louise Creighton's "Appeal against Female Suffrage," published in *The Nineteenth Century*.[146] For Lucy Cavendish, as for many other women, there was no contradiction in supporting a municipal and county franchise for women, working for women to take their places on school boards and county councils, and simultaneously opposing a national, parliamentary vote. Local politics dealt with issues that were seen as part of a woman's "natural" area of concern: public health, regulating baby farms, the housing of the working classes, schools, and parks. Women not only had a "natural" claim, they had particular expertise in these areas; imperial affairs were best left to men. Mary Ward and Louise Creighton's "Appeal against Female Suffrage" made exactly that point:

> The care of the sick and the insane; the treatment of the poor; the education of children: in all these matters, and others besides, [women] have made good their claim to larger and more extended powers. We rejoice in it. But when it comes to questions of foreign or colonial policy, or of grave constitutional changes, then we maintain that the necessary and normal experience of women – speaking generally and in the mass – does not and can never provide them with such materials for sound judgment as are open to men.[147]

We can also see Lucy's views through a letter written in November 1888 to her cousin Mary Gladstone, in which she opined, "It is not *weakness* either that differentiates between men and women. They have their own special strengths for their own special duties which men are quite devoid of." Not only had Lucy Cavendish come to a view that men were incapable of understanding certain kinds of issues, she had also come to the conclusion that, as she put it to Mary Gladstone, women's particular command of their own arena would weaken if women now spread themselves too thin by seeking to move into an imperial arena. "If women *will* undertake men's work, their own must suffer."[148]

Some found this attitude contradictory. In May of 1892 one of Lucy's old acquaintances from her days as a maid of honour to the queen, the former Miss Louisa Bowater, now Lady Knightley of Fawsley, paid a call on her, and, among other subjects, the two spoke of women's suffrage. As Lady Knightley wrote in her diary, Lucy gave two reasons for her adamant opposition. "She thinks women are 'up' to the municipal franchise but not capable of judging of imperial questions (quite as much so, I ventured to remark, as the agricultural labourer who doesn't know where Russia is), and second because women will wear themselves out with doing men's work while men are incapable of doing women's work."[149] This goes some way to explain the apparent conundrum of Lucy Cavendish's position against women's suffrage existing conterminously with her vigorous work as vice-president of the Women's Local Government Society (WLGS), formed after the 1890 legal decision in *de Souza v. Cobden* barring women from sitting as aldermen or county councillors, a decision which cut short Emma Cons's political career.[150] Lucy Cavendish not only lent her name and her time, but organized petitions, made speeches, and energetically worked for the cause of women county councillors and school board trustees. In this, she was not alone among aristocratic woman – her old friend Ishbel Marjoribanks, now Lady Aberdeen, was the president of the WLGS – but the name of Lucy Cavendish lent the WLGS both prestige and a gravitas.

Lucy Cavendish's view on women and suffrage may also have another genesis: her apprehension regarding the mottled education which she, and many women of her generation, had received. Both Lucy and her sisters Meriel and Lavinia often chided their father about the irony that, while he had spent much of his life of public service arguing and working for a systematized education for girls, his own daughters' education had been notably haphazard.[151] Thus Lucy had no background in classical languages. Her feelings about her own deficient education likely influenced her to devote much time to the Yorkshire Ladies Council of Education and to the Girls Public Day School Company and to support Morley College for Working Men and Women. It may well have also made her more determined to stay on top of so many of the political issues of the day, which she was well positioned to do. But Lucy's sense of how girls' education could be so spotty also made her more acutely aware of how deficient other women's views of the world could be. Her diary reveals her irritation with the superficiality of her acquaintances. "It made me sick yesterday, calling on that best and most sentimental of women, Lady Mary Feilding, to hear her with upturned eyes longing to go to war *now* because Russia was exhausted. I humbly asked where was the *causus belli*?"[152] In Lucy's opinion, too many of the women she encountered had received an education as slapdash as her own, leaving them with little understanding of the important issues of the day. Self-conscious about her own educational deficiencies, real or exaggerated, Lucy was quick to see the same in other women.

In taking this view, she was not alone. Sophie Bryant, principal of the North London Collegiate School for girls, made clear in an 1897 interview that she felt it "imprudent to entrust women with voting responsibilities until they have received more thorough education in political matters."[153] Notwithstanding her reservations, Sophie Bryant was also simultaneously in favour of the general principal of women's suffrage, seeing it as something which would likely evolve within the next generation as improvements in young women's education allowed them to mature into these responsibilities.

The coexistence of Lucy Cavendish's opposition to women's suffrage with her support of women's education and women's participation in local government was unremarkable for a woman of her class and time. Julia Bush, in her study of those women who actively opposed a parliamentary franchise for women, *Women against the Vote: Female Anti-Suffragism in Britain* (2007), shows example after example of women who would unite for one female-centred cause or another (women in local government, higher education for women, the defeat of the Contagious Diseases Acts, temperance), but divide on the issue of suffrage.[154] In many ways, Lucy's sense of women's capacities clarifies the views of those who saw a virtually "separate but equal" division between men and women in politics: men occupying Parliament and concerned with the greater issues of empire; women occupying local government and concerned with matters falling within their realm of expertise, those connected to health, the family, education, housing. That said, she was in the minority in the Women's Local Government Society; most of the women who worked with and supported the WLGS favoured women's suffrage as well as maternalist involvement in local government.[155] The interesting thing is that this maternalist view of women's participation in politics – that there were things that women simply did well and that men did badly, if at all – was an argument made by both Lucy Cavendish and Emma Cons, women who held diametrically opposing views of women's suffrage.

By her mid-fifties, Lucy Cavendish had acquired a multi-faceted reputation. To many, her name was synonymous with widowhood, or with Christian forgiveness; to others she was the embodiment of good works, or a combination of both, a shining example of one who could create a purpose-filled life out of devastation. But she had also acquired a broad portfolio of practical experience working with organizations that sought to help the poor. Her pattern of work was concentrated; she would adopt new organizations, such as the Friends of Armenia, the WLGS, or the Royal Victoria Hall, or expand her work, such as with the Yorkshire Ladies Council of Education, but that did not mean that she dropped others. She continued to work with the Parochial Mission Women Society well into the new century, never ceased to be involved in the St Mary's Home for reclaimed child prostitutes, and kept her seat on the Girls Public Day School Trust, which she had held virtually from its establishment. The kind of work she did varied with each philanthropy, but as she aged she gradually diminished her hands-on work with the poor and increased her organizational and management work. For example, after the age of forty, she ceased to be an active member of the Ladies Diocesan Association, no longer reading to women in workhouses. After Mrs Talbot's death in 1876, Lucy spent less time working in the field with Parochial Mission Women Society's parish workers but went on the managing committee, organizing volunteers, streamlining committee work, handling temperaments, assigning tasks, and delegating authority. But at the same time, knowing the ropes, she would pinch hit and supervise parish meetings when needed. In the same way she worked at trying to get a cooperative laundry going for girls such as those from the St Mary's Home, where they could have a steady income. And she took great satisfaction, and spent much time, in preparing individual girls at the St Mary's Home for their first communion.[156] She found, she wrote to her brother as she turned sixty, that she was "growing more interested as I get older, instead of learning detachment."[157]

One new organization with which Lucy Cavendish became involved after her return from Africa in September of 1890 was the National Union of Women Workers (NUWW). The NUWW had grown out of a series of regular conferences organized by her good friend of long standing Ishbel, Lady Aberdeen, held every eighteen months or so starting in 1888. Over its first six years, these conferences on women's work grew in both attendance and scope, while still serving as a forum for mutual support for women who were active in philanthropy. The NUWW was formally established in 1895 with Louise Creighton, wife of the Bishop of London (and co-author with Mrs Humphry Ward of the "Appeal against Female Suffrage"), installed as the inaugural president. Lucy Cavendish was enlisted as one of the vice-presidents. The NUWW had both a distinctly conservative and an Anglican constituency, but it was dedicated to promoting "the social, civil, moral and religious welfare of Women," to sharing information "likely to be of service to Women Workers," and to encouraging the organization and affiliation of women's organizations at the local level.[158] But the NUWW soon became interested in identifying and developing issues that involved women's capacity to affect policy agendas. The Manchester Conference of 1896, for example, included a session on "The Duties of Citizenship," which focused on how women might make the best use of those opportunities in local government that were currently available to them and how they might also employ well-organized philanthropic work to effect change. Described by the national press as a "Parliament of Women," a title readily adopted by its membership, the NUWW did not hesitate to encourage its members on the local level to write letters and petitions to governmental officials and discussed ways and means for women to "take up Public Work of Social Reform," as the NUWW president at the 1899 conference (Lucy Cavendish's sister-in-law Kathleen Lyttelton) observed.[159]

The NUWW did not have its own large national membership; its mission was to act as an umbrella organization for women's organizations. By 1906, the NUWW itself had only 4,300 members. But the number of women affiliated with the NUWW, through hundreds of local and national philanthropies and societies, was estimated to be somewhere around 1,600,000.[160] The NUWW enfolded virtually any women's organization that wished to join. Its membership was largely based in classic women's voluntary social philanthropy, such as the Girls' Friendly Society, the Huddersfield Inebriates Kitchen, the Church of England Temperance Society Women's Union, and the Mothers' Union, as well as associations more purposely dedicated to women's political lives, such as the Women's Local Government Society, the Women's Suffrage Society, the Women's Liberal Association, the Women's Cooperative Guild, and a group of ten women Poor Law Guardians.[161] But the leadership was adamant that the NUWW must remain aloof from politics or other factional elements that might serve to divide women. Its mandate remained firmly set on maintaining a space for the broadest possible congress of women workers, united, if only by their dedication to social reform. In spite or perhaps because of its variety of perspectives, the NUWW remained a diverse assembly of women speaking to women about how to influence the public agenda on social policy.

Lucy Cavendish had been part of the NUWW from its inception. She had attended the formative 1890 Birmingham Conference, held prior to the organization's actual incorporation. She found it stimulating, "wonderful." She had presented a paper on one of her favourite topics, proposed laundry houses for reclaimed juvenile prostitutes, and found other women's papers and the discussions first-rate. "Mrs. Maclagan (wife of the Bishop of Lichfield), Mrs. Creighton, Kathleen, Lady Georgiana Vernon, the Superior of St. Mary's either spoke admirably or read excellent papers."[162]

Royal Commissioner

By late middle age, Lucy Cavendish was known not only as an experienced administrator but also as a woman who had a broad corpus of hands-on experience. But she herself held a self-effacing, if not almost belittling, attitude towards her own work. Her brother Alfred Lyttelton took pointed exception to her modesty: "I want you to think very sanguinely about the work you do. You think so little of it and yet I feel it to be so much nobler and so much more effective and directly active for good than the work of most men. You don't rate it high enough. It does more for others than many lawyers put together."[163] His words had little effect. When, in 1894, she was asked if she would serve on the Royal Commission on Secondary Education, to be established and headed by Sir James Bryce, she wrote to her sister Lavinia that she expected to do little but support the opinions of her brother Edward.

In fact, she turned out to be an active participant on the commission, which had an important remit. The field of secondary education in Britain in the nineteenth century had not become more ordered in the century's latter half; numerous bodies, large and small, well-funded and poor, none subject to inspection, many often duplicating and competing with each other, littered the landscape. While the philosophy of laissez-faire had been eroded over the course of the nineteenth century, surmounted for example in the field of public health by a growing sense of the need for centralized organization by the state, in education this ethos remained dominant. The result was by 1894 "uncoordinated" and "illogical." The Bryce Commission was charged with enunciating the best possible scheme for conveying varying kinds of secondary education to the students of the nation. Based on her experience both with the Girls Public Day School Company and with the Yorkshire Ladies Council of Education, there were good reasons Lucy Cavendish was asked to serve.

Another aspect to this appointment is noteworthy: a woman had never been asked to sit on a Royal Commission. Ten years earlier, the cabinet debated whether to appoint Octavia Hill to the Royal Commission established to investigate the Housing of the Poor. There was no question that Hill was eminently qualified as an authority on the subject, as Gladstone's secretary, Sir Edward Hamilton, had noted in his diary. But there was no precedent, as Hamilton also noted. So, although both the president of the Local Government Board, Sir Charles Dilke, and the Prince of Wales favoured Octavia Hill's appointment, Sir William Harcourt and John Bright were "dead against it. They regard it as the thin end of the female-rights wedge."[164] Now, ten years later, Lucy Cavendish pondered the idea of becoming the first woman Royal Commissioner. She initially declined and then reconsidered. There were advantages. She would be serving with her brother Edward Lyttelton, then headmaster of Haileybury (subsequently, headmaster of Eton), which would be pleasant. And there were other reasons to accept. One was that she saw her "chief good" on the Commission as representing the Girls Public Day Schools Trust (now Company) and supporting the importance of girls' education.[165] This was also the opinion of the vice-president of the Committee of the Council on Education, Arthur Acland, who, responding to criticisms in the House of Commons that private schools were insufficiently represented on the Royal Commission, averred that the interests of private schools were secured by Lady Frederick Cavendish as a governor of the Girls Public Day School Company and so declined to enlarge the Commission.[166] But another reason for Lucy to accept lay in affirming what had now become part of her own agenda: furthering the position of women as participants in formulating public policy. As the first woman to serve on a Royal Commission, she could set a constructive precedent.

The choice of Lucy Cavendish as the first woman Royal Commissioner was not accidental in Lucy's view; the main reason she had been asked, she observed, "was not very flattering, but very cogent, *viz.*, to induce the Queen to swallow the other ladies and so inaugurate the age of Women Commissioners."[167] There would be two other women serving on the Commission, both of whom Lucy knew: Sophie Bryant, the mathematician and headmistress of the North London Collegiate School, and Eleanor Sidgwick, principal of Newnham College, Cambridge, and sister of Arthur Balfour. The commissioners were conscious that much of the nation's productivity rested on the best possible secondary education. But they were explicit that the purpose of secondary education should be, as they wrote, "to educate the mind, not merely to convey information."[168] Lucy concentrated on making clear her concerns about the scarcity of women involved as managers and governors of girls' schools, a point which was seconded by the other two women and, as well, by most of the other commissioners.[169] The Bryce Commission's Report, which came out in 1896 in many volumes, recommended sweeping changes: a new Board of Education should be created, functioning under its own minister and absorbing the various functions of the Charity commission hitherto engaged in funding some educational establishments but not others. This new Board of Education would thus become the central authority for the nation's elementary, technical, and secondary education. The Education Acts of 1899 and of 1902 embodied many of the Bryce Commission's recommendations, and national education now became the responsibility of the state.

After the death of her brother Alfred Lyttelton in 1913, Lucy Cavendish's own health suffered. She developed Parkinson's disease and gradually became confined to a wheelchair. Nevertheless, she insisted on voting in the election of 1918 and had to be wheeled to the polling station to cast her first parliamentary vote. Evidently her views had changed since she had mentioned in 1892 to Lady Knightley of Fawsley that she thought women not quite "up to" the parliamentary franchise notwithstanding the fact that Lucy had been voting in local elections since women had been granted the county council franchise in 1907. Perhaps she felt the improvements in women's education for which she had worked so diligently were now come to fruition. Perhaps she felt more confident in her own powers of political discernment. Although during the campaign of militancy conducted by the suffragettes she had heartily disapproved of breaking shop windows or setting post-boxes on fire, perhaps she had been won over to the suffrage cause by the example of women's work during the course of the First World War. Perhaps the examples of her pro-suffrage brothers Alfred and Arthur, and their wives, Edith and Kathleen, had influenced her views about women's suffrage, and perhaps also the opinions of her many friends and colleagues in charitable ventures who supported or had converted to the cause of suffrage, Emma Cons, for one, or Louise Creighton, wife of Mandell Creighton, Archbishop of Canterbury, for another. It is possible that she felt that in the election of 1918, called after the dissolution of the wartime Conservative-Liberal coalition (and complicated by the split within the Liberal Party between the supporters of Prime Minister David Lloyd George and the followers of H.H. Asquith), a vote was too important a thing to leave unused. This, however, was unlikely, as the MP for her constituency, Westminster Abbey, was a Conservative, Ashmead Bartlett Burdett-Coutts, who had held the former Westminster seat since 1885 and who was returned unopposed. Perhaps she enjoyed supporting the widower of her old colleague in philanthropy, Baroness Angela Burdett-Coutts. Or perhaps she simply felt a desire to exercise a new variety of public, political participation. Regardless, according to her niece, Lucy Masterman, Lucy Cavendish evidently enjoyed casting her first vote.[170]

Lucy Cavendish continued to pull people in to support the Old Vic. In March of 1910 she persuaded a second Prince and Princess of Wales (the future George V and Queen Mary) to attend a concert at the Hall. She elicited the Duke and Duchess of Devonshire and the wife of the Archbishop of Canterbury (by this time, Randall Davidson) to receive them together on stage with Emma Cons and the other governors.[171] She continued to be a source of advice and assistance to the Royal Victoria Hall long after Emma Cons's death in 1912. She helped shepherd Lilian Baylis through the procedure of obtaining a theatrical licence from the Lord Chamberlain.[172] Following Lucy Cavendish's death in April of 1925, the *Old Vic Magazine* reported:

> The memory of her beautiful personality would have alone made her name legendary in this theatre to which she was such a wonderful friend from the time when she stood shoulder to shoulder with Emma Cons in putting up the fight to make the Vic an influence for good. "Lady Fred," as she was affectionately known here, was the first to interest Royalty in the Vic. Work, and her buoyancy and belief greatly helped the Manager and Treasurer through the dark and troublesome days. Her love for the Vic was keen to the last, and during the first few days of the Sadler's Wells Appeal we received a cheque for £50.[173]

Lucy Cavendish's philanthropic career is representative in many ways of trends in women's philanthropy during the latter half of the nineteenth century. Her body of work in particular is useful in understanding the variety of philanthropic activities of aristocratic women. She combined direct, hands-on work with committee work, the former eventually decreasing as she gained experience in organizing and administration, but never completely disappearing. Very different was her work with the Church of England Temperance Society in the 1880s, where she discovered her gift for making speeches. Philanthropic work could allow a woman once described as "shyest" to become a woman who made two public speeches a day. Moreover, her work on temperance was not restricted to proselytizing. As is the subject of greater scrutiny in chapter 2, the Women's Union of the CETS was involved in gathering petitions, lobbying in a variety of ways, and very publicly working to alter liquor licensing laws. This experience was very useful in the 1890s when she became vice-president of the Women's Local Government Society, not only making speeches and organizing delegations to Parliament but chairing public meetings when Lady Aberdeen was absent.

Lucy Cavendish's philanthropic career also shows how women's options for charitable work significantly expanded between 1860 and 1890. As a young woman, Lucy's charitable work tended to reside with Anglican organizations and with the soup kitchens and direct help bodies established by her aunt Mrs Gladstone and her friend Mrs Talbot. But during the 1880s the options and paths open to her, as to other women, broadened significantly as we see her working with the after-care of the mentally ill, with temperance organizations, and with the Royal Victoria Hall. Her work with the Girls Public Day School Company and the Yorkshire Ladies Council of Education is also an example of how women's capacities within charities similarly grew: Lucy Cavendish sat on the governing bodies of these organizations, together with both men and women. At Morley College and the Old Vic, it was Lucy Cavendish who in fact ran the governing bodies. Thus, when she was appointed to the Bryce Commission in 1894, it was a recognition that perceptions regarding women's capacity for high-level public service had significantly changed. The philanthropic career of Lucy Cavendish serves as a good example of how, by the end of the century, women had moved well beyond simply a choice between home visiting and organizing bazaars.

2 Circumventing the Bishops: Women's Philanthropy and the Church of England

Lucy Cavendish was a great churchwoman. The Anglican Church was the bedrock of her life. In town she would usually attend services twice on Sundays, and when in the country, on weekdays as well. As her sister-in-law once affectionately said of her, "Church is Lucy's public-house, and unfortunately there's no keeping her out of it."[1] Lucy Cavendish not only derived spiritual sustenance from the Anglican Church, she found it a wholly admirable institution and was involved with it in many different aspects.[2] This was not difficult; in the latter half of the nineteenth century, the Church of England offered a variety of philanthropic avenues into which Anglican women could channel their charitable energies. But the status of women within the Anglican Church was not uniform; some of the church's philanthropies were quite loosely affiliated and gave women a great deal of autonomy, others, much less so. Some were constant in their attitudes towards women while others changed their positions over time, often shifting with the views of successive bishops and archbishops. Once again using Lucy Cavendish's activities as both exemplar and point of departure, this chapter examines three particular Anglican charities with which she was involved, the Ladies Diocesan Association, the Parochial Mission Women Society, and the Women's Union of the Church of England Temperance Society.

These three organizations flourished at a time of much discussion, both within the Church of England and in society as a whole, regarding the poor and what, if anything, ought to be done about them. In the first half of the century, the belief that poverty was not only inevitable but divinely ordained became subsumed in the debate on the sanitary needs of the nation, the efficacy of "outdoor relief" versus the workhouses mandated by the new Poor Law of 1834, and the issue of whether charity "demoralized" the working poor into a chronic state of pauperism. In the same way, Edwin Chadwick and the investigators into sanitary issues of Britain's towns and cities had focused on epidemics and their causes, but this issue had shifted by the 1860s to include the effects of slum life on character and the sense, as Anthony Wohl succinctly put it in *The Eternal Slum* (1977), "that it was the pig that made the sty and not the sty the pig."[3] During the 1860s and 1870s, the period in which the Parochial Mission Women (1860), the Ladies Diocesan Association (1864), and the Women's Union of the Church of England Temperance Society (1873) were established, the concern had moved beyond simple relief of misery and had identified, as a potential cause of poverty, the increasing social and geographical distance in British towns and cities between the classes and the absence of any salutary examples available to the poor in men and women of wealth and culture. The question now was not simply how to feed the poor, but how best to re-moralize them. Thus when the women of these three Anglican charities planned their strategy, their plans were founded on direct work with the poor. But they were far from alone. For one example, the reformer Octavia Hill purchased her first tenement in 1865, tackling its refurbishment with her friend and colleague Emma Cons, turning it into a model dwelling for the working poor with rent collected by lady visitors whose remit specifically included personal work with tenants to advise them on hygiene and thrift, and, as Octavia Hill herself phrased it, to "rouse habits of industry and effort" in the poor.[4] Similarly, the Christian Socialists, the Rev. F.D. Maurice, John Ludlow, Thomas Hughes, Charles Kingsley, and their colleagues, also believed strongly in working directly with the poor.

Christian Socialism was less a coherent movement than it was a collection of men with common views about the effects on the nation of the immense disparity in lives between rich and poor. Their concerns emerged from a confluence of the last, exhausted, Chartist demonstration of 1848 and the publication in the *Morning Chronicle* the following year of Henry Mayhew's *London Labour and London Poor*. As Hughes recalled, in his Prefatory to the 1881 edition of Kingsley's novel *Alton Locke*, Mayhew's vivid description of the hard-scrabble lives of London's poor "startled the well-to-do classes" and "made all fair-minded people wonder."[5] But it was not so much Mayhew's description of slum living conditions or the appalling exploitation of labourers that shocked the Christian Socialists so much as it was the degraded ways the poor spent their spare time.[6] Again, it was distance that had grown up between the classes that was seen as the root of the problem. To close the "gulf" that existed between the classes is an impetus that can be interpreted either as a radical, levelling ethos or as a reversion to a nostalgic Tory view of a paternalistic age where labourers enjoyed, through proximity, beneficial examples of the cultured lives of the upper classes. Arguably a confluence of the two, the Christian Socialists, in addition to their support of cooperative ventures, established the Working Men's College in 1854 to expose working men to the liberal arts culture that middle-class men took for granted, hoping to "lift up" the working poor not necessarily to a better future material life, but to a richer current one. Thus when the Parochial Mission Women, the Ladies Diocesan Association, and the Women's Union of the Church of England Temperance Society were established, they were not the only charities that grounded their mission in direct work with the poor.

As with much in Victorian life, class is involved in the overall questions of how – or if – the women who worked with these Anglican organizations were able to use them for their own ends. Like most of the elite women involved with these three organizations, Lucy Cavendish had been brought up with both access to power and an understanding of public service, since so many of her male relations were involved in governing: not only her uncle Gladstone and her cousin, the Earl Spencer, but also her father on royal commissions and her brothers in the army, Parliament, and the Anglican Church. These women understood the power structure, particularly of the Church of England and of how appointments and preferments were calculated. In particular, these women were familiar with bishops; Lucy Cavendish's brother Arthur, for example, was Bishop of Southampton, her sister Lavinia was married to the Bishop of Rochester, and two of Lucy's close friends were married to bishops. Thus, Lucy had much access to bishops. For these women, the Anglican Church was their comfortable, familiar, home turf.

But class enters the picture in another, complicating, way. With the growth of the state during the latter half of the nineteenth century and the concomitant emergence of agencies and boards charged with handling the poor, philanthropic women now had to battle an increasingly complex public apparatus, as well as private men, in asserting their position on matters of public policy. Both Frank Prochaska and M.J.D. Roberts, for example, have argued that for many women in the late nineteenth century, the increasing consolidation of social control by the state was a mixed blessing.[7] Against regulations laid down by a strengthening civil service, surely titles and personal social power would be increasingly ineffective? The exploration here of three Anglican agencies will test the authority held by elite women working both independently and in union and help us assess the power of social capital at a time when the line between professional and amateur social worker was razor thin. For all these reasons, seeing how Victorian women like Lucy Cavendish and her colleagues in various Church of England charities succeeded, or not, in negotiating their way around Anglican obstacles is important, since it involves a variety of questions concerning Victorian women and power. Without thinking too much about the repercussions and ramifications of their endeavours, did these women see the challenging of power and the pushing forward of the debate about the direction of public policy as simply another aspect of their charitable work? As Kathryn Gleadle has asked, to what extent did these women see themselves as cultural or political revolutionaries?[8] At the same time, examining how such aristocratic women fared in exercising their philanthropic muscle with the Anglican Church can serve as an instructive contrast to Lucy Cavendish and Emma Cons's vibrant and autonomous success in South London.

The Ladies Diocesan Association

In the early years of her marriage, when still in her early twenties, Lucy Cavendish became a member of the Ladies Diocesan Association (LDA), established by the Bishop of London in 1864 to organize charitable work in the poorer parishes of London. The framework of the association on the face of it was simple: the association would assign women from London's wealthier parishes to help in poorer parishes. Clergymen in these poorer parishes were unlikely to be able to afford their own curates to help with the poor. Moreover, in poorer parishes women usually either worked or were burdened by child care (or both) and thus had little discretionary time for volunteer work; hence the idea that leisured women, from wealthier parishes, would be "lent" to poorer parishes within the diocese. The Ladies Diocesan Association, although launched by the Bishop of London, Archibald Tait, was actually the brain-child of his wife, Catherine. "I remember distinctly," Tait recalled in a memoir, "her awakening me one night in our room in London House, and unfolding the scheme of the Ladies Diocesan Association, which had become impressed upon her mind. Her idea was to organize the great number of ladies who, in London, are anxious to do distinct work for Christ beyond the limits of their own families – in workhouse visitation, and in hospitals, and in ministering to the wants of the poor."[9]

The membership of the Ladies Diocesan Association was to be by invitation only and was to be almost entirely and exclusively aristocratic. The Duchess of Leeds, the Marchioness of Tavistock, the Countess of Pembroke, the Countess Spencer, the Countess Stanhope, Viscountess Downe, Lady Constance Stanley, Lady Louisa Egerton, Lady Camilla Fortescue, Lady Emma Talbot, Lady Mary Farquhar, Lady Augusta Fiennes, and the Hon. Lucy Cavendish are representative of the social echelon of the women who were enlisted as members. Each member, upon joining, was given a particular assignment and expected to attend to her duties on at least a weekly basis, while she was in London. For example, the Countess of Darnley and the Countess of Harrowby were both assigned to the Whitechapel workhouse, Lady Elizabeth Arthur to the Girls Friendly Society, the Marchioness of Ailsa to the City Road Workhouse, the Countess of Ducie to the St George's-in-the-East Workhouse, and the Countess of Waldegrave to the Dalston home for girls. These women took their duties seriously. Lucy Cavendish recorded in her diary:

> February 27, 1865. This is a day to be remembered. I attended the Bishop of London's inaugural meeting of the "Ladies Diocesan Association" which he set on foot last year, and in which ladies join to do useful and charitable work of many different kinds in the diocese. I became a member; the Bishop gave me a little book as a token of admittance. I hope to undertake small things; one is to be what they call a "supplemental lady" for the Parochial Mission Women Institution (that is, one for help on special occasions); the other, to visit St. Martin's Workhouse once a week. I have an awestruck feeling at joining people who have devoted themselves to good, and can only pray that the great blessedness of work for the poor may be mine, and that I may be helped.[10]

Catherine Tait's vision, however, was not simply to efficiently deploy otherwise idle aristocratic women among the poor of her husband's diocese; her concept was more complex. Assigning aristocratic women to poor parishes would not only relieve overburdened clergy; in this, as with so many other similar endeavours of this period, the underlying objective was to make a connection between women of entirely different classes. As her husband recalled, Catherine Tait, like Lucy Cavendish,

Emma Cons, F.D. Maurice, and many others, believed that almost "the worst growing evil of the Metropolis is the local separation between the abodes of the rich and the poor."[11] One of Catherine Tait's priorities in establishing the LDA was to let the poor of London see that they had not been entirely forgotten, that persons of note took an interest in their welfare, even if only on the most ordinary level; for example, Ladies Diocesan Association members were encouraged to bring flowers to "brighten" the workhouses they visited. Lucy Cavendish moved between three workhouses, one in Limehouse, one in Stepney, and the workhouse affiliated with her own parish of St Martin's-in-the-Fields. The duties of the workhouse visitor were varied: reading to inmates, sitting with women in the infirmary, even simply visiting and making the women feel that they had not been forgotten.

But a second, more deliberate and more important objective was to affect the perceptions of the aristocratic women themselves. Catherine Tait sought to enable her phalanx of aristocratic lady workhouse visitors to see at first hand the humanity in the poor of the workhouses and charity hospitals, to make them understand the utter squalor and desperation borne by so many of London's poor. For someone of her background, this was not entirely unexpected. Catherine Tait came from a wealthy Birmingham banking family; her father, William Spooner, was an evangelical archdeacon of Coventry whose sister, Barbara, had married William Wilberforce. The year Catherine Tait enunciated her idea of the Ladies Diocesan Association, a destitute worker, Timothy Daly, had died of infected bedsores acquired during his recent confinement to what passed for an infirmary at the Holborn workhouse. The scandal resulting from his death had heightened people's awareness of abhorrent workhouse conditions, and Catherine Tait sought to build on the momentum sparked by Daly's death by expanding the personal experiences of her aristocratic colleagues. But she also had another, more subtle and somewhat subversive objective. The aristocratic composition of the Ladies Diocesan Association was not just about bringing the classes together in understanding, neither was it simply a matter of raising the awareness of the aristocracy about conditions in workhouses. Catherine Tait's hidden agenda was to harness the power and influence of titled ladies and direct it towards workhouse reform.

Conditions in Britain's workhouses, in the 1860s, concerned many. The Poor Law Amendment Act of 1834 had centralized both workhouse policy and authority in, first, a Poor Law Commission, then a Poor Law Board, based at Somerset House in London. The purpose was to sweep away casual, local, reactive, amateur administration of the nation's workhouses, replacing a haphazard system with efficiency, rational planning, and professionalization. But better conditions in the workhouses failed to materialize. Elected Boards of Guardians and the overseers they paid to administer the workhouses were just as reluctant to admit visitors as had been the local magistrates under the old system. Louisa Twining's initial attempts to insert lady visitors into workhouses in the late 1850s had been firmly and unequivocally, if not derisively, rebuffed. Only with the greatest of difficulty, and by enlisting the influence of Lord Shaftesbury, Lord Carnarvon, and William Cowper-Temple, had Louisa Twining been able to organize her workhouse visitors into any form of effective action. Even with these influential men as sponsors, Twining's Workhouse Visiting Society encountered repeated rebuffs and accusations of undue interference with workhouse administration. These claims were not only made by disgruntled local authorities but were also heard farther up the chain of Poor Law command. Twining ran into continual obfuscation and obstacles from officials of the Poor Law Board in London itself. The apparatus of the Poor Law, from bottom to top, did not want well-meaning lady visitors in workhouses who might well point out neglect, corruption, or incompetence.

When Louisa Twining had initially attempted to organize a system of lady workhouse visitors in the 1850s, she had consulted Catherine Tait, who had experience in regularly injecting herself into the Carlisle workhouse while her husband had been dean of the cathedral.[12] When, in 1860, Catherine Tait sought to establish the LDA, she therefore did so well aware of the difficulties Louisa Twining had earlier encountered. Thus one of Catherine Tait's specific objectives in organizing the aristocratic women of the Ladies Diocesan Association was find a way to deflect, quash, or circumvent workhouse gatekeepers *ab initio*. "She knew," her husband recalled, "that such a union, under the *imprimatur* of the Bishop of London, might more effectually gain entrance for Christian visitation and kindly sympathetic influences into some of the workhouses and hospitals, in which a shrinking from such assistance had hitherto been manifested by the authorities."[13] But although the bishop might innocently assume that it was the influence of his office that his wife sought to employ, in fact, when Catherine Tait woke her husband from his slumbers that night in 1864 to broach with him her concept of a Ladies Diocesan Association, it was the power of well-connected, titled women that she saw circumventing the roadblocks encountered by Louisa Twining.

By and large, Catherine Tait's resourceful vision worked. Whether by charm, assumption, aristocratic bluster, or breezy efficiency, peeresses were, almost without exception, able to bowl their way past workhouse gatekeepers. It was no accident that the Marchioness of Ailsa had been given the City Road Workhouse or that the Countess of Darnley and the Countess of Harrowby had been assigned as a team to the Whitechapel workhouse. The Hon. Frances Georgiana Osborne, Duchess of Leeds, née Pitt-Rivers, was a force to be reckoned with. Louisa Twining acknowledged, in her 1880 memoir, that the Ladies Diocesan Association swept virtually all before it: "under such powerful influence, admission was gained into nearly all the workhouses of the metropolis." Where the ladies of Louisa Twining's Workhouse Visitation Society continued to encounter frustration when they would attempt to make their visits to workhouses, Miss Twining noted that the aristocrats of the Ladies Diocesan Association surmounted all obstacles: "at the present time there is no Board of Guardians and no chaplain who would refuse admission to the lady visitors thus introduced."[14] The Ladies Diocesan Association, by placing well-born aristocratic women of influence into active, philanthropic service, was able to accomplish three objectives. It raised the awareness of powerful women as to the real state of the nation and it used their names and connections to circumvent workhouse guardians and gatekeepers, pushing open the workhouse doors. It also enabled these well-placed women to relay their impressions of what they found therein to those who could be useful.

The network of aristocratic and powerful connections held by the members of the Ladies Diocesan Association was impressive. For example, Gladstone's ally the Earl Spencer was not only Lucy Cavendish's cousin but was married to another member of the Ladies Diocesan Association, Charlotte Spencer. The Earl of Ducie, the husband of another member (Julia, Countess of Ducie), became a great proponent of Poor Law reform, going on to serve as a reformer on the Sanitary Commission in the late 1860s.[15] Another member, Lady Louisa Egerton, was the daughter of the Duke of Devonshire. Lady Constance Stanley had sterling connections: her father-in-law was the prime minister, the Earl of Derby, but almost more importantly, her uncle, Charles Pelham Villiers, was president of the Poor Law Board from 1859 to 1866. It was the Earl of Devon (uncle of one member, Lady Camilla Fortescue, and brother-in-law of another, the Countess of Harrowby) who arranged an introduction of a deputation from the Workhouse Visiting Society who wished to discuss with Villiers the subject of competent medical inspections of workhouse infirmaries. This would have been relatively easy for Devon, as he served as permanent secretary to the Poor Law Board from 1850 to 1859.

The membership of the Ladies Diocesan Association was bipartisan and had both Tories (Countess Waldegrave, Countess Stanhope, Countess of Pembroke) and Whigs and Liberals (the Countess Spencer, Marchioness of Tavistock, Lady Camilla Fortescue, Countess of Harrowby, Lucy Cavendish). Thus when governments changed, they still had access. For example, when the Whig government fell in June of 1866 and Constance Stanley's uncle, Villiers, handed the presidency of the Poor Law Board to Jonathan Gathorne Hardy, the Ladies Diocesan Association had even easier access, as their champion, the Earl of Devon, and Gathorne Hardy now sat in cabinet together. A combined deputation of workhouse reformers armed with reports and specifics about workhouse conditions was enabled to descend on Gathorne Hardy. Indeed, the Earl of Devon himself succeeded Gathorne Hardy as Poor Law Board president.

How effective was this network of aristocratic affiliation? It is difficult to assign particular effects or results to the Ladies Diocesan Association, as the organization was established and operated in the midst of increasingly widespread concern about the state of the nation's workhouses. Certainly the formation of the LDA reflected a growing concern among the elite, as well as educated and responsible Britons generally, as to the state of the nation's workhouses and the proper role of the state vis-à-vis the most vulnerable. One particular and serious concern was the co-mingling of the sick with those who were simply poor – often, given the shortage of beds, with the two sharing sleeping accommodations. In 1861, the then president of the Poor Law Board, Charles Villiers, struck a select House of Commons committee to inquire into workhouse conditions. It would conduct hearings and gather evidence for the next three years. While this committee was in its fact-finding stage, and shortly after Catherine Tait assembled the LDA, Dr Ernest Hart, the editor of the medical journal the *Lancet*, ran a series of articles outlining both the appalling conditions in many workhouse infirmaries and the efforts of a group of doctors to secure separate medical facilities for pauper patients.[16] Florence Nightingale was one of the voices that contributed to this campaign, urging the separation of the sick, the insane, and the incurable from the general pauper population of workhouses. By 1867, Gathorne Hardy's committee had made its recommendations, many of which were incorporated into the Metropolitan Poor

Bill of that year (shepherded into being by the Earl of Devon), which brought the care of London's sick poor under the care of a new body, the Metropolitan Asylums Board. All workhouses were now required to provide hospital accommodation on sites separate from the workhouse. The Ladies Diocesan Association had been one part of this wave of reform-minded effort, but the determination of Catherine Tait's army of aristocratic ladies tells us much about how these women saw themselves as owning part of this campaign and how they were able to use their authority to combat policies and practices which they saw as destructive. The activities of the Ladies Diocesan Association also show how titled women were able to use the authority of the Anglican Church and the Bishop of London as both a shield and a sword in furthering their ends. At the same time, the LDA also shows a different aspect of the kind of philanthropic work that aristocratic women actively embraced when resident in London.

The Ladies Diocesan Association functioned in an aristocratic bubble of autonomous authority until the early years of the twentieth century, continuing to assist in workhouse visiting and various other parochial duties in London's poorer districts. Protected by the aristocratic network of women and by their affiliation to powerful men both within the Anglican Church hierarchy and without, the women of the LDA, using their high purpose and titles, were able to go where others could not. Almost more important, the Ladies Diocesan Association enabled its women to take up the same stances as did their aristocratic male colleagues. Lord John Russell, Lord Stanley, and Lord Talbot de Malahide assembled petitions for workhouse reform. The Earl of Shaftesbury, the Earl of Carnarvon, and the Earl of Devon all applied personal pressure to persuade those in power that the workhouses were in acute need of reform. In all this, aristocratic men worked to shape public policy and influence law-makers. Aristocratic women, united in the Ladies Diocesan Association, did exactly the same thing.

The Parochial Mission Women Society

As Lucy Cavendish described it in her account of its founding, the Parochial Mission Women Society was established in 1860 by four very well established "West-End ladies": Lady Laura Palmer (daughter of the Earl of Waldegrave, wife of the Earl of Selborne), the Hon. Cecily Stuart Wortley (daughter of Lord Wharncliffe, wife of Lord Montagu), Lady Wood (daughter of the Indologist Edward Moor and wife of Gladstone's first vice-chancellor, Sir William Page Wood),[17] and their leader, the redoubtable Hon. Caroline Talbot, the third member of that inseparable trio of Catherine Gladstone and her sister Mary, Lucy Cavendish's mother. Mrs Talbot's idea was to provide vicars of poor parishes, often working alone and usually overburdened, with the opportunity to acquire a helpful "mission woman" to assist with the parochial poor. The vicar would identify an appropriate, mature, and respectable woman from his parish and the Parochial Mission Women's committee of lady managers in London would remit the vicar an annual grant for this mission woman's salary. This salary was not fixed, but tailored to the needs of each particular woman. For each parish, an amount was designated by the lady managers that would give the parochial mission woman independence from having to do any other work, thus freeing her to focus completely on the mission. This generally worked out to between 8 and 14 shillings a week.[18] For example, in 1867, the older, childless, and widowed London parochial mission woman Jane Elliott was paid 10 shillings a week or £26 a year (at this time, the average mechanic in the same district could support a family on a salary of 15 to 30 shillings a week). The committee of lady managers had calculated that she would be able to pay her own rent and board on this amount.[19] By the late 1870s, the average mission woman's salary had risen to about £30 a year.[20] In 1883, this advertisement ran in the Church of England *Temperance Chronicle*: "A good parochial mission woman is wanted for a leading London parish in the W.C. district. Salary £35 per annum. The post is a very happy one, and any one many have full particulars thereof on application to the General Secretary at the offices of the CETS."[21] The funds for the mission women's salaries were raised by the lady managers and private supporters of the Parochial Mission Women Society, and very often an individual would sponsor a particular parish. The incumbent vicar was invariably asked to contribute (usually £5 per annum), but if he could not, this was not a bar.

In many ways, the Parochial Mission Women resembled the organization of missionary "Bible Women" established by Ellen Ranyard more or less contemporaneously, who went out among the poor parishes of London, spreading the message of self-help and inculcating thrift by helping the poor to save their pennies towards the purchase of Bibles. But the two organizations may be distinguished in important ways: first, Mrs Ranyard's Bible Women were part of an evangelical mission to bring the poor to the word of God by enabling them to save to purchase Bibles. In the 1870s Mrs Ranyard began to also train women to act as visiting nurses to the poor, but the main mission remained the dissemination of Bibles. The Parochial Mission Women's remit was broader and sought to inculcate practices of hygiene, thrift, and delayed gratification, assisting women to save for practical items such as blankets. Second, and no less importantly, Ellen Ranyard's Bible Women operated entirely independently; the Parochial Mission Women, by definition, were designed to be an intrinsic part of the Anglican parish structure.

The lady managers would assign a "supplemental lady" to supervise each mission woman's activities. These supplemental ladies were sometimes aristocratic (Lucy Cavendish acted as a supplemental lady and so enlisted many of her friends), but they were also often from the leisured middle class. This was not just to promote compliance with the Society's goals, nor was it simply about retaining control of working-class women who operated for the most part independently, although both of these objectives would certainly have formed part of the basis for the supplemental lady's supervision. The desire to promote the intermingling of classes was just as important. As Lucy Cavendish recounted, "here we have at once intercourse and co-operation from top to bottom of the social scale, in itself a most wholesome and desirable thing."[22] It was relatively easy for the socially well-placed committee to find supplemental ladies to supervise the parochial mission women for London parishes. Lucy Cavendish was enlisted almost as soon as she and her husband established their household in London. In other areas of the country, the committee would use its network of genteel connections or act on the recommendation of the local vicar or bishop to find an appropriate supplemental lady superintendent.

Caroline Talbot was no stranger to good works of this sort; she and Catherine Gladstone had been much involved with Louisa Twining in workhouse visiting, and it was Mrs Talbot who had been responsible for establishing the soup kitchen in Westminster where Lucy Cavendish had worked during the early years of her marriage. Lucy Cavendish became one of the five lady managers of the Parochial Mission Women in the early 1870s and was assiduous in her attendance and participation in its decision-making. After Mrs Talbot's death in 1876, the number of lady managers involved in running the Society expanded, and there were usually eight or nine women involved at each meeting. These women were as aware as any of the complexities of direct work with the poor of London, and because of this experience, the Parochial

Mission Women Society flourished. At the end of its first year of operations, eight mission women were established in six districts. Caroline Talbot's Parochial Mission Women Association soon spread beyond London to establish mission women in Penzance, Birmingham, Tyneside, and Plymouth. By 1888 there were 194 women working in 180 districts.[23] At the height of their activities, in the late 1880s, parochial mission women were placed in 300 parishes.[24]

The parochial woman's mission was specific: she was to make a connection with the poor women of the parish; she was to impart life skills to them, inculcate habits of hygiene, and, above all, thrift; she was to teach and lead the poor "to acquire habits of self-help, thrift and domestic comfort."[25] She was also to keep an eye open for cases of extreme hardship, which she was to identify for the vicar. These goals, the lady managers advised, were best accomplished through visiting, but also ought also to be pursued through weekly meetings of the parish women. Establishing a basis of trust and fellowship was important because the mission woman was charged with showing the poor women of the parish the material advantages of such middle-class values as long-term saving, delayed gratification, and planning. This goal was very like that of the lady visitors and genteel rent collectors employed by Octavia Hill and other reforming agencies. But the parochial mission woman had a distinct advantage over any sort of lady visitor and approached her task from a very different perspective. The mission woman had to be resident in the district she served and she also had to be, as the Society's literature undiplomatically put it, "bona fide of the lower class," having had herself "experience of a life of poverty."[26] This was deliberate. As Caroline Talbot wrote, the mission woman herself had the capacity to serve as a powerful model of thrifty behaviour. "She goes among them a living witness that *one of themselves* may be something better and happier than they are; and she at once puts before them encouragement to think they can do something for themselves, coupled with the cheering feeling that there is some one who takes an interest in them."[27] The point that Mrs Talbot was making, above all, was that the parochial mission woman would not be judgmental; she would understand the difficulties that women in the parish experienced, as she likely had gone through similar rough patches. This was an entirely different approach from that employed by Octavia Hill's middle-class lady rent collectors. There, an impression of condescension was inevitably inferred, despite the best of intentions. Mrs Talbot's idea, with the Parochial Mission Women, was founded in the fellow-feeling and sympathy of another woman with prior experience of poverty and personal knowledge of solutions.

Weekly evening meetings were, therefore, crucial for the parochial mission woman because of the messages she was able to personally impart to the women of the parish. Rooms were rented if a parish hall was not available, and local women were encouraged to drop in for a cup of tea and to bring their sewing with them. Needlework was also often taught; sometimes instruction in other skills, pattern-cutting for example, was given. Above all, the parochial mission woman was to instruct the women of the parish about thrift and value, to encourage them in tangible ways to save up their pennies towards making important and useful purchases. To this end, the mission woman would act as a savings bank, collecting pennies each week, cataloguing the deposits of each woman, showing her each week what her savings currently amounted to. The mission woman would also bring various useful items to the meeting and would help the women choose what they could purchase when their savings had accumulated sufficiently: blankets, Bibles, shirts, fabric for sewing. The mission women were also to encourage self-help. This they did in a variety of ways, some quite practical. For example, for those women who could sew, the supplemental lady could arrange the lease of a sewing machine. The women could acquire the machine over time on a hire-purchase arrangement, through the pennies they would deposit weekly with the parochial mission woman. Thus a variety of goals would be accomplished in one blow: thrift, sensible prioritizing, the rewards of delayed gratification, the satisfaction of gaining a self-supporting livelihood, and the ability of women to help other women.[28] Fabric for sewing would also be purchased cheaply, in bulk, by the supplemental lady and then resold at cost to the women of the parish at the weekly meeting, but in lengths they could feasibly save for. Lucy Cavendish explained in an Anglican periodical how the mission woman could inculcate a sense of the possibilities thrift could bring; she could act as the "thin end of the wedge."

> Does she find the room bare of all comforts? She tells the poor inmate in a neighbourly way of the good mattress or blanket that can be got by small weekly payments and induces her to rummage out a penny or two and thus to become a depositor. By promising to call again, an impulse is given to the new idea of making a struggle towards a better state of things: pence are put by – intercepted perhaps on their way to the gin shop – the deposits gradually accumulate and the mattress is bought. The next step

> is to persuade the poor woman to come to the weekly Mothers Meeting. It is wonderful how much the first dawn of hope tends to soften the heart once hard and despairing. The poor creature begins to feel that some one of her own sort cares about her and that there is a friendly hand to help her upwards. She goes to the Meeting, there she sees the good clothing and bedding to be had by the same payment of small weekly sums and having once tasted the pleasure of buying a good article out of her own savings she is soon tempted to begin depositing for something else.[29]

The women who ran the Parochial Mission Women central committee in London had a very clear sense of the utility of their program and the momentum it could inspire. They were convinced of both the causal connection and the cyclical aspect of poverty and drink. They saw much of the intemperance in England's slums as being partly the result of, as Caroline Talbot put it, the "physical craving for stimulants produced by the utter misery of the sanitary conditions in which they live."[30] But poverty could also be traced, they believed, to the "recklessness in the use and management of money" on the part of the poor.[31] Purposeful saving could break the cycle of drink and poverty. Saving pennies towards a new shirt or Bible or blanket, they firmly believed, could "animate the possessors to further efforts after cleanliness and economy and to breaking off habits of intemperance."[32] Thus the one invariable rule was that the mission woman was never to give charity either in the form of money or in the form of useful items from her cache; the blanket, if it was to have a lasting, transforming impact, had to be saved for, had to be anticipated, had to be earned.

This was very much in keeping with the tenets of classic Victorian philanthropy. Charity had the capacity to deform the beneficiary; if it was simply given, this would both create a dependency and rob the recipient of the incentive to help herself. This is the reason why Emma Cons would never give her tenants money; this is the reason why Mrs Talbot's Westminster soup kitchen did not give the poor food. Instead, they were given tickets which entitled them, upon their paying tuppence, to "good meat, soup, beef-tea, or pudding of at least twice the value of what they pay."[33] The parochial mission woman would not give money or goods. As her supplemental lady was supposed to continually remind her, she was in the business of showing the means to a better way of life, not to provide front-line relief.

But the parochial mission woman could do a great deal with the women of her parish aside from inculcating thrift. One mission woman, reporting to her lady manager, wrote that she had "visited a poor family where the mother of six children has been bedridden from rheumatism for three years and her mind much weakened ... she was in a miserable condition; the dirt on her poor limbs must have aggravated her suffering: I bathed them for her in warm water which seemed to ease her."[34] Similarly, another wrote, "one poor woman had two children very ill so that she could not leave them to do anything and was so poor she could not pay anyone. I offered to stay with them for an hour or two; the poor woman was so thankful."[35] In the same way, a third reported that "I had two poor things whom I went to, one from the other; they both died the same day. When I used to go creeping up the dark stairs, the poor woman would put out her hand when she could not speak; the other was a young man, and he would watch for me like a child would for its mother."[36] Much could be done by the parochial mission women aside from arranging savings for shirts.

Simply the sense of community among women had a beneficial aspect. Men were simply not part of this network; this was woman-to-woman work. Although supplemental ladies did not usually participate in the mission woman's home visiting, they invariably attended the parochial weekly meetings. One reported back to the lady managers' committee that the work was tough going at the start.

> When first our workroom was opened in April, we had to contend against a great disinclination on the part of women to avail themselves of it. Many nights passed without a single person entering the room. For six weeks I was there every Tuesday evening without meeting more than two or three old women who came merely from motives of curiosity. A person whom I had engaged to teach cutting out and fixing found her occupation a complete sinecure. In June however, a marked change took place; women began to drop in with their needlework to spend an hour in the evening. Before long about a dozen were working there regularly and a friendly feeling sprang up among themselves. On my evenings the number soon rose to twenty and upwards.[37]

The idea of women helping other women was something that the aristocratic lady managers understood, and it was the principal reason for the Parochial Mission Women's structure. One supplemental lady reported back to the committee with satisfaction at the success her meetings enjoyed exactly because they were run by a woman. "Many who would never look at a curate, now attend the women's meetings regularly."[38] In addition, although the program had its effect on the women of the working poor, it also gave the parochial mission woman herself (in addition to the no doubt profoundly welcome salary) a sense of purpose, self-sufficiency, and empowerment. Although Caroline Talbot had not specifically articulated this as one of the purposes of the organization when it was established, it was clearly one of the reasons for its success. Another effect that Caroline Talbot had not necessarily anticipated was that the Parochial Mission Women Association also gave its supplemental ladies authority, independence, and pride of accomplishment as well as training in managerial skills and the balancing of both stock inventory and personnel; supplemental ladies frequently had to smooth friction and turf conflicts between parochial mission women and their local vicars as well as the occasional curate. But the committee of lady managers who ran the association oversaw all this with an autonomy that was unusual in the 1860s.

This committee was a most peculiar institution for the Church of England, not an organization that, in the 1860s, gave women much voice. Even thirty years after Caroline Talbot had established her unusual institution, as "Women in the Churches," an article in the *Woman's Herald*, pointed out, "There is no part of social life in which the Conservative element is more powerful and tenacious than in ecclesiastical organizations."[39] But the committee that ran the Parochial Mission Women Society stood in a peculiar position of authority, since the decision-making power lay entirely with the lady managers' committee. They screened vicars' applications for grants, set the mission women's salaries, assigned supplemental ladies, and responded to complaints from mission women, supplemental ladies, and vicars. The church did not interpose a clergyman to sit with them in their deliberations, to supervise their decisions, or even to act as a liaison with the church itself. The vicars technically had authority over those Parochial Mission Women who served their parishes, but as regards the committee in London which oversaw the whole national operation, no office existed which could claim to supervise it beyond, presumably, the ultimate authority of the Archbishop of Canterbury. The Parochial Mission Women, having been established by women operating on their own recognizance, occupied an anomalous bubble outside the Anglican chain of command.

This autonomy had much to do with the fact that the women who founded the organization and served as lady managers were well-placed women on the best of terms with most of the bishops and archbishops of the Anglican Church. The Parochial Mission Women acquired many of their supplemental ladies from the Ladies Diocesan Association, thereby acquiring both working ladies and powerful allies in Archbishop and Mrs Tait. But the Parochial Mission Women already had influence of their own: their founder, the majestically steely and intimidating Caroline Talbot, was the mother of the Bishop of, successively, Rochester, Southwark, and Winchester, and Lucy Cavendish was the sister of the Bishop of Southampton, as well as the best friend of Beatrice Temple, wife of the powerful churchman Frederick Temple, successively Bishop of Exeter and London and, eventually, Archbishop of Canterbury from 1896 to 1902. Indeed, in the Parochial Mission Women's sixty-three years of existence, no churchman ever corrected, reproved, chided, or overruled them or asserted any authority whatever over them.

This anomalous bubble of authority may also be partly explained by lady managers' placing much emphasis on the idea that the parochial mission women operated entirely under the authority of the local parish incumbent. This was a message that they and their supporters continually stressed. For example, the Rev. C. Wellington Furse, at the 1862 Church Congress, observed approvingly that the parochial mission women would "in all things be subordinate to the parochial system."[40] The husband of the one of the founding ladies, Roundell Palmer, MP, wrote, approvingly, that no parochial mission woman would be employed in any parish or district "except upon application of the incumbent; who might change her or the Lady Superintendent if he saw fit; or might, if he were dissatisfied, at any time discontinue the mission."[41] Mrs Talbot and her friends thus distanced themselves from any suggestion that they were establishing a clutch of independent women like Mrs Ranyard's Bible Women, who operated independently of any organized church or parish. The Parochial Mission Women Society was strictly an Anglican organization that would work through the parochial system. By sending this message so strongly, Mrs Talbot and her committee also obviated any concerns about women of the working classes being given funds to hold unsupervised. Simultaneously, to reinforce this idea of proper control, Mrs Talbot and her three friends precluded any potential concerns about the supervision of the lady managers themselves by securing the services of "eight gentlemen whose names would inspire confidence in any assembly of Churchmen" to serve as a Committee of Reference who would supervise the lady managers.[42]

In fact, the impression of male supervision, both of the lady managers and of the parochial mission women at work in the parishes, was close to a fiction. The Committee of Reference was composed almost entirely of the husbands or sons or friends of the lady managers.[43] Its most useful function was to act as a shield. Occasionally, when a local vicar questioned a decision the lady managers had made, they would invoke the Committee of Reference as a higher power that had given its imprimatur to the decision and could not be questioned. In fact, the Committee of Reference met once a year; it audited the books (or, more likely, arranged to have professionals audit the books). As a rubber stamp for the lady managers' decisions, the Committee of Reference worked well. Similarly, although the impression was given that the parochial mission women were utterly subservient to parish vicars, in practice this was far from the case. Although the parish incumbent might nominate his parochial mission woman, she had first to be personally vetted by the committee of lady managers. Sometimes they approved the nomination; sometimes they did not.[44] The committee had no compunction in rejecting nominations of women whom they did not approve, nor did they cavil at dismissing mission women who did not measure up to the work, often in the face of vociferous opposition from the local vicar. In March of 1893, when a Mr East, vicar of St Anne's, Newcastle, suggested his wife as the supplemental lady, he was told, quite smartly, that this simply would not do.[45] The clergymen who welcomed the establishment of the Parochial Mission Women Society might well aver that vicars had authority over the parochial mission woman, but in practice the committee of lady managers governed.

The balance of power was skewed in favour of the lady managers from the start because they set the salaries of the parochial mission women and, more important, provided the funds themselves.[46] The committee of lady managers closely supervised the progress of mission women through the network of supplemental ladies. The committee would frequently summon a vicar for a meeting if there were difficulties of any kind. Similarly, the committee rarely hesitated to simply revoke grants and discontinue operations if they felt that there was undue interference from the local minister. From time to time clergymen would complain that their grants were being arbitrarily withdrawn. Sometimes the committee of lady managers would give reasons, sometimes they declined to do so, sometimes they responded simply by sending copies of the minutes of the meeting in which the decision was made.[47] Sometimes they would imply that the decision had actually been that of the Committee of Reference. Regardless, it was the lady managers' decision to make and from it there was no appeal. For example, in November of 1903, the committee was faced with a dispute from Mr Rust, the vicar of All Saints, Spitalfields, who averred that his authority over "his" mission woman was being interfered with by the committee of lady managers. Moreover, he vigorously disagreed with their rule that the mission woman was barred from giving anything away to the poor. The lady managers rather tartly informed him that the parochial mission woman would continue to obey their rules, notwithstanding Mr Rust's unhappiness, and that the rule against giving relief would not be altered. He was evidently a stubborn cleric, since, at the beginning of February of 1904, he reiterated his position to Lady Fremantle, the supplemental lady supervising the Spitalfields mission woman, making clear that he did not appreciate the lady managers' interference and that he intended to take up the matter with the Bishop of Stepney. The lady managers responded in two ways: they informed Mr Rust that they would be discontinuing their Spitalfields parochial mission, and they also simultaneously decided (perhaps as a preventive strike) to invite the Bishop of Stepney to speak at the Parochial Mission Women's annual meeting, which was to be held at the home of Lady Margaret Charteris.[48] Within weeks, Lady Fremantle reported that Mr Rust was "very satisfied" with the work of the parochial mission woman. The committee decided to keep the Spitalfields work continuing "for the present."[49] The underlying threat, as the lady managers frequently drove home, was that the money was theirs to withdraw at their sole discretion, at any time.

That this anomalous bubble of authoritative women was allowed to exist within the parochial network but simultaneously somewhat outside the Anglican Church hierarchy might also be partly explained by the fact that the Parochial Mission Women Society was an organization that brought nothing but assistance to the church and at no cost to it. The Parochial Mission Women did not receive anything from the Anglican Church; they did all their own fundraising, funded their own Parochial Mission Women, and paid for their own offices in the Strand. In this sense the lady managers truly answered to no one. If they became displeased, they could simply pack up their money and close up shop, which would leave many vicars of poor parishes without their paid assistants.

The Parochial Mission Women Society continued to be an effective organization well into the twentieth century. But by 1918, the number of parishes that still had parochial mission women had been greatly reduced. By 1922 there were only twenty parochial mission women still working in London and only three in the rest of England. Brian Heeney, the only historian to have examined the Parochial Mission Women, has argued in *The Women's Movement in the Church of England 1850–1930* (1988) that remaining fixed on their original focus of inculcating thrift and delayed gratification eventually rendered the Parochial Mission Women irrelevant, unlike Ellen Ranyard's Bible Women, who developed a secondary mission of visiting nursing with a later (from 1895) addition of training in social work.[50] But the causes for the Parochial Mission Women Society's decline are both more specific and more general. The advent of the Old Age Pension in 1909 was likely a crucial factor, since it obviated some of the most acute poverty, particularly among elderly widows, often greatly assisting their families who lived with them. Prior to the pension's introduction, the Parochial Mission Women were still thriving; in 1904, for example, the weekly meeting in Haggerston, a working-class neighbourhood in northeast London, involved over a hundred women of that parish.[51] In 1906, applications from clergymen seeking mission women for their parishes continued to come in to the London committee at the usual, regular rate. But within a year of the pension's promulgation, the number of parishes with mission women, many of which had regularly employed them since the 1860s, sharply dropped.[52]

At the same time, larger trends were also likely affecting parish life. In the five years immediately preceding the First World War, more women were working and retaining wages of their own and very likely felt much less need to be taught how to save their pennies for Bibles or blankets. Post office savings banks, introduced in the 1860s both to encourage thrift among the working classes and to help finance the public debt, had become increasingly popular. Moreover, the emergence of, first, working-class self-help organizations and, later, labour groups for women filled the need for mutual woman-to-woman assistance networks. In addition, during this period, church attendance had fallen and affiliation with one's parish diminished.[53] By 1914, many of the circumstances which had brought about the sense, shared by Caroline Talbot and her lady managers, that working-class women needed to be taught about thrift, prioritizing, budgeting, and other life skills no longer pertained. The number of applications for parochial mission women fell further during the war as munitions factories and the war effort occupied women's available time and offered better pay. The number of women attending meetings diminished, and after the war this trend continued. The Parochial Mission Women Association was wound up in 1923.

And yet, in its time, from its founding in 1860 to its dissolution sixty-three years later, the Parochial Mission Women's Society carried out its undertakings efficiently, cost-effectively, and entirely free from interference or supervision by Anglican men. Lucy Cavendish was a great believer in the effectiveness of the Parochial Mission Women's work; even in its later years, as she wrote to her sister, she still found the work of the mission women in the various parishes to be both "inspiring" and important.[54] She only retired as one of the committee of five lady managers in 1910, when her advancing Parkinson's disease made attendance difficult.

The Women's Union of the Church of England Temperance Society

As with philanthropic organizations such as the Ladies Diocesan Association and the Parochial Mission Women Society, temperance work presented an opportunity for women to acquire an associational life outside the home. But national temperance organizations dealt with their women members very differently. Within the United Kingdom Alliance, women rarely spoke and they were not at all involved in management. In contrast, quite early on, the National Temperance League entrusted three women with the task of extending temperance principles to new social groups: Mrs Fison, who organized drawing-room meetings, Miss Robinson, "the soldiers' friend," and Miss Weston, "the sailors' friend." The Church of England, characteristically, found a middle path.

The Anglican Church was late to the temperance game. Although a temperance society had been established by a handful of Anglican clerics in 1862, it was essentially ineffective and it was not an official part of the church establishment. Eleven years later, in 1873, it was reorganized, officially endorsed, funded, and entirely absorbed by the Church of England. One of the elements, however, that set the revived Church of England Temperance Society (CETS) apart was that it was quickly taken up by influential aristocrats; the Duke of Marlborough was a supporter from the start, as were the Duke of Leeds and the Earls of Chichester and Harrowby. Lucy Cavendish's father, Lord Lyttelton, was a supporter of the society from its inception as were Earl Peel, Lord Calthorpe, and Viscount Derwent.[55] The Society also attracted the support of a handful of men who would soon go on to assist Emma Cons in the Coffee Taverns Company and, subsequently, the Coffee Music-Halls Company: the Duke of Westminster and the Earls of Shaftesbury and Meath. Championing temperance was a cause for aristocratic men.

But it was not alcohol abuse among the leisured classes that these men targeted; the elite were assumed to have sufficient self-control. The main idea behind the CETS was to address the problem of drinking among the working classes. In the latter half of the nineteenth century, the message that was continually reinforced to the Victorian reading public was that drink was the root cause of crime; it was the reason the workhouses were full.[56] Abuse of alcohol was thought to be centred within the working class – those who were seen, both by those who had opinions on this matter and by those who worked with the poor, to be those least able to control themselves. Indeed, the perceived intemperance of the working classes had been used as an argument against universal manhood suffrage in the earlier part of the century. These perceptions did not fade as the century progressed. The Archbishop of York pointed out, in 1880, in the *Church of England Temperance Chronicle*, the mouthpiece for the CETS, that the working class spent most of the weekend, including Sunday, drinking themselves into oblivion. "People of the upper class," he admonished his audience, "did not go off on Saturday night and get as drunk as possible and carry it on through Sunday."[57] Whether the archbishop was accurate about either class's drinking habits, the perception remained that the poor tended to drink up their money and their future.

But although many contemporary writers couched their pleas against the abuse of alcohol in the most alarmist of all possible terms, and with the conviction that drink was a working-class problem, there actually was very good evidence to corroborate a conclusion that Britain, in the last half of the nineteenth century, had a serious drinking problem, and that a disproportionate impact fell among the working poor. A survey by the British Association for the Advancement of Science, conducted in 1881, reported that drink was the largest single item of expenditure in the working-class food budget.[58] Thus, when the Church of England Temperance Society raised high the banner, the aristocracy responded enthusiastically. But this was not simply a matter of the aristocracy seeking to control the lives of the urban working poor. A significant aspect of public concern was the fear that the nation would be adversely affected if workers could not adequately perform their jobs, either directly because of drunkenness or because wages diverted away from wholesome food resulted in a malnourished workforce. This was not hyperbolic alarm; between 1870 and 1914, two-thirds to three-quarters of all drink purchases came from the pockets of working-class men and women.[59] Charles Booth in the *Life and Labour of the People of London*

(1904) thought the working man probably spent a quarter of his wages on drink; another authority calculated that many families spent easily one-third and some a half or more on drink.[60] Temperance was clearly a crusade not only about morals or even health; it was a crusade about reclaiming a nation's pride and efficiency.

But alcohol abuse was also increasingly seen as a women's issue, and not always in a protective way. Early issues of the *Church of England Temperance Chronicle* featured numerous horror stories of drunken women falling down wells, throwing their children into fires, attacking their husbands with knives, and generally coming to a bad end. In addition to these cautionary tales, the *Temperance Chronicle* would admonish women invoking science. For example, in the spring 1880 issue, readers found an account of the Rev. J.W. Horsley's "Address to Women," given at a drawing-room meeting at Streatham, where he not only lamented women's particular weakness and liability to drunkenness and the virtual "hopelessness of reclaiming female drunkards" but also condemned women as the cause of much intemperance for leading men to intemperance and because "heredity in this matter is mainly from the mothers' side."[61]

Women also saw drink as a women's issue, though not necessarily from the same perspective. The first organization that entered the field of women working to reclaim alcoholic women and aid families beset by alcohol abuse was the British Women's Temperance Association (BWTA). Founded in 1876 by John Bright's sister Margaret Bright Lucas, the BWTA was the only organization at that time assisting other women with alcohol problems that was entirely founded by and run by women. But there was something of a geographical divide: the BWTA had established itself most strongly in the industrial centres of the Midlands and the North. There was also something of a division along religious lines: the BWTA was mainly a Dissenting organization; meetings were often held in the halls of Methodist chapels and most of the prominent leaders were Wesleyan, Congregationalist, or Quaker. The BWTA leadership thus also mainly came from the educated upper middle class, with a handful of notable exceptions: Lady Henry Somerset served as president from 1890 to 1903 and her successor was Rosalind, Countess of Carlisle, who served as president until 1921. But aside from these two, aristocratic women did not have much to do with the BWTA.[62] Anglican women who were firm on the issue of temperance initially worked with the BWTA largely because the organization was effective; the cause was good, but also there was little alternative. The BWTA still had claims on women's allegiance even after the CETS was founded, largely because the Anglican Church still had no temperance voice directed towards women specifically. The BWTA were women speaking directly to women. Emma Cons, for example, a devout Anglican, served as a vice-president of the BWTA, although there isn't much evidence of her being actively involved beyond lending her name. Lucy Cavendish was not involved with the BWTA; she involved herself with the CETS Women's Union.

Thus, the same year the BWTA was founded, the Church of England made its own attempt to organize Anglican women, haltingly at first; an inauspicious attempt at a women's auxiliary in 1876 quickly became moribund. Five years later, in 1881, with the BWTA not only making great strides but making them with Anglican women in positions of authority, the executive of the CETS, averring that it was "alarmed" at increasing female intemperance, reorganized and relaunched a women's auxiliary, creating the Women's Union of the CETS. Canon Ellison, the Queen's vicar at Windsor, was made president, but working with him, the Women's Union executive was predominantly women. Their first step was to poach away the exceptionally effective secretary of the British Women's Temperance Association, Wilhelmina Haslam. The daughter of the famously evangelical West Country minister William Haslam (who found himself converted to the evangelical cause in the midst of his own sermon), Wilhelmina Haslam's zeal and oratory was as inspiring as her father's. Although she was sure of the support of the wives of the Bishop of London and the Archbishop of Canterbury, she set out to attract titled women who had had some experience of the lives of the poor (either through the Parochial Mission Women Society or the Ladies Diocesan Association) and were likely to be attracted by the objective of women helping women to temperance. In this she was eminently successful. The Duchesses of Sutherland, Westminster, Rutland, and Manchester, Lady Rachel Howard, Lady Georgina Vernon, and Lucy Cavendish all became vice-presidents of the Women's Union. But this was not simply window-dressing. The committee which actually ran the Women's Union was equally aristocratic: the Marchioness of Tavistock, the Countess of Meath, Lady Florence Blunt, and Lady Emily Pepys. This is noteworthy, since the parent organization, the CETS, was run by an executive that was distinctly not aristocratic; with the exception of the Earl of Aberdeen, the committee was composed of middle-class clergymen. It is also worth noting the distinct overlap between the composition of the CETS Women's Union and that of the Ladies Diocesan Association.

There were three important themes that ran through the work of the Women's Union: first, the Women's Union was effective because women were appealing to other women, speaking of temperance in ways only they understood. An article in the *Temperance Chronicle* made this clear. "What does the 'Women's Union' Mean?" defined the principal purpose of the union as being mutual assistance. "Englishwomen intend to help one another to do a great work which is too hard for any one of them to do alone."[63] Second, the Women's Union was a proudly efficient organization that functioned (with the exception of the cherubic Canon Ellison) entirely under female management without recourse to the CETS. Finally, these women saw that alcohol abuse among women transcended class. Like the Ladies Diocesan Association and the Parochial Mission Women Society, explicit mention of "bridging the gulf" between classes was emphasized. This was not merely lip-service. Nor was it an attempt to put window-dressing over the idea that, when all was said and done, working-class intemperance was the real problem. The Women's Union put a good deal of effort into gathering signatures for a petition against Grocers' Licences, the idea being that although working-class women might be willing to be seen entering a pub, middle-class women would not but would simply add bottles of sherry or port to their local grocery orders.[64] In 1881 the Women's Union organized a Juvenile Union with the idea of reaching the children of the middle and upper classes at an impressionable age. The *Chronicle* featured Miss Haslam's advice to women members on how to organize an effective local Women's Union branch so as to appeal to middle-class women: "Drawing-room meetings many be held very advantageously for young women employed in shops … but similar meetings held in the afternoon will often attract ladies of the middle classes who would not think of attending ordinary temperance meetings."[65]

The issue of excessive drinking by middle-class women and even among the aristocracy was frequently discussed within the Women's Union; it was seen as an important part of its woman-to-woman mission. It was all too easy for elite women to conceal their dependence on alcohol, as Lucy Cavendish's response to the Bishop of London in 1885, mentioned earlier, reveals. The Women's Union considered this constituency when they were establishing their residential lodges for women inebriates. The women's temperance lodges, as they admitted their first patients, were structured in a way that would be, if not precisely attractive, at least not repellent for elite women. Each lodge admitted three classes of paying women inebriates: drawing-room lodgers, who paid about two pounds a week, workroom lodgers, who paid less, and kitchen lodgers, who paid still less and who were responsible for much of the lodge's manual labour, ranging from scrubbing floors to carrying coal scuttles.

Under the direction of Wilhelmina Haslam, the Women's Union grew quickly. The first local branch opened in Stepney on 17 October 1881, and others quickly followed. In its first annual report, the Women's Union reported that sixteen branches had been opened and 740 members enlisted. The following year, the annual report recounted (almost with glee) that "thirty new branches have been opened, 5,000 signatures for the women's Sunday closing petition obtained," and significant evidence had been gathered to "prove the ill effects of Grocers' Licenses among their own sex." Moreover, the Women's Union had also organized a successful, well-attended conference on the subject of drinking among the educated women of the "upper classes."[67] Miss Haslam's eloquence was just as attractive as her administrative abilities. A few months after the Women's Union was re-established, her proselytizing was reported in the *Temperance Chronicle*.

> After a short address from the Rev. Duncan Jones, Miss Haslam rose, amidst great applause and for one hour, by her earnestness and eloquence held the unflagging attention of her audience. Space would fail to report her admirable address but its effect may be judged from the fact that no sooner had she sat down than a lady rose in the hall and proposed that "it is desirable that a branch of the women's union be formed immediately in the parish."[68]

By May of 1884, Wilhelmina Haslam had opened the seventy-ninth branch. She quickly turned her attention to securing better coverage for the Women's Union in the CETS *Temperance Chronicle*. A new theme began to appear in the featured stories. Gone were the tales of drunken women falling down wells and dementedly throwing their children into the fire. Now stories were recounted of women driven to distraction by their husbands' drinking away all the family's food money, of wives and children waiting outside pubs for father to finish his drinking, or, alternatively, of women being able to proudly reclaim the respectability of their families by bringing their drunken husbands to sobriety.

The *Chronicle*, which had previously ignored the CETS women's work, now regularly and almost avidly followed the activities of the Women's Union. Every month, reports were included of the opening of new branches, drawing-room meetings in prominent houses, and speeches given by eminent clergymen or titled men to meetings of the Women's Union. A column entirely dedicated to the activities of the Women's Union soon appeared in the *Chronicle*. Miss Haslam's speeches were assiduously reported and quoted, as was the universally popular reaction to her message. "Miss Haslam, the energetic Secretary has personally attended 104 meetings, travelling as far as Durham in the North and Sussex in the South, to say nothing of journeys to South Wales. The rapid growth of the Union has made it necessary to increase the office staff notwithstanding the ready help of volunteer assistants."[69]

Miss Haslam thus secured two paid deputy secretaries to assist her. By 1886 the Women's Union offices moved to larger quarters on the second floor of the CETS Westminster headquarters opposite the House of Commons. In addition to the Women's Union's own annual report, they now put out an eight-page quarterly paper which was distributed to branches around the country. The Women's Union held its own annual conferences. They arranged temperance lectures, both in London and in the provinces. The Women's Union central office in London provided speakers for drawing-room meetings and organized meetings of women medical students. Lucy Cavendish was a tireless speaker for the Women's Union; a teetotaller herself, she often made two speeches a day, in different counties. The Women's Union did their own fundraising, and turned a small profit, which was churned back into their accounts. Much work was done by the branches: the Liverpool branch opened a home for discharged women prisoners at risk of falling back into alcohol abuse, and the Chatham branch provided tea and coffee in the barracks laundry for soldiers' wives to preclude recourse to the nearby pub.[70] In the Women's Union, educated British women had created another platform from which to assert their own position on a matter of important, national, public policy.

The same year that the Women's Union staff exuberantly moved to larger offices, however, a warning shot was heard passing across the Union's bow at its annual meeting. Addressing the assembled women, the Bishop of London, Frederick Temple, while praising their efforts, observed off-handedly that "of course the Women's Union is only a branch of the great CETS."[71] Perhaps it was the self-sufficiency of the

Women's Union that concerned the Church of England authorities. Perhaps it was the fact that their fundraising expertise had made them both a wealthy and an independently managed organization. Perhaps it was the unseemly vision of the assertive and charismatic Wilhelmina Haslam running up and down the country making speeches to enthralled audiences. Regardless, in April of 1887, the Council of the CETS suddenly reorganized the Women's Union, bringing it under the direct authority of the CETS, making it a mere department of that organization. No longer could the Women's Union hold its own funds and make its own budget; it now had to hand over the monies it raised to the financial offices of the CETS. Almost more important, the Women's Union branches set up throughout the country by Wilhelmina Haslam would no longer be run independently, but would now be subordinate to local vicars.[72] This was a sudden and an unexpected change.

The women sought clarification; they received it. The Women's Union remit was not, the CETS Council averred, being contracted but actually being improved and enlarged. The CETS had decided to refocus the objective of the Women's Union; the woman-to-woman work towards the reclamation of women inebriates was to be abandoned, and no longer would the Women's Union "be confined to helping women alone, but should be organized to further the objects of the whole Society in every other practicable way."[73] Thus their expertise in fundraising would be used to benefit the whole CETS, which would now determine how all funds were spent. This averral of a refocusing was not entirely blandwash; new and important committees were set up within the Women's Union that brought new and broader assignments. The Women's Union were to assist with the CETS mission to cabmen, an occupation seen as easily leading to intemperance through the long-standing tradition of mollifying waiting cabbies with drinks often brought out to their cabs. The Women's Union was also now to aid the CETS in its Police Court Rescue Work; it was to send its Women's Union members as delegates to police courts as missionaries, offering, when appropriate, to take in charge women found guilty of public drunkenness.[74] Finally, the Women's Union was now charged with raising funds for and establishing a shelter for inebriate women. But instead of operating on their own, all of these Women's Union committees had now "been strengthened by the addition of gentlemen" delegated from the CETS.[75] The CETS had given and the CETS had taken away. But the CETS had also made it clear that they held ultimate authority over the Women's Union.

Wilhelmina Haslam gamely began to draw up plans and raise funds for the first inebriate home for women. But the women evidently were not altogether happy with their new status of being simply a department of the CETS. Canon Ellison was at some pains to make clear, in a special address to their annual business meeting in April 1888, that the reason for bringing the central office of the Women's Union under the control of the CETS and the reason for placing the local vicars in authority over the local Women's Union branches had simply been to eliminate any potential "confusion" that might have arisen from the Women's Union raising funds for their own projects. As he explained, all this separate activity had led to "something like the idea that the Women's Union was a separate part of the CETS." Now, he pointed out, there would be no misunderstanding. This explanation evidently did not satisfy the women, particularly after Wilhelmina Haslam resigned in June of 1888.[76] Although the Bishop of London's wife, Beatrice Temple, now assumed leadership of the Women's Union under Canon Ellison (and was able to negotiate that the local dioceses and the Women's Union would split the affiliation fees as well as any new fees), the Women's Union executive sent a memorial to the CETS executive: the women were not happy with their autonomy having been taken away from them. Canon Ellison hastily expressed "great regret" that the Women's Union was disturbed. The CETS, he assured them, regarded "the Women's Union as an integral part of the society and recognize with great thankfulness the work done by the committee both in past time and in the present as one of the most important works to which they are called."[77]

As a sign of the respect in which the Women's Union was held, the CETS executive averred, the Women's Union could have back control of appointing which women would work the police courts and of determining the optimum after-care for those women the courts released to them. Although the Women's Union had to work with the CETS Police Court mission men, they now at least had authority over whom to send and how to deal with the inebriate women they found there. This was not small work; at the annual meeting in 1893 it was noted that the mission women had that year done follow-up work with more than 5,100 women charged with drunkenness. The Women's Union opened a shelter home for short stays that was often used for women just out of the police courts. "The Shelter Home has been a most valuable help," the Women's Union reported at the annual conference for 1893. "Often some poor girl or woman is brought to the office or comes herself in the most abject state of destitution through drink, but yearning for a friendly hand to help her back. Very few have friends who are able to pay for their support so for the most part they are received without any payment whatever."[78]

The Women's Union also had retained control of the lodge in Herne Hill for inebriate women, which they named Ellison Lodge in honour of Canon Ellison. A second lodge was soon opened in Torquay, named Temple Lodge after the Bishop of London, Frederick Temple. Over the course of the next ten years, four more lodges for inebriate women would be opened: the Corngreaves Hall in Erdington (Birmingham), Hammond Lodge in St Clement (King's Lynn), the Women's Temperance Home in Liverpool, and a home in Portsmouth. The Women's Union leased the homes under their own committee's direction, paid all salaries, and managed the homes themselves.

But there were difficulties with the new regime. After Wilhelmina Haslam's departure in 1888, the *Temperance Chronicle* had ceased to cover the activities of the Women's Union. The number of local branches had drastically evaporated once they became subordinate to the local vicars. Whereas there had been four hundred local branches run by women in 1889, by 1891 that number had shrunk to twenty-seven. The "friction," recorded one member of the Women's Union, "which has so often been painful" between the women of the Union and the leadership of the CETS, did not abate.[79] Canon Ellison, who had always been supportive of the Women's Union, was ousted as chairman of the CETS in 1891 and replaced by Frederick Temple, who soon proposed further alterations to the structure of the Women's Union.[80]

Bishop Temple was of the opinion, as he told the Church Congress, that women did not "work nearly so well by themselves as when they are associated with men," and he also was of the opinion that women did not keep accounts very well; "money gets into a queer condition."[81] Although he observed that women could certainly be credited with a valuable "intuitive instinct," he also pointed out that unlike men, who preferred to think about things before offering opinions, women were not "very logical in their deductions."[82] His solution to the muddle he attributed to female management was to fold the Women's Union directly into the CETS. "The Women's Union should go on," Temple announced, "but I think it should be formed in the closest connexion with the Council and the Executive and, in fact, take its orders from the

Executive."[83] The London work of the Women's Union was to be taken over by the London Diocesan Board with the understanding that women would be co-opted onto that board. A handful of women would be appointed to the CETS executive. The bishops in the provinces would be encouraged, in like manner, to bring women onto the executives of the local CETS organizations.

It was a disaster and essentially spelled the end of the Women's Union. The women knew it. At their annual meeting that July, it was observed that no negotiation was possible with the CETS. There was nothing that could actually be done. "We have only the choice of accepting the terms offered us by the CETS or of breaking away from them altogether."[84] No one wanted to do that. Their books were taken away, audited, and kept. The Women's Union offices were cleared out. The Women's Union published its last annual report at the end of that year. The CETS executive added five new seats for the new women members, but they had some difficulty finding five women from the Women's Union who were willing to serve; many declined the offer. Finally Mrs Temple found four other women besides herself.[85] Those five women, joined by two clergymen, were also constituted as "the Women's Union Board," but it was a board with no authority and with a fast-shrinking membership. They were required to ask permission of the CETS before they could start any fundraising. They began by meeting monthly. They found little to discuss and soon they reduced their meetings to quarterly sessions. By May of 1896 the only item that ever appeared on the agenda was the Ellison Lodge. By June of 1897 it was announced that the inebriate homes should now be run by a new CETS board under a central scheme. In the provinces, few dioceses appointed women to the executives of the local CETS branches. The CETS executive, rather bemusedly, wondered in the 1895 annual report why "the work of the Women's Union under the new conditions has not, so far, been taken up so warmly in the Dioceses as the Council had hoped would be the case."[86] The names of the aristocratic women who had all been part of the Women's Union Executive were now listed as vice-presidents of the reconstituted CETS. But they no longer, largely speaking, attended meetings; their names functioned as attractive ornaments. The *Temperance Chronicle* listed not one aristocratic woman on the platform at the 1899 Women's Union annual conference. By 1913, the year that the *British Journal of Inebriety* ran a comprehensive article on the lodges for inebriate women and men, all lodges were described as being run by the CETS; there was no mention that there ever had been a Women's Union.[87]

Conclusion

These three organizations, the Ladies Diocesan Association, the Parochial Mission Women, and the Women's Union of the Church of England Temperance Society, each provide different tales, some cautionary, regarding women and their relationship to power and authority within the Church of England. The oldest of the three, the Parochial Mission Women Society, established by Caroline Talbot in 1860, shows the ability of elite women to envisage, operate, and fund their own philanthropic organization within the Church of England but without actually relinquishing control. Indeed, the lady managers of the Parochial Mission Women Society were able to deploy their husbands, friends, and sons as a form of shell holding-company, making it appear as if the lady managers were closely supervised by a Committee of Reference. Moreover, these same women were also able to create the illusion that the parochial mission women answered entirely to the incumbent vicar, whereas, in fact, it was the lady managers who managed their women. Using not only their powerful connections but also their understanding of church hierarchy, Mrs Talbot, Lucy Cavendish, and the other lady managers were able to employ both class and sex to create a base of power and experience where they could simply help their parochial mission women get on about their business, free from male interference, and get their books audited for free.

The women of the Ladies Diocesan Association, founded four years later, were also able to use both their class and their sex, and in much the same way. Using their titles as both wedge and battering ram, Catherine Tait's countesses and duchesses prevailed where Louisa Twining's well-meaning men and women of the educated upper middle class were stymied. Moreover, they were able to use their status and their powerful contacts, with bishops and archbishops within the church and peers without, to remain unsupervised as they went about doing their work. But almost more important, the Ladies Diocesan Association shows a group of powerful, aristocratic women collectively asserting a position on a powerful point of public debate. In much the same way as the aristocratic women chronicled by K.D. Reynolds hosted an element of the public sphere in their drawing-rooms, so these equally aristocratic women asserted a position in the broader debate on public policy, using the knowledge they had gained by pushing open the workhouse doors. In the broader Victorian debate of what were the obligations of the state, the aristocratic women of the Ladies Diocesan Association assumed that they had a legitimate voice, and a well-informed one too.

The women of the Church of England Temperance Society Women's Union, founded seventeen years later, were not so fortunate. The original focus that Wilhelmina Haslam had so eagerly expanded, the woman-to-woman approach in reclaiming alcoholic women, was abruptly derailed after six years of simply exponential growth. Three elements distinguish the Women's Union from the other two organizations that had been able to successfully secure and retain their independence. First, the Women's Union was too big to fly under the radar as had the other two, smaller organizations; it had a large membership across the country and it had acquired a paid staff of its own. Second, and almost more important, the Women's Union had a good-sized budget, did its own fundraising, and retained control of its own, considerable, funds. The Parochial Mission Women Society and the Ladies Diocesan Association had done their own fundraising and retained their own funds, but their budgets had been quite modest, designed to break even only, and there was never a surplus. Third, the Women's Union had developed a profile of its own; press notices – beyond the *Temperance Chronicle* or the *Church Times* – of Wilhelmina Haslam's speeches up and down the country gained notice. Not only could this be viewed by some clergymen as unseemly, but it also threatened to put the work of the CETS in the shade. Temperance was not, in the opinion of the CETS executive, to be seen as a women's crusade. Frederick Temple's warning shot, "the Women's Union is only a branch of the great CETS," encapsulates much that the CETS brethren found disconcerting about their Women's Union.[88] This was, in a nutshell, the reason why the Women's Union was not going to be permitted to function independently: it was already affiliated with the CETS. The Women's Union might do its own fundraising and thus be able to make its own decisions about how to spend its money, but this and its other successes would only serve to draw attention to the very independence that was so disconcerting.

The aristocratic women who worked with the CETS Women's Union did not do much to retain its independence. The Women's Union might have had as many peeresses on its masthead as did the Ladies Diocesan

Association or the Parochial Mission Women, but when the CETS executive determined to rein them in, there was no aristocratic protest. Perhaps these women were interested in the idea of sitting on the executive of the CETS, perhaps they themselves had seen Miss Haslam as becoming too powerful, or perhaps they agreed that the work could be done more effectively in tandem with the CETS because they had always seen the Women's Union as but a branch of the CETS, or because they knew that the only alternative was to take the Women's Union out of the church. Regardless, they did not exert any of their energies to counter Frederick Temple's restraints.

The Ladies Diocesan Association and the Parochial Mission Women were able to operate unobtrusively because they had been initially established by women and because they were not actually part of any extant church organization. The Women's Union, on the other hand, had been founded by men of the CETS who wished to attract women to the cause of temperance; their independence was always conditional on the good will of the CETS executive. As such, the rules of operation were never the women's to make. In this, the charities of the Anglican Church mirror the wide variety of attitudes and patterns that have been identified in Victorian philanthropic society generally. F.M.L. Thompson maintains that women who worked with charities were invariably shunted out of leadership roles by well-meaning gentlemen and clergymen. Alan Kidd sees women as being able to command philanthropic organizations only when the charity was of their creation, as with Louisa Twining or Octavia Hill or Emma Cons. Julia Parker, conversely, points to a number of women who were able to function well at a managerial level without having had to establish charities of their own.[89] Frank Prochaska sees more change than continuity in charities devoted to bettering the lives of children and women, observing that by the end of the century many were managed by women.[90] The examples of two of these Anglican organizations (the Ladies Diocesan Association and the Parochial Mission Women Society) run akin to the trend Parker and Prochaska have identified, flourishing under female management, showing how women were able to create pockets of power for themselves within the Church of England. But we can also simultaneously see, in the story of the CETS Women's Union, much more of the state of affairs as described by Thompson and Kidd, where women could establish and keep their organization's independence within the Anglican Church, but only under certain circumstances. To retain authority, autonomy, and power within the Anglican Church, women had to be not only well connected but canny, self-funded, and in a position where the church was more in need of them than vice versa. Only when those elements were secured were women able to use a perch in the Anglican Church as a platform both to accomplish much and to successfully stake a position from which they could opine on matters of national public policy.

In a similar vein, Mary Poovey has argued that although women and many working-class men were barred from access to Parliament, that did not mean that they did not possess power.[91] Indeed, one of Poovey's main points is that the "disaggregation" of society created new "emergent" domains (such as the social) from older, "residual" domains (such as the political or the theological), domains in which new players could stake their claim to a voice. Poovey interprets the social domain as being colonized both by private individuals and, increasingly as the nineteenth century wore on, by government.[92] Thus, for Poovey, this emergent social domain was one where women could manifest the power that comes with knowledge. As an illustration, Poovey uses Ellen Ranyard's "Bible Women" as an example of women who were able to both draw on their traditional authority to minister to the poor – still present in the residual domain of the theological – and simultaneously assert a presence in the emergent domain of the social. We can easily fit the Parochial Mission Women, the Ladies Diocesan Association, and the CETS Women's Union into this analysis. Within this construct of cultural formation, one's sex is relevant, one's class, less so. Looking at these three charitable organizations run by an elite church and peopled by elite women who did not always meet with success in their attempts to retain autonomy gives us the opportunity to see if those women who in fact were successful in keeping control of their budgets and staff relied on their sex, their class, or their expertise and whether they succeeded by inserting a foot in a new domain while hedging their bets by keeping one planted in the old.

Charities could also be used as a platform from which Victorian women, striking a maternalist stance, could articulate a position on matters of public policy, but whether this was invariably a successful strategy is a matter of some debate. Kathryn Gleadle has argued that individual women of the mid-nineteenth century were often able to assert a public position through their charitable works, in the manner of, for example, Louisa Twining or Florence Nightingale, but when attempting to unite and act in concert towards a particular objective, they were often stymied.[93] Yet we have vivid examples of successful collective campaigns to affect public policy and reform laws (indeed, change patterns of public perceptions and actions) launched and maintained by women; for example, the social purity and anti-prostitution campaigns of Josephine Butler and Ellice Hopkins (a woman much admired by Lucy Cavendish). The stories of these three Anglican charities with which Lucy Cavendish involved herself show women who were able to use philanthropic branches of the church as a way of injecting themselves into the public sphere, nudging and prodding the direction of the general debate about public policy concerning the poor, but, again, successful only under particular circumstances of their own devising.

These Victorian charities can thus give us insight into many aspects of Victorian women's lives. For one, we can see the genesis of the overlapping circles of kinship and friendship made concrete as many of the women who served with Lucy Cavendish on the LDA also worked with the Women's Union of the CETS or worked as "supplemental ladies" for the Parochial Mission Women. Many of these women (and men) appear again on other committees and different campaigns. The Earl and Countess of Ducie, Lady Camilla Fortescue, the Earl and Countess of Meath, the Duke of Westminster, the Countess of Darnley, the Countess of Pembroke, Lady Elizabeth Cust, and the Countess of Lothian, all of whom had been involved in the 1860s and 1870s with one of more of the LDA, the Parochial Mission Women, or the CETS, can also be found in later years, working with Emma Cons on other philanthropic endeavours. Philanthropically, London could be a very small town.

3 Emma Cons

Aristocrats like Lucy Cavendish were not the only women who could create social networks of industrious and practical women or committees of the monied and influential. This chapter provides a case study of a resourceful woman who, although coming from circumstances of very little power or influence, was also able to create and employ overlapping circles of various philanthropic reformers, establishing her own personal "standing committee" of the powerful and well-connected on which she could repeatedly call for advice, capital, and access to power.

Emma Cons was a remarkably influential woman. When London's first county councillors assembled in 1888, their inaugural task was to nominate and elect eighteen persons to sit with them as aldermen. There were two criteria: a London residence and the ability to be useful to the councillors in their investigations and deliberations. The eighteen aldermen elected by the councillors were an impressive lot and included, among others, the eminent jurists Lord Lingen and Lord Hobhouse, the legal and social reformer Frederic Harrison, the educational reformer Quintin Hogg, the Earl of Meath, and Miss Emma Cons. She was, as one of the councillors recollected years later, "the only woman nominated as alderman and, in spite of the prejudice against the mere idea of the membership of a woman, she was elected by 58 votes in favour and only 28 against."[1] It was judged that her expertise in housing the poor was uniquely valuable, and she was immediately put onto an astonishing six crucial committees and eleven subcommittees.[2] Fifteen years later, H.H. Asquith, then home secretary, once again called on Emma Cons's unique corpus of experience when he appointed her as one of seven members of a departmental committee under the eminent senior civil servant and former permanent under-secretary at the Home

Office, Sir Godfrey Lushington, to inquire into the state of reformatories and industrial schools.[3] No one even questioned his choice.

Other women during this same period also worked to ameliorate the condition of the poor and to affect both public perceptions and public policy. The impact their efforts had was dependent on many variables, some of which lay entirely outside of their control. Women's ability to carve out influential public positions tended to depend on class and marital status. Unmarried women had an advantage in not being distracted by the needs of children or a husband, but determined spinsters could usually succeed in raising consciousness about the state of the poor only if they had independent wealth.[4] Most of the women who became philanthropic leaders in the mid-nineteenth century came from the leisured but educated upper middle class. Louisa Twining, for example, was a woman born into comfort as the daughter of the house of Twining's tea. Florence Nightingale's father had received a substantial inheritance, largely from mining interests. Octavia Hill's family situation was somewhat different; notwithstanding the financial difficulties that the Hill family suffered after the breakdown of Octavia Hill's father, James, a formerly prosperous Peterborough corn merchant, Octavia's maternal grandfather, the physician and sanitary reformer Southwood Smith, ensured that she was brought up in an atmosphere that valued education, the arts, and service.[5] In the same way, Violet Markham, Mary Carpenter, Helen Bosanquet, Mary Ward, and Beatrice Webb were all women from privileged backgrounds who devoted their lives to working with the poor.[6] There were many attractions for these women: the satisfaction gained from meaningful work, the security of collaboratively working with other women, the relative freedom of working in the East End away from neighbourly, bourgeois scrutiny.[7] In short, women of independent means, or at least from comfortable backgrounds, could carve out a satisfactory life of their own through philanthropic work. Women from working-class backgrounds, having to support themselves, likely did not have the same need to find independence, nor were they likely to have the same amount of leisure time to devote to philanthropic work. In this sense, Emma Cons is virtually unique. Even Clara Collet, who worked with Charles Booth on his monumental undertaking *Life and Labour of the People of London* and who is sometimes held up as a working-class woman who laboured with the poor, came from a background distinguishable from that of Emma Cons: Collet's father did not work with his hands, but came from a family of wealthy (although radical and free-thinking) merchants and edited the *Diplomatic Review*.

That said, opportunities for clever working-class girls were certainly expanding exponentially during this period. The Education Act of 1870 made schooling compulsory for children between the ages of five and thirteen, thereby creating a great need for teachers, an opening which many young women were quick to take advantage of. As Dina Copelman has shown in her study of women teachers, many came from skilled and sometimes unskilled labourers' families, where parents usually did not view women working as in any way demeaning.[8] But although women from working families were, through education, increasingly able to rise in society and establish themselves as schoolteachers, they did not tend to work directly with the poor in the way of Octavia Hill or Mary Carpenter. None were able to establish philanthropic endeavours in the way of Emma Cons.

Emma Cons did not bring many advantages to her career: she was a woman and came from a family that had no connection whatsoever to wealth or influence. True, she had the great advantage of being a spinster and thus could focus entirely on her career, but she did not have independent means; she had always had to earn her own living. She nevertheless transformed the knowledge gained in the course of her career into influential authority. With it she established colleges and institutions for the betterment of the working poor, raised funds, and commanded the attention of those who could make change. Hence her election as alderman in 1888 and hence Herbert Asquith's appointing her to the Lushington Committee. Nor was her influence restricted to the philanthropic or even the political world; when, in 1908, she addressed the Institute of Directors on the subject of the 4 per cent annual return on investment she invariably paid her shareholders, the directors listened. In short, Emma Cons was a woman who, by late middle age, had established a position in the public debate on what the national priorities should be. This chapter shows how, in spite of her sex and her background, she was able to place herself in such a position and how she was able to use her knowledge and expertise to carve out a place for herself and her causes by establishing and deploying her own intersecting networks of philanthropy.

Early Life

Emma Cons came from a profoundly musical family. Her great-grandfather Elias Konss had been born, brought up, and apprenticed to a maker of organ cases in the small Rhineland town of Anrath, near

Cologne. After the death of his father, he emigrated, first to France then in 1772 to England, settling in London where he married an English widow and anglicized his name to Cons. His son Frederick Cons followed his father into the craft of cabinet and piano-case making, as did Frederick's eldest son, also named Frederick, who, around 1825, was apprenticed to the leading English firm of piano makers, Broadwoods.[9] In 1833, the young Frederick Cons married Esther Goodair, the daughter of a Stockport mill-owner. They settled near the elder Frederick Cons in the vicinity of Tottenham Court Road and Goodge Street and began their family. Together they had seven children, two boys and five girls; Emma Cons was the second daughter, born in 1837. Frederick Cons's work was well regarded and he was evidently able to provide well for his family: by 1853 they had moved to a respectable address in Bloomsbury.[10]

As a child, Emma had displayed obvious artistic talent, and this was seen by her parents as a likely career path. She was sent to good art schools: first, the school run by the mother of the painter Henry Holliday and subsequently the Female School of Art, run by Louisa Gann in Gower Street.[11] Emma Cons was thus brought up in a literate, musical, artistic family of self-consciously European extraction, supported by a form of pre-industrial, exacting, hand-crafting, self-employed labour that valued education as a means of upward mobility. This is important because, although Emma Cons can be described as coming from a working-class family where her father laboured with his hands, clearly her nurturing environment was miles away from that of a factory worker or even many clerks.

But Frederick Cons became an invalid at the height of his earning power and remained so until his death in 1870. It became clear that the girls would have to make their own way and earn a living. The eldest daughter, Esther, emigrated to Australia, where she taught school; one sister, Eliza, worked for a time as a clerk before moving to South Africa; the youngest, Elizabeth, reverted to the German spelling of her surname and supported herself as the professional singer and pianist "Madame Liebe Konss." When Emma turned fourteen, she joined the Ladies Art Guild, recently set up by Caroline Hill, the daughter of sanitary reformer Southwood Smith, in Fitzroy Square as a cooperative venture to train ladies in artistic skills so as to enable them to find genteel employment. It was here that she became good friends with Mrs Hill's daughter Octavia, who was close to Emma in age. Both girls became acquainted with John Ruskin, who occasionally lectured at the Guild and who encouraged the artistic talents of the two girls, commissioning them to both restore and copy illuminated manuscripts for him.[12]

During a holiday in Switzerland, Emma Cons observed women engraving silver watch cases – a delicate skill which, she discovered, was a traditional craft of Swiss women. Upon her return, Emma and several of her friends apprenticed themselves to a watch-engraver and, after six months, they set themselves up in trade in Clerkenwell as a watch-engraving cooperative.[13] Their work was evidently good; each watch case was unique, and the women's engraving became quickly in demand from watch manufacturers, so much so, in fact, that other watch-engravers, concerned about this fresh competition, waylaid a messenger collecting a day's engravings from the girls' collective, beating and severely injuring him. Thereafter, manufacturers declined to send work their way and the cooperative was wound up. But Emma Cons's niece Lilian Baylis kept one of her watches, engraved "most exquisitely, representing a peacock with its tail outspread," and commented: "It was one of the most fascinating contradictions about her – her wonderfully minute handiwork and her big broad ideas."[14]

Emma now fell back on a craft in which she had been instructed at the Ladies Art Guild – painting on glass – seeking and gaining employment with Powells, the company that had supplied the Ladies Art Guild with glass for its classes. Here, as the first woman ever employed at Powells, she encountered vindictive sabotage by fellow workers. They would smudge her staining while it was still wet or overheat the furnace so that her work would crack. This state of affairs was only rectified by the intervention of Powell himself, who set up a separate studio for Emma, her sister Ellen, and other women who now became employed as painters of stained glass. In 1861, Ruskin recommended that Emma be seconded to help with the restoration of the windows in the chapel at Merton College, an assignment that kept her in Oxford until 1863.[15]

Philanthropic Life

When she returned to London, Emma found that her friend Octavia Hill and John Ruskin had become partners in slum renovation. Having come into his inheritance, Ruskin had purchased some all-but-derelict tenements around Cavendish Square with a view to creating model worker housing and had enlisted Octavia Hill as manager. Ruskin and Hill's vision was that the tenements would be renovated, made decent, and rented out to the "respectable" working poor. The scheme was to be operated on sound business principles with investors receiving an annual return of 4 per cent on their investment. This form of investor philanthropy was not only common during this period, it was quite popular. Charitably minded investors would buy shares in "model housing" companies that would rent to the working poor, being run on such economical lines as to produce a 4 to 5 per cent return on the shareholders' investment. The first such organization, the Metropolitan Association for Improving the Dwellings of the Industrious Classes, had been established in 1841 in Pancras Square. But the enactment of the Labouring Classes Dwelling Houses Acts of 1866 and 1867 enabled such model dwelling companies to borrow money from the government at 4 per cent, repayable over forty years. Several model dwellings companies took advantage of this.[16] Moreover, there was soon a positive efflorescence of model tenement companies run in accordance with what became known as "5 per cent philanthropy." Thirty such trusts were operating in the latter half of the century.[17] Prince Albert himself was a patron and investor, as was the Baroness Burdett-Coutts, Baron Rothschild, and a number of other wealthy and influential patrons excited by the idea of being able to combine charity, slum clearance, and an enterprising return on capital investment. The element that made Hill and Ruskin's organization different was that rents were collected weekly by a band of philanthropically minded volunteer ladies, recruited and assigned by Octavia Hill. Each lady rent collector would not only collect rents but would take on each family on her route as part of her particular case-load, advising them on thrift, hygiene, nutrition, and any other aspect of household management appropriate to the particular case.

The first two blocks of Ruskin and Hill's venture were renamed Paradise Place and Freshwater Place, and Octavia Hill set about renovations. This was hands-on work, and she enlisted the help of her school-friend Emma Cons. The two young women immediately attacked the renovations, painting, distempering, and whitewashing the rooms and reglazing the windows.[18] Octavia Hill's own description of their first glimpse of Paradise Place is vivid: "the plaster was dropping from the walls; on the staircase a pail was placed to catch the rain that fell through the roof. All the staircases were perfectly dark, the banisters were gone, having been used as firewood by the tenants ... The pavement of the back yard was all broken up, and great puddles stood in it so that the damp crept up the outer walls."[19] Nineteen-year-old Henrietta Rowland, daughter of a wealthy Clapham businessman, served as one of the volunteer lady rent collectors. Years later she described Ruskin and Hill's mutual philosophy: "a landlord of the dwellings of the poor should be responsible for both the wellbeing of the tenant and the tenement."[20]

In keeping with strict principles of classic Victorian political economy, rent was not to be discounted or let slide – even for a week – and money was never to be advanced. Adherence to these tenets was to encourage the middle-class values of thrift, planning, and the setting of priorities, steering tenants towards delayed gratification and away from frittering funds away on momentary indulgence of the senses. To do otherwise would be to encourage dependence and sloth. Emma Cons was wholeheartedly at one with this philosophy. She never gave tenants money, though she would often employ tenants or give gifts in kind, and occasionally pay for a family's holiday train tickets. This became her inflexible, lifelong rule and it came from this early work as a rent collector at Paradise Place. Years later she recalled for her niece how one day, entering a room in one of her courts during her rent-collecting rounds, she saw a stiffened figure lying under a sheet, the children, huddled, weeping with the stricken widow, who was breaking up the only stick of furniture for firewood. Moved to pity by so much misery, Emma Cons emptied her purse into the widow's hands, wondering what else she might do for them. Later, realizing that she had forgotten her umbrella, she returned to the room to find the corpse up and dancing in the best of spirits, clasping a gin bottle with the "widow," now restored to equal cheer and drinking her share from a broken teacup. Emma Cons told the story as a cautionary tale for the credulous.[21]

It was a rule of Octavia Hill's system that the often rough inhabitants of the courts must either conform to the rules of the new administration or depart. Hill and Cons both offered the residents work renovating the tenements, often using their reluctance or willingness as a gauge of their poverty or attitudes. Henrietta Rowland recalled in later years Emma Cons "mounting ladders, mixing colours, ordering and laughing at the men who, when too inexperienced, backward or perhaps indolent, would show resentment at or disinclination for the job, were made ashamed but also encouraged by seeing Miss Cons seize the brush and give an excellent lesson in distempering, painting or washing down."[22]

When a second block of flats, Barrett's Court near Oxford Street, a "mass of vile hovels," was secured by Ruskin and Hill, Emma Cons became a full-time rent collector.[23] However, Cons needed to earn her own living, and so, unlike the young Henrietta Rowland, was paid a wage.[24]

Octavia Hill trusted Cons as a right hand and made her the manager of Barrett's Court. The tenants recalled her as "a pleasant-faced young woman, with bright rosy cheeks," and the Hon. Augusta Maclagan (daughter of the sixth Viscount Barrington and the wife of the Archbishop of York), who volunteered as a Barrett's Court rent collector, remembered Cons as "the most genial and kindly of women and, may I add, the most courageous. I have seen her plunge into a street row, and forcibly separate combatants, men and women who slunk away from her indignation like whipped hounds."[25] Mrs Maclagan also leaves a good description of life in Barrett's Court as she and Cons found it:

> Every house had its own small yard with a water butt and other "conveniences" such as they were. The entrance passage was by way of being kept clean by children of the tenants, to whom 1s a week was paid if the work was well done, and the tenants on each floor were responsible for cleaning their staircase. Miss Hill began by repairing and strengthening all the front doors, and supplying latch keys to the tenants, but this soon had to be abandoned, as the tenants lost the latch keys and the drunken people in the Court burst the doors open if they were bolted, and slept in the passage or on the stairs, leaving them often in a states of indescribable filth.[26]

It was here that Emma Cons's vision of the best sort of worker housing began to deviate from Octavia Hill's rigid system of rules, and Cons began shaping her own practical interpretation of tenement political economy. Years later, A.G.E. Carruthers, a social worker with Octavia Hill and the Charity Organization Society, recalled Emma Cons's philosophy for the *Westminster Gazette*'s tribute to her at the time of her death: "Miss Hill's idea seemed to be rather to improve the houses by turning out unsatisfactory tenants, while Miss Cons' theory was to improve her building by keeping and improving the tenants and by helping them by living in the building with them."[27] This difference in policy almost certainly grew from Emma Cons's residence in the tenements she administered. She was able to see, in context and right in front of her, the difficulties and strains of life in the courts.

There were other reasons for the difference in perspective between Octavia Hill and Emma Cons regarding their clients in the courts: the two women came from different classes. Octavia Hill had experienced the pinch of shabby gentility, particularly after the complete mental and physical breakdown of her father, but she had been brought up as one of the professional and educated middle class. Emma Cons came from the upper working class.[28] Her father worked with his hands for a living. He did not have his own shop, but worked on contracted-out piecework, mainly piano keys. Had he lived to acquire sufficient capital to found his own piano-crafting establishment, employing artisans and apprentices of his own, then the Cons family would have very likely moved into the middle class, but that did not happen. That said, the Cons girls clearly had aspirations to upward mobility and were able to use their musical and artistic heritage and upbringing to create careers in the arts, usually a domain accessible only to ladies of the middle classes.[29] But just because Emma Cons's life is a good example of how women could find, on their own, various ways to rise in society (the arts, philanthropy) does not mean that she was not raised in the upper stratum of the working class as one of the family of a highly skilled artisan. As Beatrice Webb put it, Emma Cons was identifiably "not a lady by birth."[30] Her accent may have been an indicator, as the Cons girls seem not to have sought to assume more middle-class accents. Elizabeth Cons's daughter Lilian Baylis's accent was taken by more than one person (including that authority on accents, Sybil Thorndike) as cockney.[31] Emma Cons consistently failed to exhibit any middle-class reticence, distance, or stiff self-consciousness. Indeed, as the manager of model dwellings for workers, whether she was diving into fist-fights to separate combatants or tucking in her skirts and scrambling up ladders onto the roof slates to goad her tenants into helping with repairs, Emma Cons's actions were not the sort that Octavia Hill would have been likely to take. It was clear that Emma Cons was not the usual sort of lady visitor; she exuded a sense of understanding and fellowship that Octavia Hill never did and was apparently seen as being on the side of the tenants. As one elderly woman who had been, as a child, a tenant in one of Cons's tenements recalled in the 1950s, "Miss Cons was always for the 'costers."[32]

As manager of Barrett's Court, Cons first saw what she took as the cause underlying so much unhappiness and waste of resources among her neighbours. Drunkenness and alcoholism were problems among the working poor that were the subject of much discussion in Britain during the last third of the nineteenth century. Temperance societies, started early in the century, had grown exponentially as families had flooded into cities looking for work, often finding little. The public house was invariably the cheapest and most convenient source of warmth and comfort and drink the fastest relief from dreadful conditions. It was at Barrett's Court that Cons saw the havoc that drink could wreak on families and developed a reputation for handling drunken tenants. A newspaper article from 1890 recounted the memories of many of her tenants from her Barrett's Court days:

> Many stories are told of her daring in dealing with drunken and degraded people ... "you had better not go in there, Miss, he is waiting to do for you," she was once told in Drury Lane by a frightened knot of women, who were aware that a drunken and evicted tenant was watching for Miss Cons behind the door of the room with a poker in his hand. But Miss Cons went straight in, faced the man, and calmly took the poker out of his hand.[33]

Emma Cons identified incentives to sobriety and alternatives to drunkenness. She organized a total abstinence society for Barrett's Court, "The Order of the Sons of the Phoenix."[34] She arranged performances of operettas for the tenants, produced, gratis, by her sister "Madame Liebe Konss" and friends she recruited. Emma Cons started a Barrett's Court brass band for the men and an "Institute for Women and Girls," which, in addition to having classes in reading, writing, arithmetic, and needlework, also had amusements.[35] The members put on plays on winter Saturday evenings: the first, of course, was *The Winter's Tale*. Its success was followed by other plays especially written by a friend of John Ruskin's, George MacDonald, who, together with his family, organized theatricals in the basement of Barrett's Court.[36] Membership in the Institute soon swelled to eighty members. Emma Cons also arranged outings for her tenants, taking them for day trips to the country, but always carefully plotting, ahead of time, where the ramble would take her group so as to ensure they did not pass a pub.[37]

Cons's success at Barrett's Court was noticeable. Octavia Hill would, from time to time, take those interested in social work and slum reclamation around the tenement courts to show the accommodations and improvements.[38] Emma Cons was also gaining her own reputation for managing difficult tenements. In late 1869, Julia and Hester Sterling, nieces of the Christian Socialist minister F.D. Maurice, inspired by the success of Ruskin and Hill's efforts, purchased another tenement block. This court comprised thirty-eight houses in Marylebone: Walmer Street and Walmer Place. Emma Cons was appointed manager.[39] Her priorities were clear; she received a £10 donation and immediately established a library for the tenants, which soon comprised three hundred books and "sixty members, many of them lads from sixteen to twenty."[40]

By 1870, Cons had moved on to become the manager of one of Octavia Hill's larger organizations, the Central London Dwellings Improvement Company, which held and managed several tenement courts around Drury Lane. It was there that Emma Cons, together with Tom Hughes, one of the Christian Socialists and author of *Tom Brown's Schooldays*, established a temperance coffee tavern for working men, "The Cat and Comfort." This was not her first acquaintance with Tom Hughes. The Ladies Art Guild, where Emma as a girl had first encountered Octavia Hill, was one of the twelve self-governing worker cooperatives (and the only one for women) founded by the Christian Socialists. As a girl, Emma Cons had frequently accompanied Octavia Hill and her mother to hear F.D. Maurice preach in the chapel of Lincoln's Inn. One of Maurice's principal concerns, and a theme to which he constantly returned in his sermons, was the growing division between the classes. His philosophy had made a deep impression on both Octavia Hill and Emma Cons. Many of the writings of Maurice and the work and organizations established by Hughes, Charles Kingsley, John Ludlow, and the other Christian Socialists emphasized the destructive effects of the "gulf" between the classes. In later writings, Cons would refer to the importance of forging connections among persons of differing socio-economic backgrounds and, although from a different perspective from that of the Oxbridge-educated Hughes, Kingsley, and Maurice, with the same objective.

Emma Cons and Octavia Hill had both assisted in running another venture of the Christian Socialists, a "ragged school" in which very poor girls were taught how to make toy furniture. Emma and Octavia had also become friends with Tom Hughes's daughter May, who was close to them in age. Now, as an experienced manager of residences for the working poor, Emma Cons was approached by Tom Hughes and a group of associates to run a coffee tavern they hoped to open for working men. Russell Gurney, QC and MP, volunteered a house he owned in Shelton Street near the corner of Drury Lane, conveniently in the heart of the slum area encompassing the tenement courts now administered by Emma Cons.

The coffee tavern movement was not begun by Tom Hughes and the Christian Socialists; the idea had been in play long before the "Cat and Comfort" opened. There is some question as to what organization opened the first "coffee palace," since there were more than a few already operating in the North. Certainly Dr Barnardo established London's first temperance coffee establishment, the "Edinburgh Castle," in Limehouse in 1873 as a place where a working man, and occasionally his family, could obtain inexpensive, non-alcoholic refreshment.[41] Creating an alternative to the pub was an endeavour that Emma Cons, with her experience of the effects of drink on the working families in her courts, supported wholeheartedly. Two different results emerged from the "Cat and Comfort" coffee tavern: for one, challenged by a group of neighbourhood working girls, Emma Cons asked the "Cat and Comfort" committee to carve out space for a working girls' club. After an initial rough start and open hostility from the girls, this quickly grew into a permanent girls' dormitory hostel complete with piano, library, job counselling, and even crèche facilities for working mothers. The other was that the "Cat and Comfort" turned out to be a popular success. "The men," noted one observer, "called it 'the Safe Shop'; and men and women used to go there night after night, spending their evenings in a quiet chat, reading the papers or listening to a concert."[42] Tom Hughes and Emma Cons decided to try to duplicate the "Cat and Comfort" in other, similar parts of London.

By this time, Emma Cons had gathered around her a number of men and women, often of very different temperaments and social backgrounds but drawn together by a mutual desire to improve the lives of the working poor. Some, like George MacDonald, had come to know Cons through their mutual friend Ruskin. Others, like Tom Hughes, had come to know her through Christian Socialist projects. Together, they created a network of men and women mutually interested in temperance, slum clearance, the educating of poor children, and a variety of other social issues. For example, MacDonald enlisted his friend Antoinette Sterling to sing at the fêtes and parties Emma Cons would arrange for her tenants. Sterling, in turn, was a close friend of another of Ruskin's circle, William Cowper-Temple (later, Lord Mount-Temple), who stood as godfather to her son. Cowper-Temple became one of Emma Cons's staunchest supporters and he brought much with him. Simultaneously the nephew of one prime minister (Lord Melbourne) and the stepson of another (Lord Palmerston), Cowper-Temple was a Whig MP for thirty-three years, holding a succession of important and practical cabinet positions – paymaster general, president of the Board of Health, first commissioner of works – all giving him unusual insight into the state of the nation.[43] Sterling, MacDonald, and Cons all attended the evangelical and ecumenical conferences Cowper-Temple organized at his Hampshire home, Broadlands, as did Russell Gurney, the man who had purchased the house in Drury Lane wherein lodged the "Cat and Comfort" coffee tavern. It was thus logical that Tom Hughes and Emma Cons would turn to Cowper-Temple for help in expanding the coffee tavern idea.

Thus the Coffee Taverns Company was established in 1876 with Cowper-Temple as president, the Duke of Westminster as vice-president, and Tom Hughes among the directors. Certain of the company's principals had money and gave generously; it was a popular cause, and they attracted other donors. The company bought the leases of public houses at a prodigious rate, refurbished the premises, and installed new management.[44] Emma Cons agreed to supervise "The Walmer Castle," conveniently located adjacent to the dwellings she managed in Walmer Place in Marylebone which had been purchased and donated by Russell Gurney's widow. The company continued to expand; it began to publish a newsletter, the *Coffee Public-House News*. Committees were organized in other towns and cities. By 1884 there were over a thousand separate coffee tavern establishments across the United Kingdom and by 1897 there was something in excess of a hundred coffee taverns in London alone. And yet, the coffee tavern movement did not thrive. In the May 1884 issue of the *Coffee Public-House News and Temperance Hotel Journal*, prizes of five and ten guineas were offered for the best essay "satisfactorily discussing the causes of failure in the Coffee Tavern movement and the best means of rendering such places inviting to working men." This failure was largely due to two separate aspects: first, the quality of the coffee and tea was often substandard; second, competition had arisen from commercial tea-rooms and chain restaurants such as Lockharts, the Aerated Bread Company, and Pearce and Plenty, which had not existed when the first coffee taverns had been founded. Although it had been the coffee taverns that had first identified that few alternatives, aside from a pub, existed for consumers (particularly women) who sought good, inexpensive food and non-alcoholic drink, it was the commercial chains of tea-shops and inexpensive restaurants with their standardized and comfortable menus that capitalized on this consumer – and often feminine – demand. Run along directly profit-making, not temperance, lines, these institutions expanded on the customer base established by the coffee tavern movement, and by 1893 the cheerful, efficient, and standardized Lockharts was running fifty coffee rooms, the Aerated Bread Company had sixty cafés in operation, and Pearce and Plenty (which had actually started with Pearce's intermission refreshment stall in the lobby of the Royal

Victoria Hall) had twenty dining rooms throughout the UK. The well-intentioned coffee taverns could not compete.[45]

It was from this company that the idea of a "coffee music-hall" emerged. By July 1880, the *Musical Times* noted with approval that "a very powerful Council, composed of ladies and gentlemen distinguished by social position or by literary and artistic attainments is earnestly working in a thoroughly useful and philanthropic enterprise known as the Coffee Music-Halls Company."[46] The cause of temperance crossed religious lines. Although a number of clergymen were present at the company's first meeting – the meeting taking place in the Jerusalem Chamber of Westminster Abbey, chaired by Dean Stanley – the Coffee Music-Halls Company, like the Coffee Taverns Company, was non-sectarian. F.D. Mocatta, a pillar of London's Sephardic Jewish community, was an early shareholder, as were Mrs Montefiore, the Sassoons, the Goldsmids, and the Zimmermans. The Mocattas often lent their Connaught Place home for fundraising "drawing-room" events.

The objective of this united company was to turn the disreputable old "Vic" into a wholesome entertainment venue, run along temperance lines.

Reclaiming the Old "Vic"

For the newly formed offshoot of the Coffee Taverns Company – the Coffee Music-Halls Company – the Old Vic's location was auspicious, and not simply because it lay within a neighbourhood clearly in need of diversion from drink. The previous year Emma Cons had established a model worker dwellings project of her own. Her separation from Octavia Hill's organization had happened four years earlier and had been a source of some pain for her. In 1875, Hill had decided to spin off the Central London Dwellings Improvement Company, managed by Emma Cons, and create a wholly independent company. But since Hill communicated her decision either maladroitly or insensitively, or through third parties, Emma Cons inferred that she was being discarded and rejected. Hill later explained her decision in neutral, even laudatory terms: "I set her free to work towards her own standard."[47] Whether Octavia Hill intended to use corporate separation as a way of putting distance between the two women, or whether she saw increasing divergence between their philosophies of tenant management, Emma Cons was now operating her own organization.

Surrey Lodge (the former home of the late Sir James Wyatt, JP), at the northwest corner of Lambeth Road and Kennington Road, was torn down, and the quarter-acre was refashioned as the Surrey Buildings on a quadrangle with a pair of four-storied tenement flats facing each other across a central square of green and workmen's cottages at each end. Lavatories were built "well away" from the cottages and were locked, with each family given their own key. Wash-houses were built on the roof of the flats so laundry could dry in the breeze and stairways would not be encumbered by dripping lines of washing.[48]

At the Surrey Buildings, as had also been the case in the tenements she had managed for Octavia Hill, Emma Cons's sense of the havoc wreaked on family life by drink was confirmed. Living at Surrey Lodge with her tenants, she frequently had to intervene in domestic disputes and, as her niece Lilian Baylis observed, "even if the row took place at midnight, she was out of her cottage on the instant."[49] A Lambeth clergyman, reminiscing on the early years of the Surrey Buildings, noted that Emma Cons would often let mothers and children spend the night in her cottage when a drunken father had driven them from home. Although his version of one of his parishioners' recollections is summarized in dialect (likely indicating a desire to put distance between himself and his subjects), it is nonetheless revealing. "When farver came home boozed, something terrible he was, frew all the furniture over the balcony, and we're on the fifth story, mind, locked us all 'art, me and the kids and hisself in … but Miss Cons she didn't 'arf give it to him the next morning."[50] It was this understanding of the domestic situation of many of her tenants that alerted Emma Cons to the threat offered by the proximity of the raffish and disreputable Royal Victoria Theatre. A contemporary of Cons observed that "continually on Monday mornings when she collected her rents, black eyes were numerous. On enquiring the reason of this Monday carnage, she found that the men frequented music-halls on Saturday nights and drank intoxicating liquors the whole time as they listened to comic songs and foolery. They rolled home at midnight and beat their wives and little ones. Miss Cons felt it was necessary to found a music-hall on temperance lines."[51] Thus it was Emma Cons who pushed her colleagues in the Coffee Music-Halls Company to start their project by reclaiming the Old Vic. As her niece Lilian Baylis pointedly told Laurence Olivier years later, "If it hadn't been for drunken men beating their wives, dear boy, we'd never have got this place and you wouldn't be doing Hamlet."[52]

Supporters of this new venture were found, unsurprisingly, largely among the aristocracy and the professional upper middle classes, in addition to the network of socially minded persons already clustered around Ruskin, Octavia Hill, Lord Mount-Temple, and the Duke of Westminster. Some of the women were active colleagues of Lucy Cavendish in the Ladies Diocesan Association. The Marchioness of Lothian, the Earl and Countess of Meath, the Countess of Ducie, Mrs Montefiore, the Duchess of Richmond, Mrs Gladstone, and the philosopher and theologian Dr James Martineau were supporters of the Coffee Taverns Company and now turned to sustain the new company south of the river. Supporters were also found among the arts community: Sir Julius Benedict of the Covent Garden Opera House, Arthur Sullivan, and Carl Rosa, the founder of the popular Carl Rosa Opera Company, were early shareholders. Lord Frederick Cavendish was also an early shareholder in the company, and it was in this enterprise that Emma Cons, the company's secretary, first met Lucy Cavendish when she attended the company's second meeting in February 1880 with her husband. Subsequent "drawing-room meetings" were held in March of 1880, gathering further supporters from among the monied and well connected. By December 1880, the lease of the Old Vic had been secured, Emma Cons had agreed to supervise if a proper theatrical manager could be found, and renovations had commenced.

The cleaning was extensive: "literally sacks of shrimps' head and tails, periwinkle shells, nut-shells and dried orange peel" had to be shovelled out of the pit. Only basic renovations were made, but the refreshment (now temperance) bar was "beautifully fitted up" through a donation from Mrs Montefiore. The Royal Victoria Coffee Hall opened on 27 December 1880.[53] For the first year of its operations, the new incarnation of the Royal Victoria Hall attempted to retain its audience and balance its books. There were two specific challenges: ticket prices had been reduced to attract audiences, and bar revenues from the sale of non-alcoholic, and thus inexpensive, drinks (coffee, ginger beer, and cordials) added little to the balance sheet. The Hall offered mainly as broad a variety bill as it could, "freed of anything of a debasing nature": acrobats, performing dogs, the "Berisor Troupe of Roman Gladiators." Thursdays were ballad concert nights and Friday nights were reserved for a temperance lecture for which no admission was charged.[54] Reactions were mixed. The *Pall Mall Gazette* was equivocal: "The experiment is certainly one of the most interesting and admirable that has been made in the direction of giving to the workers of London some of the humanizing pleasures hitherto reserved for the idlers."[55] The *Graphic*'s correspondent was acid, but his report can serve to provide a good description of the early bill at the Hall.

> There can be no doubt that alcoholic drink is a great attraction to the working man. If, therefore, you deprive him of his beer or spirits and offer coffee and lemonade in their place, you must give him a better entertainment on the stage than he is likely to find at the ordinary music-hall ... The entertainment provided is in some respects much less stupid than that of the ordinary music-hall type; but it is, with a few exceptions, wholly lacking in the enterprise which certainly characterises the music-hall programme ... the band ... would scarcely do credit to a second-rate provincial theatre ... the "grand spectacular ballet" is, with the exception of the last scene, representing the death of Nelson, decidedly tame ... On the other hand, there is some really clever jig-dancing and skipping by Miss Hetty Towers, and a nigger entertainment of a decidedly amusing character.[56]

Emma Cons's first annual report gave an inspiring sense of accomplishment, notwithstanding: "Of the moral success of our work at the Vic, I can scarcely find words strong enough to give a true idea to anyone, except those working in the neighbourhood." The neighbouring clergy and constabulary, she wrote, initially sceptical and suspicious, now concurred that "wonderful" work was being done. "I should like you to see their letters to me: they say that the streets are quite different since we came, both for drunkenness and immorality." And indeed, the report asserted, nightly neighbourhood arrests significantly decreased from an average of forty down to four.[57] Unfortunately, notwithstanding the success of the Thursday night ballad concerts, the reformed Royal Victoria Coffee Music Hall was a conspicuous failure in terms of gross revenues, and the Coffee Music-Halls Company ended its first season £2,800 in the red. An emergency fundraising campaign among the Hall's supporters was rapidly undertaken during the summer of 1881. Sir Julius Benedict addressed the crowd on the important work of the Coffee Music Hall, the benefits of which "could not be over-rated."[58] The Marchioness of Lothian gave generously; others followed. Lord Mount-Temple undertook personal responsibility for debts incurred the next season. It was resolved that the Royal Victoria Hall would attempt another season of wholesome entertainments.

During this same period, Emma Cons was steadily gaining a reputation as a talented and efficient administrator of model housing for the working poor. Her mother had died in 1882 and thereafter Emma and her sister Ellen took two of the Surrey Buildings cottages (nos. 5 and 6 Morton Place) for their own home, Emma retaining her usual practice of living among her tenants. These two cottages became the operating headquarters for Emma Cons and the band of women she gathered about her to assist with both the running of the Surrey Buildings and the operations of the Royal Victoria Hall.

In many ways, the Surrey Buildings and the Royal Victoria Hall were deliberately structured as women's establishments. Seth Koven, in *Slumming* (2004), has observed how Toynbee Hall, peopled with young clergymen imbued with muscular Christianity, developed a homosocial, common-room atmosphere, celebrating a hearty, masculine approach to reclaiming the working poor of the East End. In much the same way, south of the river, Emma Cons created an enclave of women who interested themselves in social matters and who both worked, and often lived, together. She worked best with women and both at the Surrey Buildings and at the Royal Victoria Hall surrounded herself with women personally and professionally. Her right hand in both operations was her sister Ellen. But there were many other women who became attached and who stayed.

Caroline Martineau, whom Emma Cons had met in 1871 when they were both working with Octavia Hill as rent collectors, had joined Cons as an assistant when she established the Surrey Buildings. The niece of Dr James Martineau, Caroline Martineau had come to good works as an extension of her personal philosophy of philanthropy and fellowship: she had grown up within a wealthy and philanthropic Unitarian family. Her father, Richard Martineau, was a director and partner of Whitbread's Brewery, but he was also a good friend of the Christian Socialists Charles Kingsley and F.D. Maurice.[59] Caroline Martineau would stay over with the Cons sisters two or three nights a week when working in Lambeth. Only five years separated them in age and they were good friends as well as colleagues. Caroline Martineau's mother was a strong supporter of Emma Cons's efforts and had given £1,000 to the emergency fundraising effort at the end of the Royal Victoria Hall's first year. Mrs Martineau had previously been impressed by Emma Cons's financial common sense when she had been assisting Caroline Martineau and her mother address and stuff fundraising envelopes pertaining to a separate venture. After hours of affixing penny stamps to the letters, Emma Cons had suggested that a ha'penny stamp might suffice and had walked one down to the post office to have it weighed; a ha'penny was indeed found to be sufficient, thereby confirming Mrs Martineau's view that Emma Cons would be good with the Royal Victoria Hall's finances.[60] Caroline Martineau was a woman who had made a deliberate decision not to marry. Her choice was a conscious protest against the position of women in society. "I don't like any *spoken* protest against the position of women," she averred to a younger colleague in 1896, "when people see that we will not marry while the position of women is so unsatisfactory, they will begin to take action."[61] Caroline Martineau also brought other women into the Lambeth operations. Her sister Constance assisted at both the Surrey Buildings and the Royal Victoria Hall. Caroline Martineau persuaded their cousin, Sophia Lonsdale, to help run the Surrey Buildings. When Emma Cons's niece Lilian Baylis travelled from her home in South Africa to recuperate from an operation, it was Caroline and Constance Martineau and Emma Cons's sister Ellen who persuaded her to stay to help her aging aunt.

Intimate friendships with women also marked Emma Cons's personal life. She had been intensely devoted to Octavia Hill from the time they were girls, a friendship that Octavia's brother-in-law recalled as somewhat surprising, given Emma's boisterous nature and Octavia's reserve. "Miss Cons was so much given to romps that Octavia's fellow workers (including her sisters) were rather startled at the attraction which her new friend had for her."[62] As a girl, Emma had a frank demeanour, and this open bluntness developed into an assertive personality. After her death in 1912, Lilian Baylis asked Henrietta Barnett of Toynbee Hall, who had remained a close friend of Emma's, to write an introduction to the biographical sketch Baylis was writing as a memorial to her aunt. Barnett recalled her earliest memories of Emma Cons:

> Her personality was arresting, though often vexing; especially to one, who like myself, had been reared in close obedience to the early Victorian tenets that young ladies should speak softly, walk with short steps, agree with most things that were said by their elders, and be modestly subservient to the male members of their families ... Emma Cons spoke loudly and often aggressively, strode as if she were measuring a plot by yard steps, disliked, positively disliked, the male sex, and questioned the wisdom of many of the standards of conduct and thought accepted

> by past generations. Moreover she dressed badly, really badly, was untidy and abnormally often in a great hurry, and yet she soon captured the heart ... [63]

Baylis chose, in the end, not to include Barnett's piece, likely because of the flag of overt masculinity which Barnett's words raised and which could easily have been interpreted as indicating a lesbian identity. Baylis was at pains in writing about her aunt to use words that invoked femininity, describing her aunt as "womanly," a "beautiful, gentle little lady," and describing her "delicate little lace bonnet" and her "beautiful face lighting up with sympathy for others."[64] Yet, at the same time, Baylis evidently could not help but fall into painting her aunt in masculine tones, depicting her as "a bit of a tomboy" who "always carried a knife and a piece of string in her pocket, even when wearing evening dress," and recalling her "striding up the hill at Hever, singing in her deep contralto voice," or "tucking up her skirts and climbing on to the roof of one of her tenant's houses, to shew a recalcitrant workman how slates and gutters should be fixed." In describing her aunt's close relationship with her sister Ellen, Baylis observed that "we used to say that Emmie was like the strong husband and Ellen the devoted wife."[65]

Whether Emma Cons was one of many Victorian women who maintained intense and passionate, but essentially platonic, relationships with other women or whether she identified herself as a lesbian is difficult to determine. Nothing in her papers remains to suggest sexual relationships with other women. But this may well be the result of a sweep conducted by Lilian Baylis, who, after her aunt's death, thoroughly went through her papers, redacting and, she reported to her parents, burning a good deal. There may have been a good deal to hide.[66] Clearly the early devotion of Emma Cons to Octavia Hill grew into a passionate friendship, although it is a matter of speculation whether the relationship had an erotic aspect. If Emma Cons's sexuality is open to interpretation, so is that of Octavia Hill. A number of scholars have debated whether Octavia Hill's relationships with other women were sexual. Certainly Hill had an early and intense romance with Sophia Jex-Blake that was only disrupted by the adamant opposition of Mrs Hill. Octavia Hill went on to live with Harriot Yorke for the last thirty-five years of her life.[67] In any case, Emma Cons was utterly heartbroken in 1875 when Octavia Hill unilaterally chose to distance herself from Emma's operations at the Central London Dwellings Improvement Company. On that occasion, Emma wrote to Henrietta Barnett in bereft misery that an attempted intercession by Barnett had been ineffective. Emma's investment in her relationship with Octavia is obvious:

> All last evening and night being in such a high state of excitement and expectation of such big results from your great influence with O.H. and then on going to her this morning full of hope and getting stabbed through and through (may you never feel such). Oh it was almost too much ... You or no-one has the least idea of how I love her ... my principal dread has been her not wanting me.[68]

Whether a romance, a sexual relationship, or an intense, passionate, and long-standing friendship, her relationship with Octavia Hill clearly was enormously important to Emma Cons.

The woman with whom Emma Cons went on to share her life was Ethel Everest, the daughter of Sir George Everest, the soldier-surveyor after whom the Himalayan mountain is named. Beginning around 1882, she stayed at Surrey Lodge increasingly frequently. Like Caroline Martineau, Ethel Everest was a well-educated single woman of independent wealth. She and Emma Cons divided their time between Surrey Lodge and Everest's country home, Chippen's Bank, in Hever, Kent. Romantically or companionably, Emma Cons and Ethel Everest lived together from 1882 to Emma's death in 1912. This was accepted by all and not thought of as anything but two middle-aged, like-minded, philanthropic maiden ladies finding companionship, a not uncommon situation in Victorian Britain. Students recalled after Emma Cons's death how she and Ethel Everest invited them down to Chippen's Bank for weekends in the country.[69] After Cons's death, Lilian Baylis accorded Ethel Everest a widow's position, leaving funeral arrangements to her and raising no objections when Cons's ashes were scattered at Chippen's Bank. Baylis also reluctantly yielded to Everest's intense opposition regarding the biography of her aunt which Baylis had proposed writing, feeling free to publish only after Everest's death. Regardless of whether Emma Cons saw herself as a lesbian, regardless of whether her relationships were intensely (if platonically) romantic or sexual, her personal relationships were entirely with women. She also structured the management of both the Surrey Buildings and the Royal Victoria Hall as all-female organizations.

This was not difficult. Women were attracted to work at places like the Surrey Buildings or the Royal Victoria Hall because they offered meaningful, if badly paying, work. For example, in the years before her marriage to Sidney Webb, the young and financially independent Beatrice Potter involved herself with efforts at improving the lives of London's working poor. She joined the Charity Organization Society in 1883. This was not an unusual path for women of Beatrice Potter's milieu. The Charity Organization Society (the "COS") had been established in 1869 by a sizeable committee of eminent philanthropic individuals, including Octavia Hill, Bernard and Helen Bosanquet, Lord Shaftesbury, and John Ruskin, with the mission of coordinating the efforts of the many overlapping charities which had been gradually established during the 1850s and 1860s to help the poor. The concern of the COS was less a desire to reach an absolute efficiency in charitable effort than it was a fear that the "clever pauper" was able to cobble together a comfortable living from bouncing from one charity to another, exploiting the fact that to each he would appear as a new and desperate case. Under the COS system, a needy person would apply to the local COS committee, which would examine and question the applicant to determine whether he or she was truly needy before passing him or her on to the appropriate charity or to the local poorhouse authorities. Local COS committees were to work closely with local poor law guardians to ensure that lack of coordination between charities was not exploited. This approach, and particularly this form of examination, became responsible for the COS becoming colloquially known to many applicants as "Cringe or Starve."[70] Like the Christian Socialists, the men and women who worked with the COS believed that the separation of the classes was much to blame for the "demoralization" of the working poor. But the Christian Socialists saw "uplift" to be found in worker education, cooperative ventures, and the salutary effects of exposing the poor to middle-class values and culture. The COS saw the virtues of thrift and self-help being reintroduced via the scientific application of just enough, and just the right form of, charity, bestowed in conjunction with close, personal supervision.

In addition to her work with the COS, in 1885 Beatrice Potter became one of the first lady rent collectors at the Katharine Buildings, model worker dwellings set up that year in Cartwright Street by the East End Dwellings Company. But after only ten months, she became discouraged by the effects of the "Octavia Hill system" where lady rent collectors came and went. She saw the Katharine Buildings as an "utter failure," noting in her diary:

> They are not an influence for good. The free intercourse has here, as elsewhere in this dismal mass, a demoralizing effect. The bad and indifferent, the drunken, mean and lowering elements overwhelm the effect of higher motive and noble example. The respectable tenants keep to themselves. To isolate yourself from your surroundings seems to be here the acme of social morality; in truth it is the only creed one dare preach. "Do not meddle with your neighbour" is perforce the burden of one's advice to the newcomer ... The lady collectors are an altogether superficial thing. Undoubtedly their gentleness and kindness brings light into many homes; but what are they in the face of this collective brutality, heaped up together in infectious contact; adding to each other's dirt, physical and moral? And how can one raise these beings to better things without the hope of a better world, the faith in the usefulness of effort?[71]

That August, Beatrice Potter crossed the river to see how Emma Cons's methods employed at the Surrey Buildings differed from Octavia Hill's and to see whether the manager's being resident in a tenement court had a distinct effect. She left a vivid, if not altogether accurate, picture of Emma Cons at the age of forty-seven that tells us almost as much about the assumptions of the young Beatrice Potter as it does about Emma Cons:

> Not a lady by birth, with the face and manner of a distinguished woman, almost a ruler of men. Absolute absorption in work; strong religious feeling, very little culture or interest in things outside the sphere of her own action. Certainly, she is not a lover of fact or theory; she was not clear as to the total number of rooms, unlets or arrears. No description of tenants kept. Did not attempt to theorize about her work. Kept all particulars as to families in her head. To her people she spoke with that peculiar combination of sympathy and authority which characterizes the modern type of governing woman. I felt ashamed of the way I cross-questioned her. As far as I could make out from her books, her arrears amounted within £1 of her weekly rent – that is to say, on her working-class tenants. She lives on the premises; collects other blocks, but devotes much time to other work in connection with amusement and instruction of the people. A calm enthusiasm in her face, giving her all to others. "Why withhold any of

your time and strength?" seems to be her spirit. All her energy devoted to the practical side of the work. No desire to solve the general questions of the hour.[72]

Perhaps it was Emma Cons's focused, businesslike demeanour that gave Beatrice Potter the impression that she was entirely absorbed in the minutiae of running the Lambeth enterprises. She had certainly struck others as being utterly devoid of personal vanity and absolutely absorbed in her work. Sophia Lonsdale recalled her as "short, but strongly built, not at all handsome but her eyes were the brightest I almost ever saw and there was an eagerness of manner and address which were very striking and captivating ... She was keen, quick, very clever and very good ... with a passion for helping anyone in difficulties, absolutely careless of herself and her comfort, devoted to the people among whom she worked."[73]

This is not to say that Emma Cons was never discouraged. Although Sophia Lonsdale observed that "Miss Cons' courage and spirit and hopefulness never left her," she acknowledged that Emma Cons did have a sense of the Sisyphean nature of the struggle: "I remember walking across Lambeth Bridge with her one day and we stopped in the middle to look down the river. She said to me: 'When one thinks of all the sin and misery there is in London, what's to prevent one's throwing oneself over there except one's faith? I wish I were in heaven with the gate shut.'"[74]

Potter's assessment of Emma Cons, however, was glaringly inaccurate concerning two vital aspects of her life. She was hardly a woman of "very little culture." She had grown up in a musical household; her sister Elizabeth was a professional singer of a classical repertoire. She was also a member of the Handel Festival Choir, and contemporaries recalled her as being possessed of a good voice. Sophia Lonsdale remembered her as a "very good musician."[75] The conductor Sir Adrian Boult warmly remembered her as "a most sensitive and cultured person."[76] It was Emma Cons who, understanding the refreshing effects of an artistic culture, had put together the little operettas and theatricals at Barrett's Court. It was partly her degree of comfort in musical and performance culture that led her to take over the programming of the Old Vic. She was also a gifted and well-trained visual artist. She had supported herself as an artist, engraving silver and working in stained glass. Art, indeed, was her profession until she began to work

2 Emma Cons. Courtesy of the Morley College Archives, Borough of Lambeth Archives.

with Octavia Hill, and colour remained a passion for her. Ruskin had strongly urged her against working with Hill, but instead to continue restoring and copying illuminated manuscripts. Lilian Baylis recalled that her aunt never gave up art "as a pastime, she could not see a bare building without wanting to adorn it."[77] Emma Cons's friend May Hughes, the daughter of the author of *Tom Brown's Schooldays*, recalled, as young women, their enjoying a quiet evening's conversation in the country: "suddenly, as we looked out at the silver moon and the clouds and the sea, Emmie said, 'Did you ever think, May, that the world might have been grey? Nature could have managed it. But God gave us colour.'"[78] Emma Cons was far from a woman of "very little culture." Perhaps the young Beatrice Potter did not expect to meet culture in an efficient businesswoman from the artisan class and so she could not see it. Perhaps Emma Cons did not see the point in displaying her understanding of high culture to her young visitor, who had come to see the results of the work at the Surrey Buildings.

Beatrice Potter was also entirely incorrect in a more important aspect of Emma Cons's mission. She inferred that Emma Cons's "absolute absorption in the work" of running the Surrey Buildings left her with "no desire to solve the general questions of the hour." This was entirely inaccurate and likely the product of Potter's inexperience with worker tenements. As Lucy Cavendish, in her work with the Ladies Diocesan Association and the Parochial Mission Women, had thought much about how to eradicate the cycle of poverty, so too Emma Cons had given a good deal of thought, both during her work with Octavia Hill and subsequently on her own, to the root cause of the apparently perpetual trap of poverty among London's working poor. Like Lucy Cavendish too, it was not ideology or priggishness that had led her to temperance; Emma Cons, similarly, did not come from a temperance family.[79] But her observations during her years working with the tenants at Freshwater Place, Barrett's Court, and the Surrey Buildings led her to conclude that the ubiquity of cheap drink and a culture where drinking was not only the readiest but often the only form of amusement was largely responsible for sapping already precarious household budgets and inculcating a sense of hopelessness among tenement families. This was also a burden that usually fell disproportionately on poor wives and mothers. In the same way that Lucy Cavendish supported the woman-to-woman temperance work of the CETS Women's Union, so too Emma Cons saw her temperance work in Lambeth as reaching other women. Indeed, it was Cons's sense that most problems among her tenants could, fairly quickly, be traced back to alcohol that turned her attention to the idea of recasting the Old Vic as a non-alcoholic alternative to the pub. Cons wrote, in 1889, a concise summary of her mission and its impetus:

> So long as gin-palaces and beer-shops are to be found at nearly every street-corner in the poorer-class neighbourhoods, so long will the greatest part of the money saved by cheaper rent be spent there. And unless recreation, of intellectual and artistic merit, be brought within the reach of the mass of people (many of whom are fully able to appreciate it) and their intelligence and love of beauty, harmony and order for its own sake, are used, they will speedily reduce these new and improved dwellings to the filth and squalor of the old.[80]

Her conviction that to solve the problem of alcohol abuse was to significantly ameliorate all other problems the poor faced only grew stronger over the years. Shortly before her death, she had a conversation in a railway station with Thomas Hughes's daughter May following a committee meeting. She and May Hughes had known each other as girls, as Tom Hughes had, as a Christian Socialist, been an early supporter of Emma Cons's work. Emma and May had worked together establishing a home for "feeble-minded" girls in Bodmin; it was with May that Emma had made her observation about colour being a divine gift; Emma Cons could speak freely with May Hughes. As May later reported to Jane Cobden, theirs was a "deep and thrilling talk," and Emma "let several trains pass pouring out her pleasure" in various schemes to aid the vulnerable. But it was when the conversation came to the problems of drink that she "kindled most. Her whole being seemed searching how the "tap root drain" of this one thing was at the root of all the other evils."[81]

Eventually the young Beatrice Potter, towards the end of her time at the Katherine Buildings, also acknowledged the devastating effects of the pub's being the centre of all social life of the working poor. She noted in her diary: "as the 'Public' is the only meeting-place, the more social and generous nature is led away even by its good qualities; while the crabbed mind and sickly constitution destroys itself ... The drink demon destroys the fittest and spares the meaner nature."[82] Again, however, perhaps because she lacked Emma Cons's almost twenty years of experience with the culture of the working poor, Beatrice Potter equivocated about the difficulties posed by alcohol: "Why resist the demon drink? A short life and a merry one, why not? A woman diseased with drink came up to me screaming, in her hand the quart pot, her face directed to the 'Public.' What could I say? Why dissuade her? She is half-way to death – let her go – if death ends all. But with her go others; and these others may be only on the first step downwards."[83] Emma Cons had no doubts; she saw drink as the problem that underlay all others. She and Lucy Cavendish thus had much common ground in their mutual battle against drink, and both women saw the Royal Victoria Coffee Hall as providing a wholesome alternative enticement.

Aside from their mutual belief in temperance, Lucy Cavendish and Emma Cons were also both united in their fervent, shared Anglican faith. Emma Cons was not only deeply personally committed to the Church of England but, like Lucy Cavendish, also very specific about her religion. But they occupied positions at opposite ends of the Anglican buffet of doctrine. Whereas Lucy Cavendish was Tractarian and High Church, Emma Cons was decidedly liberal and Broad Church, in many ways influenced by her early exposure to the Christian Socialists. That said, although Emma Cons might be liberal in religious matters, her Anglicanism was not indistinct. Unitarians, for example, might be very good people, but they were not actually Christians, and to her way of thinking not appropriate for working as lady rent collectors with the residents of her Surrey Buildings. "I had a Unitarian working for me for five years," she explained to a young Sophia Lonsdale. "She knew her work thoroughly, her accounts were always right, she was most regular and punctual, but she had absolutely no influence with the people." That said, Emma Cons did not include Caroline Martineau in this general disapproval. "She is an exception – she's a Christian in heart."[84]

There is a good picture of Emma Cons's Lambeth and the men and women who were her target audience in a number of pieces of contemporary fiction. Somerset Maugham's 1897 novel, *Liza of Lambeth,* was written the previous year while Maugham was completing his obstetrical rotation at St Thomas' Hospital, Lambeth. The novel's characters, mainly women, live and work a stone's throw from the Old Vic.[85] In their everyday lives, Maugham's characters cope with the exact problems that Emma Cons saw at the Surrey Buildings: Liza's mother, with whom she lives, drinks away any of Liza's earnings she does not hide; it is Liza's encounter with beer at the local pub that leads to her getting pregnant. Her miscarriage, the cause of her death, is brought on by her getting drunk, for the first time, on whisky. Each and every female character in the book is beaten, often critically, by her drunken husband or boyfriend, a situation that is taken as normal by all. In *Liza*, the pub is the centre of all social life, even the excursion to the country, and it is easy to see the deleterious effects of its monopoly over Lambeth amusement. In the same vein, the total absence of any complex or thought-provoking artistic culture makes for a dull and virtually dehumanizing environment, as, apart from a Italian street organ grinder and a blood-and-thunder melodrama, the Lambeth of *Liza* is culturally barren.

It was with Lambeth in mind that Emma Cons tweaked the balance of the bill at the Royal Victoria Hall in its second year, decreasing the number of broad entertainments, acrobats, performing dogs, and gladiators and increasing the number of more thoughtful and artistically challenging acts. The new manager, William Poel, formerly of the Bijou Theatre, Gravesend, introduced choirs and bands on Wednesday nights, retained the Thursday night ballad concerts, and added lectures of general interest to follow the Friday night temperance meetings.[86] In her annual report for 1882, Cons noted the changes that the Old Vic's program had wrought in the Lambeth locals: "the girls known on the Surrey side as the 'Madame Blackfriars type' – girls with white aprons, mysteriously propped up hats and ridiculous fringes on their foreheads – instead of lolling on their sweethearts' shoulders and absorbing spirits and suggestions as is their wont too often at the music hall, here sit quiet and attentive."[87]

With an altered bill, the Royal Victoria Hall experienced a good increase in ticket sales. The Thursday night ballad concerts were the most popular. It was the Monday and Tuesday night variety performances that still posed a problem, and attendance continued to fall off, dragging down overall revenues. Noting the consistent success of the lantern lectures that preceded Friday night's temperance meetings, Emma Cons enlisted the aid of the scholarly scientific magazine *Nature*, which ran her appeal for scientists to speak to her audiences. She received an unexpected response: the first speaker was the established scientist William Lant Carpenter, who gave a lecture in the autumn on "The Telephone, or, How to talk to a man a hundred miles away."[88] Carpenter's inaugural lecture was followed by other speakers of significance: the astronomer Sir Norman Lockyer, the naturalist and physiologist Dr W.B. Carpenter, the president of the Royal Microscopical Society, Dr William H. Dallinger. These lectures, usually well illustrated with lantern slides, were a great success and attracted a segment of the working population of London, those of scientific tastes, who had hitherto not frequented the Hall.[89] Emma Cons formed a committee of scientists to elicit, screen, and schedule speakers and soon she replaced Tuesday night's variety bill with scientific lectures. She put Caroline Martineau in charge.

This was a logical choice. Indeed, it is likely that Caroline Martineau was originally responsible for suggesting scientific lectures to Emma Cons. And likely she was also able to secure Carpenter, the former tutor of James Martineau. Caroline Martineau was a reasonably good amateur scientist and had been from the age of seventeen when she first attended Faraday and Tyndall's lectures at the Royal Institution. In 1871 she had written *Aunt Rachel's Letters on Water and Air* as a way of introducing children to basic concepts of science. She followed that with similar books aimed at piquing children's interest in natural science: *Chapters on Sound* (1875) and *Earth, Air and Water or The World We Live In* (1881). In 1880 she was elected a member of the Physical Society, the premier organization of British physicists. She wrote a number of scholarly papers, including her last in 1900: "Shapes and Sounds: An Account of Compound Pendulum Drawings and Musical Intervals." She seamlessly combined a fervent adherence to a Unitarian form of God with a devoted belief in the theories of Charles Darwin. She was a very capable administrator of the "Penny Science Lecture" series at the Hall.

But the scientific lecture series was not without opponents. William Poel resigned at the end of the 1883 season. He thought the programming over-emphasized education and moral uplift and neglected the idea of pure entertainment. He also was of the opinion that the programming was pitched over the heads of the Hall's public.[90] Some of the directors of the Coffee Music-Halls Company shared Poel's views. Following Poel's resignation, the directors voted to do away with both the Friday night temperance meetings and the Tuesday night scientific lantern lectures. Simultaneously faced with opposition from her directors and continued dwindling revenues, Emma Cons cannily turned to a like-minded acquaintance from outside her usual circle of supporters.

When the wealthy and liberal philanthropist Samuel Morley had first been approached to generally support the Coffee Music-Halls Company in 1880, he had declined because he did not approve of music halls.[91] But over the course of the first season, he had become impressed by Emma Cons's efforts at the Royal Victoria Hall, and when the Hall was faced with its significant deficit at the end of its first season, he pledged £100 a year for five years. Now he did more. Offering £1,000 towards the purchase of the fourteen years remaining on the Hall's lease, Morley stipulated one condition: that he could choose a governing committee that would support his own views regarding temperance and worker education. Regardless of whether this condition was suggested to him by his ally in temperance, Emma Cons, Morley's pledge of £1,000 towards the purchase of the lease would save the Hall approximately £700 annual rent and was gratefully accepted. Emma Cons's companion, Ethel Everest, had already pledged another £1,000 towards the purchase of the lease, the total price of which was £4,000. With half the campaign now achieved, subscriptions came in swiftly. Caroline Martineau contributed and also successfully solicited the aid of eight further assorted Martineaus.

By June 1884 the lease had been purchased in the names of five trustees: the Duke of Westminster, Samuel Morley and his son, Charles, Sir Thomas Brassey (son of the railway contractor of the same name, Liberal MP and supporter of the cooperative movement), and Emma Cons. The Coffee Music-Halls Company was wound up and its assets were transferred to these trustees. At the first meeting of the new company, William Cowper-Temple (now Lord Mount-Temple) strenuously advocated continuing the Thursday night ballad concerts, stressing the importance of music as a civilizing influence and observing how enthusiastically they had always been received by the Hall's audiences. A working committee dedicated to temperance and programming favouring educational lectures was formed with Samuel Morley as chairman and Emma Cons as secretary. An Honorary Council of luminaries was formed to add lustre to the Hall. The Duke of Westminster became the Council's president. Lucy Cavendish was a member of this band.

The "Penny Science Lecture" series became a priority of Emma Cons, and it was well received. Subjects ranged from "Our Bones: What They Are and How They Are Made" to "Light and Colour" and "Ancient British Glaciers." Admission was deliberately kept cheap: threepence for the balcony, tuppence for the pit, and a penny for the large gallery. At the conclusion of one of the Tuesday night lectures, Emma Cons reported that "Most of the lecturers have expressed surprise and satisfaction at the interest shown by the silent attention of the audience and the evident intelligence of the applause coming at the right points – and it is certain they do not applaud out of regard for the lecturer's feelings … with them silence and applause, each in its place, are honest signs of pleasure."[92] One night, four young men from the pit approached Emma Cons to ask whether she would consider a more systematic form of regular scientific evening classes. This idea was enthusiastically supported. By the autumn of 1885, evening classes started in the backstage rehearsal rooms that were already in use by a local working men's club.

The classes, which became increasingly popular, would likely have remained simply an aspect of a working men's club had it not been for the reorganization, in 1883, of the City of London Parochial Charities. The 1883 Act allowed the charity commissioners to liberate and re-allocate funds bequeathed in previous centuries to London parishes for specific purposes by long-dead testators which had simply accumulated through diminished need. Thus bequests made centuries before, for example for the ransoming of Christian captives from Barbary pirates, towards sustaining sermons celebrating the defeat of the Armada, or for the tolling of St Sepulchre's bells at Newgate executions, could, through application of the legal doctrine of *cy-près*, now be applied towards purposes that were similar in nature and objective.[93] In the case of the Royal Victoria Hall, the charity commissioners agreed that approximately £1,000 per annum from such funds could be applied towards popular education and recreation. The difficulty was that the theatre had to be run by a charitable trust which had to own the building outright. The owner was willing to sell the trustees the freehold for £17,000 if the money was forthcoming within four months. Lucy Cavendish and the Duke of Westminster's organization of the swift campaign (concluded in August 1888 after only three and half months) had elicited support from many. Sir Thomas (soon to become Lord) Brassey gave £1,000, as did the sugar baron and benefactor of British art Henry Tate and several members of Samuel Morley's family. Ethel Everest gave £500. When the campaign was done and a new trust was established, three women, Lucy Cavendish, Emma Cons, and Caroline Martineau, sat as the trustees for the new Royal Victoria Hall.[94]

The Hall in its new incarnation now claimed more of Emma Cons's attention than did the Surrey Buildings. The Hall now had two purposes. "The Theatre shall be primarily for the holding there of public lectures and musical and other entertainments and exhibitions suitable for the recreation and instruction of the poorer classes. Admissions shall not be gratuitous, but it shall be at such prices as will make them available to artisans."[95] What now became a separate institution – Morley Memorial College for Working Men and Women – was named after Samuel Morley, who had died in 1886. Still occupying the rehearsal rooms, the new College had a particular objective: "To promote the advanced study by men and women belonging to the working classes of subjects of knowledge not directly connected with or applied to any handicraft, trade or business." The homosocial atmosphere of the Royal Victoria Hall and the Surrey Buildings was particularly marked at Morley College, which was run entirely by women. The first principal, chosen by the presiding trio of Emma Cons, Caroline Martineau, and Lucy Cavendish, was Louisa Goold, the former principal of the Working Women's College. When ill health forced her to retire after only two years, Caroline Martineau herself took over as principal, retaining this position for eleven years. Her successor, Mary Sheepshanks, daughter of the Bishop of Norwich, had studied at Newnham and worked at the Women's University Settlement in Southwark but had been attracted by the female-friendly atmosphere at Morley College. Sheepshanks recalled being asked only three questions at her interview: "Had she a sister at home to look after her parents if they fell ill? Could she stop an over-vigorous glove fight in the gym? Could she tell if a vet was too drunk to take the horse class?"[96] In 1907 she asked Emmeline Pankhurst to give a lecture on women's suffrage at the College and began the practice of organizing women-only meetings for female students as well as holding college debates and lectures on the topic of women's suffrage.[97] Emma Cons similarly appointed only women as vice-principals of Morley College. The first vice-principal, Ella Sieveking, came from a background similar to that of Caroline Martineau; her father was an eminent physician and she had studied art with Hubert Herkomer. Florence Acton, who succeeded her in 1894, was the first woman to graduate from the Victoria University of Manchester. The decision to staff Morley College entirely with women was deliberate. Caroline Martineau had once explained to a younger colleague that this was done because what Morley College needed was "an influence."[98] This was not a uniformly popular policy, but it was the choice of the deciding trio of Emma Cons, Caroline Martineau, and Lucy Cavendish. And women responded. Attracted to Morley College either because it put women in positions of authority or because of its curriculum, women students steadily increased in numbers from its first year. Morley College became a distinct part of Emma Cons's Lambeth bastion of women.[99]

Emma Cons had now been improving the lives of London's working poor for almost two decades, her efforts concentrated in Lambeth for ten of those years. The Surrey Buildings largely accomplished Cons's objective of providing stable as well as affordable and cohesive housing for the working poor of South London. The Royal Victoria Hall was proving to be an admirable and popular counter-attraction to the pub, and the emergence of Morley College from the Tuesday night "penny lectures" held promise. Her efforts attracted notice. A reporter for the *Sunday Circle* visited Lambeth in the autumn of 1909 and wrote:

> Recently the *Sunday Circle* representative found his way down Waterloo Road and into the hall, where an entertainment was in full swing. But where was the ribaldry, the profanity and the drinking for so long associated with "the Old Vic"? It is the same neighbourhood with its poverty and squalor and adjacent slums, it is the same hall and the price of admission gallery 1d and 2d, pit 4d; cushioned balcony seats 6d are within the power of the very poor. Wherein did the changed spirit of the place consist? Here and there flitted the presiding genius of the place, now in the balcony, now climbing up to the gallery to exchange a word with the audience. This was a frail gentle little lady with a sweet face and charming kindly manners.[100]

Cons observed to a newspaper which had asked her to write an article on her system at the Surrey Buildings: "I do the work but do *not* write about it. So if anyone would like to see what is being done in London, they can be taken around by one of my lady workers if your correspondents are coming to London."[101] Many took her at her word. Those interested in social welfare schemes, journalists and the occasional politician, like Beatrice Webb, came to Lambeth to view Cons's efforts. The *New York Times* correspondent, paediatrician and social reformer Henry Dwight Chapin (describing Lambeth as "a dirty, grimy section of the town"), reported that the system as applied by Emma Cons seemed to be altogether satisfactory, noting approvingly that "a bonus is returned to the tenants for regular and punctual payment of rent and thus habits of thrift are encouraged." Chapin found much to be impressed with: "one excellent feature of this enterprise, as of others similarly managed, is that ladies collect the weekly rents and thus have an opportunity to acquaint themselves with the habits and life conditions of the tenants." Making the rounds with one of the lady rent collectors, Chapin found that "it was easy to see that she was not only on friendly relations with the tenants but had a watchful eye for their welfare." Chapin also noted with approval that "The Directors have declared a dividend for the past year of four per cent free of income tax."[102] Emma Cons had made her reputation for efficiency and sensible management.

Beatrice Webb's initial judgment, that Emma Cons had not come from gentility, worked to her advantage. It gave her credibility. Middle-class ladies were unlikely to be able to show lazy workmen exactly how to patch an eavestrough or how to angle in a replacement roofing slate. Middle-class ladies did not live in tenements. Octavia Hill, for example, never took up residence in her tenements; she built a special room on the back of her house to receive tenants.[103] In this, Emma Cons's approach to her work at the Surrey Buildings, the Old Vic, and Morley College contrasted with other women's settlements of the time, most noticeably the Women's University Settlement, established in 1887 in neighbouring Southwark by women often just down from Newnham and Girton. Whereas Emma Cons lived among, and very much as, her tenants, the women graduates of the Women's University Settlement kept servants, dressed for dinner, and, instead of formulating their own objectives and projects, often worked "out" for organizations such as the Charitable Organization Society.[104] Emma Cons was also able to be frank to the point of bluntness in a way that would have been unthinkable in a well-brought-up middle-class woman of her generation. This was a quality which drew not opprobrium, but approval. "Miss Cons is plain and simple of speech, expressing her opinions incisively and without the shadow of a doubt," wrote a reporter in the *Sussex Daily News*; "she has remarkable courage, and many stories are told of her daring in dealing with drunken and degraded people."[105] Her forthright qualities, her financial acumen, her businesslike efficiency in addressing a variety of problems that beset the working poor, her ability to gather about her the aristocratic, the powerful, and the wealthy and raise funds for well-budgeted projects, all these qualities and abilities, combined in a woman who gave the impression of an almost clerical selflessness, created a reputation around Emma Cons of expertise made effective.

Emma Cons took her politics seriously and thought the Liberal Party the most likely one to bring in the cause that was dear to her heart: votes for women. She was a most active Liberal. She was president of her local Lambeth women's Liberal club. She served on the executive of the Women's Liberal Federation, which had been established in 1886 partly as a result of the passage of the Corrupt Practices Act of 1883 (which made paid political canvassers illegal and thereby women political workers invaluable) and partly as a response to the Conservative Party's Primrose League. Cons was active in local politics and, as has been said, became the first woman alderman to sit on London's first County Council. She served with two other women: Jane Cobden (daughter of the Corn Law repealer) and Margaret, Lady Sandhurst, who had both been elected as county councillors in the same inaugural election. Emma Cons had, by this stage of her career, gained a certain standing. Her work on the London County Council only enhanced her reputation as an expert in worker housing, if only because she was able to explain to her colleagues, bluntly and specifically, exactly the difficulties entailed in housing the poor. Again, Cons was able to use her class as a distinct element of her knowledge. But at the same time, she was clearly on the side of impressing her tenants with the importance of middle-class values such as hygiene and budgeting. As she wrote in an article for *County Council Magazine*, continual neglect and overcrowding, alcohol abuse, a lack of education, and familiarity only with degraded slum tenements produced tenants who would throw rubbish out the window or down any readily available hole. "I have sometimes been gravely told by a tenant that 'they are sure the drains must be very wrong as their WC is stopped up again' and on examination it has been found that the obstruction was the customary milk or preserved-meat tin, scrubbing brush, potato parings, cinders, mussel shells or, as in one case a large piece of carpet!"[106] She was at pains to make sure her colleagues became educated about the difficulties involved in managing dwellings for the working poor. Stair rails, cistern and dust-hole lids, even occasionally the stairs themselves, she wrote, were often stolen to be used as fuel, "to say nothing of the taps and lead guttering stolen and sold as soon as they are put up."[107] It is not surprising that her colleagues on the council were quick to observe her expertise.

> She knew more about the housing of the poor than any other member of the Housing Committee; she was needed for the industrial School and Lunatic Asylums; it was she who had prepared the draft scheme for the inspection of Baby Farms throughout the county. She had the work in hand and hitherto had furnished the chairman of the Sanitary Committee with a monthly report on the Baby Farms under the Council.[108]

As Jane Cobden pointed out, "it proved to be a great asset to the cause (of women in local government) that the first woman alderman on the London County Council was Emma Cons."[109]

Emma Cons emphasized her familiarity with her tenants. "Coming thus into every-day contact with the tenants, who know that at any hour of the day or night they can come to me if in trouble, and living in a cottage no better than their own, there is formed a bond of sympathy which helps us better understand their difficulties." At the same time, she also punctured any illusions her fellow councillors might have. "For those who like to picture themselves as surrounded by a grateful and admiring tenantry there will be nothing but disappointment in store."[110] Thus, when in 1895 Herbert Asquith, then home secretary, convened the Lushington committee to inquire into reformatories and industrial schools, it was quite reasonable that Emma Cons would be appointed. Asquith may have received more than he bargained for; certainly the chairman may not have expected that, over the course of fifty-three days of testimony, Emma Cons would grill the committee's witnesses quite as directly as she did.[111]

On 9 May 1912, Emma Cons stood on stage with the Bishop of Southwark and presented a bouquet of flowers to Princess Helena, who had come to attend a performance of *Tannhäuser* and to receive donations to the Royal Victoria Hall's annual fund. Twelve weeks later, Lambeth buried one of its most illustrious citizens. As befitted a well-respected member of the community (and a solid Anglican), whose reputation for public spirit was known well beyond the Borough of Lambeth, the funeral was presided over by the Bishop of Southwark. The family received hundreds of letters of condolence, many from men who had also served on the County Council, many from those who had been colleagues in helping to raise funds for various good causes. Sorrow at the loss of such an altruistic person transcended class. Lilian Baylis remembered distinctly that, as she took in Lord Stamfordham's telegram from the King and Queen, expressing their "high regard" for such a "self-sacrificing life," she received at the same time a message from a local Lambeth scavenger, saddened by the passing of such a good and selfless soul.[112] It was announced, after Emma Cons's death, that "no more appropriate means of perpetuating her memory, or one more in accordance with her wishes, could be found than by raising a fund to assist the Victoria Hall."[113] Colleagues from her time on the London County Council, Sir Richard Mevill Beechcroft and Frank Briant, Lady Frederick Cavendish, Lady Morrish and Jane Cobden, organized the fundraising; subscribers included members of the royal family, the Duke and Duchess of Devonshire, the Archbishop of Canterbury, the Duke of Westminster, numerous other peers, temporal and spiritual, students of Morley College, and residents of Southwark and Lambeth. Clearly this was a person of significance, who had accomplished much good.

Emma Cons had been able to construct a position of authority by using her knowledge and expertise as elements of power. She had done this in two ways: first, she had acquired a unique corpus of understanding of her subject because she lived among her tenants. Not even Octavia Hill, her original employer, could speak with such authority about tenement life in the hours after the pubs closed. Second, she used her background as a positive asset, attacking problems with an aggression and a practicality that seemed to point to greater familiarity with working-class life. Moreover, her disinclination to adopt the mores of middle-class femininity excused her from acquiescing in male precedence or priority. Emma Cons had a very good sense of the value of her expertise and brusquely dismissed any suggestion that a man might know better. Indeed, in the world she constructed in Lambeth, at the Surrey Buildings, the Old Vic, and Morley College, men were simply not present. Men such as the Duke of Westminster, Lord Mount-Temple, and Samuel Morley were appreciative and willing to write cheques, come to fund-raising events, allow their names to be used on letterheads, and attend the occasional performance. But the Royal Victoria Hall was actually run by Emma Cons, Caroline Martineau, and Lucy Cavendish.

Finally, in constructing such successful social enterprises, Emma Cons was not only able to galvanize local Lambeth supporters but also to enlist supporters and friends from other campaigns against squalor, despair, and drink, establishing, from the interlinked web of philanthropic sustainers, her own cabinet of ministers. Here again we see the effectiveness of the overlapping circles of philanthropic men and women, where the same names reappear under different banners. Lord Frederick Cavendish was drawn in as a shareholder of the Coffee Music-Halls Company, bringing along his wife, Lucy Cavendish, hitherto involved in the work of the Parochial Mission Women and the workhouse visiting of the Ladies Diocesan Association. Godfrey Lushington not only was the chair of the committee to inquire into reformatories and industrial schools on which Emma Cons served but had also been instrumental in helping the Christian Socialists Ludlow, Maurice, and Hughes draft their minority report of the Committee on Trade Societies and Strikes (1859) recommending compulsory arbitration in labour disputes and, even more important, that trade unions be given the legal protection of being encompassed within the Friendly Societies Act.[114] The Duke of Westminster and the Earl of Shaftestbury, both on the council of the CETS, were known to Lucy Cavendish and Emma Cons as supporters of temperance. Ruskin, Octavia Hill, Lord Mount-Temple, Lucy Cavendish, the Marchioness of Lothian, the Earl and Countess of Meath, the Countess of Ducie, the Duchess of Richmond, Mrs

Gladstone, and various Martineaus were practised in other branches of philanthropy. From their different committees and campaigns, these men and women were all enlisted by Emma Cons to support the Royal Victoria Coffee Musical Hall, the Surrey Buildings, and Morley College for Working Men and Women. Her cause was important and attracted support, but it was her competence that both retained her supporters and sustained her effectiveness.

4 Opera for Lambeth

For many late Victorian philanthropists, Congreve's notion of music possessing charms to soothe a savage breast was not simply poetry, but a practical idea whose time had come. The Rev. Henry Haweis, in 1871, wrote a slim volume of ethical musings, *Music and Morals,* articulating a philosophy wherein music itself possessed a "high mission" with the capabilities to "soothe, relieve, recreate and elevate" the people.[1] "There are great operas," Haweis wrote, "which are calculated to ennoble whilst they delight; there are songs which stir within us the finest impulses."[2] *Music and Morals* struck a chord with the reading public and the book went into multiple editions. Music was soon seen as having "humanizing" powers, as a beneficent influence on the mass of poor labourers who had not much been exposed to high culture, as being capable of bringing even the "residuum" within the embrace of civilization. Uplifting entertainment was also seen as an influence that could not only ennoble but also inculcate the respectable bourgeois values of thrift and self-help in the working poor. Canon Samuel Barnett was inspired, with his wife, Henrietta, to instil by means of music a love of beauty within the congregation of their Whitechapel church of St Jude's. They enlisted Clement Templeton, the director of the Harrow Music School, to arrange periodic concerts for their parishioners in the adjacent school room. Barnett was convinced that music had the power to develop, as he put it, "the high in the low."[3]

The Barnetts were not alone. The idea of music was deployed by a number of well-intentioned Victorians who ventured into the East End not only to "improve" the working classes but also to distract them from dangerous radical political activity.[4] Such "missionary aestheticism" led Octavia Hill's sister Miranda, among others, to found the Kyrle Society and its choir with the object of "bringing beauty home to the people."[5] Some societies presented concerts of classical music performed by often talented amateur ladies, others used professional musicians who donated their services.[6] These well-born, well-intentioned aesthetic missionaries often had conflicting motivations: part Christian spirituality, part neo-Franciscan socialism, part self-conscious benevolence, arguably part prurience. Seth Koven, in *Slumming: Sexual and Social Politics in Victorian London* (2004), has perceptively looked at waves of visitors to the East End, some to observe, some to bring help or beauty, some impelled by psychosexual motivations they often neither fully acknowledged nor entirely comprehended themselves.[7] These efforts, though always well meaning, were not always well appreciated and were frequently rebuffed and occasionally reviled. Mocking, throwing mud, trampling newly planted "beautifying" flower beds, working-class Londoners evidently rejected attempts by middle-class reformers to "improve" or "uplift" them. Henrietta Barnett recalled having dirt and stones thrown at her and her husband, the saintly Canon Barnett, following one of their Limehouse concerts.[8] Indeed, Emma Cons herself had encountered much the same reaction when establishing a club for working girls in Drury Lane in the late 1850s; the girls "marked their appreciation of the efforts made by smashing the lights, breaking the windows and tearing the inside out of the piano."[9] But when Emma Cons and the shareholders of the newly renovated and reformed Royal Victoria Coffee Hall decided to leaven the variety bill with scenes from operas and ballads performed by first-class opera singers, they soon found them to be the most popular attraction; opera consistently sold out.

What could account for this divergence? Certainly both Emma Cons and her shareholders at the Royal Victoria Hall and the Barnetts in Whitechapel were attempting to bring beauty to those who had little access to it. Put another way, programming opera at the Old Vic could be read as just as much an effort to impose elite culture and compel an internalization of the tastes of the dominant class on the working poor of Lambeth and Southwark as were the good works of Miranda Hill or the Barnetts. A number of possibilities present themselves to explain the differing audience reactions. Offering opera to working-class audiences at the Old Vic might have been seen – either by Emma Cons and her board or by their audiences – as a form of attempted *embourgeoisement*. Alternatively, Emma Cons and Lucy Cavendish might well have seen opera as a form of cultural capital, useful as a ladder providing entrée for the working class to upward mobility via the kinship of shared artistic taste, and – almost subversively – as a means of empowering their audiences. This chapter, however, will argue that quite different elements were responsible for the runaway success of opera at the Old Vic. Opera at the Old Vic, unlike the Barnetts' Whitechapel concerts, was not intended to "civilize" its audience; it did not carry a patronizing taint. Most important, however, and as is clear from the ticket sales, letters from audience members, and newspapers reports, the patrons of the Old Vic simply loved opera at the Old Vic on its own terms. They bought out the Hall opera-night after opera-night because they wanted to hear more opera, plain and simple.

The Mission of the Coffee Music-Halls Company

When, in 1880, Emma Cons and the shareholders of the just-established Coffee Music-Halls Company sat down to plan what they would put on the stage of their first venture, the raffish Lambeth theatre they had just leased, there were many among the company's shareholders who saw an opportunity for more than simply offering a lure away from the drink. They also saw possibilities for generally improving the lives of the working poor of Lambeth and Southwark.[10] This was not a new idea. Schemes to introduce what was known as "rational recreation" to the masses had been in play since at least the 1830s. But thoughts about how to elevate the working poor had encountered the emergence, in the middle of the century, of larger-scale commercial recreation and mass entertainment. These attractions often ran at cross-purposes to middle-class, philanthropic, uplifting intentions. The working classes, moreover, had a tendency to vote with their feet away from "improving" recreation and towards the pub, the penny-gaffs, and the cheaper music halls. So when the Coffee Music-Halls Company assembled to debate the most effective entertainments to put on stage at the Royal Victoria Coffee Hall in order to entice the working families of Lambeth and distract them away from the pub, their discussions took place within the general context of the challenges of rational recreation and improvement.

The Coffee Music-Halls Company's deliberations about how to program the playbill for the theatre also took place within the relatively recent proliferation of musical groups dedicated to reclaiming the poor. The musician and composer Florence Marshall, writing in *The Nineteenth Century* in February of 1881, observed the recent efflorescence of groups dedicated to bringing the civilizing influence of music to the people. "The last few years have witnessed the rapid rise and spread of people's concerts series which have been started in London and some of the chief provincial towns by a sort of simultaneous impulse and which tried at first as experiments have already in many cases developed into what seem likely to be permanent institutions."[11] Many of the Coffee Music-Halls Company's shareholders concurred and saw themselves as part of this trend. Emma Cons's colleague William Cowper-Temple, a shareholder in both the Coffee Taverns and Coffee Music-Halls Companies, observed that "people who cannot read and have a narrow conception of things about them are more open to the influence of music than to anything else."[12] Cowper-Temple was firmly convinced of the efficacy of music in rehabilitating the "residuum." Shortly after the Royal Victoria Hall opened, he assisted the Earl and Countess of Meath in forming a small committee to bring concerts to workhouses; not professionals but ladies performing a few solos and well-known hymns, "in both of which latter the audience heartily join in."[13] Commenting on the effects of music, he observed that "music had a great effect on the masses, and among the lower orders … the more violent, energetic and impulsive, the music was appreciated."[14] But if civilizing the masses and turning them towards higher things was a goal for some, all agreed that the main purpose of reincarnating the Royal Victoria Palace Theatre as the Royal Victoria Coffee Hall was to lure the working poor away from drink by providing "wholesome entertainment" that would "amuse without degrading."[15]

In 1879 the music halls and theatres of Lambeth did not provide edifying fare. In the words of the *Birmingham Daily Post*'s reporter, they presented "the lowest and most degrading representations."[16] The old Victoria Theatre's stock presentations were lurid: *Mary White, or the Murder at the Old Tabard, Jane Paul or the Victim of Unmerited Persecution,* and *The Rover's Bride or the Murder at the Bittern's Swamp* are telling titles.[17] *Dick Turpin* was a particularly big draw, since the scene where Turpin cut his horse's throat was made especially gory by the spraying of "a quantity of red ochre."[18] It had not always been so; since its opening in 1816, the Royal Cobourg Theatre, as it was originally known, had featured Kean and Junius Brutus Booth in its productions of Shakespeare; Paganini had played there. It was a well-respected, if minor, theatre. It was still eminently respectable when it was sold and renamed in 1833 in honour of the new heir, becoming the Royal Victoria Palace Theatre. But in the early 1840s with the cutting of the railway through Lambeth, the neighbourhood began a decline. The *Theatrical*

Times, a respected and well-run periodical of the acting profession, remarked in the late 1840s on "the vulgar and the ignorant such as those who throng to the Victoria to witness atrocious melodramas fit only for an audience of felons."[19] Moreover, the bar of the Royal Victoria now functioned as a second neighbourhood pub, attracting a nightly procession of prostitutes. Charles Knight, writing in his *Penny Magazine*, also in the late 1840s, observed the house with distaste. "At the *Coburg*, now called the *Victoria*, may be seen such an appalling amount of loathsome vice and depravity."[20] Over the course of the next thirty years the situation degenerated even further. On the eve of Emma Cons assuming the lease, an observer recollected that "a few nights before the old 'Vic' closed, I saw a wretched drunken woman dividing a glass of gin at the gallery bar between herself, a little boy of seven years old and a baby at her breast."[21] These were exactly the sort of persons who inspired Emma Cons and her colleagues in the Coffee Music-Halls Company.

Having started by establishing coffee public-houses, Emma Cons and her supporters in the new company focused strictly on temperance. They did not concern themselves overmuch with what was to be put on stage as long as it drew people away from the pub. At one of the earliest meetings of the Coffee Music-Halls Company, a "drawing-room" meeting held on 13 March 1880 at the home of Rosamund Davenport Hill (a noted reformer and colleague of Barbara Bodichon in the battles for women's suffrage and the Married Women's Property Act) and presided over by William Cowper-Temple, the question of how best to attract people away from the pub was debated. Most were of the opinion that the company should "simply ascertain the kind of entertainment acceptable to the masses of the people, and then, within certain limits, to give it them." All agreed that they were "not a musical elevation society. There was no use in performing music over the heads of the people."[22]

They also all agreed that the bill at the new Royal Victoria Coffee Music-Hall would be designed for the whole family. Emma Cons had found, through living in the courts with her tenants, that there were few amusements in which all members of the family could take part. As Emma Cons's niece, Lilian Baylis, put it, "Fathers sometimes went to the country for their bean-feasts in the company of other fathers; mothers went for jaunts in batches and children had school-treats of their own; but it was only with Emmie that the families made holiday together."[23] Her excursions to the country with her tenants had been established exactly as family outings. The idea was that the coffee music hall would be a similar urban entertainment. Thus the preliminary circular of the Royal Victoria Coffee Music Hall declared that it would be a place where "men may take their wives and children without shaming or harming them."[24] It was also hoped that the presence of the family would reinforce the reasons for temperance.

There was one other criterion: the programs had to at least break even, and music was almost stumbled on as an attraction for its economical aspect. As the *Musical Times* observed with amusement: "On casting about for an additional attraction, music was naturally fixed upon as at once the most seductive, the most innocent, and perhaps all things considered, the cheapest. The cheapness is evidently a point, for the different speakers at the meeting whilst enlarging on the moral benefits to their fellow men, which the promoters of the company had most at heart, were never weary of repeating that it, above all things, intended to be a commercial success."[25] In the beginning, Emma Cons and her company sought to replicate the sorts of entertainments that were usually found in ordinary music halls, weeding out those with any bawdy element. "The amusements," they declared, "would be of the lightest and most elementary nature."[26] When the coffee music hall opened on Boxing Day, 1880, it was announced that the Royal Victoria Coffee and Music Hall would present the broadest (and likely the most profitable) possible variety: "Dusoni's Troupe of Performing Dogs, Monkeys and Goats," historical *tableaux vivants*, magicians, acrobats, and minstrel shows.[27]

"The Better the Music, the More It Is Appreciated"

At the same time the Coffee Music-Halls Company was, almost otiosely, averring that it was "not a musical elevation society," there were shareholders and supporters who saw a more promising opportunity. If, while entertaining the people of Lambeth and diverting them from the public house, the company could simultaneously elevate them, it would be all to the good. As the Coffee Music-Halls Company shareholders made clear at their inaugural April 1880 meeting, "if music of a high class was found to be appreciated it might be gradually introduced."[28] The *Musical Times* noted somewhat wryly that it was clear that the company "has seized upon music as a moral agent, direct or indirect."[29] But improving people's morals by diverting them from the drink was the primary goal; inculcating a taste for elite music only secondary.

Emma Cons had good experience with the utility of the performing arts in slums. When first established as the manager of Barrett's Court in the 1860s, she had, in addition to her sister's operatic recitals and the dramatic group organized by the writer George MacDonald, also enlisted the first-rate American contralto Antoinette Sterling, whom she knew as a temperance advocate.[30] Octavia Hill, perhaps inspired by these activities, had also, from time to time, put on concerts for her tenants. On one notable occasion, in 1874, she hosted three hundred costermongers from Drury Lane for a concert of opera. It was evidently a "grand success," as Hill's mother, Caroline, wrote the next morning to a friend. "The people thoroughly enjoyed themselves. Of course they did ample justice to the tea and liked the music so much – poor people. Miss Antoinette Sterling sang beautiful, rather solemn music in her rich alto voice. When she and her friend came in opera cloaks, the people cheered; 'it was all the opera cloaks,' she said to Octa."[31] For Emma Cons, who had grown up in a musical household, the beneficial powers of the performing arts were obvious.

Emma Cons was therefore quite receptive when one of her shareholders, Alice Hart, volunteered to organize a concert of classical music featuring sung ballads for the first Thursday night of the new Royal Victoria Coffee Hall. Having heard her sister, Henrietta Barnett, waxing rhapsodical about the elevating effects of her and her husband Samuel's concerts at St Jude's, Whitechapel, Alice Hart had become converted to the idea of the missionary properties of music and the redemptive power of beauty.[32] The concert she organized for the Royal Victoria's first Thursday night drew an enthusiastic response from the audience. The following morning, Emma Cons called on two acquaintances: Sir Julius Benedict and Madame Charlotte Sainton-Dolby, two persons who would have been able to summon good musical talent. Benedict was a composer of note (*The Lily of Killarney*) but also conducted seasons of opera at Drury Lane and the Lyceum. Charlotte Sainton-Dolby was acknowledged to be "the greatest contralto of her day." Mendelssohn had composed the contralto arias in *Elijah* for her; she was "unrivalled as an interpreter of English ballads and oratorio."[33] Between the two of them, they arranged for a number of well-known vocal artists to donate a performance for a series of Thursday evening ballad concerts.

The ballad concerts were consistently respectfully and enthusiastically received. A stagehand from that first season recalled the sincere and intense response of the gallery to the singers. "On one occasion, during a ballad sung by Sims Reeves, 'no smoking' was requested.

A young fop in the gallery, ignoring the order, calmly went on with his pipe. Thereupon two typical costermongers, regular gallery patrons, took the matter up. Once more the fop was asked quietly but firmly to chuck it. When again he refused one seized him by the shoulder, another by the legs and without more ado they chucked him down the gallery staircase."[34] On another occasion in the same season, the manager of the evening was too apprehensive of what the crowd's reaction might be to ask them to stop smoking; that evening's performer, the contralto Antoinette Sterling, took charge herself and walked onto the stage, smiled sweetly at the audience, and said: "'I want to sing to you, but if I do, all this smoke will hurt my voice. Now if you like your pipes better than my singing, why, you go on smoking.' And every pipe was knocked out."[35]

Notwithstanding the success of the ballad concerts, the first season, as a whole, was a financial disaster. The income from the bar of the reformed Royal Victoria Coffee Hall, which now, instead of beer, wine, and spirits, sold coffee, "sparkling rubine, gingerette, raspberry and peppermint, tobacco, cigars, sausages, seed and currant and fancy cakes and Bath and plain buns," was significantly less than it had been in its alcoholic days.[36] But a fall-off in overall attendance was also responsible for the new Hall's financial difficulties. Following the resignation of her manager, William Poel, who felt that Emma Cons was "aiming too high," Cons enlisted her cabinet of supporters (Samuel Morley, the Duke of Westminster, William Cowper-Temple, and Lord Shaftesbury) and, commandeering both the administration and programming from her committee, reconstituted the Hall's governance and organized the purchase of its lease.[37]

Now in control and with greater financial breathing room, Emma Cons reviewed her attendance and decided she would entirely take charge of the programming herself. She found that the Thursday night ballad concerts were consistently better attended than the magicians, dog shows, minstrels, and acrobats. The correspondent for the *Illustrated London News* had observed the same phenomenon. "The hard-working enthusiastic dwellers in the New Cut crowd the place to suffocation to hear Sir Julius Benedict play and Miss de Fonblanque sing. The better the music, the more it is appreciated; and the rough working men are as courteous and enthusiastic as the fashionable folk in St. James' Hall."[38] Emma Cons also observed that the audience tended to be more interested in operatic arias than in drawing-room ballads. She began programming, on alternate Thursdays, bills wholly devoted to excerpts from operas, sung in English.

Presenting opera at the Hall (in particular, opera sung in English) was heartily encouraged by three men who had recently come to sit on the committee of the Coffee Music-Halls Company: Sir Julius Benedict, the opera company director Carl Rosa, and the composer Sir Arthur Sullivan.[39] Opera, either composed in English or sung in translation, was experiencing a surge in popularity at this time, and each of these men was significantly responsible, in his own way, for this growing taste among the opera-going British public.[40] These three men hoped that presenting English opera at the Old Vic would involve the Victoria Hall's audience more than opera sung in Italian or German. They also hoped that opera sung in English would further include the working poor of Lambeth in what they saw as a growing, national art form.

The operas performed at the Hall were not full-length. That would have contravened the Hall's licence, which was for a music hall, exclusively. A theatrical licence, which would have permitted both full-length plays and operas, would have necessitated a number of expensive structural repairs and would have prohibited smoking, something to which the Hall's audiences were deeply attached. Thus scenes from the most popular operas were strung together, featuring favourite arias. Moreover, in order not to contravene the music hall licence, these scenes would have to be presented as tableaux, with the curtain rung down between them. Lilian Baylis gave an example from *Faust*: "a soprano would sing the 'Jewel Song', leave the stage and would next be seen sitting at the spinning-wheel."[41] The audience's program would give synopses of each scene. Thus in the first two seasons, for example, the Hall offered "Selections in costume from Beethoven's *Fidelio*" and "Scenes from the Italian opera, sung in English under the direction of Signor Garcia." Verdi was favoured, as were Mozart and Balfe, largely because they were in the public domain.[42] Amateur musicians, often of wildly varying quality, were enlisted as the orchestra. George Bernard Shaw leaves an account of his time, initially as pianist, then as bell-ringer in *Il Trovatore*, where he was instructed to do what he could with "a length of gaspipe on a string and an old poker to hit it with."[43] Thursday nights also featured amateur choirs, enlisted as the chorus for the operas.[44] In spite of, or because of, the "greatest hits" aspect of presentation, opera at the Hall quickly became the most popular item on the bill.

Some were not impressed. Beatrice Webb wrote in her diary early in November of 1885: "Went with two fellow-workers to the Vic; managed by that grand woman, Miss Cons. To me a dreary performance, sinking to the level of the audience, while omitting the dash of coarseness, irreverence and low humour which give the spice and the reality to such entertainments. To my mind the devil is preferable, and in every way more wholesome, than a shapeless mediocrity."[45] Not all would have agreed. Charles Kingsley had made clear, in his Chartist novel *Alton Locke* (1850), his sense of the direct connection between the quality of what was put on stage and the moral growth of the audience.[46] The hero of the novel and his companion observe one night, as they are passing by the previous incarnation of the Old Vic, the audience flowing in "to their low amusement from the neighbouring gin-palaces and thieves' cellars," and point out the demoralizing effect of such a place on the "herd of ragged boys, vomiting forth slang, filth and blasphemy" who "pushed past us, compelling us to take care of our pockets."

> Look there! Look at the amusement, the training, the civilization which the Government permits to the children of the people! These licensed pits of darkness, traps of temptation, profligacy and ruin, triumphantly yawning night after night! And then tell me that the people who see their children kidnapped into Hell are represented by a government which licenses such things! Give us the Charter and we'll send workmen into Parliament that shall find out whether something better can't be put in the way of the ten thousand boys and girls in London who live by theft and prostitution than the tender mercies of the Victoria – a pretty name! They say the Queen's a good woman, and I don't doubt it! I often wonder if she knows what her precious namesake here is like.[47]

George Bernard Shaw evidently agreed with the idea of aiming high, notwithstanding his experience as bell-ringer for *Il Trovatore*. After two or three more visits to the Hall in 1883, he suggested that "the management underestimates, rather than overestimates, the critical capacity of its audiences." One concert had been attended by about 1,500 people, and Shaw pointed out, "if the whole of them had been skilled musicians, the verdict on each item could not have been more discriminating. The demeanour of all present was equally remarkable, perfect silence being preserved while the music was being performed."[48] Independent observers tended to agree with Shaw and, by extension, with Emma Cons's choices in programming. Certainly audiences for the Hall's opera nights grew steadily. One reporter in 1888 wrote, "Last night there must have been 2,000 people in the pit, boxes, galleries and stalls. A wonderful sight it was ... Mademoiselle Lang with her violin and *Nocturne* of Chopin. Dead stillness, of course, while the skilful performance lasts, followed by a roar of applause that comes swelling up to us from the depths."[49] For that reporter, "the depths" would certainly have been metaphoric as well as literal.

The "People's Opera House"

By the end of the 1880s, opera, presented in selected scenes, was the most consistently popular feature on the bill. As time went on and as the Hall became better known for its operas, "it was nothing for an audience of two thousand to crowd into the Vic for an opera."[50] This likely had a good deal to do with the quality of the singers (who were persuaded to either donate their services or perform for a significantly reduced fee). Opera drew the most consistent, and the most appreciative, crowds. One reporter who visited the Hall in November of 1889 reported that the working men and women who came to the Hall were eager. "The long-abused, despised, condemned lower class of London who fill the theatre every night, listen with delight to music of the best masters and to lectures upon art by the best orators. Mothers with their children are there, boys and girls at the 'dangerous ages,' working men and slaving women and over all hangs an atmosphere of purity and truth which must cause rejoicing in heaven, for Emma Cons has found the way to console and pacify the troubled soul."[51] Faced with a growing audience, Cons presented opera increasingly more frequently. In the 1891–2 season, for example, she presented scenes from *Mignon*, *Cavalleria Rusticana*, *I Pagliacci*, *Il Trovatore*, Gounod's *Faust*, *La Sonnambula*, *The Daughter of the Regiment*, *The Bohemian Girl*, *Maritana*, *The Lily of Killarney* (part of the "English Ring Cycle"), *Fra Diavolo*, and *Nydia*, by George Fox, based on the popular novel *The Last Days of Pompeii*. The public voiced its approval robustly. An observer writing to the *Musical Times* in 1894 noted the "enthusiastic audience, chiefly of the lower middle and lower classes," which "amid an atmosphere of decency and domesticity gave ear to good music."[52] The reputation of the Hall for good productions of opera, enthusiastically received, grew.

Another reporter, visiting in 1909, described the audience's reaction to Verdi: "The gallery was packed from end to end with men, one could hardly have placed a pin between them."[53] The working poor of Lambeth embraced this ostensibly elite art form as their own. The Hall became known as the "People's Opera House," and it was a title the management revelled in.[54] The noted Shakespearean actor Harcourt Williams recalled, in his history of the Old Vic, how he was "once introduced to a family in Camberwell. The father, who was a clockmaker, invited me to have a cup of tea with them at the evening meal. When the friend who had brought me there told them that I was married to the daughter of Antoinette Sterling, they all rose from their seats. 'We always stand when that name is mentioned,' explained the old man."[55] Emma Cons proudly included in the Hall's annual report for 1890–1 a letter written to Madame Nordica following a Thursday operatic recital:

> Madam – I feel I must write and thank you for your singing last night, it was more than kind of you to sing so many songs and it has done me such a lot of good, as my life for the last three years has been a very hard struggle, but after last night I shall never seem weary again of struggling. Pray don't think me a sentimental girl, as I am a hard-working woman with four children and my only regret is that my husband was not there, and again, most humbly thanking you,
>
> I remain,
>
> A Woman of the People[56]

In 1886, the charity commissioners were deliberating how much of the consolidated funds of the City of London Parochial Charities to allocate to the Old Vic. They were most impressed not by the presentation made by Lord Mount-Temple and the members of the committee but by a petition, organized by thirteen residents of Lambeth who took time off work to gather over two thousand signatures, which they laid before the commissioners. As was reported in the *Daily News*, "the Commissioners have spoken since of the impression which the intelligence and earnestness of these working men deputies left upon their minds. All that ought to be known. It speaks volumes. 'We have a love for the old "Vic"' say these men; 'it is a favourite institution of the neighbourhood'."[57] The charity commissioners were inspired to give the Hall an annual grant of £1,000.

The allegiance to the Hall did not fade. An article in *Musical Opinion*, "Apollo in the New Cut," featured a profile of an audience member:

> Here is a burly patron: if appearances count for ought, might be a burglar off duty. From time to time he gives in a hoarse whisper explanatory

> comments on the Opera to a youthful companion … A hard-bitten veteran, stretching himself at the interval, he tells me he has been a regular attendant at the "Vic" on Thursdays for several years, formerly he lived in the neighbourhood. He has moved since to north-east London but still comes over every week, *walking one way!*[58]

The report for 1911–12 was now entitled "The Royal Victoria Hall (People's Palace for South London) Formerly the Royal Victoria Theatre and generally known as the 'Old Vic'." The annual report featured a portrait of another patron who frequented the upper galleries. "Ask him what he has seen and heard since that great night when his friend Joe Smith introduced him to the now familiar gallery railing, and don't be astonished if he talks to you about Wagner, Gounod and Grand Opera generally. He knows 'Maritana' and 'Rigoletto' by heart and whistles the song of the Toreador about his work. Ask him where he lives and you will be surprised to hear that his enthusiasm necessitates his tramping it from Haggerston; his boots are not over sound, but he has a soul and he's 'orf to the opera.'"[59]

It was not simply the more melodic Italian operas which were popular. The Hall presented *Tannhäuser* as soon as it came into the public domain in 1904 and the audiences lined up around the block; ten years later it was just as popular, as can be seen from the cartoon in the *Daily Graphic* (see cover image). That working men and women enjoyed opera should not have come as the surprise it evidently did. One of the most telling and illustrative examples Jonathan Rose brings to his discussion of working-class intellectual life is the intensely blissful intellectual communion of the young, self-taught Mancunian clerk Neville Cardus with his comrades in culture.

> We never went straight home after a new play by Shaw, after *Gerontius*, after the A flat symphony, after Kreisler had played the Elgar violin concerto for the first time, after *Tristan*, after Strauss' *Salome* with Aino Akté in it. We walked the city streets; we talked and talked … not to air our economic grievances, not to "spout" politics and discontent, but to relieve the ferment of our minds, or emotions after the impact of *Man and Superman*, *Elektra*, *Riders to the Sea*, *Pélleas and Mélisande*, *Scheherazade*, *Prince Igor*.[60]

Cardus's recollections of young working men's artistic tastes provide an even more instructive story when contrasted with those of Lucy Cavendish, who did not much partake of the culture that was, for her, within easy reach. She had never visited the British

Museum – and expressed astonishment that anyone would. Her favourite novelist was Charlotte Yonge and her favourite work was *Chaplet of Pearls*, Yonge's historical romance set at the time of the St Bartholemew's Day Massacre.[61]

Canon Barnett Tries to Bring Out the "Manlike Qualities in Those Who Live Like Animals"

In contrast, Henrietta and Samuel Barnett's cultural enlightenment work in the East End was neither accepted nor loved by the residents of Whitechapel in anything like the way the Old Vic was seen as simply part of the life of Lambeth and Southwark. The Barnetts had soon regularized Clement Templeton's occasional St Jude's concerts into the People's Concert Society, which presented a series of six concerts, inexpensive at the Chelsea workingmen's club and free at St Jude's.[62] The Barnetts went on, in 1884, to establish the university settlement house of Toynbee Hall, a few blocks away from St Jude's, where, as part of their efforts to lift up their East End neighbours, they offered weekly concerts, an annual art exhibition, and regular lectures by such speakers as Leslie Stephen (the editor of *Cornhill* magazine and editor of the DNB) and the noted jurist and historian Frederic Harrison. But their lack of success may have been the result of their often patronizing attitude towards their audiences.

George Lansbury, who had grown up in Whitechapel and who in the 1880s lived slightly further east, in Bow, loathed Toynbee Hall. He found the Barnetts' obviously sincere good intentions, concerts, lectures, and Oxbridge settlement workers tainted by their association with the Charity Organization Society, which had been welcomed to make its headquarters at Toynbee Hall. The policies of the COS were, for Lansbury, "malignant." He saw the Barnetts' efforts to "civilize" the poor of their parish as nigh unto contemptible and found their work both "heartless and brutal in its effect on the lives of the poor."[63] Toynbee Hall was entirely different from the Old Vic. Although both establishments had analogous objectives, the Barnetts approached their goals from a different angle than did Emma Cons. More important, each saw their clientele through different eyes. As Canon Barnett put it, his aim, in bringing music to Whitechapel, was to bring out the "manlike qualities in those who live like animals."[64] Emma Cons would never have described the tenants among whom she lived as animals. Even when frustrated beyond containment with her tenants, as, for example, when they blocked up the drains by using them to dispose of untenable objects (sardine tins, small bottles), she always saw and described her tenants as individuals.

But there was often a certain lack of comprehension among many of the middle and upper class about working-class culture. This was something that both the philanthropists who worked for the East End and those who supported the Royal Victoria Hall often held in common. At a meeting of supporters of the Royal Victoria Hall, held at the Duke of Westminster's house in June of 1884, Lord Mount-Temple attempted to help the assembled philanthropists understand just how barren the lives of Lambeth residents were, by announcing the shocking statistic that in the parish surrounding the Hall there were "9000 people not wealthy enough to keep a servant."[65] Although this was likely the closest Lord Mount-Temple could come to understanding the often desperate lives of the working poor, this was not the way Emma Cons, who had grown up among people who worked for a living, who had always had to support herself, whose father and grandfather had been artisans, and whose own family more often than not could not afford to keep a servant, would have thought of her audiences. Nor is it a view that Lucy Cavendish, with her work in the Whitechapel and Limehouse workhouses and with the reclaimed juvenile prostitutes in Kent, would have shared.

The Power of Opera

There are several reasons why opera was so wholeheartedly adopted by the Old Vic's Lambeth audiences. The theatre historian George Rowell speculates, in his history of the Old Vic, that opera might have become such an immediate favourite of Lambeth audiences because the colour and excitement of the plots reminded them of the "blood-and-thunder" melodramas of the Vic's earlier incarnation, particularly since many of the operas presented had originated as melodramas.[66] This is a reasonable supposition. But the popularity of opera at the Old Vic probably rests on more than familiar reminiscence of action, spectacle, or the sentimental. Part of the attraction of opera at the Vic would simply have been the high quality of the artists Emma Cons presented. They were not the second string. Sims Reeves, who sang at the Hall regularly, was Great Britain's foremost tenor from the 1850s through the early 1880s and did not retire from the concert stage until 1891.[67] Hermann Klein, the musician, noted critic, and prolific writer on the subject of musicians of the late nineteenth century, recalled that "to hear him, long after he had passed the age of seventy, sing 'Adelaide' or 'Deeper and Deeper Still' or 'The Message' was an exposition of breath control, of tone-colouring, of phrasing and expression, that may truly be described as unique."[68] "Fancy hearing Sims Reeves for threepence!" observed one contemporary journalist.[69] Charles Santley, who also sang at the Hall, is considered by opera scholar Julian Budden to have been "one of the most brilliant baritones of the second half of the nineteenth century and certainly one of the greatest English singers of all time"; the conductor Sir Eugene Goossens concurred, asserting that Charles Santley was "unquestionably the greatest English baritone of his day."[70] The Welsh tenor Ben Davies was equally well respected, and James Foli was thought of by the reviewer in the *Era* as "in many respects the finest basso of the day."[71] The women who sang at the Hall were no less eminent. Belle Cole, Ada Crossley, Lillian Nordica, and Antoinette Sterling were certainly in the first tier of singers in the 1880s when they sang at the Hall. Janet Monach Patey ("Madame Patey") succeeded Madame Sainton-Dolby as the leading contralto of her time, and both sang at the Royal Victoria Hall.[72] A reporter, observing the upper gallery at a performance of opera, noted the quality of the artists. "The most amazing production for the prices paid. Several of the singers were Covent Garden favourites of world-wide fame and the audience listened breathlessly. Here indeed was a sufficient denial to the theory that coarse and vulgar entertainments are demanded by the people, and that the manager who dared to give them anything else would be ruined."[73]

There are likely other reasons for the popularity of opera at the Old Vic. Chris Waters has argued, in *British Socialists and the Politics of Popular Culture* (1990), how early British socialists also saw music as a means of personal regeneration. Jonathan Rose, in *The Intellectual Life of the British Working Class*, has also made the case that, for many workers, the pursuit of elite culture was seen as a refutation of its being the exclusive property of the rich. Attending the touring orchestras of Hallé and Thomas Beecham and the touring opera companies of Moody-Manners and Carl Rosa, which performed their operas in English, was seen as an assertion of working-class identity. Rose points to sponsorship of arts organizations by working men's clubs; for example, the Glasgow Independent Labour Party organized a small orchestra to play classical interludes before its lectures, which included a talk by Charles Manners of the Moody-Manners Opera Company that attracted an overflow crowd of seven thousand.[74] Arguably, since both the Moody-Manners and Carl Rosa opera companies presented operas in English, allegiance could also be a statement of robust national pride contrasted to the foreign, the elite, and the effete. This all the more so since the opera patronized by the upper classes gave the impression of having been colonized by either the Italians (Covent Garden had been known since 1870 as the Italian Opera House) or the Germans. The Royal Victoria Hall's being known both for presenting English operas by English composers and for presenting much (although not all) of its foreign operas in English could have been interpreted as its being the true national opera house in addition to being "the People's Opera House." In short, working-class interest in high art may have been surprising to the philanthropic elite, but to the working poor themselves it was not.

Another equally important reason for the popularity of opera at the Old Vic likely lies in the secular sacrament of shared emotions. Whether the men and women who went to the Old Vic to hear the operas were conscious of it or not, one of the most compelling attractions was likely the power of the communal, collective catharsis offered by the performances. Communion among the audience, created by the vivid emotions conveyed by the human voice, would be a potent draw. This would not have been lost on Emma Cons. A woman of profound religious beliefs, she was also a woman who knew the power of art, visual and vocal. Just as she saw colour as a deliberate creation of God's, she saw the human voice in the same light. In the same way that Lucy Cavendish hesitated before attending Bach's *St. John Passion* during Lent because of the intensity of the joy she knew it would incite within her ("she knew she would enjoy it so much as almost to disqualify it as a Lenten occasion"), so Emma Cons, from her time in the Handel festival choir, would have seen opera at the Old Vic as something divine.[75] Not only was it God's way of diverting the men and women of Lambeth from drink, but opera, shared among the audience, was also a transcendent and euphoric experience. Both of these women knew the power of communion and understood instinctively the transformative capacity of art not only performed, but shared. At a time when music halls generally were becoming less rowdy and more respectable, with seating in rows replacing café tables, the audience at the Old Vic could still experience the thrill of consuming passion, but under the *imprimatur* of a temperance enterprise.[76]

Communion can also be a powerful way of transcending class barriers both in the sense that all classes take religious communion together and in the sense of communion as a response to art. And a sense of a growing division between the classes was a concern that preoccupied many in the latter half of the nineteenth century. Benjamin Disraeli's 1845 novel, *Sybil, or Two Nations,* had grappled with the growing chasm between those who could afford a reasonable life and those who found it increasingly unattainable. F.D. Maurice had been quite vocal on the subject in his sermons and writings in the mid-1850s. Bridging the "gulph," inculcating "fellowship" between men of different classes, was one of the main reasons why he and the other Christian Socialists had founded the Working Men's College in 1854.[77] He was not alone. In 1861, the Bishop of London, speaking in Stepney, declared that "if there was one evil that destroyed a nation more than another it was that there was a separation of classes."[78] An editorial in the *Daily News* in July of 1874 noted a similar caution, made by the Dean of Westminster, concerning the same perceived threat: "the separation of classes in England" "is a great misfortune to them all but there are gulfs that cannot be bridged over by philanthropical pontoons."[79] In his sermon "Phoebe, the Servant of the Church," given in 1873, Edward Benson White (not yet Archbishop of Canterbury, but honorary chaplain to the Queen) drew a direct and cautionary comparison between the present day and the "First Imperial Age of Rome" in the growing "separation of classes by pecuniary forces."[80] Similarly, the Bishop of Bedford in 1884 announced that "the great danger which threatens our modern life is the separation of classes."[81] This was not only a matter for the higher clergy; speaking to his colleagues at the Midland Farmers' Club in June of 1872, T.B. Wright of Birmingham spoke about his concern regarding "a strong feeling growing up – a feeling which would lead to a separation of classes which would lead to serious consequences."[82] Praising a prominent Darlington businessman for his efforts at industrial peacemaking, the *Newcastle Courant* wrote that Mr David Dale had done much to "bridge that horrible gulf between the classes which is one of the curses of society."[83] Some took a different view; in 1874, the paymaster-general, Stephen Cave (Conservative MP for New Shoreham), denounced the very idea as subversive. "I do not believe in the gulf between class deepening and widening. I believe there never was a time in which there was more sympathy between them; but no doubt clever and unscrupulous agitators by pandering to and tempting the half-educated do much to widen any such gulf."[84] And yet the idea of a dangerously widening separation of the country into two nations was one which became accepted as virtually self-evident. No less a person that the Prince of Wales himself, in a speech given on the occasion of the inauguration of the Royal College of Music on 7 May 1883, concurred with both the reality of class estrangement and its causes. "The time has come when class can no longer stand aloof from class, and that man does his duty best who works most earnestly in bridging over the gulf between different classes which it is the tendency of increased wealth and increased civilization to widen."[85]

No one would have been more attuned to the dangers of a increasing alienation between classes than Emma Cons. Writing in the Hall's annual report for 1884, she made clear her sense of the Hall as creating a fellowship that brought together persons from different classes. She appealed to her supporters for more than simply money. She wanted, she declared, to encourage their attending the Hall's performances with the working people of Lambeth. "The Hall might be made," Emma Cons wrote, "a valuable means of linking together classes whose wide separation all agree in considering a crying evil."[86]

But a growing division between the classes could mean different things to different people. The Rev. Benson had been specific in his cautionary sermon: bridging a rift between rich and poor was not merely a moral imperative; he was warning about class warfare. "It is a terrible problem in this England of ours, that awaits a solution somewhere in the future – the disunion of classes. And while many talk of the problem and judge that the collisions which have been are but the prelude to a real collision – nay, an engagement all along the line – between the everyday increasing masses who have nothing to lose and the lessening classes into whose very laps the tide of all wealth comes sweeping ..."[87] Benson was not alone. Samuel Taylor, writing in 1858 about "Literary and Musical Entertainments for the People" for the National Association for the Promotion of Social Science, wrote specifically about how the working classes needed to be distracted from drink not simply for their own intellectual uplift but for the benefit of property-holders.

> In a community like ours where the mass of the people pass the greater part of their lives in one ceaseless round of exhausting toil there must exist the desire for occasional relaxation and pleasurable excitement and it must, and will, be had of some kind somehow and somewhere. "All work and no play make Jack" not only a "dull" but in times of excitement a "dangerous fellow." He contrasts his own dreary existence with the ever varying pleasures enjoyed by his superiors and discusses with his fellows over his pipe and his beer the causes of such a widely different fate.

> Unable to solve the social problem, he regards the rich man's lot with envy and curses his own, temporarily, drowning too often, alas, the recollection of his supposed wrongs and subduing his rancour by drinking confusion to all his wealthier neighbours, the sad end being too frequently his own ruin and that of his innocent family.[88]

For many, speaking of "separation between the classes" was barely hidden code for fear of a disgruntled or militant working class. For Emma Cons it was a call to show the upper classes their commonality with the working poor of Lambeth. We can read this in her annual reports where she urges those who wished to support the Hall not simply to write cheques, but to come down for performances, as Lucy Cavendish did regularly. Both women were clear about how the Hall could become a beneficial and neutral territory:

> The mere fact of filling a box at a ballad concert or a lecture has its value in showing that there is some community of taste between those who have more education and means of recreation and those who have less, and the people think much more of a performance if "the gentry" are there and applaud. "It's all right – there's *our* Lady Cavendish again", said a bricklayer in the gallery who recognized the occupant of one of the boxes.[89]

The instrument Emma Cons used to inculcate fellowship was the shared emotions of the audience. Whether they were delighted or moved to tears by the performers on stage, all felt the communion of emotions, the shared catharsis. The Old Vic could emphasize social unity by creating emotional communion and thereby moderating class difference, but never in a way that attacked the established social order. From her box, the Hon. Lucy, Lady Frederick Cavendish could, together with the audience of the Old Vic, enjoy and feel Madame Antoinette Sterling's performance, both observed approvingly by the bricklayer in the pit.

The opera and classical music which Emma Cons programmed at the Old Vic differed in other important ways from the civilizing mission of Clement Templeton, the Barnetts, the various People's Concert Societies, and the Countess of Meath's ladies who sang in workhouses. The music at the Royal Victoria Hall was not charity; it was not benevolently offered for free; if you wanted to attend you had to pay at the door, just as under previous licensees of the Vic. This provided a respectful, level playing field to the Old Vic's audience. Emma Cons understood this. So did Samuel Morley: "People like to pay; they don't like these things done for nothing."[90] At the Hall, there was no condescension. In the same sense, a no less important aspect was very likely the audience's satisfaction in knowing that Emma Cons was providing for them exactly the same artists who regularly performed for the elite at Covent Garden and played before the Queen. Similarly, when Lucy Cavendish took a box and brought her friends to the Hall, it was to hear singers who were unquestionably first-rate and whom her guests would certainly enjoy.

Another aspect lies in the person of Emma Cons herself. Her accent declared her origins. Her father had worked with his hands and she had too. Unlike Octavia Hill, she lived with her tenants in their courts. As this background had given her a path of communicating with her tenants at Barrett's Court and later at Surrey Lodge, it also gave her greater entrée and ease with the patrons of the Old Vic. She was a strong temperance advocate, but again, temperance for Emma Cons was not a prescription given from a woman of the elite to the poor; temperance was a cause embraced by all classes. She was also very frank in her way of speaking. She was clearly seen to be on the side of her audience, but not in a condescending or patronizing way.

Another aspect that set the music at the Old Vic apart from the concerts offered at Toynbee Hall was that, aside from the professional musicians who played on stage, the Old Vic had its own orchestra largely peopled by local Lambeth residents. Emma Cons had pointed this out to Sir Julius Benedict in June of 1884. As was reported in the *Coffee Public-House News*, at the first meeting of shareholders following the assumption of the Royal Victoria Hall's lease, Benedict, planning for the Hall's future, observed that he "should like to see an orchestra of working men playing in the Victoria Hall." To which Emma Cons called out from the other side of the room, "There is one!"[91] Thus audiences at the Hall were able to enjoy a real degree of local ownership of the Old Vic while at the same time they could also enjoy and be complimented by the presence of top-tier talent on stage.

After Emma's death in 1912, Lilian Baylis was faced with having to navigate programming on her own. She knew her audiences still loved opera. This was something Lucy Cavendish, still on the Old Vic's Board of Governors, was also sensitive to. Writing to her sister in 1913, she noted that "It is maddening to think of £100,000 being paid into this silly Olympic games nonsense when £5,000 would provide poor South London with the good music which it so wants and loves."[92] Lilian Baylis took steps to obtain a theatrical licence from the Lord Chamberlain, enlisting the assistance of Lucy Cavendish. They were successful, and now the Hall could present full-length opera. In the spring of 1913, Lilian Baylis did away with the opera scene concerts altogether and replaced them with full-length operas every Thursday. The following year she featured operas on Saturday nights as well. She was somewhat apprehensive, but her concerns were quickly dispelled. "On the first Saturday night of the opera, we were crowded out and this has been the rule ever since."[93] The allegiance of the working men and women of Lambeth and Southwark to opera at the Old Vic did not lessen but continued under Lilian Baylis's direction in the 1920s and 1930s. The noted mezzo-soprano Edith Coates, who sang at the Old Vic in the 1920s, recalled three generations of Lambeth residents who regularly attended operas, plays, lectures, and classes at the Old Vic and at Morley College as well. Moreover, now that the Old Vic could present full-length operas and theatrical plays under its new licence, Lilian Baylis began to produce Shakespeare, which was well received from the start. The *Daily Telegraph*'s theatre critic during that period, W.A. Darlington, was of the opinion that the Old Vic's audiences were the only theatrically intelligent audience in London.[94] But when Lilian Baylis attempted to bump the operas in April of 1914 and present a series of Shakespeare's plays in their stead, the result was dismal. As she explained it, by that time the "Vic opera had a large and steady public which was loathe to dispense with its music."[95] Opera maintained its pride of place at the Old Vic until 1931, when Lilian Baylis secured Sadler's Wells theatre and made it the exclusive home for productions of Vic opera and ballet.

Emma Cons and the group of men and women of the Coffee Music-Halls Company whom she assembled around her established the Royal Victoria Coffee Music Hall as a means of luring the working men and women of Lambeth away from the pubs and the licensed music halls that pushed their customers to buy alcohol. They saw drink as the fount of virtually every social evil among the working poor; any means that might divert the residents of Lambeth from the drink was all to the good. When one of their number, Alice Hart, organized, in that first week, a concert of "good" music featuring sung ballads, the consensus among the shareholders was that anything that steered the audience away from drink should be identified and repeated. Even if Hart's agenda was closer to the "civilizing" mission of her sister Henrietta

Barnett, the rest of the shareholders were more single-minded about their purpose. Here again we can see the recurrent role of the connected circles of philanthropic men and women. In the case of the Old Vic, they not only established and funded and defined the Hall's mission, but also participated in programming what initially went on stage.

The Hall's mission, however, could be interpreted differently by those who came to see the performances. A reporter for the *Illustrated London News* saw the declared mission of the Hall in 1883 as part of classic, condescending philanthropy. It was "an acceptable institution for the purpose of culture in the present imperfect stage of development among the English working-class population; we must commend the wisdom, as we do the kindness of the promoters of this undertaking, themselves persons of high intellectual refinement, in so readily providing whatever materials of innocent mirth and unreflecting wonderment can give any pleasure to the simplest minds."[96] But Emma Cons had never seen the people of her courts as simple-minded, capable only of "innocent mirth and unreflecting wonderment." She saw a temperate life as the first step to improvement. As many did, she saw "great" music as a means by which the men and women she lured away from the pub could be diverted from lives centred on what she saw as the pursuit of destructive sensation. Like the Rev. Henry Haweis, Emma Cons saw great music and opera as a means by which "the inner life may be reached, awakened or created: the excitement of higher emotions – those touched by music, poetry and painting – is a legitimate means of stirring the sense within and arousing mankind to the necessity of an inner as well as an outer and merely mechanical life."[97] She had a vision of the men and women of her courts brought to lives filled with purpose, delayed gratification, thrift, and advancement, both spiritual and material. But hers was not simply a vision of *embourgeoisement*. In the operas she produced and presented at the Old Vic, Emma Cons saw a way of bringing her audience within the community of British civilization. She saw her audiences transcending class conflict, becoming citizens of a national culture through the communion and shared catharsis offered by great art.

But Lucy Cavendish and Emma Cons had another agenda at the Old Vic. It was not hidden; they were explicit about it. They wished to create a space where both the leisured and the working classes could encounter each other in neutral territory. Whereas Toynbee Hall explicitly attempted to "civilize" those of the darkest East End whom they could lure into their concert hall and tame with the Countess of Meath's ballad-singing ladies, Lucy Cavendish and Emma Cons sought to make "the gentry" understand that they were seated with fellow citizens. In the same way, by their giving the working poor of South London the elite knowledge and cultural capital of opera nights at the Old Vic, Emma Cons and Lucy Cavendish acted as agents of subversion. They created a space where the boundaries of class were deliberately blurred. But, in addition, they created an experimental zone, where the working poor of South London could test and try on the cultural garments of the elite. We can also see a space that enabled the Old Vic audience to explore new configurations of inclusion and participation. Thus the Old Vic can be interpreted not only as a literal space, deliberately made inclusive for the working poor of South London, but also as a metaphoric space where still-excluded identities of citizenship could be put on, even if only for the evening.

5 The Citizens of Morley College

In October 1885, four young men presented themselves at the side door of the Royal Victoria Hall. They were enrolled in the first regular scientific classes which were being attempted as an experiment, growing out of the interest shown in the Friday night "penny science lectures." The courses offered were in mechanical drawing, geometry, and electricity and magnetism. Since all four students worked during the day, classes were held in the evening in one of the Old Vic's spare dressing rooms, and tuition for the season was two shillings and sixpence.[1] The classes quickly grew in popularity; the original four young men quickly became sixty students, and more teachers, giving other courses, were added. By the winter, classes had expanded into the rehearsal rooms, the basement, several of the Hall's dressing rooms, and what had once been the saloon bar.[2] Emma Cons's assistant at the Surrey Buildings, Caroline Martineau, who had originally conceived of and organized the Friday night science lectures at the Royal Victoria Hall, was the logical person to take charge; and she did. Within three years, in consultation with the charity commissioners, Emma Cons set out a scheme.

Her objective, as articulated in the College's establishing documents, was to "promote the advanced study by men and women belonging to the working classes of subjects of knowledge not directly connected with or applied to any handicraft, trade or business."[3] Even if the objective had not been spelled out, it would have been clear from the sort of courses offered that the studies were, in the words of an early instructor and supporter, to be "pursued for themselves alone and the pleasure rather than the pecuniary profit."[4] The charity commissioners approved the scheme and scheduled the Hall for an annual grant of £1,000, part of which was to go towards classes. The Hall's Board of Governors decided to name this new college in memory of Samuel Morley, who had given so much money and time and taken such pleasure in the Friday night "science penny lectures."[5] Thus "Morley Memorial College (For Working Men and Women)" officially opened its doors in September 1889. The entrance to the College was made, very appropriately, through the Hall's side door, off the Waterloo Road, under a terra cotta half-moon frieze (locally made by Doulton's Lambeth potteries), showing Samuel Morley engaged in discussing texts with students.

In its first year as a College, the courses it offered were quite mixed. There were classes in reading, writing, arithmetic, Latin and French, biology, algebra, and geometry. The fundamental classes in reading, writing, and arithmetic were seen as temporary measures, until the students got themselves up to speed and were able to tackle the more advanced subjects.[6] Instruction in the violin and in singing was also offered. Over the course of the next few years, many more courses were established in literature, history, economics, political science, logic, music, and art. By offering the working poor of Lambeth and Southwark studies in the liberal arts and not simply vocational training, Morley College was clearly sending a different signal. It offered its students knowledge as power – tools with which to engage in critical thinking. But seen another way, it could equally be interpreted as offering them a prescribed, middle-class curriculum, acceptance of which would entitle them to rise materially in what was arguably becoming a homogenized, national culture.

A good deal has been written on working-class claims to higher education. Much of the debate turns on different aspects of this single issue. One school of thought maintains that worker education was simply a way of offering higher learning for those hitherto denied the opportunity to engage in non-vocational, academic inquiry.[7] Others maintain that adult worker education was a means whereby workers' striving for learning was harnessed and shaped by elitist forces that blunted and conformed it into a respectable, reformist, working-class model. John Reed has pointed out that F.D. Maurice and the other founders of the Christian Socialists' Working Men's College sought not to assist working men to enrich themselves and thereby rise into the middle classes, but to cultivate their inner selves – to be better men – while encouraging them to remain in the social positions they then occupied.[8] Roger Fieldhouse has made the case that many educational programs for workers were either created or promoted by an elite that sought to divert the working classes away from any potential Marxian-tinged militancy.[9] Conversely, Lawrence Goldman and Ross McKibbin have argued that, regardless of whether such diverting was deliberate, the late Victorian and Edwardian working-class educational movement largely reflected the essentially moderate, socially conservative, and upwardly mobile aspirations of much of the British working class of this period.[10] But these were also contemporary questions, as can be seen both from the founding in 1908 at Oxford of the Plebs League, an organization dedicated to independent worker education along Marxist lines, and from the strike at Ruskin College the following year, led by students apprehensive about what they perceived as the growing assimilation of authentic, often assertive, working-class minds into non-oppositional collaboration. The strike at Ruskin College led directly to the forming of the Central Labour College, which sought to establish worker education free from any control or direction from Oxford University. This chapter is, therefore, more than simply the story of how the women who established and administered Morley College sought to help their students realize their inner potential, and to enable and encourage them to move into the middle class. This chapter will also argue that some of their intentions and objectives – and those of the instructors and their students – were more subversive.

A Growing Sense of the Need for Worker Education

In its curriculum, Morley College carved out new territory while simultaneously standing on the foundational work of various earlier educational establishments. The idea of higher education for working men did not originate with Emma Cons and Lucy Cavendish and the Board of Governors of the Royal Victoria Hall. The Working Men's College, originally located in London's Great Ormond Street, had been established in 1854 by the Christian Socialists, John Ludlow, the Rev. F.D. Maurice, Thomas Hughes, Charles Kingsley, and their colleagues. It had grown out of the various cooperative ventures they had set up in the 1850s, such as the Ladies Cooperative Guild, where Emma Cons had first met Octavia Hill. Leading authorities in their fields came to lecture and teach at the Working Men's College: Ruskin taught drawing, Rossetti taught painting, and the legal philosopher James Fitzjames Stephen taught history, as did the Lushington twins, Godfrey and Vernon, both later eminent public servants. In keeping with its Christian Socialist origins, the Working Men's College sought to increase workers' intellectual and cultural scope, introducing them to the liberal arts, offering courses of study that would both personally enrich and challenge the students' minds and better prepare them vocationally. But the Christian Socialists' Working Men's College itself had precedents.

The Mechanics Institute, for example, established in Glasgow in 1823, had been founded by Dr George Birkbeck to give mechanics both the opportunity to study the scientific principles behind the industrial machines at which they worked and the means by which they could understand current and potential practical applications. In much the same way, Kneller Hall, a teacher training college founded in 1845, was established to train young men from the upper stratum of the working class to become teachers of pauper boys in the series of district schools that the Whig government of the day sought to create. The idea was to lift up both teacher and, subsequently, student. First headed by Lucy Cavendish's great friend Frederick Temple, Kneller Hall held great promise for its first graduates. But the comprehensive system of district schools in which Kneller Hall's graduates were to teach did not materialize, and after a decade of profound disappointment, during which its graduates were sent to teach in workhouse schools, it was closed in 1854.[11] Similarly, the idea of extending the reach of Oxford and Cambridge universities had germinated in the middle of the century. These universities had instituted, in the late 1850s, a system of local examinations for boys who were not able to leave home to attend university, and, out of this, university extension lectures unofficially began in 1867. A young Cambridge don, James Stuart of Trinity College, was asked by the North of England Council for the Promotion of Higher Education for Women to give a series of lectures on astronomy to about 550 women who were contemplating becoming schoolmistresses. Emerging from this, the first official university extension lectures were established in 1873 and proved remarkably popular. They were often given, particularly in the provincial towns, in the evenings, after work, and were held under the auspices of working men's associations, cooperative societies, or Mechanics Institutes. Audiences were composed largely either of tradesmen and their families or working men. "These," in the words of an early teacher, "are the rank and file of Extension centres."[12] Thus, the notion of adult education was an idea that grew through much of the nineteenth century.

But after the passage of the Second Reform Act of 1867, the number of voters almost doubled overnight (from 1.5 million to nearly 3 million), and, more to the point, a significant number of working men could now vote.[13] People became increasingly focused on the implications and concerns that grew about the capacity of the newly enfranchised, given the state of education among workers, to cast an informed vote. The point made by an adamant Liberal opponent of the Act, Robert Lowe, regarding the importance of an educated electorate possessed of a capacity to make informed choices has apocryphally come down to us as the pithy "we must educate our masters."[14] The Liberal government of the day enacted the Elementary Education Act of 1870, which made primary schooling compulsory for all children to the age of ten (subsequently raised to the age of twelve). But the idea of adult education for the working classes was also fairly uniformly applauded. For many, the only questions were what sort of education they ought to receive and who should set the course of study.

At Morley College the curriculum was purposefully broad. In the first year of the college's independent existence, even with its limited resources, a broad menu of courses in the liberal arts was offered and eagerly accepted. But the liberal arts curriculum was not conceived of by Emma Cons alone. The College's principal, Caroline Martineau, was instrumental in shaping what courses would be offered in its first official year. Being well versed in science, she established a curriculum that quickly weighted towards the scientific. These courses were popular; one of the early teachers later recalled that "always we found a great desire for subjects usually of a scientific nature lying outside of daily experience."[15] Both pure and applied science courses soon formed the bedrock of the College's curriculum: botany, elementary physiology, chemistry, electricity and magnetism, arithmetic, geometry, and Euclid were offered. Astronomy was a favourite subject, and a university extension course was established, "Suitable to Artizans." But social science courses were also requested, and in the next few years, courses in economics, political science, logic, and history were established. Music became popular (singing, orchestra, and violin), as did early Italian art (which included field trips to the National Gallery), sculpting, and drawing. Modern languages were offered almost from the start. German and French were particularly popular; Spanish was added in 1892.[16]

"A very small and select number" were interested in learning classical languages, and, in response to this demand, Latin was offered; Greek was added later.[17] This latter offering is significant, since knowing Greek was viewed as the exclusive purview of educated elite men; it was the essence of learning for its own sake, the farthest thing from the practical or profitable. At the same time, not having studied classical Greek was also a practical bar in one sense; for example, the Foreign Office, even well into the twentieth century, tended to recruit entirely Oxbridge graduates who had read Classics. A display of Greek, a superfluous knowledge, was also a way for men to signal or confirm to each other their status as part of the freemasonry of the elite. This was not simply a matter of class exclusion, it was also an exclusion of sex. Not knowing Greek was seen by many otherwise well educated women of Lucy Cavendish's generation as a significant handicap that excluded them from the world of the truly educated and cultured.[18] Writing to her niece Lucy Masterman in 1903, Lucy Cavendish applauded her: "Only think of your learning Greek!!!! Eve and Gwen are the only she's of your generation who have flown so high."[19] Thus Morley College's offering not only Latin but also Greek gave it a Promethean dimension, establishing it as an institution which made inaccessible knowledge available to men and women of the working classes.

The response was enthusiastic from the beginning. "Early in the evening the students came streaming upstairs, pausing at the top to enter their names in the roll book – boldly stating the classes they wished to join, whether they appeared in the programme or not."[20] Those who had belonged to the earliest classes that had been held in the Royal Victoria Hall signed O.V.S. (Old Vic Student) after their names, "as proudly as though the letters stood for some distinguished degree."[21] Declared one student, signing in: "We'll make that as good a degree as any of them."[22] This was a common feeling among the students. Emma Cons wrote in her first annual report, "there is no false shame about those who are earnest students. They come to learn and mean to do it … their eagerness is very gratifying; and the progress they make shows what the best class of working men can do. Their determination to understand thoroughly ought to put all teachers on their mettle."[23]

Striking a Balance between the Liberal Arts and Practical Knowledge

Morley College's objective of worker education in the liberal arts for its own sake, not vocational training, was noteworthy at the time: it explicitly distanced Morley College from those institutions which trained men and women to become better and more skilled workers. This was deliberate. In 1888 a committee of socially prominent men, following Quintin Hogg's lead, was struck to look into the establishing of a polytechnic south of the river to promote "industrial skills and general knowledge to young men and women belonging to the poorer classes ... and give instruction in the general rules and principles of the arts and sciences applicable to any handicraft, trade or business." It also stated that it should provide instruction "suitable for persons intending to emigrate."[24] Both Morley College and Lambeth's Borough Polytechnic sprang into being the same year. But Morley College deliberately went in a direction diametrically opposed to the Polytechnic. If the Polytechnic's declared objective was to give instruction "applicable to any handicraft, trade or business," Morley College's Board of Governors enunciated their mission as providing advanced study for the working classes of subjects of knowledge "not applicable to any handicraft, trade or business." They could not have made their meaning clearer. In sum, the idea of Morley College came from Emma Cons's, Caroline Martineau's, and Lucy Cavendish's vision of broadening the horizons of workers, not relegating them to vocational training.

Nevertheless, Morley College also, in addition to courses in the liberal arts, offered classes in "subjects that might more or less directly tend to better the chances of students in regard to the earning of their daily bread": shorthand, machine drawing, building construction, and bookkeeping.[25] The commercial courses pointed towards upward mobility for the labouring poor who, it was hoped, would be attracted to Morley College. The idea was that if the College could draw students by means of a shorthand class, they might well stay for the class on political science or French. One of the most popular classes was on the care of horses; run by a series of veterinarians, it was attended by cabbies, horse owners, and handlers alike. Classes in cookery and dressmaking were added to the curriculum in 1891 at the express request of women students. Emma Cons and Caroline Martineau did not contest this.

This inclusion of practical courses of study goes directly to the issue of what was the best sort of education for Britain's working classes, which was the subject of heated debate at this time. Ought educators to focus on greater technical training to enable workers to improve their skills and enrich themselves? Technical training at this time was very much seen as the way for Britain to surpass Germany in the race for scientific, industrial, and, thereby, economic supremacy, and a surge of interest in technical training for British workers grew and gathered momentum. In the mid-1880s, Quintin Hogg had assumed leadership of the Polytechnic in Regent Street and revived the movement to establish similar institutions. There were many, however, who held quite divergent opinions. Should not there be some attempt to expose the working classes to the liberal arts? Was it not better for the nation if all could be as well educated as possible? There were strong advocates on both sides and infinite gradations in between.

An 1875 article on "The Education of Workmen" in *Capital and Labour* (a London-based periodical with an annual subscription of £1, describing itself as a "journal with a large circulation among manufacturers, ironfounders, engineers, colliery owners, and other employers of labour") argued that it was in the nation's best interest for the workman to understand the principles behind his application of craft and machinery. Moreover, the contributor argued, the working man had a "direct interest in extending his knowledge beyond the sphere of his particular employment, in cultivating his mind on the broad scale of humanity and reason and in acquiring such extended information and power of thinking as shall not only be a solace to himself in all circumstances but fit and qualify him the more for all the relations, duties and honours of life." But at the same time, the author also pointed to the folly of trying to inject "French, or any other lingo or parrot education into a secondary school mainly designed for the working classes."[26] Similarly, an editorial in *The Times* on the subject of technical education pointed out the difficulties inherent in teaching the working classes beyond rudimentary education, although "a lad, after learning to read, write and cipher, should acquire some facility in drawing and should be familiar with elements of physical science." The point was that "his skill in applying the processes of his craft will vary in great measure with his knowledge of the scientific principles on which they depend." But little need existed, in the same writer's opinion, to educate the sons of handicraftsmen in the liberal arts; teaching, for example, French or German would likely "greatly hamper the vigour and elasticity … of an ordinary lad's mind."[27] Even the liberal and philanthropic Earl of Meath, in a letter to *The Times*, wrote with great concern that trying to teach the working classes the humanities, particularly foreign languages, brought strictly technical education into disrepute and left the children of the working classes "desirous of engaging in work which is neither manual nor what is mis-termed menial."[28] Another letter to *The Times* put it: "the country wants handicraftsmen and we produce scriveners. The colonists are crying out for men who can handle a plough, shoe a horse and mend a cart and we send them out clerks or would-be gentlemen."[29] An 1888 book, *Prosperity or Pauperism*, was entirely compiled of letters to various editors and essays reprinted from periodicals and newspapers on exactly this vigorously debated subject of educating the working class.[30]

This debate did not automatically divide along class lines. One inclusion in *Prosperity or Pauperism* was an essay entitled "A National Necessity" by Edward J. Watherston, a silversmith, member of the National Association for the Promotion of Social Science, and vociferous author on the subject of British commerce. Watherston vigorously challenged the wisdom of educating the working class in the liberal arts. "How much Latin, French or physiology could be taught to or retained by a child of twelve in a school for the children of the working classes? I submit that the moment a child has reached a fair standard of proficiency in the three R's, such child should become a half-time scholar, spending one half his time in the literary department where instruction in drawing and mathematics should be the main features and the other half in a workshop school."[31]

Not all concurred. Writing at the same time, Graham Wallas, Fabian and university extension lecturer (future co-founder of the London School of Economics and president of Morley College from 1928 to 1933), was of a different opinion. "The workmen themselves … feel that the only hope for the working classes lies in their future *intellectual* education … their way of looking at the question is very difficult for an ordinary middle-class politician to understand. To him the need of technical education, 'if we are to compete with foreigners' is perfectly obvious, the need that the working classes should be taught to think is not obvious at all."[32]

His was not a lone voice.[33] The idea of helping working men to think for themselves was the very basis of the Workmen's Social Education League, established in 1876 by the Rev. Henry Solly for the purposes of "imparting information and forming a sound public opinion on questions relating to Capital and Labour, Trade and Technical Education, Cooperation, Government, etc., upon the basis of History, Social Science and Political Philosophy."[34] It quickly gained a number of eminent and well-positioned supporters at both Oxford and Cambridge, including Lucy Cavendish's brother, the Rev. Arthur Lyttelton (soon to be made Master of Selwyn College, Cambridge, a devoutly Christian foundation for students of modest means), and her sister Lavinia's husband, Edward Talbot, the first Warden of Keble College, Oxford, both of whom applauded the League's objective of "organizing lectures and discussion, especially at Working Men's clubs and Institutes on history, social political and economic science, in order to assist in the formation of instructed and intelligent opinion among the people on these and kindred subjects."[35] This sort of education for the working classes had nothing to do with training in technical skills. It had everything to do with inculcating workers' awareness of the stake they held in society, of the degree of control (or lack thereof) over public policy and the course of their careers that they possessed, of their becoming engaged in the body politic; in short, with workers becoming citizens.

Citizenship

For those working men and women who came to the Royal Victoria Hall, either for the performances or the classes at Morley College, possessing citizenship in the sense of possessing both a right and duty to participate in civil society was not an abstract notion. At the time Morley College was founded – and even after the Third Reform Act of 1884 – approximately 35 per cent of Britain's poorest men (and all of Britain's women) still did not have the vote. These were men who paid less than 10 pounds a year in rent, or who moved so often they did not meet the twelve-month residency requirement for rate-paying; as Emma Cons noted in the College's first annual report, her students tended to move house frequently. "The working class population of London is distinctly nomadic in its habits," she wrote, "and moves hither and thither in search of work, or cheaper or more convenient lodgings. The erasures in our address books prove how frequently the students change their abode."[36] Mostly, however, the unenfranchised were young men who were not "heads of households," those who did not have the wherewithal to leave their father's house and acquire their own lodgings, even if they were over twenty-one. These people were exactly the audience of the Old Vic and exactly the men and women who came at night to Morley College. For these men and women, the question of whether to be trained or educated was important because one path led to inclusion and citizenship whereas the other might well not. For exactly these reasons of accessibility and inclusion, Emma Cons was a strenuous advocate of keeping the scale of College fees as low as possible. Her idea was that the College should "keep with us those real earnest students whose means were small." The fee for the first set of classes was set at one shilling; a second or third course could be added for an additional sixpence each.[37] Classes were held in the evening to allow working men and women to attend.

The theme of citizenship ran like a ribbon through much of Morley College's curriculum. Emma Cons, Caroline Martineau, and Lucy Cavendish had an instinctive understanding of the connection between an education in the liberal arts and citizenship. We can glean this not only from Emma Cons's own words but from the political participation of the women who ran Morley College. All three were members of the Women's Local Government Society, which agitated for women's election to school boards and to town and county councils. Mary Sheepshanks also ran for the County Council (unsuccessfully) while vice-principal of Morley College; when she eventually left the College in 1913, it was to edit the international women's suffrage journal, *Jus Suffragi*. These women understood and valued participatory citizenship and, more to the point, understood what it was to be barred from it. This understanding of the significance of participatory citizenship intrinsically coloured their construction of Morley College.

Sir Frederick Black recalled that Emma Cons "had a remarkably clear conception of what such a College as Morley could do for working men and women ... her ideal in education was that which brought out all that was best capable of development in men and women intellectually and in character."[38] One student recalled the "delighted interest" Caroline Martineau took "in the growth of the young minds about her!"[39] The principal objective of the founders was clearly not to provide the students with information but to teach them to think and reason for themselves. To offer, for example, a woman of the working classes in 1888 a course in how to be a better dressmaker is a perfectly good thing. But to teach her Latin and history and music and economics and literature is not only to show her that her mind is an innately valuable thing but also to teach her to think, to question, to construct theories, and to think critically. Lord Curzon encapsulated this idea perfectly when he described the value for artisans of, as he put it, "that liberal and humane scheme of mental training ... which they regard as indispensable for the part that they desire to play in the national life; thus the best among them seek that training in citizenship which the study of political and economic science and of social and industrial history will give."[40] But Curzon was writing in 1909 when, after the 1902 Education Act's consolidation of educational authorities and the subsequent efflorescence of secondary schools, the idea of workers seeking higher education and increasing their understanding of their citizenly capacities was a more widely accepted position. Morley College's classes had started in the rehearsal rooms in the mid-1880s, at a time when the wisdom of educating working men and women in the humanities so that they might think for themselves – more fully appreciate their citizenship (or their exclusion therefrom) – was a more contentious issue. Then the view of many, even the most well-meaning, was that it was self-indulgent, impractical, pointless, and even bad for both the country and the empire to teach languages or literature or history or Greek to the labouring classes.

The idea of inciting students' citizenly participation was part of Emma Cons's dedication to one of her favourite preoccupations: bridging the gulf between the classes. This same sense also led her, in her annual report for the Royal Victoria Hall for 1884, to ask benefactors and those who would donate money instead to cross the river and play games with the students in the College gymnasium, preside over a class, or simply chat with the students in the refreshment area and share their experiences. As with the operatic performances on stage at the Old Vic, Emma Cons wanted her benefactors to connect with Morley College's students and see their kinship for themselves. As she put it, she wanted them to meet with minds "essentially like their own, but differently shaped by the different circumstances and experiences to which they have been subjected. It has well been said that the old Roman fable of the gulf in the Forum applies to the gulf between classes in our modern life. What is needed to fill it up is not gold nor armour nor any material thing but the best life of the nation. In places where that is forthcoming, the gulf closes."[41]

Her words again echo those of the founder of the Working Men's College, F.D. Maurice, who, as previously discussed, preached of "closing the gulph between the classes."[42] This is not surprising; Maurice's words had been a great influence on Emma Cons since she and Octavia Hill, as teenaged friends, had accompanied Mrs Hill to hear him preach. But we know that Maurice's vision was one of fellowship within a defined patriarchy. When he and the other Christian Socialists established the Working Men's College in Great Ormond Street, it was to *preclude* the growth of Chartist frustration into a more pernicious strain of radicalism, not to encourage or enable working men to question the established societal structure or their place in it. The fellowship which F.D. Maurice sought to bring to them was spiritual and moral, not political or economic, one where all men, regardless of class, could recognize their commonality beneath one heavenly Father.[43] Indeed, these words echo those of the Barnetts at Toynbee Hall or of Octavia Hill. It was a most Victorian ethos. But as a woman who understood exclusion and knew manual labour, Emma Cons questioned authority from a different perspective. Her upbringing had not been as cushioned as that of the genteel Barnetts or Octavia Hill or any of the middle- and upper-class women who felt the "magnetic pull" to work with London's poor.[44] Unlike Octavia Hill or the Barnetts, or Beatrice Webb, what Emma Cons determinedly established at the side door of the Old Vic was both a specific and a virtual space where Lambeth's working men and women could taste the intellectual exercises of the elite, creating new practices of inclusion and participation.

But when Emma Cons spoke of bridging the gulf between classes, her purpose – and her perspective – was diametrically different from that of the Rev. F.D. Maurice or Octavia Hill or the Barnetts. Emma Cons understood what it was to support yourself by working with your hands; she simply did not see working men and women in the same way as her more leisured colleagues.[45] Although many may well have thought her intention in asking Morley College supporters to play games with the students or chat over tea was simply to expose her students to refined minds, lives, and manners (and indeed that was certainly an ancillary objective), in fact her main goal was the converse. She wanted the College's elite benefactors, by meeting "minds essentially like their own," to realize their kinship with working men and women.[46]

This same sense of pushing together people from different levels in society also led Emma Cons to ensure that, one way or another, Morley College would subsidize its students' attendance at the summer convening of university extension students held at both Oxford and Cambridge. Attendance at these sessions (varying from ten days to a month in length) was dependent on the student's passing the examination at the conclusion of the university extension course and securing a scholarship – £7 for a month in Cambridge and £5 for a fortnight in Oxford – and, always the most difficult, getting time off work. Emma Cons repeatedly put the touch on regular contributors to make special donations towards Oxbridge summer session bursaries: "If those who read this Report could only realize the delight and stimulus which are afforded by these peeps into a life of leisure and culture, we think the funds would not be long in coming."[47] In 1892 eight male Morley College students took part in the Cambridge session – two pipe fitters (who had studied machine-drawing), a carpenter's improver and a pattern-maker (who both took building construction), and three clerks and a shorthand-writer (who had, among them, studied history, astronomy, French, German, and Spanish) – and one woman, a music teacher who gained her place on the basis of passing examinations in two courses in Shakespeare.

The students evidently found the sessions not only a welcome break from work but also genuinely intellectually interesting. One student who attended the 1892 session in Cambridge wrote back to Emma Cons: "I went to two lectures on the Revival of Parliament by Dr. Lawrence. They were very interesting lectures and were mainly about Oliver Cromwell and Charles the Second. The lecturer placed Cromwell in quite a different light to what, as a rule, he is placed … It seems surprising how much more interesting History can be made by listening to a good lecturer than by reading."[48] Another who attended the same session wrote: "Such a visit tends more than anything I can think of to widen one's experience and mental outlook, and I believe we had all added considerably to our stores of information, developed in some degree our mental faculties and learned to appreciate more fully than before the advantages set before us in classes, reading and refined cultured society."[49] The Oxford and Cambridge university authorities were also quite assiduous about entertaining their extension guests. One student who spent ten days at Cambridge in 1891 received invitations to tea every day and was invited to luncheon by the Master of Peterhouse, to a reception by the Master of Trinity, to luncheon by a don at King's, to a dessert by the Master of Selwyn, and to a garden party at Downing.[50] Emma Cons, in pushing her students to venture out of the familiar world of Lambeth, to risk the potential social pitfalls and petty humiliations of luncheons with dons, was encouraging them to assert their own inclusion as participants and citizens. But her vision of fellow citizenship was accomplished not simply by changing how the students saw themselves but also by changing how the elite saw the working persons she sent to Oxford and Cambridge. Consciously or not, she diverted F.D. Maurice's rhetoric for her own purposes. But when she spoke of bridging the gulf between classes she also meant inculcating in her students a sense of their right to inclusion.

The Female Citizens of Morley College

Contemporary debate regarding adult education for working people also involved discussions of educating women. Women's education had been part of the original agenda of the founders of the Working Men's College in 1854. Octavia Hill, in her pre-tenement-work days, had been employed by the Rev. F.D. Maurice as part-time secretary to the College's women's classes. Although those classes grew into the Working Women's College, a division of opinion soon arose over the question of whether both sexes should be permitted to attend its classes or whether they should be kept for women alone, and the Working Women's College foundered.[51] The movement to establish colleges for workers was sincerely alive to the need to enrich their inner lives through a "liberal, humane education." But, as June Purvis and Elizabeth Bird have observed in their studies of adult education, women of the working class tended not to be integrated into this movement.[52] Even those reformers who were firmly convinced of the uplifting properties of a liberal arts education were not necessarily also of the opinion that this was the optimum course of study for women of the working class. Women were typically offered courses that were either vocationally oriented or, more typically, fashioned to fit a world of domesticity and given in single-sex classes.[53] Classes in cookery, dressmaking, domestic economy, and hygiene aimed at making working women either better workers or better housewives. Even courses given by the Women's Co-operative Guild, an organization which expressly aimed at educating women and giving them a "wider life," emphasized classes in sick nursing, millinery, cookery, laundry, and singing as appropriate for women students.[54] But very often these were classes which working-class women themselves had requested.[55]

Classes given through the university extension program were also problematic for women of the working class. With universities still effectively inaccessible to most young women in the mid-1880s, the conveniently located, cost-effective, and accessible university extension lectures quickly became popular with middle-class women.[56] For working-class women, university extension courses, building as they inevitably did on a significant pre-existing corpus of education, were intimidating, rarely nearby, and often simply not feasible. The university extension movement resulted largely in working-class men but only middle-class women gaining access to courses in the liberal arts, given in classes composed of both sexes. Indeed, June Purvis sees the entry of middle-class women into higher education as driving a wedge between middle-class and working-class women, who were often left without educational resources. Emma Cons and Lucy Cavendish clearly saw Morley College as helping to fill this gap.

Lucy Cavendish was more familiar than was Emma Cons with efforts to educate women and provide them with access to vocational training, and with the merits of both. She had been involved not only with the

3 The Morley College Gymnasium Team, circa 1895. Courtesy of the Morley College Archives, Borough of Lambeth Archives.

Girls Public Day School Trust since taking over her father's seat in 1874 but also with the Yorkshire Ladies Council of Education since her husband's election as MP for the West Riding of Yorkshire in 1865; indeed, she had become more actively involved since his death, becoming president of the Council in 1886.[57] Founded in 1871 by a group of elite Leeds women concerned about women's access to education in Yorkshire, the Yorkshire Ladies Council attempted, and fairly successfully too, to meet the needs of many different kinds of women. It directly provided classes in cookery, sewing, and laundry skills, which were very popular among mill girls and workhouse children.[58] But if the Council was affiliated with the Cookery and Domestic Science School, they were more closely involved with the Yorkshire College of Science (which was to grow into Leeds University). The Council vigorously promoted young women's access to higher education. They were instrumental in founding the Leeds Girls High School in 1876. They established a library for girls taking the Cambridge local examinations. They exhorted women to take advantage of the opportunities in higher education that already existed, encouraging them to attend courses first at Leeds College, then, subsequently, Leeds University (particularly after the establishment of its Day Training College in 1896). The Council promoted university extension lectures and managed women's taking of university extension examinations at the end of various courses of study.[59] It also provided bursaries for students at Leeds Girls High School to continue their studies at universities. It established annual examinations to decide which girls would receive Council scholarships for study at Girton; Emily Davies herself attended the examination in 1887. Lucy Cavendish was well aware of how the two streams of women's education could beneficially affect women's lives, but she was also, as she mentioned in more than one of the Yorkshire Ladies Council's annual reports, highly conscious of the danger of vocational and domestic training "swamping" the "higher instruction" and continually cautioned the Council not to neglect the aims of higher education.[60]

Lucy Cavendish's views on this subject formed the basis of her address to the Council's annual meeting in 1894, the same year she was appointed to the Royal Commission on Secondary Education.

> Two opposing tendencies have to be noted in the theories of the day as to girls' education. There was the strong desire to promote higher instruction in literature, the classics, science and mathematics on the one hand, and on the other an equally strong feeling in favour of home arts and

> domestic science. She thought they might welcome both those tendencies. They would correct each other where it was advisable they should do so, and if both claimed their proper share of attention they would see proper play given to the capacities of girls all round. Could they doubt that the higher subjects were most necessary and most desirable in their secondary schools for girls?[61]

At the same meeting she also took a direct swipe at the Darwinian psychologist George Romanes, who had asserted a few years earlier, in an article popularizing Darwinian science in *The Nineteenth Century*, that women's brains, weighing less than men's, were inferior in capacity and function.[62] Praising the results of the Yorkshire Ladies Council's efforts, she observed that "perhaps the most far-reaching result of all had been the recognition of the fact that girls' brains differed little in degree, and not at all in kind, from the brains of boys."[63] Likely even more than did Emma Cons in the early 1880s, Lucy Cavendish understood not only the importance of offering a variety of education to girls and women but also, in particular, the impact and importance of encouraging women to pursue higher learning, not merely vocational training.

Emma Cons, Caroline Martineau, and Lucy Cavendish each felt strongly about the importance of women's education and how valuable a college for working women could be. Lucy Cavendish, in particular, was both self-conscious about the deficiencies of her own education and attuned (through her work with the Girls Public Day School Trust and the Yorkshire Ladies Council of Education) to how education could open doors for women. Thus the new courses of liberal arts study that Morley College offered were explicitly available for working women as well as working men, a point Lucy Cavendish drove home in a speech she gave at the Hall on 15 May 1888 expressing her opinions on the importance of the admission of women to Morley College. Similarly, Emma Cons's appointing Caroline Martineau as principal was an explicit sign of the level playing field accorded women that she sought to create at Morley College. It is also a good example of the dynamic of power between Emma Cons and her Board of Governors; they did not much question her recommendations. "Dominating but not domineering" was how one early supporter described her.[64] Emma Cons, Caroline Martineau, and Lucy Cavendish not only made sure that classes were explicitly open to women but also that it was stipulated in the College's organizing charter that the Governing Council should always include at least three women. This was easily accomplished; Caroline

Martineau, Lucy Cavendish, and Emma Cons were appointed as the College's first governing councillors. Among the three of them, Morley College was run by women.[65]

"Leonard Bast"

Morley College's first annual report painted a very good portrait of the 1,270 men and women who enrolled that first year. Most were men. Most were local; students consistently came from Lambeth and Southwark right up to 1914.[66] Many were clerks, occupying the grey area between the working class and the lower middle class. For example, 211 students, identifying themselves as clerks of one type of another (law clerks, conveyancing clerks, junior clerks), enrolled in the College's first year, as did a governess, a corn merchant, 2 journalists, 3 apothecaries, 2 chemists, 2 dentists, 10 teachers, 2 missionaries, a teacher of pianoforte, 2 policemen (and a detective), and a woman who simply described herself as "a Lady." But many students also worked with their hands: 6 masons enrolled, as did 22 printers, 31 warehousemen, 19 who identified themselves simply as "labourers," 4 bricklayers, and 3 brushmakers, in addition to numerous other occupations involving manual labour. Many worked with the railroads, likely out of nearby Waterloo terminus; 87 students described themselves as engineers.

There were also a significant number of skilled artisans in the first year: 8 were tailors, 2 made musical instruments, 12 students bound books, 6 were draughtsmen, 14 were carpenters, 13 were joiners, 5 were engravers, 6 made scientific instruments.[67] The women's working hours generally ran very late and the hours of the classes, which generally started at eight o'clock, acted as a deterrent. That said, at least 40 either identified themselves as women (including 9 women machinists) or had occupations traditionally taken up by women (nurses, for example). But Emma Cons was herself pleased with her demographic breadth: proudly listing the occupations of her students, she noted that they "prove that this College has really reached the class it was formed to help, working people."[68] The general youth of the students in the first year can be readily seen, 10 identifying themselves as "boys" or "lads" ("post boy," "entering lad"); 27 other students identified themselves either as apprentices or as junior assistants in one sort of skilled trade or another. Of the 1,270 students who took classes in the first year, about 45 per cent were under twenty, another 45 per cent were between twenty and thirty. The remainder were over thirty, including three mature students, aged sixty-four.[69] There was a drop in the College's second year as the initial flurry of interest shook out those students who had overestimated their capacity, interest, or available time, but annual enrolment soon settled at just under a thousand, where it stayed until 1913 when it rose again to around 1,200.

Some students had interesting pedigrees. John Garibaldi Sparkhall was a young clerk when he took classes at Morley College in its first year. He was also the son of Isaac Sparkhall, a "fashionable silk and felt hat-maker" of decidedly radical views who had been a good and trusted friend of the radical Charles Bradlaugh. Isaac Sparkhall had been a campaigner against the enclosure of Victoria Park in 1855 and an organizer of the Hoxton Secular School Rooms.[70] Given the way that Isaac Sparkhall named his son, it is not surprising that Sparkhall Senior was also one of the chief organizers, in 1862, of the Working Men's Garibaldi Committee. Young John Garibaldi Sparkhall was one of the pillars of Morley College. He had been one of the original four young men who approached Emma Cons about setting up regular classes out of the penny science lectures. He was the only student in the college to successfully conclude the ambitious three-year course of study devised by Caroline Martineau to cover courses in literature, mathematics, languages, and science with exacting examinations at the conclusion of each year, requiring first-class standing before a student could progress to the next level. He was also one of the first students to have his name inscribed in the Honour Roll of Associates of the College.

We also have portraits in fiction. E.M. Forster was giving a series of lectures at Morley College at the very time he was building, in *Howards End*, the character of Leonard Bast, a young clerk at the "extreme verge of gentility ... not in the abyss, but he could see it" from where he stood.[71] Leonard Bast loved beauty, played a bit of piano, liked Grieg, attended lectures, and hoped to "come to Culture" as evangelicals hoped to come to Jesus. He felt that "if he kept on with Ruskin, and the Queen's Hall concerts, and some pictures by Watts, he would one day push his head out of the grey waters and see the universe."[72] The description of Bast's country walk into the dawn could have been taken almost verbatim from the reports of the Morley College Walking Club, which was devoted to long-distance hiking. In its first outing, members undertook a "night tramp" of forty miles from Purley to Brighton, returning by rail, finding it "intensely interesting walking along the well-known road during the 'wee sma' hours o' the morning.'"[73]

There are many aspects of Forster's Leonard Bast that recall the sort of young man who attended classes at Morley College. That said, the character of Leonard Bast probably tells us more about how Forster saw his students than about what his students were actually like. As Jonathan Rose comprehensively demonstrated in his examination of the richness of late nineteenth- and early twentieth-century British working-class autodidact and intellectual culture, workers who sought out intellectual activity, the classics, and culture were often not as insecure as Bast was painted.[74] They usually had a more solid sense of their own worth and their experience of literature, history, theatre, and music was more often consistent, passionate, and joyous. One of the great strengths of Rose's work is that it is packed thick with working-class memoirs showing the texture and depth of appreciation that Edwardian workers often held for ostensibly elite education: W.J. Brown, the young clerk who usually spent his "glorious" hours of freedom after work at the Post Office Savings Bank reading Dostoesvksy in the Battersea Public library; young Allen Clarke, who worked in the Lancashire textile mills but who also spent his spare hours in the public library, devouring Chaucer, Marlowe, Shelley, and Goldsmith; A.E. Coppard, the laundrywoman's son and clerk who used prize money from running races to buy Shakespeare, Homer, and William Morris. These portraits, more than the depiction of Leonard Bast, are close to the reality of Morley College's students.

Similarly, the character of *Mrs. Dalloway*'s shell-shocked Septimus Smith tells us more about Virginia Woolf than it does about her students at Morley College. Like Leonard Bast, the character of Septimus Smith was taken from a student of Woolf's to whom she taught Keats in 1907. Woolf's journals and contemporary correspondence give us a picture of a young poet in one of her classes who "rants and blushes, and almost seizes my hand when we happen to like the same lines."[75] As Woolf constructed him in *Mrs. Dalloway*, Septimus Smith had come to London from Stroud before the First World War, "shy and stammering," "anxious to improve himself," and "in love with Miss Isabel Pole, lecturing in the Waterloo Road." Omnivorously hungry for knowledge, Septimus Smith studied in an unsystematic but joyous way, was writing a masterpiece of his own late into the night, "running out to pace the streets, fasting one day, drinking another, devouring Shakespeare, Darwin, *The History of Civilization*, and Bernard Shaw." Septimus Smith also affected his teacher, Miss Isabel Pole, who wondered whether he was like Keats, corrected his love poems in red ink, and "reflected how she might give him a taste of *Antony and Cleopatra* and the rest; lent him books; wrote him scraps of letter; and lit in him such a fire as burns only once in a lifetime."[76] Like Leonard Bast, Septimus Smith could in some ways have stepped directly from the pages of the *Morley College Magazine*.[77] At the same time, real Morley College students tended to be more resilient than Septimus Smith, and it can be seen, both from Jonathan Rose's case studies and from the *Morley College Magazine*, that they tended to be more systematic and less simple-mindedly reactive in their approach to learning than either Septimus Smith or Leonard Bast.

Providing an Intellectually Stimulating Social Life

Just as the bill at the Royal Victoria Hall was designed to divert the working poor of Lambeth from alcohol, so Morley College also offered recreational activities as an alternative to the pub for young working men and women. An early teacher recalled that Emma Cons had a very good idea that an institution such as Morley College could provide working men and women "on the social and recreational sides."[78] From living in the courts she managed, Emma Cons understood that working men often suffered from social isolation, with few opportunities beyond the pub to mix in collegial, let alone intellectually stimulating, company. This disruptive situation was even more difficult for lonely, isolated young working women trying to lead a "respectable" life. As she delicately put it in her annual report, shortly after the College opened:

> Those who have been brought up from childhood in cultivated homes, surrounded with intellectual society, may perhaps find it difficult to imagine what life would be without these blessings, to the girl or young man in a lonely lodging, or the dwellers in a crowded room where quiet is impossible. "We can't make friends in our rank of life" said a shoemaker with ten children. "How can I tell my boys to bring home a pal in the evenings? We've not room for it!"[79]

This isolation was particularly marked in those who held upwardly mobile ambitions or who had already had some education. This may have been most evident among the 45 per cent of the College's students under the age of twenty who would have been the first generation to have benefited from compulsory elementary education introduced in

1870 and who may well have developed a thirst for knowledge. Emma Cons observed in her annual report for the College's second year, describing the sort of student the College was attracting, that "there are not a few working men whose education is far ahead of that possessed by the companions of their daily work and their lives are apt to be very lonely."[80] Changing lodgings frequently, as many of London's working poor did, could exacerbate the isolating effect. Managing the tenements had made Emma Cons particularly sensitive to the ripple effects on an individual or family of uprooting and losing the supporting network of neighbours, particularly for women who often lacked a similar workplace network. These detrimental effects were a concern, since they would affect Morley College students' ability to thrive. Clearly Emma Cons understood how the College could provide not only a social life but also a set of connections for many of its students, drawing them out of their isolation and into greater involvement and participation. "If we can bring into the lives of our students, books and an intelligent interest in the affairs of the world and the beauties of nature, we do much for them. If we make friendship possible to them, we do perhaps still more."[81]

Thus, a common room was established and kept open to all students before and after classes. Lucy Cavendish donated rugs and chairs and made sure to pass on her copies of *Punch* when she had finished with them.[82] A refreshment stand was established in the basement so that students coming directly from work could have their tea and relax a bit before class. A smaller room was rigged up as a library and stocked books donated by members of the Governing Council. From the start, the College established various clubs for the students. Some were more successful than others; those involving sport were invariably well attended. The cricket club was continuously popular and fielded both a First and a Second Eleven team, for both of which Lucy Cavendish arranged permission to practise in the grounds of Lambeth Palace, the home of the Archbishop of Canterbury. They tended to do well; in 1894 the First Eleven won fourteen out of eighteen matches. Two swimming clubs met at the nearby York Baths – the men's club met twice a week and the women's club met once a week. Emma Cons's companion, Ethel Everest, served as president of the women's club and offered a challenge cup. A women's games club was established in 1894 that met in a nearby garden for croquet and aimed at finding tennis courts. A women's basketball team was organized (see figure 3). Walls were knocked out and a gymnasium set up with hours ensured for both men and women and gymnastics classes established with gold, silver, and bronze medals awarded at competitions. By 1894, the men's gymnastics class was so popular it had to be divided into two groups.

Clubs devoted to intellectual or cultural stimulation were established. Art exhibitions were organized with first-rate pictures lent and exhibited. Lucy Cavendish was involved with these from the beginning, tapping the Marquess of Lorne to open one exhibition, enlisting the support of her old friend Princess Helena to open another, and prevailing upon her sister May's old beau, Arthur Balfour, to lend pictures. A Natural History Club organized outings, for example to the Royal Botanic Society, Kew Gardens, or Regent's Park. The archaeological society took field trips to such places as the Tower of London and Westminster Abbey. All lectures given at the Royal Victoria Hall were free to Morley College students and half-price to any friends they took with them. An astronomy club, a literary society, and a chess club were also established, although they were not as consistently popular.

Outings to the country were thought of as tremendously important. Emma Cons organized day trips for students, often either to Caroline Martineau's Maidenhead country house or to Chippen's Bank, the Kent home Emma Cons and Ethel Everest shared. But there were also long weekend rambles when the students were invited to spend the night. One student recollected that at Chippen's Bank "we slept on hay in the barn, and I can remember, though it's nearly sixty years ago, Miss Everest and Miss Cons visiting us in the middle of the night with storm lanterns to see if all was well"[83] (see figure 4). The students themselves set up both a cycling club and a rambling field club for both men and women. Morley College thus presented a way for working men and women to meet each other in reputable, even laudable surroundings, on a level playing field. Aside from church activities, there were very few opportunities for young men and women to make friends with the opposite sex or meet suitable partners. The clubs and common room had the great advantage of being unsupervised by college authorities. Students were trusted to govern themselves. A Student Social evening was held once a month on Saturdays. These were organized by the students themselves and usually featured their own songs and recitations.

The issue of citizenship and inclusion was a common theme in extracurricular activities at Morley College just as much as it was a theme in the curriculum. If Morley College sought to inculcate in its students

4 Morley College outing, 1911. Courtesy of the Morley College Archives, Borough of Lambeth Archives.

an intelligent interest in the affairs of the world, there were different ways to do it. A college magazine was set up in 1892 and appeared monthly during the term. At first it was edited by one of the younger members of the Governing Council, but it was later ceded to the students to run themselves. Students were co-opted onto the Governing Council. A colleague of both Lucy Cavendish and Emma Cons from the Women's Local Government Society, Walter McLaren, MP for Crewe (and John and Jacob Bright's brother-in-law), organized the Debating Club; early subjects of debate included the superiority of Thackeray to Dickens, the wisdom of the eight-hour day, and women's suffrage. Judging from the resolutions they passed, students seem to have held broad-minded political philosophies, but, certainly in the early years of the College, more liberal than socialist. Students supported an imperial federation but were simultaneously "anti-militarist"; they were in favour of "women's rights" generally and women's suffrage specifically; the power of the House of Lords should be curtailed; MPs should receive a salary, but the formation of an Independent Labour Party, the society resolved, was "neither necessary nor desirable."[84] Notables would often send in papers for students to study and debate; Auberon Herbert, philosopher, sometime MP for Nottingham, and supporter of the cooperative movement, offered his paper on the "Foundation of the Voluntary State" for discussion.[85] When Walter McLaren stepped down as chairman, his place was taken by C.P. Trevelyan, not yet the Liberal (and subsequently, Labour) MP he would become.

Teaching Working Men and Women to Think for Themselves

The students felt strongly about Morley College. This is obvious not simply from the rapidity with which students enrolled, although the steady increase in numbers after the College's third year give a good indication of its popularity. Average nightly attendance in 1892 rose from 127 to 157 and the following year increased again to 178. From their first class, students caught the idea that Morley College was offering not simply classes but a chance at a different sort of life; students offered to give away the College's first prospectus in the streets, "as if they were tracts."[86] Letters from former students received by Emma Cons after only a few years attest to a sense of gratitude for how the college enabled them to "rise in life."[87] Her annual reports make frequent mention of the students' "eagerness."

It was clearly not simply the classes that incited loyalty and a sense of belonging. In the annual report for 1892, Emma Cons wrote that "many and touching are the proofs which we have of the place our College holds in the life and affections of the students."[88] It was often, as she put it, "something less tangible but certainly not less important, a grateful acknowledgement of awakening intellectual life, or sympathy in intellectual interests which are already awake ... such men speak most warmly not only of the means of further study afforded by the classes, but of the Society of those like-minded with themselves to be found in the Clubs and Common Room."[89] When, in 1905, the LCC proposed to transfer many of Morley College's technical and scientific courses to the Borough Polytechnic (and conversely transfer the Polytechnic's humanities courses to Morley College), many of the students objected that this segregation would strike at the heart of Morley College's identity. Graham Wallas and George Trevelyan were also considerably concerned. "You will not be able to get the science students at Morley to go to the Polytechnic," wrote Trevelyan to Wallas, "they are Morley men, just as I was a Trinity man; the esprit de corps, which means the social and intellectual life is real and valuable at the Morley; it arises from the mixture of science and the Humanities."[90] Clearly, Morley College gave the men and women of Lambeth a sense that they were of significance, that their opinions had merit, their minds were worth cultivating. The students' loyalty and affection was the return of respect. Emma Cons wrote in the 1893 annual report: "as to the spirit prevailing among our students, we cannot speak too thankfully of it. We always try to make them feel that the College is *theirs*; that it exists for their benefit, and that its success depends mainly on them. And they respond heartily. 'I never felt so much at home anywhere in my life,' said one."[91]

That said, and likely as a result of concern regarding the youth of many of the students, Emma Cons and Caroline Martineau kept an eye on students' recreation. Seeing the college as theirs, students often had views that crossed the intentions of the administration. The first student representatives to the Consultative Committee were vocal in voicing their disagreement with, for example, the authorities' veto of a dancing club and a proposed roller-skating club in the gymnasium, both seen as too frivolous and possessing neither educational, cultural, nor athletic qualities. Student protests led to the ban on smoking in the basement refreshment room being lifted. In 1893 their protests persuaded the Council to permit scenes from plays to be performed, on the condition there was no "dressing up," something which was seen as potentially embarrassing to working women unable to afford finery.[92] The following year, students united to reject the principal's *ex officio* seat on all student clubs, arguing that it was undemocratic; the secretary of the Swimming Club threatened to immediately adjourn any meeting which the principal attempted to attend.[93] That same year, a quarter of the students protested and petitioned, unsuccessfully, against the firing of a popular member of staff. Caroline Martineau and Emma Cons, likely conscious of their obligations as *de facto* chaperones, evidently sought to create certain barriers between the sexes: women were not permitted to enter the basement refreshment room which functioned as an informal club for the men students.[94] It was not until after Emma Cons's death that students were permitted to hold a dance at Morley College.[95] But the students were increasingly assertive of their own stake in the College, and the Consultative Committee often had to work hard to retain a state of equipoise.

Emma Cons and Lucy Cavendish had delegated the choosing of teachers to Caroline Martineau, and several of her hires were exceptional. For example, the Fabian and experienced university extension lecturer Graham Wallas first came to Morley Memorial College in November of 1893 when he gave a series of lectures on "The English Citizen Past and Present." Like Emma Cons and Octavia Hill, Graham Wallas had been influenced by John Ruskin and his fusion of aesthetic, moral, and social teachings,[96] so it was easy for Caroline Martineau to persuade him to include Morley College as part of his university extension lecturing. Beatrice Webb was of the opinion that young Wallas was "an admirable and most popular University extension lecturer," and certainly his lectures at Morley College were well attended and well regarded by the students.[97] Wallas, too, regarded his students favourably, writing to Caroline Martineau that "the average of intelligence is, I think, higher than in any of my other centres."[98] Wallas was not simply being polite; F.W. Maitland, Downing Professor of Law at Cambridge (and acknowledged father of English legal history), who served as the external examiner of the English Citizen students, held a high opinion of Wallas's students: "I am well satisfied with the results of the examination. I consider the subject a very difficult one for those who have had no previous training in history or law."[99] Wallas had not only prepared his students well, but had given them the confidence to sit a difficult paper which they knew would be read by an elite and demanding judge.

As Caroline Martineau became increasingly unwell in the late 1890s, many of her duties were taken up by the vice-principal, Mary Sheepshanks. Sheepshanks also increasingly became the *de facto* principal of the College, as Caroline Martineau's successor, Charles Roden Buxton, appeared to view the job as part-time at best. Immediately after accepting the position of principal of Morley College, he ran for Parliament and was elected for the constituency of East Hertfordshire; thereafter he was infrequently seen at the College.[100] Mary Sheepshanks was responsible for a number of exceptional appointments of her own. It was she who secured the Cambridge historian George Trevelyan to lecture on various aspects of his subject.[101] She was also responsible in 1907 for hiring the young Gustav von Holst (not yet a renowned composer but still a well-thought-of young teacher of music, who would, drop the "von" during the First World War) to create a music department and set up the Morley College orchestra. In fact, Holst was not her first choice. Ralph Vaughan Williams had lectured at the College as a visitor in 1905 and had returned, together with Cecil Sharp, the great reviver of English folk music and country dancing, to give a series of recitals on "The English Folk Song." Vaughan Williams was approached first, but, being too busy, had suggested his friend Holst, with whom he had studied at the Royal College of Music. Mary Sheepshanks was also responsible for persuading Leslie Stephen's children to teach at Morley College. Vanessa Stephen taught drawing; her brother Thoby and his friend Clive Bell taught Latin; Adrian Stephen taught history and Greek and Virginia Stephen (not yet the published author Virginia Woolf) was recruited to teach English composition. Although the others soon drifted away from Morley College, Virginia Stephen stuck and continued to teach both British history and English for four years.

Virginia Woolf approached her students much as an anthropologist studying a distant tribe: "On the whole they were possessed of more intelligence than I expected; though that intelligence was almost wholly uncultivated. But of this I am convinced; that it would not be hard to educate them sufficiently to give them a new interest in life; they have tentacles languidly stretching forth from their minds, feeling vaguely for substance, & easily applied by a guiding hand to something that [they] could really grasp."[102] Woolf's diaries at this time reveal good intentions. But they also show an almost complete absence of understanding of Morley College's mission. "Ain't it ridiculous – teaching working women about the ancient Britons!"[103] Considering a course of eight lectures which George Trevelyan was offering on the subject of the

French Revolution, she questioned, "And what, I ask, will be the use of that? Eight lectures dropped into their minds like meteors from another sphere impinging on this planet, & dissolving into dust again. Such disconnected fragments will these eight lectures be: to people who have absolutely no power of receiving them as part of a whole, & applying them to their proper ends."[104] Virginia Woolf found her students difficult and frustrating. In a letter to her friend Violet Dickinson, written at the start of her teaching at Morley, she expressed her dissatisfaction:

> [O]n Wednesdays I have English Composition; 10 people: 4 men and 6 women. It is, I suppose the most useless class in the College; and so Sheepshanks thinks. She sat through the whole lesson last night and almost stamped with impatience. But what can I do? I have an old Socialist of 50, who thinks he must bring the Parasite (the Aristocrat, that is you and Nelly) into an essay upon Autumn; and a Dutchman who thinks – at the end of the class too – that I have been teaching him Arithmetic; and anaemic shop girls who say they would write more but they only get an hour for their dinner, and there doesn't seem much time for writing … Oh Morley College is a fine place and – can you end the quotation?[105]

She became increasingly less satisfied with her work at Morley College. After two years, she still looked on her students with puzzlement. "I have been teaching a Milkman to write English for 2 hours; and the effect is so singular that I had better say no more. It is like floating your brains in cold mist."[106] Tentatively offered the position of librarian by Mary Sheepshanks, Virginia Woolf declined and concluded her work at Morley College.[107]

If Virginia Woolf failed to grasp the purpose of Morley College, the young Gustav Holst understood it entirely. But Holst came from a very different social bracket than did Woolf. Like Emma Cons, Holst came from an emigrant, continental, musical family; his father was a music teacher and composer, descended from generations of music teachers and composers. Also like Emma Cons, Holst was a believer in art and education for working men and women. He was enthusiastic about the works of Walt Whitman and George MacDonald (the Scottish visionary who had written plays for Emma Cons's tenants at Freshwater Place). Holst became a member of William Morris's Hammersmith Socialist Society, headquartered at Kelmscott House, where Holst conducted the Hammersmith Socialist Society choir.[108] He was a good fit with Morley College.

He accepted all comers to the orchestra he established there in 1907, which initially consisted of two violins, a flute, three clarinets, a cornet, and a piano. No one would be turned away because they were "not good enough"; the only condition was that they be prepared to work hard. Indeed, the orchestra was very much proof of Holst's practice of inclusion: the second violinist had a paralysed right arm and used to play by leaning against the wall, holding what would have been her bowing arm rigid, while moving her violin back and forth with the other.[109] The Morley College orchestra and chorus soon became popular and were evidently competent. Their 1909 performance of Purcell's *King Arthur* was well received by at least one critic, who described an "energetic young conductor" extracting a performance that "was admirable in many ways."[110] Within four years the orchestra had grown to a size where they could, in 1911, give the first concert of Purcell's *Fairy Queen* performed since 1697.[111]

Holst's students did not simply absorb and recite the music he taught them; he encouraged the development of their critical faculties and their growth as musicians and composers. He insisted on including at least one student composition at every Morley College concert. He also had them tackle challenging pieces: Handel's *Acis and Galatea*, Monteverdi's *Dido and Anaeas*, Mendelssohn's *Hebrides Overture*, Beethoven's Second Symphony, Bach's *Magnificat*, works by Schumann, Haydn, and Dvořák, and symphonies and operas by Mozart.[112] Morley College students could also, evidently, appreciate musical humour, as can be seen from a College concert featuring a "Futuristic Tone Poem in H," which Holst conducted with two batons.[113] On one occasion, a journalist, Miss Katharine Eggar, sat in on a rehearsal for an article she was writing for the *Music Student*, remarking on the program which, in addition to the student composition, included Beethoven's *Choral Fantasia*, Brahms's *Song of Destiny*, and a Morley College student's new translation of Bach's B minor Mass. She observed Holst's pleasure at his students' developing discernment. As they turned from the Bach to the Brahms, "the conductor wheeled round again to his visitor. 'Did you see that? Their faces fell! Some of them don't like Brahms – they'd like to go on singing Bach all night! ... *Ha!* But I always do learn from my pupils.'"[114] Holst thought highly of his "resourceful" Morley College performers.[115] During the time he taught there, he spent his weekends at a small cottage in Thaxted, Essex, where he began, in 1916, to train the choir of the parish church. He would often bring his pupils from Morley College down to combine with the Thaxted choir in Bach and Purcell at the

Whitsun festival.[116] Holst's pedagogical vision of inclusion, his holding his students to high standards, and his encouraging their development as musicians and composers was very much part of the Morley College ethos.[117]

Gustav Holst, E.M. Forster, George Trevelyan, Ralph Vaughan Williams, Virginia Woolf, Clive Bell, and Adrian, Thoby, and Vanessa Stephen were not the only notable and often eminent teachers Mary Sheepshanks secured for Morley College; she tended to aim high. For example, the historian John Holland Rose (noted biographer of Napoleon) lectured there in, or around, 1900. During the same period, Goldsworthy Lowes Dickinson was prevailed upon to give a class in philosophy. The zoologist Peter Chalmers Mitchell was the secretary of the London Zoological Society when he began to teach at Morley College in 1903.[118] Similarly, G.E. Moore's defence of the evidence of an external world was first articulated in a series of lectures he gave at Morley College in 1910–11.[119] The young R.H. Tawney became a member of Morley College's Governing Council. Tawney would go on to a distinguished career as an economic historian and, after the First World War, was one of the Labour Party's chief theorists on educational policy. Mary Sheepshanks was indefatigable in persuading good minds that it was worthwhile sharing their thoughts with Morley College students.

Inculcating Fellowship or Teaching "Discontent"

The presence of so many elite instructors raises the issue of whether Morley College sought to divert its students away from Marxian radicalism and direct them towards upwardly mobile assimilation and conformity. Not only did many of the courses implicitly prepare students for citizenly participation, but many lecturers returned repeatedly and specifically to the subject of the inclusion of the working class in political and public life. In 1909, the economist J.A. Hobson took charge of Morley College's first University Tutorials in economics, starting with the subject "Making and Sharing Wealth." The "earnest and lively" young Fabian, Graham Wallas, gave more than simply his one series of lectures on the English citizen; he gave one series of lectures on government generally, another on "The Making of the English Constitution," and a third on the English citizen of the nineteenth century.[120] Moving systematically through British history, Wallas consistently used as his pivot point the struggle of the English working class to gain and retain the "rights of freeborn Englishmen." He stressed the subversive aspects of working-class struggle to become active citizens. For example, in his sixth lecture, on the effects of the French Revolution on English working men, he described how "colliers in the mines would go out at night on the moor, light a peat fire and sit down and read Tom Paine hour by hour through the night – taking care after the meeting to bury the proscribed book down in the peat."[121] This particular lecture Wallas concluded with the question which he threw out to his students of "whether electors should expect their M.P.'s to think or simply be delegates." Two weeks later, he brought his students back to much the same place, observing in his lecture on the evolution of Britain's Poor Law that "no nation can be wealthy in which the individual citizens themselves do not feel their own responsibility."[122] Similarly, the following week, speaking on the battle to bring public elementary education to the working class of Britain, Wallas deliberately chose for his lecture some of the most provocative quotes from the House of Commons debates concerning Samuel Whitbread's 1807 Bill ("What produced the French Revolution? *Books!*"), observing that the Bill had been derided in the House as "jacobinical" and quoting Sir Samuel Romilly's observation in debate that "the fact is, the greater part of the House desire that the people should be kept in a state of ignorance."[123] In these lectures, Wallas engaged just as much in raising the consciousness of his Morley College students as in instructing them in a narrative of British history.[124]

If that was the objective of Wallas and, indeed, of other Morley instructors, were they successful? The responses of some students seem to suggest so, or alternatively that Morley College attracted those predisposed to hear the message. C.H. Hartley, one of the first student representatives to the College's Consultative Committee, recalled of himself and his student colleagues, "the most ardent of Socialists were we all."[125] Alfred Arnold, who enrolled in the College in 1892, described himself as "an active Socialist propagandist," and indeed, he was not only a member of H.N. Hyndman's Social Democratic Federation but also contributed to its weekly journal, *Justice*.[126] Arnold was an active debater and successfully led the argument, at one of the debating society meetings in 1893, in favour of "Socialism" and, as he put it, "astonished certain worthy people by the vigorous manner in which I maintained my opinion on the subject, notwithstanding the fact that the Principal of the College had expressed herself against it."[127] Virginia Woolf, writing to Lady Robert Cecil, described one of her students as "a good working man – who is a socialist, of a kind."[128] There were other indications that some of the students of Morley College were politically and critically alert. At the conclusion of a gymnastics display in 1892, when the band struck up the national anthem, a "vigorous hissing" was heard and attributed to "republican" students.[129] When the Earl of Lytton spoke on imperialism a few years later, he was heckled.[130] The advertisements of Johnson and Son ("first-class tailors") in the *Morley College Magazine,* conscious of the readership, prominently averred that they employed no sweated labour and invited inspection of their workshops.[131] In 1889 when, following the end of a bitter dock strike, a demonstration was held to aid dock-workers' families, the *Daily News* reported that the organizers chose to "muster at the Morley College for Working Men and Women [and] with Bands and banners, perambulated the streets and roads of Lambeth and Southwark, gathering in great quantities of copper and silver as they went."[132] If one of the objectives of Morley College had been steering students away from working-class consciousness, it wasn't working.

One of the things that made Morley College different was that it was not part of the construction of adult worker education by Oxbridge men and other reform-minded intellectuals of the day. First, it was established and entirely run by women. Secondly, although the original shareholders of the Coffee Music-Halls Company and the Board of Governors of Morley College were certainly part of the elite, the College was not their brain-child. It had spontaneously grown from the desires and interests of the audience for the Friday night penny science lectures. In the debate about the underlying purpose of offering higher education to working persons, it is important who created and shaped this education. Had Morley College, notwithstanding its having been founded and run by disenfranchised women who felt strongly about citizenly participation, become an instrument of elite power, attempting to steer working-class educational ambitions away from Marxian militancy and towards respectable reformism? Was Morley College's liberal arts curriculum designed to transmit the kind of cultural capital that would enable the working men and women of Lambeth and Southwark to assimilate more easily into the middle class, away from working-class consciousness? Emma Cons may have been a daughter of the artisanate, very familiar both with the working poor and the aspirational clerks of London, but Caroline Martineau, Mary Sheepshanks, and Lucy Cavendish were not. Even Graham Wallas, Fabian though he was, bent on raising the consciousness of his students, was still, like Tawney and Hobson, part of a tradition of elite, Oxbridge-educated reformers.

We have the evidence that, increasingly, more Morley College students were clerks of one kind or another, men and, increasingly, women who made their living by their pens and their minds, not by heavy lifting or manual labour. The number of manual labourers at the College declined as the number of clerks rose. These were men and women who likely would have had upwardly mobile aspirations and who often occupied the grey area between the working class and the lower middle class. These were men like Leonard Bast or John Garibaldi Sparkhall. By 1901, Caroline Martineau was concerned that those who worked with their hands no longer enrolled in their former numbers. As one of the College's earliest students, F.W. Jacob, recalled after Caroline Martineau's death: "Her great wish was to help men and women to help themselves and to aid them to lift themselves out of the mire of their surroundings. The classes at the old 'Vic' offered them the means, and it hurt her to know they were despised by the very men they were intended to benefit."[133] For some, the College and its courses of liberal arts study had become, perhaps, too middle class. By 1913, the year after Emma Cons's death, clerks comprised almost one-third of the College's students, the remaining two-thirds continuing to be evenly split between skilled and unskilled workers.[134] But "clerk" is a broad term, particularly when employed in self-identification, and would have included, for example, young women shop-clerks who stood behind a counter just as much as black-coated scriveners. The increase in clerks registered at Morley College may likely also have much to do with the exponential increase in their numbers: from 95,000 to 843,000 between the years 1850 and 1914.[135] Moreover, women during this period were becoming clerks at a faster rate than were men, from 2,000 in 1850 to 166,000 by 1914.[136] The increase in the number of clerks at Morley College may also have been as much a factor of a simple increase in women's enrolment. In the College's first year, men had outnumbered women four to one; by 1913, women made up half the College. Many clerks of either sex, however, would likely have attended classes at Morley College precisely because they already sought to better their lives materially and socially, as we can see from letters to Emma Cons from former students, grateful at having been enabled to "rise in the world." That would be consistent with the steady popularity of elocution classes, introduced in Morley College's second year of operations.[137] Bettering one's presentation, and one's accent, was axiomatic with upward mobility. This picture of Morley College's students would entirely comport with Lawrence Goldman and Ross McKibbin's depiction of the prevalence of upwardly mobile aspirations among the late Victorian working class.[138]

Morley College, in the first decade of the new century, became a main centre of the activities of the Workers Education Association (WEA), an organization founded in 1903 by a cooperative cashier, Albert Mansbridge, stirred by his belief that university extension courses had been colonized by the middle classes and were no longer as inviting to working-class students as they once had been. The WEA was a reformist and progressive organization, dedicated to bringing workers within the embrace of middle-class, liberal, humane, educational norms and culture. The WEA also perfectly fitted with Emma Cons's mission to use both great art on the stage of the Old Vic and the classics in the classrooms at Morley College to break down the isolation of the British working class and integrate them into a national culture. To the Plebs league and the strikers at Ruskin College, the WEA was seen as assimilationist, seeking to strip the working class of its sense of self. But the WEA found a home at Morley College; from 1909 onwards, one of the WEA's most enthusiastic champions was R.H. Tawney, a member of Morley College's Governing Council.

That said, clearly not all Morley College students held upwardly mobile, assimilationist views; the College had radical as well as liberal students. The resolutions of the debating society can again be instructive: they show a trend, at least among debating students, to the left. If in the early years of the College students had resolved that an Independent Labour Party was "neither necessary nor desirable," by the turn of the century one debate resolved that the Boer War was "unnecessary" and another unanimously voted in favour of the utility of supporting and joining trade unions.[139] The following year, the first resolution in favour of "Socialism" was passed. This is not altogether surprising considering the political complexion of many of the popular speakers that Caroline Martineau and Mary Sheepshanks brought to the College to address the students between 1889 and 1913: the suffragette Charlotte Despard argued for providing school dinners for children; the Fabian (and later, historian) Robert C.K. Ensor spoke on the necessity of minimum wage laws; a young Herbert Morrison spoke on children's care committees; Christabel Pankhurst and Margaret Bondfield each spoke on women's suffrage; and Amber Pember Reeves debated Free Will, in what the club secretary described as "the best discussion we've ever had."[140] Thus, by the start of the First World War, the student body was more bourgeois and more female, but also more socially and politically critical. But if Morley College students were becoming politically more radical than had been the College's earliest students, this might equally reflect an increasingly liberal political temperament in Britain generally, between 1889 when the College opened and 1913. Moreover, liberal or even radical political views can easily be held by those who wish to better their material position.

Some Morley College students went on to interesting and likely prosperous lives afterwards. James J. Denton, a student of the technical classes, began in 1895 to teach his own class on practical electricity. But Denton also made his mark in science as an assistant to John Logie Baird in his invention of the television and his first television broadcast out of Hastings. Denton was a founding member of the Faraday Society, devoted to making further advancements in radio and, in 1927, helped found (and was the first honorary secretary of) the newly organized Royal Television Society.[141] The young clerk John Garibaldi Sparkhall became something of an inventor of anti-bacterial agents.[142] R.W. Bowers, one of the earliest Morley College students, had attended the Friday night penny science lectures at the Royal Victoria Hall and was one of the students who helped to gather signatures for the original petition to the charity commissioners. He was also, at the time of Morley College's establishment, a secretary of the working men's club that met in the former saloon bar of the Royal Victoria Hall. A printer's apprentice when a student, Bowers went on to a career as a successful printer and became, in middle age, senior alderman on the London County Council representing Southwark.

Thus we can see in Morley College alumni those who reflect the upwardly mobile aspirations of much of the Edwardian British working class. But others show us a lively interest in courses which do not axiomatically lead to better jobs and can serve as good examples of students searching for a "higher life" through more, and higher-quality, education. The words of the students from the student-edited *Morley College Magazine*, the kinds of clubs students formed, their letters to Emma Cons from their summer courses in Oxford and Cambridge, and their observations reported in the College's annual reports all indicate an active interest in acquiring greater familiarity with elite learning and culture, but not necessarily solely for the purpose of directly increasing their material well-being. Moreover, during its formative years, the classes Morley College offered became less vocational, not more so: Spanish, history, geography, and logic were introduced in 1891, the following year courses in Italian and Greek were added, in 1894 physiography, geology, and art history were offered for the first time, and in 1896 courses were offered in poetry, psychology, and ethics.[143] The featured presentation at the 1913 College prize-giving ceremony was a production of Sophocles' *Antigone*, with a cast of forty women students who had spent "many months" studying not only their parts but also "Greek art and culture with Professor Richardson."[144] Becoming comfortable with culture hitherto monopolized by the elite might or might not lead to the middle class, but it gave its own satisfactions.

But this revives the essential question regarding Morley College: was its purpose assimilation or emancipation or something in between? Did Emma Cons, Caroline Martineau, and Lucy Cavendish see lectures on the English citizen, ancient Britons, and Shakespeare and classes in Latin and art as means of giving the workers of Lambeth and Southwark the kind of cultural capital that would enable them to rise in the world? Did they see Morley College as a way of drawing their students more firmly within a national culture? Or did they have a more subversive intention? Did they see Morley College's education as a way of awakening its students to their citizenly capacities? Jonathan Rose, in *The Intellectual Life of the British Working Class*, has made the interesting argument that, for many workers, the pursuit of elite culture was not indicative of assimilation, but was often an act of rebellion against the strictures and confines of the British class system. Internalizing literature and classics often sharpened, not blunted, their radicalism. In exactly this way, learning Greek and Latin and Shakespeare could be seen by Morley College students and their teachers not only as a worthwhile activity in its own right but also as a way of gaining access to "forbidden" power. Penelope Corfield has made the compelling argument that the professions, particularly law, medicine, and apothecaries, retained much of their power in the nineteenth century through their use of Latin, Greek, and law French, keeping their knowledge as a mystery known only to the initiated. In the same way, if Shakespeare and Milton and Greek are what the ruling elite learned and read for pleasure, then that was what was wanted at Morley College. Certainly David Vincent's study of nineteenth-century working-class autobiography, *Bread,*

Knowledge and Freedom: A Study of Working Class Autobiography (1982), reveals a consistent belief among his working-class autodidact subjects that knowledge was power.[145]

The liberal arts courses at Morley College suggest that Caroline Martineau and Emma Cons were aware of the power of elite knowledge and of the subversive aspects of giving working persons access to it. Emma Cons, Caroline Martineau, Lucy Cavendish, and Mary Sheepshanks structured Morley College to have great inclusive capacity; it could bring different things to people with different needs and aspirations. Certainly some students sought to use its classes as a means of rising in society. Others wanted the personal fulfilment that comes from learning new things well. These personal ambitions and the cultivating of a more radical consciousness, however, are not mutually exclusive. Some students surely sought the satisfaction in mastering hitherto forbidden knowledge. The founders' intentions were not wholly directed towards giving their students a prescribed, middle-class curriculum, acceptance of which would enable them to enrich themselves and rise in the world. Neither was their intention solely to provide students with a form of cultural capital that would enable them to flourish, although that may well have been seen as an adjunct goal. Rather, their objective was to create Morley College as a big tent that could encompass all those objectives and more, because they also sought to offer students knowledge as a kind of power, giving them the tools with which they could engage in clear, inevitably critical thinking, enabling them to engage in public affairs as citizens. In short, the purpose of Morley College was not simply *embourgeoisement*; it was just as much concerned with empowering. The students could use the power as they saw fit.

We know that these women who ran Morley College wanted to teach their students how to think and how to question. During his time as president, from 1928 to 1933, Graham Wallas had an opportunity to reflect on what Morley College, since its founding in 1889, had contributed to the lives of the working men and women of Lambeth and Southwark. In a lecture he gave in November of 1931, he suggested that one of the most important things it brought to Lambeth was that it made its students discontented.

When Ferdinand Lassalle, seventy years ago, attempted to organise the recently industrialized men of South Germany, he implored them in the new crowded and bewildering factory towns to escape from their own

> "damned wantlessness". Here at Morley, owing first to the genius of that little bright-eyed artist-saint Emma Cons, our founders set themselves to create and quicken "wants" among the "wantless" inhabitants of the dreary streets and drearier workshops ...[146]

Inculcating discontent is not an element of assimilation or *embourgoisement*. Whether wholly consciously or not, in their passing on elite knowledge and cultural capital to the working poor of South London through Morley College, Emma Cons and Lucy Cavendish can be seen to have acted as Promethean agents of subversion.

6 Philanthropy and Citizenship

"What is True Charity? Helping people to help themselves and become good Citizens."

Church of England Temperance Society, Annual Report, 1887

Women's good works for the first half of the nineteenth century were understood as being a well-accepted, indeed laudable, variety of female associational life. "Charity is the calling of a lady; the care of the poor is her profession … it is her bounden duty to administer to them." Hannah More had the character Mrs Stanley make this affirmation in her 1808 novel, *Coelebs in Search of a Wife*.[1] This was an accepted view then and it prevailed without much challenge for at least another fifty years. We hear it again, virtually unchanged, from Louisa Twining, who wrote in 1858 in a pamphlet on *Workhouses and Women's Work* that women, possessed of hearts full of "love for young and old, sick and poor because they are a sacred charge committed to her care," were "fittest" to tend to "the sick and aged, children, the outcast and the fallen."[2] For many Victorian men and women, God had ordained that woman's highest calling was to care for the sick, the poor, and the helpless. Indeed, those women who publicly opined on matters of national interest grounded their standing to do so in their moral indignation, invoking Christian conscience as an extension of their natural sphere of authority. Duty, Christian self-sacrifice, the overflow of domestic, maternal love directed outwards to society, this is a familiar view of Victorian women's philanthropy, and it is quite correctly descriptive. Jane Lewis, in writing about the life and work of Octavia Hill, maintains that "self-giving as a manifestation of Christian obligation" was central to Hill's view of philanthropy, a view echoed by Gillian Darley.[3] Lewis, Kathryn Gleadle, and others see much the same picture at the end of the century. Indeed, the overall tone of Angela Burdett-Coutts's introduction to an 1893 compilation of women's philanthropic organizations, *Woman's Mission*, is one of Christian charity.[4] Maternalism, taken together with Christian duty, wrapped in high moral authority, created a powerful and enduring ethos.

But in the late 1860s, in other quarters, and not even radical ones, the stirrings of an upheaval could be detected. Whether consciously or not, certain women began to detach the idea of charity from its roots as a quasi-religious commitment and recast it as civic, not personal, virtue, couched not in terms of Coventry Patmore's "angel in the house" now venturing beyond the threshold, but of women's philanthropy as the assumed obligations of a citizen. This did not arise in a vacuum. In the last third of the nineteenth century, the issue of citizenship, particularly that of the unenfranchised working class, was in play in a way that had not been the case earlier in the century. Indeed the link between citizenship and service was made explicitly in that context. Part of the argument made by reformers in the debates leading up to the Second Reform Bill of 1867 was that the franchise was a "trust" bestowed upon those who had earned it by financial standing and established residence, endowments indicating that the head of such a household would exercise his vote both rationally and free from improper influence and thus would productively contribute to the benefit of the nation. In a debate held in 1865 at a Social Meeting of the Working Men's Club and Institute Union (presided over by Lucy Cavendish's father, Lord Lyttelton), the Rev. F.D. Maurice gave a talk on "The Duties of Citizenship" in which he observed, "The citizen is the reverse of 'slave', but identical with 'servant'; his service is civil service, and that is the very condition of every man's existence as a citizen."[5] The connection between the franchise and the obligation it entailed was part of an overall network of civic obligation. At this time, two supporters of votes for women, John Stuart Mill and Barbara Bodichon, unsuccessfully petitioned to bootstrap women into the franchise expansion of the 1867 Second Reform Bill, basing their argument on the notion of women as citizens who were capable of valuable service.

But the case for women as citizens did not fade. Two years later, Harriet Taylor and John Stuart Mill argued in *The Subjection of Women* that Britain should not foolishly deprive itself of the abilities of women and the service they could render to the national good. Louisa Shore published an article in 1874 entitled "The Citizenship of Women Socially Considered" in the *Westminster Review*, reasoning that women's service to the nation gave them title to legitimate and equal standing as citizens.[6] The struggle through the late 1870s for married women to retain their own earned wages, successfully culminating in the Married Women's Property Act of 1882, was also partly based on the argument that retaining one's own wages was the right of a citizen. Similarly, Frances Powers Cobbe's 1878 article in the *Contemporary Review*, "Wife Torture in England" (part of her campaign for passage of the Matrimonial Causes Act of 1878), used a variety of theories to make her argument for a woman's right to possession and security of her own body. One was based on the principle that a woman already possessed a kind of citizenship – but one that had been placed in an inferior position. "The position of a woman before the law as wife, mother and citizen remains so much below that of a husband, father, citizen, that it remains a matter of course that she must be regarded by him as an inferior."[7] The idea of women as citizens was also intrinsic to Josephine Butler's campaign in the 1870s and 1880s against the Contagious Diseases Act (whereby doctors could snatch women off the streets and subject them to forced medical examinations simply on suspicion of their being prostitutes). Butler used the rhetoric of citizenship, arguing that the Contagious Diseases Act nullified for women the doctrine of *habeas corpus*, thus entirely vitiating their citizenship.[8] Women's claims to citizenship surfaced and resurfaced continually during the 1870s and 1880s as women gained the right to own property, enter into contracts, secure maintained separation from their assaulting spouses, become eligible for election first to school boards, then as poor law guardians and on vestries and town councils, and then in 1888 sit as councillors of the new county councils. The idea of women as citizens was a part of public discourse from the time of the Second Reform Act debates.[9]

In the last quarter of the nineteenth century, questions of citizenship preoccupied many thoughtful persons. Julia Parker, in *Citizenship, Work and Welfare* (1998), has looked at how progressive Victorian thinkers, Arnold Toynbee for example, or T.H. Green, John Ruskin, and William Morris, increasingly saw citizenship as intrinsically connected to an individual's public service; this was a view increasingly embraced by women.[10] Lydia Murdoch, in *Imagined Orphans: Poor Families, Child Welfare and Contested Citizenship in London* (2006), has shown how, for example, those engaged in social welfare work saw no anomaly in sharply distinguishing between middle-class citizens and working-class parents who might or might not have fulfilled the requirements for citizenship.[11] Jane Rendall and Anna Clark have observed that the question of exactly who was qualified for citizenship in late Victorian and Edwardian Britain was also a deeply gendered issue, arguing that, as citizenship became synonymous with voting rights, it solidified as a male preserve.[12]

Women frequently made the argument that they already fulfilled any requirements of citizenship by virtue of their contribution to the country. Frances Powers Cobbe, in a series of lectures given in 1880 entitled (and later published under the title) *The Duties of Women*, explicitly made the connection between women's philanthropy as public, not personal, service, outlining the duty of women to the state in her final lecture, "Woman as a Citizen of the State." "What is this, after all, my friends, but *public spirit* – in one shape called patriotism in another, philanthropy – the extension of our sympathies beyond the narrow bounds of our homes."[13] Cobbe was not alone; in the first issue of the *Plymouth High School for Girls Magazine*, an editorial drew the same connection: "It seems quite simple and obvious that women have duties towards the States which are just as binding as those other duties on which so much stress has been laid ... How is it then that we hear and think so little of a woman's duties as a member of a state?"[14] But men, too, made the same argument. In a sermon preached on "Citizen Sunday" 1895, the Rev. S. Farrington spoke to his assembled congregation of the connection between service and citizenship. "This morning I wish to speak of women as citizens ... what women can do as members of the community, as members of the nation, to contribute to its welfare and to the development of a better life, which is the fundamental duty of every citizen."[15] Walter McLaren, MP, pointed out at an 1890 constituency meeting, "whenever woman had been called upon to do any public work she had done it in an excellent manner, and women were now fulfilling every duty of citizenship except that of voting at Parliamentary elections."[16] At a meeting of the General Council of the Birmingham Liberal Association in January of 1891, the speaker explicitly drew the connection between women's service to the nation and citizenship. "[W]omen had already most emphatically proved their claim to the rights of citizenship by their services on School Boards and on Boards of Guardians and one of the most important committees of the Birmingham city Council had acknowledged the help ladies had rendered in promoting the health of the people."[17] Women were not alone in grounding their claims to citizenship in the service to society they rendered through their philanthropic activities.

The connection between women's philanthropic public service and citizenship was increasingly made. At the Conference of the National Union of Women Workers in Manchester in 1896, Miss Gwenllian Morgan of Brecon, a poor law guardian, addressed the conference on "The Duties of Citizenship." "It is a subject for rejoicing that every year women are awakening more and more to a sense of their responsibility as citizens." She further observed that women's duties as citizens had now moved beyond philanthropy and they must exercise the votes they had to prudently elect the best local councillors: "it is a very solemn responsibility that rests upon us as women to use our votes at every election."[18] The Boer War reignited the assertion that women could not be given the vote because they were incapable of offering the nation military service. The response quickly came that such public service as was offered by such women as Florence Nightingale or Octavia Hill more than met any requirement for citizenship.

Victorians understood this notion of a correlation of service to citizenship because it was cast in the mould of the ancient Greek civic tradition emphasizing the virtues of participation in the public sphere: the notion of *virtu* as the admirable attribute possessed by the civically engaged, public-spirited citizen.[19] We hear this clearly in the address given by Mrs Mallett, a candidate for the London School Board, who spoke to a meeting of the Hornsey Women's Liberal Association in November of 1891. Her address was on the subject of women's duties of citizenship and in it she referred to the Greek and Roman idea of citizenship, observing: "it was the duty of a citizen, in the Olden Time, to sacrifice life itself, if need were, in defence of the State. The same ideal of citizenship is ours today. The foes which menace us are hunger, vice, pauperism, ignorance and apathy. Our weapons are the strength of united service."[20] Similarly, the suffragist Mrs Wynford Phillips wrote, in a pamphlet for the Women's Liberal Association, *An Appeal to Women*:

> Women: your sphere is your home! Yes, but you have a double duty. First of all to your family, and secondly to the wider family, the world of human beings outside, and you fail in one of your most solemn obligations, if you devote yourself solely to your own home and your own children, unmindful of the fact that thousands of poor men and women have no homes, or

> live in dark degraded homes and that hundreds and thousands of little children are growing up uncared for, untaught, unthought-of, in slums and alleys or the streets of our great cities.[21]

This was a message that the women's suffrage movement vigorously encouraged.[22] An article written in *County Council Magazine* in 1889 by "A Lady" made the point that an active interest in public matters was a positive obligation for both genders. "There are only two classes one would be glad to see sitting with folded hands, and taking no interest in public matters – the vicious and the stupid – but for men and women of principle and intelligence to fall into such apathy is to fail in patriotic duty."[23] Similarly, the suffragist Laura Ormiston Chant made the same point in the May 1899 issue of *The Nineteenth Century*.

> When one passes in review the lives and teaching of the women who have made this century famous for reforms in the treatment of the criminal, the lunatic, the blind, the poor, the sick, the orphan, the outcast and the drunkard and have stirred in the fellow women not only a yearning for recognized citizenship but enthusiasm for such of its duties as prejudice could not withhold from them ... [24]

Similarly, in September 1903, Bertha Mason, poor law guardian, suffrage worker, and daughter of the wealthy Liberal MP for Ashton-under-Lyme, gave a speech to the junior branch of the British Women's Temperance Association. In it she emphasized for her audience the importance of women understanding their obligations as citizens: "You are parts of a whole, you *are* citizens of a State, whether you know it or not ... if you are to be citizens in the best sense of the word, it is your duty – you have no choice – to feel a personal concern, and to take a personal interest in the life of the community in which you dwell." In linking personal obligation with citizenship, Bertha Mason invoked the entire roster of social care-taking of the vulnerable that formerly was seen entirely as a woman's Christian duty: "You will come to realize that the housing of the poor, the protection of infant life, the safeguarding of the workers, the care of the aged, the mentally afflicted, the education of the young, are your business, your concern." She then went on to expressly link the citizen's obligation towards those most at risk not only with citizenly philanthropic participation but also with the citizenly act of voting: "If you girls will only care enough about this great subject of citizenship … to train yourselves to serve on Boards of Guardians, to use the franchise as a weapon to be used for the protection of your fellow-citizens."[25]

But this was not only a matter for suffragists or those of radical persuasions; women of fairly moderate views saw the link between philanthropy and women's citizenship. In late 1884, Ann Lindsay read a paper at the Christian Women's Union Congress held in Glasgow. In it, the idea of women as citizens is taken virtually as acknowledged: "Christian women as citizens are bound to take a thoughtful and intelligent interest in the affairs of their country and to assist in the formation of public opinion about them."[26] Similarly, the members of the Council of Congregational Women were admonished at their 1898 meeting by one of their speakers about fulfilling their obligations as citizens: "In their factories, workhouses, lunatic asylums and police courts, competent women were minister to their fellow-sisters, playing a large part in citizenship."[27] Even women of a distinctly conservative bent also began to see philanthropic service as a correlative of citizenship. At Queen Victoria's Golden Jubilee in 1887, three women were asked to attend the ceremonies at Westminster Abbey in their own right: Florence Nightingale, Josephine Butler, and Octavia Hill. The common denominator was service to the nation.

Even women who actively opposed women's suffrage acknowledged the link between service and women's citizenship. Mrs Humphry Ward's "Appeal against Female Suffrage," published in *The Nineteenth Century* in 1889 to argue against the idea of votes for women, made explicit the relationship between the service women could render to the nation and their citizenship. "Citizenship is not dependent upon or identical with the possession of the suffrage. Citizenship lies in the participation of each individual in effort for the good of the community."[28] Lucy Cavendish was a signatory to this appeal and it was an ethos she wholeheartedly endorsed. The idea of women's philanthropic service, what was now widely termed "women's work," was increasingly seen by mainstream society less as the Christian duty of the selfless woman, undertaken without thought of recompense, and more as public service – a fulfilment of citizenship. Louise Creighton was the wife of the Bishop of London, the historian Mandell Creighton, and, like Lucy Cavendish, was active in the National Union of Women Workers; she served as president three times. Also like Lucy Cavendish, she was a signatory to Mrs Humphry Ward's appeal. But when Creighton addressed the meeting for young women at the annual Anglican Church Congress in 1897, her message was one of citizenship for young women and, for a bishop's wife, it contained an oddly radical streak:

> It was in the home that the woman's duty must first be done. But they ought not only to consider how to bear the home burdens. They must remember also that they were citizens. When the French people rose against the nobles of the land, the title in which they delighted was that of citizens, each claiming to have a share in the State and in the management of its affairs. Women nowadays should bear in mind that they, too, were citizens, and have regard, not only to their rights, but to their duties as such.[29]

Louise Creighton went on to exhort her young women to be serious in thinking about how best to offer service to their country. "Girls ought to know a little of the way in which that country was governed. Some of them perhaps already have the power of using the municipal vote. And when the voting time came, how were they going to use their power?" At the same time she was also explicit about how, to her way of thinking, citizenship and public service had little to do with electing parliamentary representatives. "It had not yet been thought right, and I for one hope it never will, to give women the parliamentary franchise. Again, what was that gift that each woman had to offer her country? Herself."[30] Although Louise Creighton would go on to revise her views on women's suffrage (indeed, she used her speech to the National Union of Women Workers' 1906 Annual Conference at Tunbridge Wells as the vehicle to publicly declare her change of allegiance), her views on the link between women's public service and citizenship did not change.[31] For Lucy Cavendish and for Emma Cons both, their work took place within this ongoing evolution in the discourse of citizenship.

This shift from philanthropy as self-sacrificing duty to philanthropic work as the qualification for citizenship did not jettison the notion of duty, but repositioned it as further evidence of "women's work" as the *quid pro quo* of the rights of citizenship. Looked at in another way, it is a rewriting of the contract: previously philanthropy is duty given without thought of recompense; now it stands as part of a fair trade for citizenship. For some this is a conscious revision; for others, likely both Emma Cons and Lucy Cavendish among them, it is more of a subtle, subconscious shift of emphasis. This particularly as Emma Cons and Lucy Cavendish sat rather in the mid-stream of late Victorian sensibility. For them to embrace the idea of women's philanthropic work as an act of citizenship is significant. Lucy Cavendish's view is of particular note because nothing in her self-effacing personality or her very established background would have prepared her to actively assert or display anything, let alone her citizenship. Similarly, Emma Cons came from the Octavia Hill, Henrietta Barnett school of selfless, ameliorative work and so would have been more likely to remain committed to the view of settlement work as an act of personal virtue. And yet, whether they would have recognized it as such or not, their work can be read as a revealing example of philanthropy as a display of citizenship.

The personal philanthropic trajectories of both Lucy Cavendish and Emma Cons can again act as good case studies. Their philanthropic work, although it may have begun as an expression of personal duty, serves as an example of how late Victorian women reconstructed the idea of women's philanthropy, recasting it as civic, not private, virtue. In the 1860s and 1870s, Lucy Cavendish worked with charities that can be seen as extensions of a nurturing woman's natural, maternalist, sphere – the Soho House of Charity, the Home for Epileptic and Incurable Women, a penitentiary laundry for young prostitutes, directly ministering to the poor through the Ladies Diocesan Association and the Parochial Mission Women. Emma Cons similarly worked with the Mental After-Care Association and the Coffee-Taverns Association, and as a rent collector for Octavia Hill. But starting in the early 1880s and until Emma's death in 1912, Lucy Cavendish and Emma Cons devoted the majority of their efforts towards the Old Vic, Morley College, lobbying for reform of temperance laws, and the cause of electing women to local government bodies, chiefly the newly established local county councils. Again, we see, in the stories of these two Victorian women, their shift away from improving the lives of the poor within an unchanged social welfare framework to either publicly advocating change or building organizations such as the Old Vic and Morley College that empowered the poor. This development may be partly explained by the reticence of youth maturing into the self-confidence of middle age and the increased abilities of these two women to express and assert their views. But it also suggests a broader, societal shift in how women saw themselves as citizens.

From whence did this shift emerge? Is philanthropy's transition from being an element of a woman's Christian duty to being a citizenly variety of public service a reflection of a society in the process of secularizing? That is a viable argument, but the threshold question is whether religion was actually in decline in Victorian society. The generally received impression is of a steady decline in religious attitudes and church attendance through the latter half of the nineteenth century.[32] Jonathan Rose argues in *The Edwardian Temperament 1895–1919* (1986) that Darwinism sapped Christianity of much of its credibility among educated people. Pointing to a persistent fading of Londoners' attendance at church, a steady decline in the number of men entering the Anglican priesthood, and a sharp drop in the number of books published on religion, Rose makes the case that the decline of religion and the increasing secularization of British society had far-reaching effects.[33] More recently, Jeremy Morris in "The Strange Death of Christian Britain: Another Look at the Secularization Debate" (2003) points to the fading of evangelical messages and characters in children's literature and boys' magazines, *inter alia*, as indicating a secularizing society. Callum Brown, however, in *The Death of Christian Britain: Understanding Secularization 1800–2000* (2009), maintains that although church attendance dropped from the 1880s onwards, church affiliation did not. For Brown, although Christian protocols and practices may have eased, the broader religious discourse points to Britain's remaining a firmly Christian nation up to the year of 1963.[34] Women's philanthropy, detached from its place as part of charitable Christian duty and repositioned as "our bit," could be seen as a part of this pattern. This interpretation would stand as one with Morris's notion of the process of late Victorian secularization being not so much a decline as "cultural displacement."[35]

But regardless of whether late Victorian Britain was becoming a less religious nation, secularization had nothing to do with the life of either Lucy Cavendish or Emma Cons. Both were utterly devout Christians and specifically devoted to the Church of England. Although one was High Church while the other was Broad Church, one of the bonds between these two women was their sincere and complete devotion to the Anglican Church as an all-encompassing force for good. But this sincere religious conformity to the different ends of the Anglican spectrum did not prevent both women from being part of philanthropy's general shift from being a Christian obligation to being the public service of a citizen. Lucy Cavendish clearly came to see her philanthropic works as the duties of a citizen. As she herself simply and succinctly put it, in an article for the March 1890 issue of the *New Review* (written to encourage support for a cooperative laundry for girls taken off the street), it is "the duty of all citizens to work for the good of all."[36] Emma Cons was no less explicit: in an 1891 speech to the Society for Promoting the Return of Women as County Councillors, she declared that "we are not here tonight to advocate for women's rights, but for every woman's right to do her duty to her sex and her country."[37] The duty to which both women referred was not then that of a Christian but that of a citizen. This view, for both Lucy Cavendish and Emma Cons, had nothing to do with secularization. It also impelled both of them to campaign for the expansion of women's arena for public service.

Barbara Bodichon and John Stuart Mill's attempt to win women the vote in 1867 did not have much support in the country, among either men or women; Lucy Cavendish at the time had dismissed it as an "odious and ridiculous notion."[38] But by the 1880s, as women increasingly connected public service with citizenship, interest in the more explicit actions of citizens also grew. Exercising the civic duty of a citizen was clearly the argument behind suffragists' attempts to include women in the Third Reform Bill of 1884. This having been unsuccessful, the idea of women's contributions as citizens became the driving force behind the founding in 1888 of an organization which was directed at civic engagement in a different venue: the Society for Promoting the Return of Women as County Councillors, in which both Emma Cons and Lucy Cavendish served as vice-presidents. Although Emma Cons was a committed suffragist, whereas Lucy Cavendish did not support votes for women beyond the level of local government, they both gave their names (each of which, by 1888, held considerable weight) and their time to the cause of getting women elected to local government bodies, particularly after Emma Cons's foray into politics.

Women had been directly involved in Britain's local government since 1869 when Jacob Bright slipped in an amendment during a late-night session of the House of Commons debating borough electoral qualifications (an Act tidying up questions left over from the hurried Second Reform Act of 1867). This gave women ratepayers the vote in local government elections. The following year local school boards were established, and women both voted for and served as school board trustees. The first woman was elected as a poor law guardian five years later. Thus, by 1888, when the Local Government Board attempted to consolidate London's chaotic squirrel's nest of overlapping agencies, vestries, and boards into the first London County Council, rate-paying women were qualified to vote for city councillors.

Whether they were themselves entitled to stand for election was less clear. The 1888 County Councils Act did not expressly exclude women, and so, on 9 November 1888, a group of like-minded, liberal women gathered together to explore the possibilities.[39] The Society for Promoting the Return of Women as County Councillors identified four women who it believed could win County Council elections: two in London, two in the counties. The two women who ran in the London districts – Jane Cobden, in Bow and Bromley, and Margaret, Lady Sandhurst, in Brixton – were successfully elected in January of 1889.[40] Both had sterling progressive credentials; Jane Cobden was the daughter of Richard Cobden, one of the founders of the Anti-Corn Law League; Lady Sandhurst was the widow of William Mansfield, Lord Sandhurst, a distinguished military officer. One of the newly elected Council's first orders of business was to elect those persons to serve with the councillors as aldermen. As a practical matter, since the Progressives, a confederation of Liberal, radical, and Labour councillors, held the majority of council seats, nominations for aldermen brought forward by the Progressive caucus would likely be elected. The Society for Promoting the Return of Women as County Councillors, which soon became the Women's Local Government Society (WLGS), sent a resolution to the Progressive members of the London County Council expressing the hope that they would nominate two women as aldermen. The WLGS suggested three names for consideration: Lady Frederick Cavendish, Miss Emma Cons, and Mrs Massingberd, one of the women who had run for a provincial county council seat (Lindsey, in Lincolnshire), failing by only twenty votes, but who kept a London residence.[41]

Lucy Cavendish was a logical choice. By 1889 she was known for her work with the Girls Public Day School Company and the Yorkshire Ladies Council of Education. The public was also aware of her work with Emma Cons on behalf of the Royal Victoria Hall. She was known to be a good committee member, able to chair meetings efficiently. Since her husband's death she had also become known for championing progressive causes, women's education, and the Royal Victoria Hall, and for making good speeches, mainly on the subject of temperance. For the same reasons that she had been asked to become Mistress of Girton, hers was a reasonable nomination. But by the time her name was debated by the Progressive councillors, Lucy Cavendish was on her way to Africa to visit her brother the Rev. Albert Lyttelton in his South African parish and to recuperate after the death of her infant nephew Christopher Lyttelton, and her name was not further considered.

Emma Cons's name was an equally logical nomination and, moreover, one of the newly elected Progressive councillors was able to speak from personal acquaintance, having known her for more than ten years.

Jane Cobden and Emma Cons had first met at the opening of the Coffee Tavern that Emma Cons had established in the Marylebone Road and they had come to know each other better through working together on a variety of good causes. Cons was known as a political person; she galvanized her local Lambeth Women's Liberal Association. When asked by Jane Cobden if she would let her name stand for an alderman, Cons had responded that she thought her "experience would be useful."[42] She was not self-effacing, did not engage in false modesty, and had a very good sense of what "thirty years of experience gained by me in hard and practical work for the improvement of the houses and the amelioration of the lives of the poorer classes" could bring to such an institution as the London County Council.[43] Thus, at the first meeting of the Progressive caucus where the names of various potential aldermen were debated, Jane Cobden was able to speak warmly in favour of Emma Cons. Her work in housing for the poor and in reclaiming the Royal Victoria Hall was well known; it spoke for itself. In the end Emma Cons was the only woman nominated as alderman and was elected by a wide margin.[44]

Emma Cons's corpus of experience garnered in her decades of managing worker housing was openly acknowledged as greatly surpassing that of the vast majority of her colleagues, and, as she wryly put it, "the result of this practical experience has been that at the last election of committees I was, during my absence from Town, elected to six committees and eleven sub-committees." Reasonably enough, given her experience, Emma Cons was automatically placed on the committees for theatres, industrial schools, parks, sanitation, and the housing of the working classes. Her work with Lucy Cavendish and Drs Hawkins and Tuke with the Mental After-Care Association gave her far better understanding of the problems of the mentally ill than virtually any other councillor, and so she was also immediately placed on the Asylums Committee.[45]

Her understanding of the practicalities of residential institutions was invaluable. The Earl of Meath, one of her fellow councillors and a member of the Housing of the Working Classes committee, recalled that during their committee's official inspection of a County Council institution, Emma Cons was not to be found when the time came to depart and had to be searched for. She was discovered, emerging from the basement, having found "a serious leak in the drainage system which, if permitted to continue would in all probability have exposed the inmates to serious disease and possible death." The committee, having already given "complete approval of the way in which the institution was being carried on from every point of view," was obliged to reverse its opinion.[46]

Emma Cons had a very clear conception of what she could do on the London County Council. Writing to the *Morning Post* in November of 1890, she opined that what women brought to the County Council was nothing short of invaluable. She was quick and clear to play up the maternalist argument, emphasizing the unique contribution women could bring to local social administration.

> If the ratepayers only realized the crying need of women's help on the County Council, especially in the industrial schools, the lunatic asylums, the baby farms, the housing of the poor, a need that makes my heart quite sick to think of it; if they could have seen the little lad of 14 "quite incorrigible" brought up again, brazen-faced before the committee, for sentence; if they could have seen the little fellow afterwards break down and sob because, meeting him quietly by myself, I said I could not bear to see him in disgrace, and asked him again to get rid of the bad conduct badge before I came again ...[47]

The issue of women serving on county councils had the interesting effect of often uniting suffragists in common cause with women who were opposed to female suffrage. Octavia Hill, for example, an adamant opponent of women's suffrage, was an enthusiastic supporter of Emma Cons's work on the Council. Writing to her mother on 26 April 1889, she described Emma Cons's work as entirely satisfactory: "Miss Cons seems to be doing beautiful work at the L.C. Council, inspiring everyone and keeping herself in the shade."[48] Lucy Cavendish took exactly the same position. Women on county councils were simply exercising their "house-keeping" expertise on a slightly broader canvas. For her, and clearly also for Octavia Hill, local government gave women the platform to do what they did best. Both recognized the maternalist aspects of public service and both firmly supported women's election to county councils. Lucy Cavendish also saw much county council work as being the kind that, as she put it, men were "incapable" of doing.[49] Writing to her cousin Mary Gladstone, shortly after Emma Cons's election, Lucy Cavendish observed that men were "quite devoid" of the special capabilities and strengths that women possessed.[50] But both Lucy Cavendish and Emma Cons also recognized that service as poor law guardians, on school boards, and on county councils could give women greater capacity to affect public policy more broadly.

The opposition to women as councillors began immediately after the women's election. Lady Sandhurst's defeated opponent Charles T. Beresford-Hope petitioned at once that her election be declared invalid. The court of first instance ruled that if Parliament had not explicitly declared them as eligible to stand for office then women must perforce be construed as not eligible.[51] Lady Sandhurst's appeal was dismissed and Beresford-Hope assumed her seat. Jane Cobden's election had not been challenged, and Emma Cons's election as alderman by the county councillors themselves was entirely different, but both women knew that they stood at risk of being unseated.[52] It was at this stage that the WLGS swung into action, hoping to extract a favourable outcome from Parliament, notwithstanding the Conservative government. Walter McLaren, together with a number of other sympathetic MPs, introduced a bill in the House of Commons qualifying women as county councillors. The Earl of Meath, a member of the County Council himself, introduced a similar bill in the House of Lords. The WLGS also worked behind the scenes; it was thought that a deputation to Lord Salisbury would be advisable, and it was proposed that Lucy Cavendish would be the perfect candidate. Emma Cons volunteered to sound her out.[53] Lucy Cavendish's diary records no such meeting with Lord Salisbury and, in any event, clearly the authorities in both houses were not sympathetic; they did not employ Whips, and both bills were defeated by large margins.

The question now arose of whether Jane Cobden and Emma Cons could continue to sit. Electoral law at the time declared that although persons might be improperly elected, if they were not successfully challenged after twelve months, their election was deemed to be proper. Thus the strategy now became for both women to keep a low profile, not attend council meetings, and wait for twelve months to pass. Emma Cons immediately resigned her committees and subcommittees and was at once asked by her colleagues to resume her activities as an unofficial co-opted visitor. As soon as the twelve-month period ended and the two women resumed their position on committees and voted, the Tory faction in the council initiated proceedings against them for having acted as councillors – voting when not qualified. Emma Cons declared openly that she would rather go to prison than pay any fine and, in order to avoid creating a sympathetic martyr, the court was persuaded to hear *De Souza v. Cobden* first on the question of voting when not qualified to do so. Emma Cons's companion, Ethel Everest, offered the WLGS (of which she was both a member and staunch supporter) a guarantee of £500 against expenses not defrayed by donations. The court ruled against the women, although it decreased the amount of the fine from £250 to £5 per vote cast.[54] Thus both women were in the invidious position of being able to sit as councillors but not to act as such. Both resumed their seats. Emma Cons wrote to the council that she did so for three reasons: "firstly, as a protest on behalf of the ratepayers and the restricting of their right to choose their representatives, secondly, as a protest on behalf of women against the courts ignoring their 'rights of citizenship' and, probably most importantly, to give the council and the public an opportunity of judging for themselves as to the competency of women to discharge the duties required by the county Council."[55]

The difficulty was that in addition to their being now barred from voting, the women were now also deprived of the ability to actually do the work on the committees. This placed Emma Cons in the enormously frustrating position of being the one member of the Housing of the Working Classes Committee who actually had practical experience with the housing of the working classes. Similarly, it was Emma Cons who had prepared the draft scheme for the inspection of London's baby farms and it was she who had been tasked with furnishing the chairman of the Sanitary Committee with a monthly report on that subject.[56] Moreover, her work on her six committees (and eleven subcommittees) had been a source of great satisfaction to her and had enabled her to influence a number of younger members, most notably W.H. Dickinson, councillor for Wandsworth, and John Benn, who represented Finsbury East.[57] Both would go on to careers as Liberal members of Parliament and to promote significant progressive legislation of their own. The difficulty was temporarily addressed by asking the women to sit on their committees as co-opted visitors, which both were willing to do in order to accomplish the committees' objectives. But by the summer the issue was moot. The council was dissolved and new elections were held to which the women did not have access.

The WLGS now reoriented its efforts from canvassing and campaigning to lobbying. It was at this stage that Lucy Cavendish, returned from Africa, fell into the new work of the WLGS with vigour. Together with her old companion from her late husband's Yorkshire campaigns, Sir James Stansfeld (MP for Halifax), she was unanimously elected vice-president of the WLGS at the March 1895 annual general meeting. Both she and Emma Cons gave their names and their efforts to the cause of women in local government; both spoke at the well-attended public meeting held at St Martin's Hall in February 1896. Lucy Cavendish chaired the annual general meetings of the society and lent her Carlton House Terrace house for them. At the 1899 meeting of the WLGS, in her opening remarks as chair, she reminded her audience "of the importance of women availing themselves of the offices already open to them, since showing capability for public office was the surest means of ultimately procuring their legal eligibility to those greater bodies from which they were as yet excluded."[58] In this, however, she was not referring to the parliamentary franchise but to women standing for poor law guardians and school board guardians (a practice then also under attack), in order to pave the way back to county councils.[59]

This same shift from the personally virtuous Christian duty to the *quid pro quo* of public service for citizenship can be seen concurrently taking place in the development and maturing of a number of the women's philanthropic organizations with which Lucy Cavendish and Emma Cons were affiliated. Formerly concentrating entirely on improving conditions, but not much interested in changing people's attitudes or amending the legislative framework, during this same period some women's charitable organizations began to recognize new priorities and, perforce, employ different methods to attain new ends. Incorporating advocacy within their mission, women's philanthropic organizations started raising the consciousness of, first, the public, then persons of influence, finally lobbying politicians for changes to legislation. We can see a good example of this in the British Women's Temperance Association (in which Emma Cons served as vice-president), which began as an organization devoted to bringing individuals to an abstinent life and which, beginning in the early 1880s, conducted increasingly vigorous campaigns not only to raise public awareness about alcohol's ill effects but also to change Britain's liquor laws. This is an important and revealing shift in priorities and tools because lobbying, petitioning, and advocating for change are all actions taken by citizens asserting their standing to do so.

The same shift occurred, as we have seen, in the Women's Union of the Church of England Temperance Society, which Lucy Cavendish (vigorously) and Emma Cons (quietly) both supported. The Women's Union had been initially established to address drunkenness among women, as female intemperance was widely seen as a growing problem. But like the British Women's Temperance Association, the CETS Women's

Union expanded its methods as it grew. It not only posted members in the police courts to take into care women who had been brought up on charges of public drunkenness, and established and managed the five residential lodges for the reclamation of inebriate women, but around 1880 it also began to advocate for changes in liquor laws. In 1882, its members gathered over 5,000 signatures as part of their effort to aid in the multi-organizational British Women's Petition in favour of the pending Sunday Closing Bill, a petition which in total contained over 159,000 women's signatures and was "over a mile long."[60] By 1884, the Women's Union was campaigning vigorously against the licensing of grocers to sell alcohol. They gathered doctors' opinions and evidence of inebriation for presentation to parliamentary committees and assembled names for petitions to Parliament; in 1884 they solicited over 47,000 signatures. The Women's Union published a pamphlet, *The Evils of Grocers' Licences*, which was circulated widely.[61] They worked vigorously not only to raise public awareness of the dangers to women of licensed grocers but also to affect the votes of members of Parliament. "Legislative Work" quickly became "the most popular element" of the Women's Union mission.[62] The *Temperance Chronicle* reported with satisfaction in May of 1884 on the advocacy effort of the Women's Union. "The state of public business in the House this session has so far blocked the course of Temperance legislation, but the Union may be depended upon to keep this matter before the public until grocers' shops are restored to their legitimate purposes."[63] Whereas, in the 1860s and 1870s, more traditional women's charities such as the Ladies Diocesan Association had used the connections and influence of well-born women to try to improve conditions in workhouses, by the mid-1880s, "Legislative Work" was a separate, and sizeable, section in the Church of England Temperance Society Women's Union Annual Report.

Women were becoming increasingly better trained in organizing through working with charities. Steven King, in his work concerning the philanthropic Mary Haslam of Bolton, *Women, Welfare and Local Politics 1880–1920* (2006), argues that through philanthropy, women were able to acquire and hone important administrative experience: how to chair a meeting, how to streamline authority, how to budget and keep books, how to hold an annual meeting of shareholders and supporters. One of the most important lessons women learned was not to automatically defer to the opinions of the men with whom they sat on committees. In a letter to her sister, Meriel, Lucy Cavendish commented that she had often had to face men, sometimes holding opposing views, at the committee table.[64] Thus many suffragettes, for example, entered the struggle for the vote already well trained in how to organize a campaign. But women came to that struggle feeling increasingly secure about the legitimacy of their citizenly right to attempt to affect public policy. And they joined that fight with sufficient experience in public advocacy and campaigning. The shift in focus by philanthropies from the uncritical and strictly ameliorative to a mission that included advocacy, awareness-raising, and lobbying had broader implications.

This emerging energy and impetus of women's philanthropies to advocate and lobby for change as part of their mission ran concurrent with the emergence of political bodies either established by women, such as the Women's Liberal Federation, founded in 1886, or the Primrose League, which Conservative women could join, founded in 1883. These overtly political bodies were often staffed by the same philanthropic women. Indeed, during this period, many of the same women moved from charity committees to advocacy campaigns and back again, creating a mutually constructive cross-pollinating effect. Experience would be shared, attitudes shaped, tactics for campaigns pooled. This effect can be seen even through looking only at cross-section as small as acquaintances of Emma Cons and Lucy Cavendish: Ishbel, Lady Aberdeen, Louisa Hubbard, the Countess of Meath, Ethel Everest, Louisa Twining, Lady Knightley of Fawsley, Mary Sheepshanks, and Rosalind, Countess of Carlisle all moved back and forth between groups, steering and supporting a variety of women's philanthropies and advocacy groups.[65] This effect is clearly seen in women's political work with official parties. Rosalind, the Countess of Carlisle (president of the BWTA), Helen Gladstone, Lady Aberdeen, and Jane Cobden, together with Emma Cons, formed the executive of the Women's Liberal Federation. Emma Cons held her own with her titled colleagues, often chairing the executive meetings; she brought a great deal to the table. In her memoirs, Lady Aberdeen recalled that whenever she had had to act as chairman at a public meeting where she knew a strong opposing element would be present, she would always be apprehensive until she knew "wonderful" Emma Cons would be there, "and then she always felt a certainty of winning."[66]

Victorian women's growing sense of the legitimacy of their standing to challenge public policy emerged partly through their philanthropic work. The increasing willingness of women who worked with charities to publicly engage in the citizenly activity of attempting to affect legislation also had ripple effects. Women's views of what was acceptable and legitimate advocacy changed. So too, the public's sense of what were permissible limits for women's campaigning also broadened. For much of the nineteenth century, women had used charitable activity as a virtuous shield behind which they could test the limits of acceptable public advocacy. By the end of the century, the sort of private discussion of policy previously restricted to the drawing rooms of elite women had turned into a much more accessible and public debate. This development is an important aspect of identity-formation for Victorian women and is arguably a more significant emergence than a collective turn towards women seeking a vote in parliamentary elections. This public emergence of campaigning women affected how agenda items were determined and what could stand as valid policy. Women's increased public voice shifted the discourse.

But late Victorian women did not focus their efforts solely on "legislative work" or lobbying men on councils and in Parliament. Women spent a great deal of time talking to other women about public policy. Dina Copelman has observed how women's advocacy groups, the Women's Trade Union League, the National Federation of Women Workers, the Anti-Sweating League, shared office space – and common cause – in Mecklenburgh Square.[67] Increasingly, in the last third of the nineteenth century, we see the proliferation of associations organized for the express purpose of women's speaking to each other on matters of social work and social policy. The National Union of Women Workers, the "Parliament of Women" in which Lucy Cavendish served as vice-president, was entirely focused on bringing together women working with different philanthropic organizations and in different campaigns who could offer support and encouragement, share experience in establishing, running, and improving the efficiency of charities, compare lobbying tactics, and learn from each other's experience. The NUWW's committee devoted to law reform and lobbying was extremely popular. At NUWW conferences, women were able to discuss, entirely among themselves, how to work more effectively in their own philanthropies in order to change the landscape of social work among the nation's needy and vulnerable. They heard each other's papers on social reform and the best direction for the nation. The NUWW gave women a forum wherein they could speak to each other about how to affect policy.

In the same way, women established journals aimed exclusively at a female readership, publishing articles on "women's work" (philanthropy) as well as public policy, providing news of meetings and the establishment of new women's associations. *The Women's Penny*

Paper, Woman's Signal, The Englishwoman's Review of Social and Industrial Questions, Waverley, Work and Leisure, The Englishwoman's Year Book, and *Shafts: A Magazine for Progressive Thought* were all established by women, edited by women, and largely written by women, offering fora for discussion of national policy.[68] It is important to note that this substantial genre was entirely separate from the equally significant contingent of women's magazines directed at issues surrounding the cause of women's suffrage.

In short, it was at the point when British women started to speak seriously *to each other* about national policy and how to effect change that they produced a public sphere of their own wherein they could assert a presence, enunciate positions, promote agendas, organize campaigns, and claim an audience of like-minded women citizens.

Conclusion

This book has attempted to illuminate a number of aspects of the Victorian philanthropic world. Primarily, it has sought to represent a picture of the men, and particularly the women, who came together time and again to form and re-form into committees and campaigns, creating the Venn diagrams that made up the interconnected circles of Victorian philanthropy. Using the lives and endeavours of Lucy Cavendish and Emma Cons as a dual case study was not a random choice. Mapping the social geography of philanthropic Victorian society without a frame of reference would have been excessively unwieldy. The lives and philanthropic careers of Lucy Cavendish and Emma Cons created a two-sided point of departure for examining this particular slice of Victorian society. The two women came from very different backgrounds and worked, both together and individually, in many different endeavours over twenty years, providing an excellent perspective from which to analyse how a woman from the elite and a woman from the artisanate approached working with the poor of London. Both women, moreover, were not only part of this web of committees, associations, and campaigns; they are exemplars of those women who knew well how to establish, cultivate, and deploy these networks to further their charitable causes.

Moving from charity committees to advocacy campaigns and back again, men and women created overlapping networks of mutual assistance as they went, establishing lists of who could be called upon to canvass, to chair meetings, to speak, to organize volunteers, to assign work, to mobilize delegations to MPs, and to arrange audits, *gratis*. This can be seen even just looking at a handful of the acquaintances of Emma Cons and Lucy Cavendish. We encounter the same names again

1. Pit and Galleries: An Appreciative Audience.—2. Stalls and Boxes: Burnt-Cork Minstrelsy.—3. The Café: "The Cup which Cheers but not Inebriates."

THE ROYAL VICTORIA COFFEE PALACE AND MUSIC HALL

5 The Royal Victoria Coffee Palace and Music Hall. *The Graphic*, 20 August 1881, 196.

and again. The Earl of Meath was not only an early supporter of Emma Cons in the Coffee Taverns Company but also her colleague on the London County Council. His wife, the Countess of Meath, was not only a supporter of the Old Vic but also sat with Lucy Cavendish as a member of the Women's Union of the CETS. The Countess of Ducie was not only a supporter of the Old Vic but also served with Lucy Cavendish as one of the door-opening aristocrats of the Ladies Diocesan Association. The Duke of Westminster and the Earl of Shaftesbury not only sat on the executive of the CETS but were drawn by Emma Cons to become financial benefactors and governors of the Royal Victoria Hall. Similarly enlisted was the host of the evangelical Broadlands conferences, Lord Mount-Temple, and those who, with Emma Cons, attended his discussions: the contralto (and star of the Old Vic) Antoinette Sterling, for example, the author George MacDonald, and the lawyer, diplomat, and parliamentarian Russell Gurney – the man who had purchased the house in Drury Lane wherein lodged the "Cat and Comfort" coffee tavern that Emma Cons once managed. Alice Hart, who organized the first ballad concert at the Old Vic, was married to Dr Ernest Hart, the editor of the *Lancet*, whose investigation into the state of workhouse infirmaries had worked in tandem with the Ladies Diocesan Association. Lady Lothian, Louisa Twining, Lady Knightley of Fawsley, Ethel Everest, Lady Aberdeen, Louisa Hubbard, Mary Sheepshanks, the Countess of Carlisle, all slid from committees to campaigns, steering and supporting a variety of philanthropies and advocacy groups. In many ways the philanthropically minded formed a kind of village of neighbours where everyone knew whom to call on in time of need.

But overarching this discussion has also been the sense of change, not continuity; that women, in the last third of the nineteenth century, were able to employ their philanthropic work not only to affect the broader debate on public policy, but also, in the process, to construct new identities as citizens. Thus the varied experiences of this complex of women and their colleagues in philanthropy can also serve as entry points through which we may more fully understand the shifts and changes in perceptions of women's identity, role, and place in society during a complicated period.

Emma Cons matured step-by-step with her friend Octavia Hill, both women working in exactly the same enterprises, but Cons developed her own, quite different, philosophy of how to better the lives of the working poor. Emma Cons's origins in the working class (albeit the highest echelon thereof), just as much as her years of experience with her tenants, enabled her to understand the capacities of the men and women who came to the Royal Victoria Hall in ways that Octavia Hill simply did not. It was this same awareness and her forthright practicality that made Cons's judgment and opinion so highly valued for campaigns and on committees. But it was her experience as well as her judgment that enabled her to step out of the pack of temperance advocates and convene and redirect the great and powerful advocates of temperance to help her establish her base of operations in Lambeth. It was this understanding that was responsible for her offering not just engineering, mathematics, and physics, but French and Latin as well as history and literature and politics at Morley College. It was this empathy and comprehension of what her tenants were capable of, as well as her own musical background, that similarly allowed her to see how and why opera could be a great attraction at the Royal Victoria Hall. If others saw entertainment for the masses as a means to distract or possibly pacify, that was a view diametrically opposed to Cons's intention. Where Miranda Hill's Kyrle Society and the attempts by Canon and Henrietta Barnett to bring great music to the East End were frequently received by their intended audiences with indifference or even, occasionally, anger, the opera at the Old Vic was enthusiastically embraced. This was no mystery to Emma Cons. Whereas the dignified chamber music of Toynbee Hall appeared to be detached, icy, and patronizingly free of charge for the poor, the opera at the Old Vic gave its audiences full-throated human passion and the satisfaction of communal, cathartic release – as well as the pleasure of knowing that they were paying threepence for the same singers as sang at Covent Garden. This was something to which the middle-class Hill sisters or the genteel Barnetts or Beatrice Webb never, evidently, twigged.

Lucy Cavendish had interesting and revealing capacities of her own, some of which could be expected from Lord Lyttelton's daughter and some of which are surprising. There was little in her background that would have prepared her for a career in the sort of gritty philanthropy she adopted. The shyness of her youth and the reluctance with which she met the ghoulish celebrity emanating from her husband's murder became transformed into a sort of power. It enabled her, quite comfortably, to prepare former child prostitutes for their first communions, vigorously campaign for women's place in local government, and make speeches, sometimes two a day, on temperance as a women's issue. But, although Cavendish's life was unusual in many respects, in other ways it was also representative. We can see, with Lucy and her aristocratic colleagues, how women of the nobility embraced hands-on work with the poor, even when resident in London, away from their estates and their tenants – when the urban poor in question were not "their" poor. In the same way, we can also see how these women grew in their social awareness, moving from the short-term amelioration of tickets for beef tea and coal into browbeating workhouse gatekeepers and obdurate beadles, progressing to petitions, lobbying, and addressing public rallies. Lucy entirely understood Emma's developing both Morley College's liberal arts curriculum and the Old Vic's program of opera, alternately cajoling and coercing the board of governors of the Royal Victoria Hall into supporting Emma Cons's judgment and decisions. When Lucy Cavendish, to repeat the *Old Vic Magazine*'s obituary, "stood shoulder to shoulder with Emma Cons in putting up the good fight," these two women were a powerful force.[1] Lucy Cavendish's story, just as much as that of Emma Cons, is based in horizons, expanding.

The two women's philanthropic endeavours, specifically their work to affect legislation and policy, placed both of them in the centre of the public sphere. Both women were able to shoulder their way into the debates on public policy but via different paths and employing different implements. Emma Cons's decades of hands-on experience establishing, funding, and managing model worker housing gave her a well-deserved credibility. It was this earned expertise, as much as her perspective as a woman from the upper stratum of the working classes and her innately sound judgment, that gave her access to a variety of public platforms, including an alderman's seat on the London County Council and a chair on the Lushington Committee. Lucy Cavendish had the advantage of social capital through her network of aristocratic connections. Here the presence of the Hon. Caroline Talbot among Lucy's colleagues is most instructive, as she provides a vivid and personal link with the late Georgian world of petticoat politics. Ostensibly the latter had been a time of greater female involvement in the politics of the day, but comparing Mrs Talbot's experience and Lucy Cavendish's political life suggests that mid-Victorian political wives, even those who did not set themselves up as great hostesses in the Glencora Palliser style, were indeed politically involved.

But Lucy also held powerful public celebrity as the nation's "other" public widow – the one who did not shut herself away to mourn her husband for decades, but instead turned herself entirely outwards towards good works. In many ways, Lucy Cavendish did not so much insert herself into the public sphere as the public sphere intruded into her life. First as a part of her husband's and her uncle's political circles, later as her support of worthy causes gave her life purpose, Lucy Cavendish's speeches were reported and read in newspapers. Willingly or not, her life was publicly held up for examination and emulation. In very different ways, using very different equipment, both Lucy Cavendish and Emma Cons planted their voice and presence into the highly charged Victorian debate on what was the optimum public policy for the good of the poor, for women, and for the nation.

But this participation in public dialogue, by both these women, and by their colleagues, highlights a broader shift that took place after the failure of the Second Reform Act to include women as franchise holders. Prior to 1867, women generally tended to express their moral outrage about, for example, the working conditions for children in mines by invoking a "maternalist" indignation arising out of their understanding of (and their seisin over) their own "natural," domestic sphere. Subsequent to the debate over including women in the Second Reform Act, women began to see "women's work" as an effort in furtherance not only of a parochial, but of a national, good. The shift, for many, from women's work as personal Christian duty to women's work as "our bit," as a display of their civic engagement, the *quid pro quo* of women's service to women's citizenship, is a recasting we can see both in the words and the deeds not only of Lucy Cavendish and Emma Cons but also of many others in their circle.

The early stirrings of this shift are evident in the related emergence in the work, for example, of the Ladies Diocesan Association and the Church of England Temperance Society Women's Union. From one perspective, their work might have appeared to be conventional women's "maternalist" charity. But from another, the activities of the women working with these organizations involved identifying laws that were ripe for repeal or reform, gathering petitions, testifying before commissions, pressuring members of Parliament; in short, what they themselves described as "legislative work," all hallmarks of citizenly activity.

In much the same way, this shift is also a part of the formation during this period of a distinct women's public sphere, the emergence of which can be seen in the proliferation of organizations meeting the needs of women to discuss policy matters among themselves. The founding of women's journals of substance, edited by women, featuring articles written by women, points to a desire for women to speak to other women on women's work and how such work affects the state of the nation. The founding (again by women, for women) of associations such as the National Union of Women Workers, or the Women's Union of the Church of England Temperance Society, shows how women created a space where they could discuss among themselves matters of policy and national direction as well as ways and means of implementation.

It is the cautionary tale of the Women's Union of the Church of England Temperance Society that shows how a women's public sphere became increasingly necessary to women during the later nineteenth century. The Ladies Diocesan Association and the Parochial Women's Society, established in the 1860s, relied on stealth and guile to circumvent bishops. By virtue of their small size, their self-financing status, and their network of aristocratic connections, these organizations were able to successfully avoid Anglican authorities. The Women's Union of the CETS, established in 1881, was not so fortunate. Partly because of its size but also because of its high profile and energetic, somewhat glamorous director, the CETS Women's Union was, politely but unequivocally, decapitated, diluted, and absorbed. But unlike the Ladies Diocesan Association and the Parochial Mission Women Society, the CETS Women's Union hadn't much leeway from the start because it had been founded expressly as an auxiliary to, as Archbishop Temple put it, "the great CETS." The women of the CETS Women's Union could be forgiven for forgetting, in their ardour and zeal, that they had to tread lightly or risk hobbling.

But although Lucy Cavendish and Emma Cons serve well as representative case studies, they also bring individual and distinctive colour to the picture. Between the two of them, Emma and Lucy encompass much of the nineteenth century. Emma Cons was born in the first year of Queen Victoria's reign; at the other end, Lucy Cavendish lived to cast a vote in the parliamentary election of 1922, wheeled to the polling station in her bathchair, delighted to vote almost in spite of herself. Both women lived lives filled with philanthropic endeavours and civic activity and both were part of that army of over a million philanthropically engaged women that emerged in the last third of the nineteenth century, grappling with how to better the lives of the vulnerable. But that does not mean that these two women saw their mission as strictly ameliorative; they understood gathering the troops to effect change. They knew how to budget, how to organize, how to encourage supporters, they had access to money, they could command from the stage of a hall. They knew how to mobilize women and men to move boulders out of the path. Likely more than many of their colleagues in these various committees and campaigns, Lucy Cavendish and Emma Cons also understood the capacities of the working poor, both by conviction and by experience. At a time when almost 70 per cent of Britons could not vote for their member of Parliament, these two women grasped the effect of seeding ambition and even, as Graham Wallas put it, discontent in Lambeth. At the Royal Victoria Hall, Lady Frederick Cavendish and Miss Emma Cons, each typifying a different aspect of utterly respectable Victorian womanhood, together waged a campaign of the utmost subversion and in doing so reconstructed much more than their own sense of citizenship.

Notes

Introduction

1 Angela Burdett-Coutts, *Woman's Mission* (London and New York, 1893), 364.
2 Frank Prochaska's *Women and Philanthropy in Nineteenth-Century England* (Oxford, 1980) remains the foundational work on Victorian women's charitable involvement, delineating how Victorian women could move beyond a strictly domestic sphere by engaging in philanthropic work, finding purpose and identity for themselves outside the home while still cloaking themselves in the respectability of virtuous, selfless charity. Julia Parker, in *Women and Welfare: Ten Victorian Women in Public Social Service* (London, 1989), furthered this position, posing ten case studies investigating the motivations of those women who involved themselves so wholeheartedly in philanthropic works. See also Lenore Davidoff, *Worlds Between: Historical Perspectives on Gender and Class* (New York, 1995); Geoffrey Finlayson, *Citizenship, State and Social Welfare in Britain 1830–1990* (Oxford, 1994); Steven King, "WE Might be Trusted," in *Women, Welfare and Local Politics 1880–1920* (Eastbourne, 2006).
3 The Lyttelton peerage dates from 1756, and the baronetcy had been conferred in 1618. The first Baron Lyttelton built Hagley Hall in 1751, although the Lyttelton family had held substantial lands in that area of Worcestershire since the thirteenth century.
4 Lady Knightley Fawsley, *The Journals of Lady Knightley of Fawsley*, ed. Peter Gordon (London, 2005), 23 March 1896, 193.
5 Cicely Hamilton and Lilian Baylis, *The Old Vic* (London, 1926), 262.
6 Lucy Masterman, unpublished biography of Lucy Cavendish, 243, Lucy Masterman Papers, Lucy Cavendish College Archives, Cambridge University.

7 Fawsley, *The Journals of Lady Knightley of Fawsley*, 9 May 1892, 193–4.
8 *Old Vic Magazine*, April 1925, 4.
9 Parker, *Women and Welfare*; Prochaska, *Women and Philanthropy in Nineteenth-Century England*.
10 Alan Kidd, *State, Society and the Poor in Nineteenth-Century England* (London, 1999); F.M.L. Thompson, *The Rise of Respectable Society* (London, 1988).
11 Sophia Lonsdale, *The Recollections of Sophia Lonsdale*, ed. Violet Martineau (London, 1936), 160–6.
12 Patricia Hollis, *Ladies Elect: Women in Local English Government 1865–1914* (London, 1987); Elizabeth Schafer, *Lilian Baylis: A Biography* (Hatfield, 2006); Jonathan Schneer, "Politics and Feminism in 'Outcast London': George Lansbury and Jane Cobden's Campaign for the First London County Council," *Journal of British Studies* 30, no. 1 (January 1991): 63–82.
13 John Booth, *A Century of Theatrical History 1816–1916: The Old Vic* (London, 1917); Richard Findlater, *Lilian Baylis: The Lady* of *the Old Vic* (London, 1975); George Rowell, *The Old Vic Theatre: A History* (Cambridge, 1993).
14 Denis Richards, *Offspring of the Vic: A History of Morley College* (London, 1958).
15 Sheila Fletcher, *Victorian Girls: Lord Lyttelton's Daughters* (London, 1997).
16 Betty Askwith, *The Lytteltons: A Family Chronicle of the Nineteenth Century* (London, 1975).
17 Susan Burman, *Fit Work for Women* (New York, 1977); Lenore Davidoff and Catherine Hall, *Family Fortunes* (Chicago, 1987); Martha Vicinus, *Suffer and Be Still: Women in the Victorian Age* (Bloomington, 1972).
18 The intrinsic identification of domesticity with the middle classes is also contested. Domesticity and evangelical rectitude, it is now argued, were not the exclusive purview of the middle classes in the late eighteenth and early nineteenth centuries; Linda Colley and Peter Mandler point to a cultivating of domesticity, religious observance, and "high morality" among the British landed elite at the turn of the century as a means to consolidate their own authority. Linda Colley, *Britons: Forging the Nation, 1707–1837* (New Haven, 1992), 188–93; Peter Mandler, *Aristocratic Government in the Age of Reform: Whigs and Liberals 1830–1852* (Oxford, 1990). Dror Wahrman similarly sees a cult of domesticity cutting across class lines prior to 1832 and a "colonizing" of the haven of the private sphere by the middle classes, subsequently. Dror Wahrman, *Imagining the Middle Class: The Political Representation of Class in Britain c. 1780–1840* (Cambridge, 1995).
19 Amanda Vickery, "Golden Age to Separate Spheres? A Review of the Categories and Chronology of English Women's History," *Historical Journal (Cambridge, England)* 36, no. 2 (1993): 383–414. See also Kathryn Gleadle,

Borderline Citizens: Women, Gender and Political Culture in Britain 1815–1867 (Oxford, 2009); Eleanor Gordon and Gwyneth Nair, *Public Lives: Women, Family and Society in Victorian Britain* (New Haven, 2003); Clare Midgley, *Feminism and Empire: Women Activists in Imperial Britain 1790–1865* (Abingdon, 2007); M.J. Peterson, "No Angels in the House: The Victorian Myth and the Paget Women," *American Historical Review* 89, no. 3 (June 1984): 677–708; Martin Pugh, *The March of the Women: A Revisionist Analysis of the Campaign for Women's Suffrage 1866–1914* (Oxford, 2000); Jane Rendall, "Women and the Public Sphere," *Gender and History* 11, no. 3 (1999): 475–88; Pat Thane, "Late Victorian Women," in *Later Victorian Britain*, ed. Terry Gourvish and Alan O'Day (London, 1988).

20 K.D. Reynolds, *Aristocratic Women and Political Society in Victorian England* (Oxford, 1998). See also Kathryn Gleadle and Sarah Richardson, eds., *Women in British Politics 1760–1860: The Power of the Petticoat* (Basingstoke and New York, 2000).

21 Jane Rendall, "Citizenship, Culture and Civilisation: The Languages of British Suffragists 1866–1874," in *Suffrage and Beyond: International Feminist Perspectives*, ed. Melanie Nolan and Caroline Daley (Auckland, 1994); "The Citizenship of Women and the Reform Act of 1867," in *Defining the Victorian Nation: Class, Race, Gender, and the Second Reform Act of 1867*, ed. Catherine Hall, Jane Rendall, and Keith McClelland (Cambridge, 2000). Citizenship could also be a matter of class; Lydia Murdoch, in *Imagined Orphans: Poor Families, Child Welfare and Contested Citizenship in London* (London, 2006), argues that social welfare authorities saw significant distinctions between working-class and middle-class citizenship.

22 Anna Clark, "Gender, Class and the Nation: Franchise Reform in England, 1832–1928," in *Re-reading the Constitution: New Narratives in the Political History of England's Long Nineteenth Century*, ed. James Vernon (Cambridge, 1996).

23 Julia Parker, *Citizenship, Work and Welfare: Searching for the Good Society* (Basingstoke, 1998).

24 Eugenio Biagini, "Liberalism and Direct Democracy: J.S. Mill and the Model of Ancient Athens," in *Citizenship and Community: Liberals, Radicals and Collective Identities in the British Isles 1865–1931* (Princeton, 1996), 21–44. This theme of public duty has also been explored by a variety of historians in Peter Mandler and Susan Pedersen's *After the Victorians: Private Conscience and Public Duty in Modern Britain* (London, 1994). Frank Prochaska has also recently contributed to the study of citizenship with *Christianity and Social Service in Modern Britain: The Disinherited Spirit* (Oxford, 2006) and the smaller study *Schools of Citizenship: Charity and Civic Virtue* (London, 2002).

25 Laura Nym Mayhall, *The Militant Suffragette Movement* (New York, 2003); Marian Sawer, "Gender, Metaphor and the State," *Feminist Review* 52, no. 1 (1996): 118–34. See also Stefan Collini, *Public Moralists: Political Thought and Intellectual Life in Britain 1850–1930* (Oxford, 1991); Susan Pedersen, "Gender, Welfare, and Citizenship in Britain during the Great War," *American Historical Review* 95, no. 4 (October 1990): 983–1006; Susan Pedersen, *Eleanor Rathbone and the Politics of Conscience* (New Haven, 2004).

26 This anti-suffrage position was not all that uncommon among women, and debate about the "antis" has become a livelier issue since Brian Harrison's 1978 account of the opponents of women's suffrage, *Separate Spheres: The Opposition to Women's Suffrage* (London, 1978), was recently joined by two contributions by Julia Bush: *Women against the Vote: Female Anti-Suffragism in Britain* (Oxford, 2007) and "The National Union of Women Workers and Women's Suffrage," in *Suffrage outside Suffragism*, ed. M. Boussahba-Bavard (Basingstoke, 2007).

27 Colley, *Britons*, 280.

28 Keir Hardie would disagree. In a 1905 article entitled "The Citizenship of Women," published in the *Review of Reviews* (and later, separately, in 1906, as a pamphlet), he had averred that following the unsuccessful attempt to bootstrap women into the Second Reform Act, all discussion of women's citizenship had died away. Keir Hardie, *The Citizenship of Women* (London, 1906).

29 Ian Fletcher, "Some Aspects of Aestheticism" in *Twilight of the Dawn: Studies in English Literature*, ed. O.M. Brack, Jr (Tucson, 1987).

30 Diana Maltz, *British Aestheticism and the Urban Working Classes 1870–1900* (Basingstoke, 2006); Ruth Livesey, *Socialism, Sex and the Culture of Aestheticism* (London, 2006).

31 These are also elements which Seth Koven has also addressed in greater detail in his work on "The Whitechapel Picture Exhibitions and the Politics of Seeing," in *Museum Culture*, ed. D. Sherman and I. Rogoff (Minneapolis, 1994), as have Geoffrey Budge in "Poverty and the Picture Gallery: The Whitechapel Exhibitions and the Social Project of Ruskinian Aesthetics," *Visual Culture in Britain* 1 (2000): 43–56, and Giles Waterfield in his catalogue for the Dulwich Picture Gallery exhibition, *Art for the People: Culture in the Slums of Late Victorian Britain* (Dulwich, 2000).

32 Michael Lang, *Designing Utopia: John Ruskin's Urban Vision for Britain and America* (Montreal, 1999); Peter Stansky, *Redesigning the World: William Morris, the 1880's and the Arts and Crafts* (Princeton, 1985); Gill G. Cockram, *Ruskin and Social Reform: Ethics and Economics in the Victorian Age* (London, 2007); Sharon Aronofsky Weltman, *Performing the Victorian: John Ruskin and Identity in Theater, Science, and Education* (Cleveland, 2007); David Craig, *John Ruskin and the Ethics of Consumption* (Charlottesville, 2006).

1. Lucy Cavendish

1 Lady Frederick Cavendish, *The Diary of Lady Frederick Cavendish*, ed. John Bailey (New York, 1927), 1:192, 4 December 1863.

2 Ibid., 1:194.

3 K.D. Reynolds, *Aristocratic Women and Political Society in Victorian England* (Oxford, 1998), 111, 112; Kathryn Gleadle, *British Women in the Nineteenth Century* (London, 2001).

4 Reynolds, *Aristocratic Women*, 111, 112.

5 17 February 1887, Lyttelton Family Papers, 29/2/2/48, Hagley Hall Archives.

6 The particular ability of aristocratic women to use Anglican charitable works as a wedge with which to gain entry into public life is discussed more fully in chapter 2, "Circumventing the Bishops: Women's Philanthropy and the Church of England."

7 Lenore Davidoff and Catherine Hall, *Family Fortunes* (Chicago, 1987); Martha Vicinus, *Suffer and Be Still: Women in the Victorian Age* (Bloomington, 1972); and Susan Burman, *Fit Work for Women* (New York, 1977).

8 Kathryn Gleadle, *Borderline Citizens: Women, Gender and Political Culture in Britain 1815–1867* (Oxford, 2009); Kathryn Gleadle and Sarah Richardson, eds., *Women in British Politics 1760–1860: The Power of the Petticoat* (Basingstoke and New York, 2000).

9 Reynolds, *Aristocratic Women*.

10 Lucy Masterman, unpublished biography of Lucy Cavendish, Masterman Papers, Lucy Cavendish College Archives, Cambridge University, p. 1.

11 Sheila Fletcher, *Victorian Girls* (London, 1997), 2.

12 Ibid., 13.

13 Cavendish, *The Diary of Lady Frederick Cavendish*, 1:70, 75.

14 Lord and Lady Aberdeen, *Reminiscences* (London, 1926), 1:135.

15 Ibid.

16 Cavendish, *The Diary of Lady Frederick Cavendish*, 1:252.

17 Hugh McLeod, *Class and Religion in the Late Victorian City* (London, 1974), 201.

18 Betty Askwith, *The Lytteltons: A Family Chronicle of the Nineteenth Century* (London, 1975), 48. Lord Lyttelton was also, at a time when he could ill afford it, one of the strongest of supporters of the Canterbury Association, a group headed by the Archbishop of Canterbury and involving a number of peers and bishops, who organized the establishment of a small but resolutely middle-class Anglican colony of 107 settlers on the South Island of New Zealand. Hence the naming of the port of the Canterbury Region as Lyttelton Harbour.

19 D.W. Bebbington, *Evangelicalism in Modern Britain: A History from the 1730's to the 1980's* (London, 1989), 2–12; see also Boyd Hilton, *The Age of Atonement: The Influence of Evangelicalism on Social and Economic Thought 1795–1865* (Oxford, 1988).
20 Askwith, *The Lytteltons*, 51, 162.
21 Cavendish, *The Diary of Lady Frederick Cavendish*, 1:127.
22 Lucy and her sister Meriel made their débuts in 1861, together with their cousin Agnes Gladstone, from the Gladstones' house, 11 Carlton House Terrace. Memoirs of Meriel Talbot, née Lyttelton, Talbot Family Papers, U1612 F104, Centre for Kentish Studies, Kent County Archives, Maidenhead; Georgina Battiscombe, *Mrs. Gladstone* (London, 1957), 116, 117.
23 John Bailey, Introduction to *The Diary of Lady Frederick Cavendish*, 1:xiv. See also Lady Lyttelton, *Correspondence of Sarah Spencer* (London, 1912).
24 Cavendish, *The Diary of Lady Frederick Cavendish*, 1:165.
25 Lady Knightley Fawsley, *The Journals of Lady Knightley of Fawsley*, ed. Peter Gordon (London, 2005), 68, 9 January 1864.
26 Ibid., 69, 11 January 1864.
27 Cavendish, *The Diary of Lady Frederick Cavendish*, 1:198, 14 January 1864.
28 The Hon. Lucy Lyttelton and Lord Frederick Cavendish were third cousins, Lord Lyttelton having been second cousin to Lord Frederick's mother, but there is no indication that the two met until a year or so prior to their becoming engaged.
29 Cavendish, *The Diary of Lady Frederick Cavendish*, 1: 246, 27 October 1864.
30 It was here that Lucy Cavendish first became acquainted with the Bristol philanthropist Samuel Morley, who would become such a great benefactor of both the Old Vic and Morley College. See chapters 4 and 5.
31 The three women, as recalled by Lucy's sister Meriel, had first met in 1852 when Mrs Talbot's husband, John Chetwynd Talbot, had unexpectedly died during a visit to Brighton. "Mrs. Gladstone, who knew them a little, happened to be also staying at Brighton and with the warm-hearted sympathy which was such a strong characteristic of her, she went at once to see if she could be of any comfort to Mrs. Talbot alone in the hotel. This naturally led to a great friendship, first with the Gladstones and afterwards with my parents." The Talbots and the Lyttletons visited each other frequently and also took holidays together at St Leonards, "Mrs. Talbot reading *Kenilworth* to us." During her last confinement, Lucy's mother was nursed by Mrs Gladstone and Mrs Talbot, and "I cannot say how much and in how many big and little ways dear Mrs. Talbot helped and cheered my mother during the last years of failing health." Lucy's two sisters,

Meriel and Lavinia, went on to marry Mrs Talbot's two sons, John and Edward. Memoirs of Meriel Talbot, née Lyttelton, Talbot Family Papers, U1612 F104.

32 Battiscombe, *Mrs. Gladstone*, 95. Mrs Talbot was also the great-granddaughter of the great traveller Lady Mary Wortley-Montagu.

33 Fletcher, *Victorian Girls*, 45

34 The Parochial Mission Women Society is the subject of study in chapter 2, below.

35 23 February 1877, Correspondence of Lucy Cavendish, Lyttelton Family Papers, 33/2/49.

36 Cavendish, *The Diary of Lady Frederick Cavendish*, 1:298, 13 February 1866.

37 Ibid., 1:300, 301, 2 March 1866.

38 The Ladies Diocesan Association is the subject of greater scrutiny in chapter 2, below.

39 Cavendish, *The Diary of Lady Frederick Cavendish*, 2:25, 20 February 1867.

40 Ibid., 1:253, 10 March 1865.

41 The hamper was evidently greatly appreciated, particularly the wine and arrowroot, according to the entry of 17 March 1865.

42 Ladies who were part of the Ladies Diocesan Association.

43 Lucy Cavendish's friend Charlotte Seymour had, in 1858, married the fifth Earl Spencer (the "Red Earl") and become Countess Spencer. Cavendish, *The Diary of Lady Frederick Cavendish*, 1:255, 17 March 1865.

44 Aberdeen, *Reminiscences*, 1:148.

45 Cavendish, *The Diary of Lady Frederick Cavendish*, 2:80, 26 February 1870.

46 Ibid., 2:31, 29 April 1867.

47 Ibid., 2:7, 15 May 1866.

48 Ibid., 1:114, 115, 24 and 29 April 1861.

49 Pat Jalland, *Women, Marriage and Politics 1860–1914* (Oxford, 1986).

50 Elaine Chalus, "That Epidemical Madness: Women and Electoral Politics in the Late Eighteenth Century," in Hannah Barker and Elaine Chalus, *Gender in Eighteenth-Century England: Roles, Representations and Responsibilities* (London and New York, 1997); Linda Colley, *Britons: Forging the Nation, 1707–1837* (New Haven, 1992); Dror Wahrman, *Imagining the Middle Class: The Political Representation of Class in Britain c. 1780–1840* (Cambridge, 1995); Amanda Foreman, *Georgiana, Duchess of Devonshire* (London, 1998).

51 Diaries of Caroline Talbot, Talbot Family Papers, U1612 F29.

52 There is greater certainty and consensus that after the passage of the Corrupt Practices Act of 1883, which barred the paying of canvassers, women instantly became political creatures, as once again they held both election duties as unpaid canvassers and the power that went with candidates' reliance on same.

53 K.D. Reynolds and Peter Mandler, "From Allmack's to Willis': Aristocratic Women and Politics 1815–1867," in *Women, Privilege and Power: British Politics 1750 to the Present*, ed. Amanda Vickery (London, 2001).
54 G.E. Maguire, *Conservative Women: A History of Women and the Conservative Party, 1874–1997* (London, 1998); James Vernon, *Politics and the People* (Cambridge, 1993); Gleadle and Richardson, eds., *Women in British Politics 1760–1860*; Jalland, *Women, Marriage and Politics 1860–1914*.
55 Cavendish, *The Diary of Lady Frederick Cavendish*, 1:276, 13 July 1865.
56 Ibid., 2:246, 247, 5 April 1880.
57 Ibid., 1:272, 24 June 1865.
58 Ibid., 2:8, 31 May 1866.
59 Battiscombe, *Mrs. Gladstone*, 177.
60 Gladstone's principal private secretary, Sir William Hamilton, also received his information of Gladstone's abating reluctance to accept a peerage not directly, but from Lucy Cavendish, in May 1883. *Diaries of Sir Edward Walter Hamilton 1883–1885*; ed. Dudley Bahlman (Oxford, 1972), 435.
61 Cavendish, *The Diary of Lady Frederick Cavendish*, 2:83, 17 June 1870.
62 Ibid., 1:303–4, 13 April 1866.
63 Ibid., 2:199, 2–8 October 1876.
64 *Diaries of Sir Edward Walter Hamilton*, 2:594.
65 Cavendish, *The Diary of Lady Frederick Cavendish*, 1:xvi.
66 John Booth, in his history of the Old Vic, maintains that the idea of renting the Royal Victoria Theatre came from John Hollingshead of the Gaiety Theatre, who approached the committee hoping to become the theatre's manager. John Booth, *A Century of Theatrical History 1816–1916: The Old Vic* (London, 1917), 59.
67 Ibid., 52.
68 A.E. Dingle, "Drink and Working-Class Living Standards in Britain 1870–1914," *Economic History Review* 25, no. 4 (1972): 608.
69 Account of the annual meeting of the Women's Union, CETS, 2 May 1890, Church of England Temperance Society (CETS) Archives, Lambeth Palace.
70 Cavendish, *Diary of Lady Frederick Cavendish*, 2:194, 6 February 1876.
71 Masterman, biography of Lucy Cavendish, 147–9.
72 Lyttelton Family Papers, 33/3/1.
73 Diary of Lady Frederick Cavendish, vol. 14, Cavendish Family Papers, Chatsworth Archives.
74 19 September 1885, Lucy Cavendish to Meriel Talbot, Lucy Cavendish Correspondence, LCCA/LR7/1, Lucy Cavendish College Archives, Cambridge University.

75 *Pall Mall Gazette*, 31 October 1892, 5. Lucy Cavendish came to know Beatrice Temple well through their common Devonshire connection, as Beatrice's elder sister Emma had married Lord Frederick Cavendish's brother William; Beatrice used to accompany her sister to Chatsworth for Christmas and other family occasions. The two young women first became acquainted in 1864, when Lucy Lyttelton married Lord Frederick Cavendish, and they quickly became good friends, Lucy's letters to "dear old B" showing a level of jolly intimacy not used with anyone else except her sisters; writing to her aunt Mrs Gladstone in 1897, Lucy recounted that "Beatrice Temple's account of the state of the Lambeth drains is enough to make one's hair stand on end." 11 February 1897, Lyttelton Family Papers, 29/10/36.

76 Recollection of the Bishop of London, *Church of England Temperance Chronicle*, 28 May 1885.

77 *Funny Folks*, 15 October 1892, 330.

78 Masterman, biography of Lucy Cavendish, 149–150a. See also letter to Mrs Flower (Lady Battersea), 10 November 1903, Add. Man. 47911 ff101, British Library, declining to make speeches for an organization to which she had no connection.

79 CETS *Temperance Chronicle*, 3 April 1896.

80 Upon the death of her brother Arthur Lyttelton, Bishop of Southampton, in 1903 and that of his wife, Kitty Clive, four years later, Lucy Cavendish happily took in their daughter, Margaret, making the arrangements for her marriage to Launcelot Becher in 1914. Masterman, biography of Lucy Cavendish, 149–150a.

81 Ibid.

82 *Daily News*, 10 February 1882.

83 This association continued to the next generation as Princess Christian's daughter, Princess Marie Louise, became not only a great supporter of the Hall but its official patron.

84 *Morning Post*, 5 December 1885, 5.

85 Annual Report of the Royal Victoria Hall, 1884, 5, Old Vic Archives, Bristol University.

86 Old Vic Archives, OVEC/000180/5. This idea of silk farming had also intrigued Lucy Cavendish, who had attempted to interest the Irish in starting a sericulture cooperative.

87 Dr Hack Tuke, *A Dictionary of Psychological Medicine* (Philadelphia, 1892), 56.

88 Alexander Walk, *Psychiatry in the 1870's: A Centenary of the Mental After-Care Association*, excerpt from the first paper read by Dr Henry Hawkins, 5 June 1879.

89 Masterman, biography of Lucy Cavendish, 96.
90 Sheila Fletcher has speculated that it was to avoid exactly this occurring that Lord Lyttelton threw himself over the staircase banister when his valet was distracted. Fletcher, *Victorian Girls*, 191–4.
91 His appointment had surprised some. Sir William Harcourt saw Lord Frederick as not only a "man whom all like and respect" but also as being actually "too good for the job." Lucy Masterman notebooks, 46/3/1, Masterman Family Papers, University of Birmingham Archives. His son, Lewis Harcourt, was characteristically waspish: "I can't conceive of a worse appointment at a time like this ... but I suppose it is all the result of Lady Frederick's being Mrs. Gladstone's niece." Patrick Jackson, *Harcourt and Son: A Political Biography of Sir William Harcourt, 1827–1904* (Cranbury, NJ, 2004) 105. Lewis Harcourt's Journal, Bodeleian Library, Oxford, 4 May 1882. But Lewis Harcourt did not much like Lucy Cavendish; he found her "a bit of a prig and a good deal of a prude," *Loulou: Selected Extracts from the Journals of Lewis Harcourt (1880–1895)*, ed. Patrick Jackson (Danvers, Mass., 2006), 31, 5 November, 1881.
92 Masterman, biography of Lucy Cavendish, 138.
93 *Diaries of Sir Edward Walter Hamilton 1880–1885*, 266.
94 *Punch*, 2 May 1882; *Journal du Grande Monde*, 1 June 1882.
95 *Pall Mall Gazette*, 9 May 1883, 3.
96 *Court and High Life*, 1 June 1882, 10.
97 *Moonshine*, 3 February 1883. Nine months later, as the conspirators' trial opened, the whole cycle of morbid fascination began anew: for example, the *Penny Illustrated Paper* ran "Illustrations of the murderers and their haunts. Maps of their routes to Phoenix Park." 24 February 1883, 116.
98 Earl Spencer included Lucy Cavendish's letter in his address to, among other institutions, the Belfast Chamber of Commerce, and it was published broadly through the empire, appearing in, for example, the *New Zealand Tablet* 10, no. 483 (14 July 1882): 5; the *Calcutta Liberal and New Dispensation* 1, no. 23 (11 June 1882): 1; and a Boston periodical for the Roman Catholic community, *Donohoe's Magazine* 8 (July 1882–January 1883): 90.
99 Letter from Mary Gladstone, Add. Man. 46235, fo. 217, British Library.
100 Stephen Gladstone, "A Life Given for Ireland: A sermon preached at the dedication of a memorial window erected by the men employed in the iron and steel works to the late Lord Frederick Cavendish" (London, 1883).
101 The sermon, drawing parallels between the sacrifices of Lord Frederick Cavendish and Christ, was published as a bound pamphlet by Rivington's.

102 Pat Jalland, *Death in the Victorian Family* (New York, 1996); Philip Ariès, *Western Attitudes towards Death, The Hour of Our Death* (New York, 1981); David Cannadine, "War and Death: Grieving and Death in Modern Britain," in *Mirrors of Mortality: Studies in the Social History of Death*, ed. J. Whaley (London, 1981).

103 Lucy Cavendish's niece Lucy Masterman recalls, in her biography of her aunt, how Lucy Cavendish came to London in 1914 to hear the Third Reading in the House of Commons of the Home Rule (for Ireland) Bill from the Ladies Gallery, procured for her by Lucy Masterman's husband, Charles Masterman, then an MP. "He and my mother were standing in the lobby with Lucy when John Redmond, the leader of the Irish Nationalist cause came by. My mother, who had a taste for historical occasions, whispered to my husband, 'introduce Aunt Lucy to Redmond.' He did so, they shook hands and she congratulated him on what seemed the final success of the Home Rule Bill. He accepted this formally at first, but as she moved away he turned on my husband and said, 'Who did you say that was?' When he was told, he stood dumb-founded for a moment and then said, 'Well, that's the most generous thing I have ever known.' He looked as if he was in church, my mother said." Masterman, biography of Lucy Cavendish, 234.

104 17 February 1883, Lyttelton Family Papers, 29/2/3/5.

105 Cavendish, *The Diary of Lady Frederick Cavendish*, 1:xxviii.

106 Diary of Lady Frederick Cavendish, vol. 14, Cavendish Family Papers.

107 Masterman, biography of Lucy Cavendish, 257.

108 Ibid., 145.

109 Talbot Family Papers, U1612 Q19. This was a common feature of penitentiaries. See Paula Bartley, *Prostitution Prevention and Reform in England 1860–1914* (London, 2000), 25–38; Rebecca Lea McCarthy, *Origins of the Magdalene Laundries: An Analytical History* (Jefferson, NC, 2010).

110 *Man about Town*, 9 June 1883; *Country Gentleman*, 9 June 1883, 678; *Vanity Fair*, 23 June 1883, 339.

111 *Diaries of Sir Edward Walter Hamilton*, 2:453.

112 *Diaries of William Ewart Gladstone*, 11 March 1883.

113 Masterman, biography of Lucy Cavendish, 145.

114 9 August 1898, Lyttelton Family Papers, 29/10/47.

115 Fletcher, *Victorian Girls*, ix.

116 Add. Man. 46235, fo. 227, British Library.

117 7 July 1884, Lavinia Talbot to Mary Gladstone, Add. Man. 46238, fo. 223, British Library.

118 9 July 1884, Lucy Cavendish to Mary Gladstone from Bolton Abbey, Skipton, Add. Man. 46235, fo. 228, British Library.
119 Lord Lyttelton had been one of the original founders of the Girls Public Day School Trust (soon incorporated as the Girls Public Day School Company) but had proposed that his daughter Lucy should assume his position on the Executive Committee soon after.
120 5 November 1874, Lucy Cavendish to her father, Lyttelton Family Papers, 25/8/65/1.
121 She remained president until 1912.
122 Archives of the Yorkshire Ladies Council of Education, WYL5045, Leeds University.
123 It was for her work with the Yorkshire Ladies Council of Education that the University of Leeds bestowed its first LLD *honoris causa* on Lucy Cavendish in 1904.
124 Edith Lyttelton, *Alfred Lyttelton – An Account of His Life* (London, 1917), 161.
125 10 September 1888, Masterman, biography of Lucy Cavendish, 159.
126 Mrs Massingberd, a woman who had failed by only twenty votes to secure election as county councillor for Lindsey in Lincolnshire and who had a residence in London, was the third name that was suggested to the Progressives at this time. *Miss Emma Cons and Miss Jane Cobden*. Local Government 1889, Cobden MSS 348, Cobden Family Papers, West Sussex Record Office.
127 Masterman, biography of Lucy Cavendish, 203.
128 1 November 1909, Old Vic Archives, OVLB/000047/2.9/1/B2.
129 12 April 1897, Old Vic Archives, OV/M/000002.
130 30 January 1904, Old Vic Archives, OV/M/000004.
131 13 May 1913, Lyttelton Family Papers, 33/3/84. Morley College Archives, IV/224/1/1/2, Borough of Lambeth Archives.
132 22 October 1913, Lyttelton Family Papers, 33/3/87.
133 Old Vic Archives, OV/M/000015/1.
134 Denis Richards, *Offspring of the Vic: A History of Morley College* (London, 1958), 124. Morley College Archives, IV/224/1/1/2.
135 5 May 1911, Old Vic Archives, OVEC/000132.
136 22 October 1913, Lucy Cavendish to Lavinia Talbot, Lyttelton Family Papers, 33/3/87.
137 1 January 1904, Old Vic Archives, OV/M/000002-13; OVEC/000132.
138 17 February 1904, Old Vic Archives, OV/M/000002-13.
139 21 January 1904, Old Vic Archives, OVEC/000133.

140 This was a thankless task and likely no one wanted it, but the point is that Lucy Cavendish was trusted not to make a muddle of it. Old Vic Archives, OVLB/000047/2.9/1/B2.
141 Archives of the Women's Liberal Federation, DM1193/4/2, University of Bristol Archives.
142 16 March 1892, Masterman Family Papers, L. Add/122, University of Birmingham Archives.
143 A point of some frustration and sorrow for Lucy's cousin Mary Gladstone, a suffrage supporter.
144 15 January 1867, diary of Lady Frederick Cavendish, vol. 14, Cavendish Family Papers.
145 Neither did those of her sisters, Lavinia and Meriel, who shared her views. Interestingly, their much younger brother Alfred, arguably being almost of another generation, was a strong supporter of votes for women, as was their next younger brother, Arthur Lyttelton, Bishop of Southampton, who supported his wife, Kathleen, in her suffrage work.
146 Another co-signatory was Beatrice Webb, then Miss Potter. Although Beatrice Webb later repudiated her signing, Lucy Cavendish never did.
147 Mrs Humphry Ward et al., "An Appeal against Female Suffrage," *The Nineteenth Century* 25 (June 1889).
148 27 November 1888, Lucy Cavendish correspondence with Gladstone family, Add. Man. 46235 fo. 239, British Library.
149 Fawsley, *The Journals of Lady Knightley of Fawsley*, 1:37, 9 May 1892.
150 The WLGS was the new name for the Society for the Promotion of Women as County Councillors.
151 Fletcher, *Victorian Girls*, 50.
152 22 February 1878, Lyttelton Family Papers, 33/2/61.
153 "Mrs. Sophie Bryant, D.Sc.," *The Woman at Home*, 1897, p. 197.
154 Julia Bush, *Women against the Vote: Female Anti-Suffragism in Britain* (Oxford, 2007).
155 The most comprehensive account of the WLGS is found in Patricia Hollis, *Ladies Elect: Women in Local English Government 1865–1914* (London, 1987).
156 It was here that Lucy Cavendish met Bertha Christian, the woman who would be her secretary and companion until her death in 1924. According to Lucy Cavendish's niece, Lucy Masterman, Bertha Christian's father had run through the entirety of his capital, and on his death his daughter was left destitute. Having no other means of support, she went to the St Mary's Home to work with the street girls. But, "having no knowledge

of prostitution or the facts of life," she was very unhappy, and so Lucy Cavendish took her to London as a companion and secretary, a position she evidently discharged very satisfactorily. Lucy Masterman notebooks, Masterman Family Papers, 46/3/1, University of Birmingham Archives.

157 18 September 1901, Lucy Cavendish Papers, Lucy Cavendish College, Cambridge.

158 Report of the Annual Meeting, 1901, 24, Archives of the National Union of Women Workers, Fawcett Library. For works which analyse the role of the NUWW in greater detail, see Frank Prochaska, *Women and Philanthropy in Nineteenth Century England* (Oxford, 1980); Hollis, *Ladies Elect*; Serena Kelly, "A Sisterhood of Service: The Records and Early History of the National Union of Women Workers," *Journal of the Society of Archivists* 14, no. 2 (1993): 181–3, Julia Bush, "The National Union of Women Workers and Women's Suffrage," in *Suffrage outside Suffragism*, ed. Myriam Boussahba-Bruard (Basingstoke, 2007); and Daphne Glick, *The National Council of Women of Great Britain: The First One Hundred Years 1895–1994* (Ipswich, 1995).

159 Mrs Arthur Lyttelton quoted in Glick, *The National Council of Women*, 11.

160 Julia Bush has observed that this figure may involve some double-dipping, as women not infrequently belonged to two member organizations. Bush, "The National Union of Women Workers and Women's Suffrage," 130n40.

161 For a thorough discussion of the impact of the suffrage movement on the NUWW, see ibid.

162 Late autumn 1890, diary of Lady Frederick Cavendish, Cavendish Family Papers, vol. 14.

163 31 July 1888, Alfred Lyttelton to Lucy Cavendish, Lucy Cavendish Papers, Lucy Cavendish College, Cambridge University.

164 *Diaries of Sir Edward Walter Hamilton*, 2:564.

165 6 March 1894, Lucy Cavendish to Lavinia Talbot, Lyttelton Family Papers, 33/4/47.

166 Thursday, 19 March 1895, Mr Arthur Acland, Hansard, House of Commons Debates, vol. 31, c. 1423.

167 2 March 1894, Lucy Cavendish to Lavinia Talbot, Lyttelton Family Papers, 33/3/46.

168 ED12/11–12; ED 24/1864; ED90/144, National Archives, Royal Commission on Secondary Education, 1895, 140–1.

169 Ibid.; Joyce Goodman, "Constructing Contradiction: The Power and Powerlessness of Women in the Giving and Taking of Evidence in the Bryce Commission 1895," *History of Education* 26, no. 3 (1997): 287–306.

170 Masterman, biography of Lucy Cavendish, 240.
171 Richard Findlater, *Lilian Baylis: The Lady of the Old Vic* (London, 1975), 98; Booth, *A Century of Theatrical History*, 68.
172 Findlater, *Lilian Baylis*, 101.
173 *Old Vic Magazine* 6, no. 7 (May 1925): 4.

2. Circumventing the Bishops: Women's Philanthropy and the Church of England

1 The speaker was the wife of Lucy's brother, General Neville Masterman. Lucy Masterman, unpublished biography of Lucy Cavendish, Lucy Masterman Papers, Lucy Cavendish College Archives, Cambridge University, p. 244; Lady Frederick Cavendish, *The Diary of Lady Frederick Cavendish*, ed. John Bailey (New York, 1927), Introduction, xxiii.
2 Lucy Cavendish participated actively in Church Congresses and corresponded with the Archbishop of Canterbury, who frequently solicited her counsel on a number of subjects, including the Deceased Wife's Sister Bill and the disestablishment of the Welsh Church.
3 Anthony Wohl, *The Eternal Slum: Housing and Social Policy in Victorian London* (London, 1977), 8–9. See also Boyd Hilton, *The Age of Atonement: The Influence of Evangelicalism on Social and Economic Thought, 1795–1865* (Oxford, 1988) and Gertrude Himmelfarb, *The Idea of Poverty: England in the Early Industrial Age* (New York, 1985).
4 Octavia Hill, *Fortnightly Review* 6 (November 1866): 682.
5 Thomas Hughes, Prefatory to Charles Kingsley, *Alton Locke* (Edinburgh, 1881).
6 Edward Norman, *The Victorian Christian Socialists* (Cambridge, 2002), 8.
7 Frank Prochaska, *Women and Philanthropy in Nineteenth Century England* (Oxford, 1980), 171–3; M.J.D. Roberts, "Feminism and the State in Later Victorian England," *Historical Journal* 38, no. 1 (1995): 85–110.
8 Kathryn Gleadle, *British Women in the Nineteenth Century* (Basingstoke, 2001), 67.
9 William Archibald Tait, *Catherine and Craufurd Tait, Wife and Son of Archibald Campbell, Archbishop of Canterbury, a Memoir, edited at the Request of the Archbishop*, ed. William Benham (London, 1882), 38.
10 Cavendish, *The Diary of Lady Frederick Cavendish*, 252.
11 Tait, *Catherine and Craufurd Tait* (London, 1882), 38.
12 Louisa Twining, *Recollections of workhouse visiting and managing during twenty-five years* (London, 1880), appendix 1, 103.
13 Tait, *Catherine and Craufurd Tait*, 38.

14 Twining, *Recollections of workhouse visiting*, 90.
15 The Earl and Countess of Ducie purchased seven of the tenements at Barrett's Court that Octavia Hill turned over to Emma Cons's management.
16 Ernest Hart was also the husband of Alice Hart (Henrietta Barnett's sister), the colleague of Emma Cons who, in the first week of performances at the reconstituted Old Vic, had volunteered to organize concerts of classical music. See chapter 4, p. 141.
17 Lady Frederick Cavendish, "Parochial Mission Women," *Mission Life*, vol. 10, part 2 (London, 1878), 449–56, 450. The Society's name was loosely applied; sometimes in their literature it was referred to as the Parochial Mission Women Association; more often, as the Parochial Mission Women Society.
18 Vice-Chancellor Sir William Page Wood, "Parochial Mission Women," paper read at the Church Congress, 15 October 1863, 10.
19 Jane Elliott, *A Servant of the Poor, or Some Account of the Life and Death of a Parochial Mission Woman* (London, 1874) 17.
20 Cavendish, "Parochial Mission Women," 455.
21 *Church of England Temperance Chronicle*, 17 March 1883.
22 Cavendish, "Parochial Mission Women," 450.
23 Roundell Palmer, *Memorials, Part I, Family and Personal 1766–1865* (London, 1896), 355.
24 Parochial Mission Women, MS 1691, Church of England Archives, Lambeth Palace.
25 Palmer, *Memorials*, 354.
26 Rules for Parochial Mission Women, Tait 389 ff49, Church of England Archives. This phrase had, on one occasion, "deeply hurt the feelings" of one mission woman who had inadvertently been shown the Society's rules of operation. November 1903, Parochial Mission Women, MS 1691, Church of England Archives.
27 Caroline Jane Stuart Talbot, *Parochial Mission Women: their work, and its fruits* (London, 1862) 7. See also Mrs Edward Liddell, *Work in Dark Places* (London, c. 1890).
28 Elliott, *A Servant of the Poor*, 32.
29 Cavendish, "Parochial Mission Women," 452.
30 Tait Ff50, Church of England Archives.
31 Ibid.
32 Ibid.
33 13 February 1866, Diary of Lady Frederick Cavendish, vol. 9, Cavendish Family Papers, Chatsworth Archives.
34 Talbot, *Parochial Mission Women*, 26.

35 Ibid., 27.
36 Ibid., 29.
37 Ibid., 39, 42.
38 Ibid., 21.
39 *Women's Herald* 6, no. 207 (15 October 1892): 1.
40 Church Congress Record, 1862, quoted in Brian Heeney, *The Women's Movement in the Church of England 1850–1930* (Oxford, 1988), 53.
41 Palmer, *Memorials*, 354.
42 Wood, "Parochial Mission Women."
43 For example, Lady Laura Palmer, Mrs Hardcastle, and Mrs Oldfield enlisted their husbands, Mrs Talbot enlisted her son, John, and Camilla Fortescue enlisted her uncle, the Earl of Devon.
44 Elliott, *A Servant of the Poor*, 18.
45 9 March 1893, Parochial Mission Women, MS 1689, p. 268, Church of England Archives.
46 Cavendish, "Parochial Mission Women," 451.
47 Parochial Mission Women, MS 1682, 1689, 1691, Church of England Archives.
48 At the time of Mr Rust's complaint, in 1904, Stepney was remarkably fortunate in its bishop; Cosmo Gordon Lang had worked at Toynbee Hall as an undergraduate and was thus not unfamiliar with some of the rhythms of working-class neighbourhoods. He was a liberal clergyman, who made (as a newly appointed Archbishop of York), in his maiden speech in the House of Lords in 1910, a vigorous attempt to persuade his fellow Lords to abandon their intention to vote against Lloyd George's "People's Budget."
49 February 1904–April 1909, Parochial Mission Women, MS 1692, Church of England Archives.
50 Heeney, *The Women's Movement in the Church of England 1850–1930*, 46–55.
51 Parochial Mission Women, MS 1691, Church of England Archives.
52 Parochial Mission Women, MS 1692, Church of England Archives.
53 There is a lively debate as to whether the undisputed decline in church attendance translated into outright secularization. Jeremy Morris, "The Strange Death of Christian Britain: Another Look at the Secularization Debate," *Historical Journal (Cambridge, England)* 46, no. 4 (December 2003): 963–76; Jonathan Rose, *The Edwardian Temperament 1895–1919* (Athens, Ohio, 1986); Callum Brown, *The Death of Christian Britain: Understanding Secularization 1800–2000* (Abingdon, 2009). See also Callum Brown, *Religion and Society in Twentieth Century Britain* (Harlow, 2006).
54 October 1905, Lyttelton Family Papers, 33/3/76, Hagley Hall Archives.

55 For a thorough discussion of establishment support of the CETS in general and aristocratic support in particular, see Gerald Wayne Olsen, "Drink and the British Establishment," unpublished manuscript, 2009.

56 Axel Gustafson, *The foundation of death: a study of the drink-question* (London, 1884).

57 *Church of England Temperance Chronicle*, 16 October 1880, 659, 600.

58 Anthony Wohl, *Endangered Lives: Public Health in Victorian Britain* (London, 1984), 59.

59 A.E. Dingle, "Drink and Working-Class Living Standards in Britain 1870–1914," *Economic History Review* 25, no. 4 (1972): 608–22.

60 Seebohm Rowntree thought these figures excessive and pegged his estimate closer to one-sixth. Ibid., 609. See also Wohl, *Endangered Lives*, 60.

61 *Church of England Temperance Chronicle*, 27 March 1880, 197.

62 Carlisle and Somerset are also hardly representative of aristocratic women; Rosalind Stanley, Countess of Carlisle was a radical and outspoken supporter of temperance, women's suffrage, and religious free-thinking. Similarly, Lady Henry Somerset, daughter of the Earl and Countess Somers, had divorced her husband, Lord Henry Somerset, on the grounds of his homosexuality. She had (successfully) fought an unpleasantly public custody battle for her son but was, in many sections of aristocratic society, blamed for having made the battle so public and for essentially hounding her husband out of the country to escape sodomy laws. The Prince of Wales, for one, would not hear her name. She was accused (unfairly) of using temperance as a way of rehabilitating her position in society.

63 *Church of England Temperance Chronicle*, 17 May 1884, 31

64 The lobbying efforts of the CETS Women's Union is the subject of further scrutiny in chapter 6, "Philanthropy and Citizenship."

65 *Church of England Temperance Chronicle*, November 1883.

66 Annual Report, CETS Women's Union Archives, "Address of the Bishop of London, May 28, 1885 at Grosvenor House to the Women's Union of the CETS," H5013.T3, Church of England Archives.

67 Annual Report of the Women's Union, H5013.T3, Church of England Archives.

68 *Church of England Temperance Chronicle*, 4 February 1882.

69 *Church of England Temperance Chronicle*, 17 May 1884.

70 Annual Reports, CETS Women's Union, 1882–8, H5013.T3, Church of England Archives.

71 Report of the Annual Meeting, CETS Women's Union, 1886, H5013.T3, Church of England Archives.

72 Annual Report, CETS Women's Union, 1887, H5013.T3, Church of England Archives.

73 Report of the Autumn Council, 1888, MS 2030, p. 84, Church of England Archives.
74 This developed into the modern practice of probation. See Maurice Vanstone, *Supervising Offenders in the Community: A History of Probation Theory and Practice* (Aldershot, 2004), 1–18.
75 Report of the Autumn Council, 1888, MS 2030, p. 84, Church of England Archives.
76 Wilhelmina Haslam appears to have become the secretary of the Church of England Women's Mission to Palestine.
77 Annual Report, CETS Women's Union, 1887, H5013.T3, Church of England Archives.
78 Women's Union Report of the Annual Conference, 5 May 1893, H5011.C4, Church of England Archives.
79 Letter of Miss Ayerst, Annual Report, CETS Women's Union 1894, H5011. C4, Church of England Archives.
80 This change in CETS leadership was evidently the result of a revolt by a radical wing led by Basil Wilberforce. Olsen, "Drink and the British Establishment," 47; See also Jack S. Blocker, Jr, David M. Fahey, and Ian R. Tyrrell, eds., *Alcohol and Temperance: A Modern History: A Global Encyclopedia* (Santa Barbara, 2003), 216.
81 Report of the Church Congress, 22 October 1894, MS 2031, pp. 8, 9, Church of England Archives.
82 The annual reports of the Women's Union for that year actually showed little muddle. In 1893 they turned a net profit of £11, which, put towards the deficit from previous year, reduced their cumulated total debt to 6 pounds; this, running lodges which brought in income of approximately a thousand pounds each.
83 Report of the Church Congress, 22 October 1894, MS 2031, pp. 8, 9, Church of England Archives.
84 12 July 1894, CETS Annual Meeting, MS 2051, Church of England Archives.
85 Mrs Cholmeley, Mrs Symes Thompson, Miss Townend, and Mrs Carus Wilson.
86 Annual Report of the CETS, 1895, p. 24, MS 2051, Church of England Archives.
87 Rev. Gerald Thompson, "The Church of England Temperance Society's Homes for Inebriates," *British Journal of Inebriety* 10, no. 3 (January 1913): 141–4.
88 Report of the Annual Meeting, CETS Women's Union, 1886, H5013.T3, Church of England Archives.
89 F.M.L. Thompson, *The Rise of Respectable Society* (London, 1988); Alan Kidd, *State, Society and the Poor in Nineteenth-Century England* (New York, 1999);

Julia Parker, *Women and Welfare: Ten Victorian Women in Public Social Service*.(London, 1989).

90 Prochaska, *Women and Philanthropy*, 144.

91 Mary Poovey, *Making a Social Body: Cultural Formation 1830–1864* (Chicago, 1995), passim.

92 Poovey sees the social domain as situated apart from the political or economic domain.

93 Kathryn Gleadle, *Borderline Citizens: Women, Gender and Political Culture in Britain, 1815–1867* (Oxford, 2009) 59.

3. Emma Cons

1 *Miss Emma Cons and Miss Jane Cobden Local Government* 1889, Cobden Family Papers, MSS 348, West Sussex Record Office. The councillors elected Emma Cons over four other possible aldermen to represent Lambeth: the local philanthropic potteries businessman Sir Henry Doulton, the engineer Sir Douglas Galton, the organizer of wounded troop evacuation Sir Vincent Kennett-Barrington, and the Duke of Abercorn.

2 Emma Cons served on the following seven committees: Housing of the Poor, Asylums, Industrial and Reformatory Schools, Parks and Open Spaces, Sanitation, Special Purposes, and Theatres.

3 Following his retirement from the civil service in 1898, Lushington served as an alderman on the London County Council.

4 Eleanor Gordon and Gwyneth Nair, *Public Lives: Women, Family and Society in Victorian Britain* (New Haven, 2003).

5 Barbara Corrado Pope, "Angels in the Devil's Workshop: Leisured and Charitable Women in Nineteenth Century England and France," in *Becoming Visible: Women in European History*, ed. Renate Bridenthal and Claudia Koonz (Boston, 1977). See also Caroline Morrell, "Octavia Hill and Women's Networks in Housing," in *Gender, Health and Welfare*, ed. Anne Digby and John Stewart (London, 1996).

6 Kathryn Gleadle, *British Women in the Nineteenth Century* (Basingstoke, 2001); Kathryn Gleadle, *Borderline Citizens: Women, Gender and Political Culture in Britain 1815–1867* (Oxford, 2009); Pat Jalland, *Women, Marriage and Politics 1860–1914* (Oxford, 1986); Jane E. Lewis, *Women and Social Action in Victorian and Edwardian England* (Stanford, 1991). See also Morrell, "Octavia Hill and Women's Networks in Housing.

7 Deborah Epstein Nord, *The Apprenticeship of Beatrice Webb* (Amherst, Mass., 1985); Martha Vicinus, *Independent Women: Work and Community for Single*

Women 1850–1920 (Chicago, 1985); Seth Koven, *Slumming: Sexual and Social Politics in Victorian London* (Princeton, 2004); Katharine Bradley, *Poverty, Philanthropy and the State: Charities and the Working Classes in London, 1918–79* (Manchester, 2009).

8 Dina Copelman, *London's Women Teachers: Gender, Class and Feminism 1870–1930* (London, 1996).

9 Richard Findlater, *Lilian Baylis: The Lady of the Old Vic* (London, 1975), 24.

10 Old Vic Archives, OVEC/000218, Bristol University. At his death, Frederick Cons was proudly recorded as being "of 38 Torrington Square." Findlater, *Lilian Baylis*, 37.

11 A good description of Emma Cons's family life can be found in chapter 2 of Elizabeth Schafer's biography of Emma Cons's niece: *Lilian Baylis: A Biography* (Hatfield, 2006). For a thorough discussion of the significance of the Female School of Art, see Patricia Zakreski, *Representing Female Artistic Labour 1848–1890: Refining Work for the Middle-Class Woman* (Aldershot, 2006), 86n62.

12 Gillian Darley, *Octavia Hill* (London, 1990), 52, 53.

13 Cicely Hamilton and Lilian Baylis, *The Old Vic* (London, 1926), 259.

14 Sophia Lonsdale, *The Recollections of Sophia Lonsdale*, ed. Violet Martineau (London, 1936), 162; Hamilton and Baylis, *The Old Vic*, 258, 260.

15 Ibid., 255–62.

16 Anthony S. Wohl, *The Eternal Slum: Housing and Social Policy in Victorian London* (London, 1977), chapter 6, "Philanthropy at Five Per Cent," 142–78.

17 Ibid., 146.

18 Darley, *Octavia Hill*, 91.

19 E. Moberley Bell, *Octavia Hill, A Biography* (London, 1942), 78.

20 "Emma Cons: An Appreciation by Canon and Mrs. Barnett," *Westminster Gazette*, 29 July 1912.

21 Hamilton and Baylis, *The Old Vic*, 266.

22 Henrietta Barnett, typescript of proposed introduction to Lilian Baylis's memoir of Emma Cons, Old Vic Archives, OVEC/000231/1-11.

23 Hamilton and Baylis, *The Old Vic*, 265.

24 Darley, *Octavia Hill*, 126; Lewis, *Women and Social Action in Victorian and Edwardian England* (Stanford, 1991), 55.

25 Darley, *Octavia Hill*, 133, 135.

26 Ibid., 133–5.

27 "Emma Cons: An Appreciation by Canon and Mrs. Barnett," *Westminster Gazette*, 29 July 1912.

28 *Octavia Hill and the Social Housing Debate: Essays and Letters by Octavia Hill*, ed. Robert Whelan (Bury St Edmunds, 1998), editor's introduction, 9.
29 This had been the whole objective of the Ladies Art Guild established by Octavia Hill's mother – to provide genteel artistic remunerative work for ladies of the middle classes.
30 Beatrice Webb, *The Diary of Beatrice Webb, Volume One 1873–1892*, ed. Norman and Jeanne MacKenzie (London, 1982), 136.
31 Dame Sybil Thorndike, *Lilian Baylis as I Knew Her* (London, 1938), 28; Sir Cedric Hardwicke, *A Victorian in Orbit: The Irreverent Memoirs of Sir Cedric Hardwicke* (London, 1961), 100; Peter Roberts, *The Old Vic Story: The Nation's Theatre* (London, 1976), viii.
32 J.C. Winnington-Ingram, "A Glimpse of London in the Last Century," *Quarterly Bulletin of the Society of Housing Managers* (April 1954), quoted in Findlater, *Lilian Baylis*, 35.
33 *Sussex Daily News*, 2 February 1890.
34 Findlater, *Lilian Baylis*, 33; Darley, *Octavia Hill*, 138.
35 Hamilton and Baylis, *The Old Vic*, 265.
36 Darley, *Octavia Hill*, 139. MacDonald is possibly better remembered as the author of the children's classics *The Princess and the Goblin* and *The Princess and Curdie*.
37 Hamilton and Baylis, *The Old Vic*, 269.
38 On these occasions, Octavia and Emma would often divide the group between them because, as Octavia put it, Emma "can and does tell and show as well or better than I." Darley, *Octavia Hill*, 137.
39 Hamilton and Baylis, *The Old Vic*, 268.
40 Emily Maurice, *Life of Octavia Hill* (London, 1914), 367.
41 Lloyd George deliberately chose "The Edinburgh Castle" in Limehouse as the venue for his July 1910 speech defending the "People's Budget."
42 Hamilton and Baylis, *The Old Vic*, 272.
43 Cowper-Temple was also involved in shepherding to passage the 1870 Education Act, which established Board schools throughout England and was responsible for the insertion of the Cowper-Temple clause permitting parents to withdraw their children from religious education in these same schools.
44 Their first London coffee tavern, "The Rose and Crown" in Knightsbridge Road, was refurbished and opened at the end of the first year. "The Glass House" in Edgware Road started business in the spring of 1877 and in June another coffee tavern was established at the Billingsgate Market. The same month, Samuel Morley, the MP for Bristol and supporter of the temperance movement, funded the opening of "The People's Café" in Gracechurch Street, near Eastcheap.

45 See Derek Oddy and Derek Miller, *The Making of the Modern British Diet* (London, 1976), 163.
46 *Musical Times and singing-class circular*, July 1880, 325. See also Denis Richards, *Offspring of the Vic: A History of Morley College* (London, 1958), 42.
47 Octavia Hill, *Letters to Fellow Workers, 1872–1911* (London, 2005), 65.
48 Findlater, *Lilian Baylis*, 36.
49 Hamilton and Baylis, *The Old Vic*, 270
50 Old Vic Archives, OVEC/000251.
51 John Booth, *A Century of Theatrical History 1816–1916: The Old Vic* (London, 1917), 61.
52 Findlater, *Lilian Baylis*, 47
53 Ellen Barlee, *Pantomime Waifs or A Plea for our City Children* (London, 1884), 204; Hamilton and Baylis, *The Old Vic*, 276: Richards, *Offspring of the Vic*, 50; George Rowell, *The Old Vic Theatre* (Cambridge, 1993), 61.
54 Findlater, *Lilian Baylis*, 48.
55 Richards, *Offspring of the Vic*, 52.
56 *Graphic*, 20 August 1881, 102, first column, "The Victoria Coffee Music Hall."
57 Royal Victoria Hall Annual Report 1881, General Reference Collection 10348.f.1, British Library; Old Vic Archives, quoted in Richards, *Offspring of the Vic*, 53, 54.
58 *Church of England Temperance Chronicle*, 30 July 1881.
59 He believed in the ideals of Christian Socialism, so much so that he placed the education of his son John in their hands. Richard Martineau was also related to the writer Harriet Martineau, who was his first cousin.
60 *Old Vic Magazine* 4, no. 5 (February 1923): 5, Old Vic Archives, OV/MAG/000004/4.
61 Richards, *Offspring of the Vic*, 137.
62 Maurice, *Life of Octavia Hill*, 15.
63 Henrietta Barnett, introduction to proposed biography of Emma Cons, Old Vic Archives, OVEC/000231/1-11.
64 Hamilton and Baylis, *The Old Vic*, 252, 253.
65 Ibid., 250, 252, 256, 258.
66 Old Vic Archives, OVLB/000017.
67 Catriona Blake, *The Charge of the Parasols: Women's Entry into the Medical Profession* (London, 1990), 196–7; Rosemary Auchmuty, "By Their Friends We Shall Know Them: The Lives and Networks of Some Women in North Lambeth 1880–1940," in *Not a Passing Phase: Reclaiming Lesbians in History 1840–1985*, ed. Lesbian History Group (London, 1989), 80; Nicky Hallet, *Lesbian Lives: Identity and Autobiography in the Twentieth Century* (London, 1999), 88–90.
68 2 March 1875, Old Vic Archives, OVLB 000017.
69 Richards, *Offspring of the Vic*, 134.

70 Gareth Stedman Jones, *Outcast London: A Study in the Relationship between Classes in Victorian Society* (Oxford, 1971), chapter 12, "The Deformation of the Gift: The Problem of the 1860's," 241–70.
71 Beatrice Webb, *My Apprenticeship* (Cambridge, 1979), 277
72 Beatrice Webb, *Diary, Volume Two*, ed. Norman and Jeanne MacKenzie (London, 1982), 136.
73 Lonsdale, *Recollections of Sophia Lonsdale*, 160–6.
74 Ibid., 214.
75 Ibid., 166.
76 Adrian Boult Centenary Festival Souvenir, quoted in Findlater, *Lilian Baylis*, 93. Boult served on the Hall's Board of Governors.
77 Hamilton and Baylis, *The Old Vic*, 262.
78 Ibid., 263.
79 Although Richard Findlater, in his biography of Lilian Baylis, hints that two of Emma's sisters, Elizabeth and Esther, had problems with alcohol in their later years. Findlater, *Lilian Baylis*, 38.
80 Emma Cons, "Model Dwellings," *County Council Magazine* (April 1889).
81 May Hughes to Jane Cobden, Jane Cobden Papers, DN 851, letters 1910–May 1917, Bristol University.
82 Webb, *My Apprenticeship*, 268.
83 Ibid., 268.
84 Lonsdale, *Recollections of Sophia Lonsdale*, 166.
85 W. Somerset Maugham, *Liza of Lambeth* (London, 1953). There is a rich vein of literary works of the 1890s that depict urban working-class culture, both in the East End of London and south of the river. Arthur Morrison's more bluntly violent *Lizerunt* (London, 1894), written two years before his more famous *Child of the Jago* (London, 1896), is arguably just as much an influence on Maugham as were his experiences as a young Lambeth physician.
86 Rowell, *The Old Vic Theatre*, 62.
87 Royal Victoria Hall, Annual Report, 1882. We can see fair descriptions of Emma Cons's "Madame Blackfriars type" in Arthur Morrison's heroine from *Lizerunt*: "Lizerunt worked at a pickle factory, and appeared abroad in an elaborate and shabby costume, usually supplemented by a white apron ... her cheeks were very red ... and her fringe was long and shiny." P.J. Keating, *Working-Class Stories of the 1890's* (London, 1971), 29. We can also see her in Somerset Maugham's Liza: "a young girl of about eighteen, with dark eyes and an enormous fringe, puffed-out and curled and frizzed, covering her whole forehead from side to side and coming down to meet her eyebrows. She was dressed in brilliant violet with great lappets of velvet and on her head an enormous black hat covered with feathers." Maugham, *Liza of Lambeth*, 8.

88 Richard, *Offspring of the Vic*, 58.
89 Ibid., 59
90 Robert Speaight, *William Poel and the Elizabethan Revival* (Cambridge, Mass., 1954); Richards, *Offspring of the Vic*, 55.
91 Morley was the president and sole owner of the prosperous Nottingham hosiery firm I & R Morley, and Liberal MP for first Nottingham (1865) and subsequently Bristol (1868–85). Interested in education and temperance, Morley devoted many of his later years to supporting worthy causes, giving away often £20,000 to £30,000 per annum. Lord Shaftesbury once remarked to Morley's biographer Edwin Hodder: "There is that dear man Samuel Morley, content to be anything or nothing, so that good is done." Offered a peerage by Gladstone in 1885 in the warmest terms ("I do not know that I have ever had a more genuine pleasure in conveying a proposal of this nature than now, when I make it to one who had earned so many irrefragable titles to the honourable regard of his country-men"), Morley declined the honour, since he disapproved of an unelected, hereditary chamber being involved in governing the nation. Edwin Hodder, *The Life of Samuel Morley* (London, 1887), 462–6.
92 Richards, *Offspring of the Vic*, 68, 69.
93 The doctrine of *cy-pres* is, in Law French, "*cy-près comme possible*," the notion of applying the funds of a failed charitable trust to that object which is as close to the testator's original object as possible.
94 Emma Cons must have been sure of her supporters: George Rowell records the transfer of the freehold as being dated 31 March 1888, about a month before the fundraising campaign started. Rowell, *The Old Vic Theatre*, 76.
95 Royal Order in Council 23 February 1891; Rowell, *The Old Vic Theatre*, 76.
96 Richards, *Offspring of the Vic*, 142.
97 "The best discussion we have ever had" followed the speech on women's suffrage made by Amber Pember Reeves in 1909. Ibid., 159.
98 Ibid., 148.
99 It remained so until 1950. Mary Sheepshanks's administration was followed by that of Clare Brennand, who was in turn succeeded by, successively, Barbara Wootton, Eva Hubback, and Amber Pember Reeves.
100 "Transforming a Music Hall," *Sunday Circle*, 18 September 1909.
101 Darley, *Octavia Hill*, 224.
102 He also observed generally, of London's various housing schemes for the poor, that "to an American, the most interesting and instructive feature of this subject of housing the poor is the part that is being taken by the Governing Council of London. This is nothing more or less than an expression of municipal socialism." *New York Times*, 2 September 1894.

103 Pamela K. Gilbert, *The Citizen's Body* (Cleveland, 2007), 108.
104 Vicinus, *Independent Women*, 229. See also Lewis, *Women and Social Action in Victorian and Edwardian England*.
105 *Sussex Daily News*, 2 February 1890.
106 "Model Dwellings," *County Council Magazine* 1 (July 1889): 136–42.
107 Ibid.
108 *Miss Emma Cons and Miss Jane Cobden Local Government* 1889, Cobden Family Papers, Cobden MSS 348.
109 Ibid.
110 "Model Dwellings," *County Council Magazine* 1 (July 1889): 136–42.
111 DSC Report on the Reformatory and Industrial Schools (1896), OP-fC.8204, British Library.
112 Schafer, *Lilian Baylis*; Richards, *Offspring of the Vic*, 174.
113 "The Emma Cons Memorial," OVEC/000143/2, Old Vic Archives.
114 P.N. Backstrom, Jr, "The Practical Side of Christian Socialism in England," *Victorian Studies* 6, no. 4 (1963): 305

4. Opera for Lambeth

1 Rev. H.R. Haweis, Music and Morals, 3rd ed. (London, 1873), 563.
2 Ibid., 67.
3 Samuel Barnett, "Human Service," reprinted in Practicable Socialism, 2nd ed. (London, 1894), 286.
4 Peter Bailey, *Leisure and Class in Victorian England: Rational Recreation and the Contest for Control 1830–1850* (London, 1987). See also Brad Beaven, *Leisure, Citizenship and Working-Class Men in Britain, 1850–1945* (Manchester, 2005).
5 Diana Maltz, *British Aestheticism and the Urban Working Classes 1870–1900: Beauty for the People* (Basingstoke, 2006), 209.
6 Paula Gillett, *Musical Women in England: Encroaching on All Man's Privileges* (New York, 2000), 46.
7 Seth Koven, *Slumming: Sexual and Social Politics in Victorian London* (Princeton, 2004). See also Nigel Scotland, *Squires in the Slums: Settlements and Missions in Late Victorian London* (London, 2007).
8 Gillett, *Musical Women in England*, 46.
9 Cicely Hamilton and Lilian Baylis, *The Old Vic* (London, 1926), 268.
10 The Old Vic, situated on the Waterloo Road, lay right at the border of Lambeth and Southwark, both poor, working-class neighbourhoods.
11 Florence Marshall, "Music and the People," *The Nineteenth Century* (February 1881): 271.

12 Richard Findlater, *Lilian Baylis: The Lady of the Old Vic* (London, 1975), 59.
13 Countess of Meath, *Diaries of Mary, Countess of Meath*, ed. Reginald Brabazon (London, 1900), 14.
14 *Coffee Public-House News and Temperance Hotel Journal*, 1 July 1884, 85.
15 "Coffee Music Hall Company," *Coffee Public-House News and Temperance Hotel Journal*, no. 18, 1 April 1880, 328.
16 *Birmingham Daily Post*, 29 November 1889.
17 John Booth, *A Century of Theatrical History 1816–1916: The Old Vic* (London, 1917), 50.
18 Ibid., 47.
19 Ibid., 52.
20 Ibid.
21 Findlater, *Lilian Baylis*, 49.
22 "Coffee Music Hall Company," *Coffee Public-House News and Temperance Hotel Journal* no. 18, 1 April 1880, 328.
23 Hamilton and Baylis, *The Old Vic*, 269.
24 Preliminary circular of the Coffee Music-Halls Company, 1879; Denis Richards, *Offspring of the Vic: A History of Morley College* (London, 1958), 42; Booth, *A Century of Theatrical History*, 59.
25 *Musical Times* 21, no. 449 (1 July 1880): 325.
26 *Birmingham Daily Post*, 29 November 1889.
27 George Rowell, *The Old Vic Theatre: A History* (Cambridge, 1993), 61.
28 *Coffee Public-House News and Temperance Hotel Journal* no. 18, 1 April 1880, 328. But it was the morals and the social habits of the audience that were to be improved, not their musical taste. When the Rev. P.H. Wicksteed, in an early meeting of the Coffee Music-Halls Company shareholders, referred to the average man knowing the difference between "bad music and good music, and preferred the good," he was not referring to a preference for complex tonality, cascading polyphony, lyrical fugues, or well-constructed, multifaceted harmonies; he meant the difference between a bawdy song and sacred music. When he went on to state that, in his experience, "he had discovered with surprise that the better the music provided, the better the people were pleased," he was referring to his successful experience in presenting well-attended performances of religious oratorios and anthems on Sunday evenings to working people.
29 *Musical Times* 21, no. 449 (1 July 1880): 325.
30 Elizabeth Schafer, *Lilian Baylis: A Biography* (Hatfield, 2006), 52.
31 26 March 1874, Mrs Caroline Hill to Mrs Edmund Maurice, C. Edmund Maurice, *The Life of Octavia Hill As Told in Her Letters* (London, 1913), 303.

32 Alice Hart was also interested in aesthetics for the home. In 1903, she purchased the magazine *The House: An artistic Monthly for those who manage and Beautify the Home* (England's first periodical on home decorating), swiftly reinventing it as *House Beautiful and the Home: A Journal for those who Design, Beautify, Furnish and Inhabit Houses*, which quickly became a platform for those who sought to bring beauty to the homes of the poor. Deborah Cohen, "Why Did *The House* Fail? Demand and Supply before the Modern Home Magazine, 1880's–1900's," *Journal of Design History* 18, no.1 (2005): 35–42; Maltz, *British Aestheticism and the Urban Working Classes 1870–1900*, 27.
33 Hermann Klein, *Great Women Singers of My Time* (London, 1931), 162; Gillett, *Musical Women in England*, 53; *Monthly Musical Record*, 1 March 1885, 67; Hamilton and Baylis, *The Old Vic*, 277.
34 "Reminiscences of a Stagehand," Old Vic Archives, OVSB 1913-192, Bristol University.
35 Rowell, *The Old Vic Theatre*, 93.
36 *Judy or the London Serio-Comic Journal*, 1 October 1885, 196.
37 Robert Speaight, *William Poel and the Elizabethan Revival* (London, 1954); Richards, *Offspring of the Vic*, 55.
38 *Illustrated London News*, 2 April 1881.
39 Better known for his light operettas composed with W.S. Gilbert, Sir Arthur Sullivan also composed serious operas in English, e.g., *The Martyr of Antioch* (1880), *The Golden Legend* (1886), *Ivanhoe* (1890).
40 Carl Rosa's company had been founded in 1875 expressly to present opera in English. Richard D'Oyly Carte attempted to encourage English grand opera by building, at his own expense, the Royal English Opera House in Cambridge Circus and launching it with the premiere of Arthur Sullivan's *Ivanhoe* in 1891. This trend in English opera would continue; the Moody-Manners company was established in 1898 as part of this wave in popularity of opera sung in English.
41 Hamilton and Baylis, *The Old Vic*, 191.
42 As Lilian Baylis put it, economy dictated that "non-copyright works were the rule." Ibid., 191.
43 Findlater, *Lilian Baylis*, 60.
44 George Rowell speculates that these choirs acted as operatic choruses from the start; Richard Findlater is of the opinion that choruses were not added to the operas until the spring of 1894, when the choir from the Church of the Sacred Heart in Camberwell was enlisted to perform in the opera *Robert Macaire* by George Fox. Findlater, *Lilian Baylis*, 60; Rowell, *The Old Vic Theatre*, 71.

45 Beatrice Webb, *My Apprenticeship* (Cambridge, 1979), 264.
46 Kingsley was a Christian Socialist and a colleague of F.D. Maurice, who had been such an influence on Emma Cons, Octavia Hill, and Lord Frederick Cavendish. Kingsley was also a friend of George MacDonald, who had helped Emma Cons put on plays for her first tenants at Barrett's Court.
47 Charles Kingsley, *Alton Locke* (London, 1881), 305.
48 *Musical Review*, 10 March 1883, quoted in Findlater, *Lilian Baylis*, 60.
49 *Daily News*, 11 May 1888, 6.
50 Hamilton and Baylis, *The Old Vic*, 191.
51 *Birmingham Daily Post*, 29 November 1889.
52 "Middle Class," *Musical Times*, 1 November 1894, 770.
53 "Transforming a Music Hall," *Sunday Circle*, 18 September 1909.
54 Rowell, *The Old Vic Theatre*, 89.
55 Harcourt Williams, *The Old Vic Saga* (London, 1949), 20.
56 Annual Report 1890–1, Royal Victoria Hall and Coffee Tavern, 4, Old Vic Archives, Bristol University [Theatre Archives].
57 *Daily News*, 11 May 1888, 6.
58 Annual Report 1911–12, Royal Victoria Hall, 4.
59 Ibid., 5.
60 Jonathan Rose, *The Intellectual Life of the British Working Classes* (New Haven, 2001), 410.
61 Lucy Masterman, unpublished biography of Lucy Cavendish, Masterman Papers, Lucy Cavendish College Archives, Cambridge University, p. 243.
62 Henrietta Barnett, *Canon Barnett, His Life, Work and Friends* (London, 1918), 96.
63 Samuel Barnett, "Human Service," 286; George Lansbury, *My Life* (London, 1931), 132. But see Seth Koven's insightful comment pointing out a younger Lansbury's more favourable comments concerning many East End philanthropists. Lansbury's views on the Old Vic's opera are not known, but he was a great supporter of Emma Cons in her brief political life as the first woman alderman on the London County Council and he ran the 1888 campaign of her colleague Jane Cobden. Koven, *Slumming*, 286. See also Jonathan Schneer, "Politics and Feminism in 'Outcast London': George Lansbury and Jane Cobden's Campaign for the First London County Council," *Journal of British Studies* 30, no. 1 (January 1991): 63–82.
64 Samuel Barnett, "Human Service," 286.
65 Annual Report, Royal Victoria Hall, 1884, Old Vic Theatre Reports and Pamphlets, SFX; 1014043, General Reference Collection, British Library.
66 Rowell, *The Old Vic Theatre*, 70.
67 C.E. Pearce, *Sims Reeves – Fifty Years of Music in England* (London, 1924).

68 Hermann Klein, *Thirty Years of Musical Life in London 1870–1900* (New York, 1903), 462.
69 William Towell in the *Sporting Times*, 21 April 1888, 2.
70 Goossens's father (confusingly, also a conductor, named Eugène Goossens) had worked with Santley. Marcello Conati, Julian Budden, and Richard Stokes, *Encounters with Verdi* (Ithaca, 1984), 54; Eugene Goossens, *Overture and Beginnings*, 8; see also Klein, *Thirty Years of Musical Life*, 203, a contemporary of Santley's who recalled his voice as "eminent and evergreen."
71 *Era Almanack* (1875): 22.
72 Booth, *A Century of Theatrical History*, 66.
73 "Transforming a Music Hall," *Sunday Circle*, 18 September 1909.
74 Rose, *The Intellectual Life of the British Working Classes*, 200.
75 Masterman, biography of Lucy Cavendish, 243.
76 The seating at the Old Vic (originally established as a theatre, not a music hall) was always in theatre rows, and Emma Cons, not seeking to emphasize refreshment, did not alter that configuration when she took over the theatre. Thanks to Peter Bailey for pointing out this connection.
77 Frederick Maurice, *The Life of Frederick Denison Maurice, Chiefly told in his own letters* (London, 1884), 304.
78 *Standard*, 18 January 1861, 3.
79 *Daily News*, 23 July 1874, 5.
80 Edward White Benson, "Phoebe, the Servant of the Church," 11 May 1873, 8, given at St Peter's Kensington as part of a fundraising effort for the Parochial Mission Women.
81 *John Bull*, 2 February 1884, 82.
82 *Birmingham Daily Post*, 7 June 1872, 6
83 *Newcastle Courant*, 19 March 1880, 7.
84 *Royal Cornish Gazette and Falmouth Packet*, 21 November 1874.
85 *Musical Times*, 1 June 1883, 310.
86 Annual Report, June 1885, Royal Victoria Hall, Old Vic Archives, Bristol University [Theatre Archives].
87 Benson, "Phoebe," 16.
88 Samuel Taylor, "Literary and Musical Entertainments for the People," *Transactions of the National Association for the Promotion of Social Science, London 1858* (London, 1859), 646.
89 Annual Report, Royal Victoria Hall, 1884, 10, Old Vic Theatre Reports and Pamphlets, SFX; 1014043, General Reference Collection, British Library.
90 Ibid.
91 *Coffee Public-House News*, 1 July 1884, 85.

92 22 October 1913, Lucy Cavendish to Lavinia Talbot, Lyttelton Family Papers, 33/3/87, Hagley Hall Archives.
93 Findlater, *Lilian Baylis*, 101.
94 "Almost a University," from the memoirs of H. Powell Lloyd, Old Vic Archives, OVSB/000537.
95 Hamilton and Baylis, *The Old Vic*, 195.
96 "The Royal Victoria Coffee Hall," *Illustrated London News*, 10 February 1883.
97 "The Reverend Hugh Reginald Haweis at Home," *John Bull*, 16 November 1876, 745.

5. The Citizens of Morley College

1 Denis Richards, *Offspring of the Vic: A History of Morley College* (London, 1958), 72–3.
2 Indeed, one of the College's first teachers recalled that they taught "not only at the back of the stage but under it, over it and at each side of the stage – for the lecture hall was built over the stage, classrooms were at each side and the gymnasium and refreshment rooms were underneath." *Reminiscences of Sir Frederick Black*, Old Vic Archives, OV/M/000012/4, Bristol University.
3 Morley College Archives, IV/224/5, Borough of Lambeth Archives.
4 Old Vic Archives, OV/M/000012/4.
5 Samuel Morley had recently died (1886), and not only was his loss deeply felt by Emma Cons, Lucy Cavendish, and Caroline Martineau, but it was also thought that no better memorial could be established to honour his memory.
6 Richards, *Offspring of the Vic*, 96.
7 J.F.C. Harrison, *Learning and Living 1790–1960: A Study of the English Adult Education Movement* (London, 1961).
8 John Reed, "Healthy Intercourse: The Beginnings of the Working Men's College," *Browning Institute Studies* 16, special issue on Victorian Learning (1988): 77–90.
9 Roger Fieldhouse, *A History of Modern British Adult Education* (Leicester, 1996); *The Workers' Educational Association: Aims and Achievements, 1903–1977* (Syracuse, 1977). See also Sylvia Harrop, *Oxford and Working-Class Education* (Nottingham, 1987).
10 Lawrence Goldman, *Dons and Workers: Oxford and Adult Education since 1850* (Oxford, 1994); Lawrence Goldman, "Intellectuals and the English

Working Class 1870–1945: The Case of Adult Education," *History of Education* 29, no. 4 (2000): 281–300; Ross McKibbin, "Why Was There No Marxism in Great Britain?" in his *The Ideologies of Class: Social Relations in Britain 1880–1950* (Oxford, 1990), 1–41. See also S.K. Roberts, *A Ministry of Enthusiasm: Centenary Essay on the WEA* (London, 2003); Brian Harrison, "Oxford and the Labor Movement," *Twentieth Century British History* 3 (1991): 236; Sheila Rowbotham, "Travellers in a Strange Country: Responses of Working-Class Students to the University Extension Movement," *History Workshop Journal* 12, no. 1 (1981): 88.

11 Peter Bingham Hinchliff, *Frederick Temple, Archbishop of Canterbury: A Life* (Oxford, 1998).

12 H.J. Mackinder, *University Extension: has it a future?* (London, 1890), 37–9.

13 The Second Reform Act of 1867 gave the vote to all urban, adult, ratepaying male householders and to male lodgers annually paying £10 for unfurnished rooms. This had the effect of enfranchising about 1,500,000 new men.

14 Lowe's actual statement was: "I believe it will be absolutely necessary that you prevail on our future masters to learn their letters." Hansard HC Deb 15 July 1867 vol. 188 cc1549. Lowe had also previously made the similar statement, "We cannot suffer any large number of our citizens, now that they have obtained the right of influencing the destinies of the country to remain uneducated."

15 *Reminiscences of Sir Frederick Black*, Old Vic Archives, OV/M/000012/4.

16 Ibid.

17 Ibid.

18 R. Fowler, "On Not Knowing Greek," *Classical Journal* 78, no. 4 (April–May 1983): 337–49. For example, Sir William Harcourt, replying to Gladstone concerning Sir Frederick Cavendish, wrote: "F. Cavendish is like the *άμν'μονεc*, a man whom all like and respect ..." Alfred Gardiner, *The Life of Sir William Harcourt*, Vol. 1 (London, 1923), 433.

19 23 April 1903, Masterman Family Papers, CFGM 1/17/5/6, University of Birmingham Archives.

20 First Annual Report, 1890, 8, IV/224/1/19, Morley College Archives.

21 Ibid.

22 Richards, *Offspring of the Vic*, 85.

23 First Annual Report, 1890, 10, IV/224/1/19, Morley College Archives.

24 "Polytechnic," "Scheme of the City Parochial Charities Act pertaining to educational institutions," *Encyclopaedia Britannica* (Cambridge, 1911), 22:40.

25 Richards, *Offspring of the Vic*, 110.

26 "The Education of Workmen," *Capital and Labour* 2 (26 May 1875): 237.
27 *The Times*, 4 December 1877, 9, col. C
28 *The Times*, 11 October 1886, 3, col. C.
29 Ibid.
30 Earl of Meath, ed., *Prosperity or Pauperism* (London, 1888).
31 Edward J. Watherston, "A National Necessity," in ibid., 182.
32 Graham Wallas, "Socialists and the School Board," *Today* 10 (November 1888).
33 For example, Thomas Burt, the miner and trade unionist who served as Liberal MP for Morpeth from 1874 to 1918, declared in May of 1883 that "he was more and more convinced every day, and every page of history went to show, that you could not raise a man, or a community, by giving better material advantages unless at the same time you improved their intellectual and moral condition." *Leicester Chronicle and Lincolnshire Mercury*, 19 May 1883, 1.
34 *Cambridge Review*, 10 December 1879, 139.
35 *Jackson's Oxford Journal*, 28 February 1880, 5.
36 Morley Memorial College, First Annual Report, 1890, 9, IV/224/1/19, Morley College Archives.
37 Old Vic Archives, OV/M/000012/4; Morley Memorial College, First Annual Report, 1890, 18, Morley College Archives.
38 *Reminiscences of Sir Frederick Black*, Old Vic Archives, OV/M/000012/4.
39 Old Vic Archives, OV/M/000015/4, p. 14.
40 George Curzon, *Principles and Methods of University Reform* (London, 1909), 50.
41 Annual Report, Royal Victoria Hall 1884, Old Vic Theatre Reports and Pamphlets, SFX; 1014043, General Reference Collection, British Library.
42 Frederick Maurice, *The Life of Frederick Denison Maurice as chiefly told in his own letters* (London, 1885), 304.
43 Reed, "Healthy Intercourse."
44 Ellen Ross, *Slum Travellers: Ladies and London Poverty 1860–1920* (Berkeley, 2002).
45 Beatrice Webb, *My Apprenticeship* (Cambridge, 1979), 266, 12 August 1885.
46 Annual Report, Royal Victoria Hall 1884, Old Vic Theatre Reports and Pamphlets, SFX; 1014043, General Reference Collection, British Library.
47 Morley College, Annual Report, 1893, 7, Morley College Archives.
48 Morley College, Annual Report, 1892, 10, Morley College Archives.
49 Morley College, Annual Report, 1892, 6, Morley College Archives.
50 Richards, *Offspring of the Vic*, 116.
51 One faction broke away to form the College for Working Women. This institution did not last and was eventually absorbed into the Working

Men's College. The remainder became part of a quickly renamed College for Working Men and Women, which wound up operations in 1901.

52 June Purvis, "Working-Class Women and Adult Education in Nineteenth Century Britain," *History of Education* 9, no. 3 (1980): 204. See also June Purvis, "Separate Spheres and Inequality in the Education of Working Class Women 1854–1900," *History of Education* 10, no. 4 (1981): 227–43; June Purvis, *Hard Lessons: The Lives and Education of Working-Class Women in Nineteenth-Century England* (Cambridge, 1989); June Purvis, "Towards a History of Women's Education in Nineteenth Century Logical Analysis," *Westminster Studies in Education* 4, no. 1 (1981): 45–79; Elizabeth Bird, "To Cook or to Conjugate: Gender and Class in the Adult Curriculum 1865–1900," *Gender and Education* 3 no. 2 (1991): 183–97.

53 Ibid.

54 Purvis, "Working-Class Women."

55 Similar requests were made by Morley College women as well.

56 See an article on the London Society for the Extension of University Teaching by "An 'Extension' Student" in the *Girls Own Paper*, 30 November 1889, 135.

57 Archives of the Yorkshire Ladies Council of Education, WYL5045, Leeds University.

58 The Council was affiliated with the Yorkshire Training School of Cookery and Domestic Science, which not only trained women in cooking, dressmaking, laundry work, and millinery, but also provided certificate and diploma classes to prospective teachers of these subjects.

59 The annual report for 1880 announced that year's results as "Very Successful, both as regards the numbers attending and certificates granted." Annual Report, 1880, Archives of the Yorkshire Ladies Council of Education, WYL5045, Leeds University.

60 Annual Report, 1887, 1890, Archives of the Yorkshire Ladies Council of Education, WYL5045, Leeds University.

61 Annual Report, 1894, Archives of the Yorkshire Ladies Council of Education, WYL5045, Leeds University.

62 George John Romanes, "Physiological Selection," *The Nineteenth Century* 21 (1887): 59–80.

63 Annual Report, 1894, Archives of the Yorkshire Ladies Council of Education, WYL5045, Leeds University.

64 Richards, *Offspring of the Vic*, 172.

65 Morley College was administered by women until 1950, either by vice-principals Mary Sheepshanks and Clare Brennand (1899–1925) or by principals Barbara Wootton, Eva Hubback, and Amber Pember Reeves (1926–50).

66 Richards, *Offspring of the Vic*, 170.
67 Morley College, First Annual Report, 1890, 9–12, IV/224/1/19, Morley College Archives.
68 Ibid., 12.
69 Ibid., 9–12.
70 Edward Royle, *Victorian Infidels: The Origins of the British Secularist Movement 1791–1866* (Manchester, 1974), 193.
71 E.M. Forster, *Howards End* (New York, 1921), 45.
72 Ibid., 50.
73 Report of the Walking Club in the *Morley College Magazine* 12, no. 3 (December 1902): 48. The Club's second venture was no less daring, walking from Barnes to Dorking, via Leatherhead, returning by Boxhill. Leonard Bast, in *Howards End* (1910), makes a similar night tramp, paying particular note to the coming of the dawn.
74 Jonathan Rose, *The Intellectual Life of the British Working Classes* (New Haven, 2001), chapter 12, "What Was Leonard Bast Really Like?"
75 Virginia Woolf, *Flight of the Mind: The Letters of Virginia Woolf 1888–1912*, ed. Nigel Nicolson (London, 1975), 313, 321; Melba Cuddy Keane, *Virginia Woolf: The Intellectual and the Public Sphere* (Cambridge, 2003), 85. See also Beth Rigel Daugherty "Morley College and Virginia Woolf," in *Virginia Woolf and Her Influences*, ed. Laura Davis and Jeanette McVicker (London, 1998).
76 Virginia Woolf, *Mrs. Dalloway* (New York, 2005), 83, 84.
77 Melba Cuddy Keane speculates that the student in question was likely Cyril Zeldwyn, whom Woolf described as "a poet; but also very clever and enthusiastic, and he can write short hand, and is a good man at accounts, and has a testimonial," and whom she tried to help secure a position, obtaining him an interview with Lord Robert Cecil. Keane, *Virginia Woolf*, 84. See also Woolf, *Flight of the Mind*, 321.
78 Old Vic Archives, OV/M/000012/4.
79 Richards, *Offspring of the Vic*, 139.
80 Morley Memorial College, Annual Report, 1892, 4, IV/224/1/20, Morley College Archives.
81 Richards, *Offspring of the Vic*, 139.
82 Executive Committee Minutes, IV/224/1/1/2, Morley College Archives; Richards, *Offspring of the Vic*, 124.
83 Ibid., 134.
84 MPs did not receive a salary until 1911.
85 Morley Memorial College, Annual Report, 1894, 6, IV/224/1/22, Morley College Archives.
86 Richards, *Offspring of the Vic*, 73.

87 Morley College, Annual Report, 1892, 3, Morley College Archives.
88 Ibid.
89 Ibid., 4.
90 George Trevelyan to Graham Wallas, 7 December 1906, Graham Wallas Papers, 1/32, LSE Archives. Caroline Martineau's successors were less inclined towards the sciences than she had been and tended more towards the humanities; thus, when the London County Council proposed to transfer the technical and more scientific courses to the Borough Polytechnic, they did not resist much. Morley College's technical and mechanical classes were transferred to the Borough Polytechnic while its music and Shakespeare classes were transferred to Morley College.
91 Morley College, Annual Report, 1893, 7, 8, Morley College Archives.
92 Richards, *Offspring of the Vic*, 134.
93 In this instance a diplomatic compromise was reached which satisfied both students and College authorities.
94 This ban was in effect until 1910.
95 That said, College dances could be – and had been – held off premises, the first having been organized by the Cycling Club in 1905 in Caterham.
96 During Wallas's first year at Corpus Christi College, Oxford, he attended Ruskin's lectures, "and for a short time, saw him almost every day." Ian Britain, *Fabianism and British Culture: A Study in British Socialism and the Arts* (Cambridge, 2005), 72.
97 Beatrice Webb, *Our Partnership* (Cambridge, 1975), 38.
98 Morley College, Annual Report, 1893, 4, Morley College Archives.
99 Morley College, Annual Report, 1893, 12, Morley College Archives.
100 Richards, *Offspring of the Vic*, 149.
101 Trevelyan also directed a Shakespeare reading circle during the 1907–8 academic year. Richards, *Offspring of the Vic*, 154.
102 Quentin Bell, *Virginia Woolf* (New York, 1972), appendix B, "Teaching at Morley College," 202–4.
103 May 1905, Virginia Woolf to Violet Dickinson, in Woolf, *Flight of the Mind*, 191.
104 Bell, *Virginia Woolf*, appendix B, "Teaching at Morley College," 203.
105 May 1905, Virginia Woolf to Violet Dickinson, in Woolf, *Flight of the Mind*, 192.
106 February 1907, Virginia Woolf to Lady Robert Cecil, in ibid., 281.
107 The position was given to the young Stella Browne, who held the post from 1907 to 1912, before going on to establish a reputation as a thoughtful advocate for free love, birth control, and available and inexpensive abortion.

108 Imogen Holst, *Holst* (London, 1974), 19–23.
109 Ibid., 88.
110 *The Times*, 7 June 1909, 8.
111 The full score of the work had been lost shortly after Henry Purcell's death and remained lost until 1901, when John Shedlock, a lecturer at the Royal Academy of Music, found it in the Academy's music library. It was published by the Purcell Society and, soon thereafter, revived by Holst at Morley College. Bruce Wood and Andrew Pinnock, "The Fairy Queen: A Fresh Look at the Issues," *Early Music*, February 1993.
112 Harvey Grace, "Gustav Holst – Teacher," *Musical Times* (August 1934): 691.
113 Ibid.
114 Holst, predictably, did not care overmuch for Brahms. Ibid., 692; Imogen Holst, *Holst*, 31; Katharine Eggar, "How They Make Music at Morley College," *Music Student* (March 1921).
115 Imogen Holst, *Holst*, 47.
116 Imogen Holst, *The Music of Gustav Holst* (London, 1951), 54.
117 Holst had a distinct soft spot in his heart for Morley College and remained fond of it and its mission long after ill health compelled him to retire. On his death, Ralph Vaughan Williams organized a subscription for a Gustav Holst Memorial, which was to take the form of a music room at Morley College, observing that he was sure it was a purpose of which Holst would heartily approve. *Musical Times* 76, no. 1106 (April 1935): 349.
118 He would go on to be knighted and serve as the biology editor of the eleventh edition of the *Encyclopedia Britannica*.
119 G.E. Moore, *Some Main Problems of Philosophy* (London, 1958).
120 Morley Memorial College, Annual Report, 1893, 4, Morley College Archives.
121 Graham Wallas Papers, 6/3, lecture VI, delivered at Morley College, 8 November 1893, LSE Archives.
122 Graham Wallas Papers, 6/3, lecture VIII, 22 November 1893, "The Poor Law," LSE Archives.
123 Graham Wallas Papers, 6/3, lecture IX, 29 November 1893, "Public Elementary Education," LSE Archives.
124 This focus on working-class citizenship in his lectures at Morley College was not simply Graham Wallas's external consciousness-raising, it was part of his own research. Just before he came to give his series of lectures at Morley College, while researching Chartism in the reading room of the British Museum, he discovered a large and as yet uncatalogued collection of the papers of the radical London tailor Francis Place. This research was

to grow into his biography of Place, published in 1898. Martin Wiener, *Between Two Worlds: The Political Thought of Graham Wallas* (Oxford, 1971), 41.

125 *Morley College Magazine* (1902): 15, Old Vic Archives, OV/M/000015/4.

126 Alfred William Arnold, "The Old Guard Dies but Never Surrenders," *Justice*, 15 October 1913; "Bandê Mataram," *Justice*, 15 September 1907.

127 *Special Supplement to the Morley College Magazine* (April 1902): 13, Old Vic Archives, OV/M/000015/4.

128 December 1907, Virginia Woolf to Lady Robert Cecil, in Woolf, *Flight of the Mind*, 320.

129 *Morley College Magazine*, 1 June 1892, 4, Morley College Archives.

130 Richards, *Offspring of the Vic*, 159.

131 *Morley College Magazine*, July 1901, Morley College Archives.

132 "Termination of the Great Strike," *Daily News*, 16 September 1889. This fund to aid the families of striking dockworkers was a cause to which Lucy Cavendish contributed.

133 *Special Supplement to the Morley College Magazine*, April 1902, 11, Old Vic Archives, OV/M/000015/4.

134 Richards, *Offspring of the Vic*, 170.

135 Meta Zimmeck, "Jobs for the Girls: The Expansion of Clerical Work for Women, 1850–1914," in *Unequal Opportunities: Women's Employment in England, 1800–1918*, ed. Angela V. John (Oxford, 1986), 153–77.

136 Ibid., 154.

137 Richards, *Offspring of the Vic*, 71.

138 Goldman, "Intellectuals and the English Working Class 1870–1945"; McKibbin, "Why Was There No Marxism in Great Britain?"

139 *Morley College Magazine* (December 1902): 16.

140 Richards, *Offspring of the Vic*, 159.

141 Bob Greenlee, *John Logie Baird, the Man Who Invented Television* (Bloomington, 2010), 111.

142 He was also, in 1924, brought up on charges of practising dentistry without being registered.

143 Richards, *Offspring of the Vic*, 110–11.

144 Ibid., 161.

145 David Vincent, *Bread, Knowledge and Freedom: A Study of Working Class Autobiography* (New York, 1982); Penelope Corfield, *Power and the Professions in Britain 1700–1850* (London, 1995).

146 Graham Wallas Papers, 2/11, lecture at Morley College, 14 November 1931, LSE Archives.

6. Philanthropy and Citizenship

1 Hannah More, *Coelebs in Search of a Wife* (New York, 1810), 12.
2 Louisa Twining, *Workhouses and Women's Work* (London, 1858), 32.
3 Jane E. Lewis, *Women and Social Action in Victorian and Edwardian England* (Stanford, 1991), 28; Gillian Darley, *Octavia Hill* (London, 1990).
4 Kathryn Gleadle, *British Women in the Nineteenth Century* (Basingstoke, 2001), 154–7; Angela Burdett-Coutts, *Woman's Mission* (London, 1893).
5 F.D. Maurice, "The Duties of Citizenship," *John Bull*, 24 June 1865, 408.
6 Louisa Shore, "The Citizenship of Women Socially Considered," *Westminster Review* (July 1874).
7 Frances Powers Cobbe, "Wife Torture in England," *Contemporary Review* 32 (1878): 55–87.
8 Josephine Butler, *The Constitution Violated* (Edinburgh, 1871).
9 Keir Hardie disagreed with this view and saw a desert for women's citizenship following 1867; see note 28 to the Introduction, above.
10 Julia Parker, *Citizenship, Work and Welfare: Searching for the Good Society* (Basingstoke, 1998).
11 Lydia Murdoch, *Imagined Orphans: Poor Families, Child Welfare and Contested Citizenship in London* (London, 2006).
12 Jane Rendall, "Citizenship, Culture and Civilization: The Languages of British Suffragists 1866–1874," in *Suffrage and Beyond: International Feminist Perspectives*, ed. Caroline Daley and Melanie Nolan (New York, 1994); "The Citizenship of Women and the Reform Act of 1867," in *Defining the Victorian Nation*, ed. Catherine Hall, Keith McClelland, and Jane Rendall (Cambridge, 2000); Anna Clark, "Gender, Class and the Nation: Franchise Reform in England, 1832–1928," in *Re-reading the Constitution: New Narratives in the Political History of England's Long Nineteenth Century*, ed. James Vernon (Cambridge, 1996).
13 Frances Powers Cobbe "Woman as a Citizen of the State," *The Duties of Women* (London, 1881), 182.
14 Quoted in the *Englishwoman's Review* 13 (15 May 1882): 209.
15 Women's Local Government Society Archives, WLGS/A/WLG/32, London Metropolitan Archives.
16 *Women's Penny Paper*, 5 April 1890.
17 Reported in the *Women's Herald*, 31 January 1891, 5.
18 Gwenllian E.F. Morgan, "The Duties of Citizenship: The Proper Understanding and Use of the Municipal and Other Franchises for Women," in *Before the Vote Was Won*, ed. Jane Lewis (London, 1987), 468.

19 Eugenio Biagini, "Liberalism and Direct Democracy: J.S. Mill and the Model of Ancient Athens," in *Citizenship and Community: Liberals, Radicals and Collective Identities in the British Isles 1865–1931* (Princeton, 1996), 21–44.
20 *Woman's Herald* 4, no. 161 (28 November 1891): 918.
21 Mrs Wynford Phillips, *An Appeal to Women*, Westminster Women's Liberal Association Leaflet, c. 1890, Women's Library, London Metropolitan University.
22 Laura Nym Mayhall, *The Militant Suffragette Movement* (New York, 2003); Marian Sawer, "Gender, Metaphor and the State," *Feminist Review* 52, no. 1 (1996): 118–34; Stefan Collini, *Public Moralists: Political Thought and Intellectual Life in Britain 1850–1930* (Oxford, 1991).
23 "Lady Councillors" by A Lady, *County Council Magazine* 1 (February–July 1889) (London, 1889): 21
24 Laura Ormiston Chant, "Woman as an Athlete," *The Nineteenth Century* (May 1899): 752.
25 "Good Citizenship," a speech given by Miss Bertha Mason, *White Ribbon* 7, no. 11 (September 1903): 173.
26 *Englishwoman's Review* 140 (15 December 1884): 556.
27 *Woman's Signal*, 22 October 1898.
28 Mrs Humphry Ward, "An Appeal against Female Suffrage," *The Nineteenth Century* 25 (June 1889): 781–8.
29 CETS Archives, Annual Church Congress Meeting for Young Women, 30 September 1897, H502.C4, Church of England Archives, Lambeth Palace.
30 Ibid.
31 James Thayne Covert, *A Victorian Marriage: Mandell and Louise Creighton* (London, 2000).
32 Alan Haig, *The Victorian Clergy* (London, 1984); Robert Currie, Alan Gilbert, and Lee Horsley, *Churches and Churchgoers* (Oxford, 1977); Callum Brown, *The Death of Christian Britain: Understanding Secularization 1800–2000* (Abingdon, 2009); Jeremy Morris, "The Strange Death of Christian Britain: Another Look at the Secularization Debate," *Historical Journal (Cambridge, England)* 46, no. 4 (December 2003): 963–76; W.R. Ward, *Religion and Society in England 1790–1850* (London, 1972).
33 Jonathan Rose, *The Edwardian Temperament 1895–1919* (Athens, Ohio, 1986), 1. One of the more telling statistics that Rose cites is the fact that at the beginning of the 1840s Balliol sent half its undergraduates into the priesthood; by the 1890s, only 4 per cent.
34 Brown, *The Death of Christian Britain*; Callum Brown, *Religion and Society in Twentieth Century Britain* (Harlow, 2006). See also Hugh McLeod, *The*

Religious Crisis of the 1960's (Oxford, 2006); Philip Larkin, "Annus Mirabilis," in *Collected Poems*, ed. Anthony Thwaite (New York, 2004), 146.

35 Morris, "The Strange Death of Christian Britain."

36 Lucy C.F. Cavendish, "What is to be done with the Morally Deficient?," *New Review* (March 1890): 212–20.

37 "Enthusiastic Meeting at Westminster Town Hall," *Women's Herald*, 14 February 1891.

38 Lady Frederick Cavendish, *The Diary of Lady Frederick Cavendish*, ed. John Bailey (New York, 1927), 2:22, 15 January 1867.

39 Among them were Annie Leigh Browne, Lady Aberdeen, Florence Balgarnie, and Eva McLaren.

40 George Lansbury organized Jane Cobden's campaign in Brixton; see Patricia Hollis, *Ladies Elect: Women in Local English Government 1865–1914* (New York, 1989), 1; Jonathan Schneer, "Politics and Feminism in 'Outcast London': George Lansbury and Jane Cobden's Campaign for the First London County Council," *Journal of British Studies* 30, no. 1 (January 1991): 63–82.

41 *Miss Emma Cons and Miss Jane Cobden Local Government* 1889, Cobden Family Papers, MSS 348, West Sussex Record Office.

42 Jane Cobden Papers, DN 851, Women's Liberal Federation Archives, Bristol University.

43 Emma Cons's letter to the LCC following the judgment in *Cobden v. De Souza*, *Miss Emma Cons and Miss Jane Cobden Local Government* 1889, Cobden Family Papers, MSS 348.

44 *Miss Emma Cons and Miss Jane Cobden Local Government* 1889, Cobden Family Papers, MSS 348.

45 Emma Cons was also placed on the council-chamber and offices committees, the schools committee, and the following subcommittees: housing, parks, baby farming, Millbank housing.

46 *Miss Emma Cons and Miss Jane Cobden Local Government* 1889, Cobden Family Papers, MSS 348, tribute of the Earl of Meath, 12 March 1923.

47 "Miss Cons and the County Council," *Morning Post*, 1 December 1890, 3.

48 Emily Maurice, *Life of Octavia Hill* (London, 1914), 489.

49 Lady Knightley Fawsley, *The Journals of Lady Knightley of Fawsley*, ed. Peter Gordon (London, 2005), 9 May 1892.

50 27 November 1888, Add MSS 46235 FF. 239, British Library. See also the discussion in chapter 1, above, of the view of Lucy Cavendish, Sophie Bryant, and likely other women that women's education in broad matters of foreign policy and economics was not currently "up to" the stage where they could effectively assess MPs.

51 In doing so the court relied on the 1868 decision in *Chorlton v. Lings*, L.R. 4 C.P. 374, where the court of common pleas ruled that unless expressly stated, statutes using the words "men" or "man" would not be construed to encompass women.
52 Jane Cobden's opponent, E. Rider Cook, a Liberal, had, immediately after the election, written to her that he would in no way challenge her victory and graciously offered her any assistance he might be able to provide. Letter from E. Rider Cook, 21 January 1889, Cobden Family Papers, quoted in Hollis, *Ladies Elect*, 310.
53 Minutes of the WLGS, May 1889, Fawcett Library.
54 Since the objecting councillor, Walter de Souza, was in the position of acting as a common informant, he pocketed half the proceeds of the women's fine, a situation which the Progressive faction in council did not hesitate to taunt him with.
55 *Miss Emma Cons and Miss Jane Cobden Local Government* 1889, Cobden Family Papers, West Sussex Record Office, MSS 348.
56 Ibid.
57 John Williams Benn is more familiar as the grandfather of the Labour politician Tony Benn.
58 Annual Report WLGS, 10 March 1899 A/WLG/27, WLGS Archives, Fawcett Library.
59 *Woman's Signal*, 24 March 1898, 184.
60 *Church of England Temperance Chronicle*, 15 July 1882, 450.
61 *Church Worker* 2 (1883): 42; *Family Churchman*, 20 February 1884, 767.
62 *Church of England Temperance Chronicle*, 17 May 1884, 30.
63 Ibid.
64 Lucy Masterman, unpublished biography of Lucy Cavendish, Lucy Masterman Papers, Lucy Cavendish College Archives, Cambridge University, 202.
65 For example, Mary Sheepshanks, while vice-president of Morley College, also ran for London's County Council in 1909; Lady Knightley of Fawsley was active in the Society for the Promoting the Employment of Women, the Central Society for Women's Suffrage, the Ladies Sanitary Association, and the British Women's Emigration Society; Lady Aberdeen was president of the Society for Promoting the Return of Women as County Councillors, the Women's Liberal Federation, and a variety of directly ameliorative philanthropies.
66 Lord and Lady Aberdeen, *Reminiscences* (London, 1926), 273; Old Vic Archives, OVEC/000232/5, Bristol University.

67 Dina Copelman, "The Gendered Metropolis: Fin de Siècle London," *Radical History Review* 60 (Fall 1994): 38–56.
68 Michelle Tusan, *Women Making News: Gender and Journalism in Modern Britain* (Champaign, Ill., 2005).

Conclusion

1 *Old Vic Magazine* (April 1925): 4.

Bibliography

Archives

British Library, London
Archives of the British Women's Temperance Society, Rosalind Carlisle House, Solihull
Cavendish Family Papers, Chatsworth Archives
Church of England Archives, Lambeth Palace
Church of England Temperance Society (CETS) Archives, Lambeth Palace
Cobden Family Papers, West Sussex Record Office
Jane Cobden Papers, Women's Liberal Federation Archives, Bristol University
Lyttelton Family Papers, Hagley Hall Archives
Lucy Masterman, Biography of Lucy Cavendish, mss, Lucy Masterman Papers, Lucy Cavendish College Archives, Cambridge University
Masterman Family Papers, University of Birmingham Archives
Morley College Archives, Borough of Lambeth Archives, London
National Archives, Royal Commission on Secondary Education, 1895
Archives of the National Union of Women Workers, Fawcett Library
Old Vic Archives, Bristol University
Talbot Family Papers, Centre for Kentish Studies, Kent County Archives, Maidenhead
Graham Wallas Papers, London School of Economics, London
Archives of the Women's Liberal Federation, University of Bristol Archives
Archives of the WLGS (Women's Local Government Society), Fawcett Library
Archives of the Yorkshire Ladies Council of Education, Leeds University

Primary Sources

Aberdeen, Lord and Lady. *Reminiscences*. London, 1926.

Barlee, Ellen. *Pantomime Waifs or A Plea for our City Children*. London, 1884.

Barnett, Henrietta. *Canon Barnett, His Life, Work and Friends*. London, 1918.

Barnett, Samuel. "Human Service." Reprinted in *Practicable Socialism*, 2nd ed., 285–93. London: Practicable Socialism, 1894.

Blackburn, Helen. *A Handbook for Women Engaged in Social and Political Work*. London, 1895.

Burdett-Coutts, Angela. *Woman's Mission*. London and New York, 1893.

Butler, Josephine. *The Constitution Violated*. Edinburgh, 1871.

Cavendish, Lady Frederick. "The Dangers of the Luxury of Modern Life." Women Workers: The Official report of the Conference held at Croydon, 53. London, 1897.

– *The Diary of Lady Frederick Cavendish*. 2 vols. Ed. John Bailey. New York, 1927.

– "Parochial Mission Women." *Mission Life*, vol. 9, part 2. London, 1878.

Chant, Laura Ormiston. "Woman as an Athlete." *The Nineteenth Century* (May 1899): 752.

Cobbe, Frances Powers. "Wife Torture in England." *Contemporary Review* 32 (1878): 55–87.

– "Woman as a Citizen of the State." *The Duties of Women*. London, 1881.

Cons, Emma. "Model Dwellings." *County Council Magazine* (April 1889).

Curzon, George. *Principles and Methods of University Reform*. London, 1909.

Elliott, Jane. *A Servant of the Poor, or Some Account of the Life and Death of a Parochial Mission Woman*. London, 1874.

Encyclopaedia Britannica. "Polytechnic" "Scheme of the City Parochial Charities Act pertaining to educational institutions," 22:40. Cambridge, 1911.

Escott, T.H.S. "Popular Culture in the Crucible." In *Social Transformations of the Victorian Age*. London, 1897.

Fawsley, Lady Knightley. *The Journals of Lady Knightley of Fawsley*. Ed. Peter Gordon. London, 2005.

Forster, E.M. *Howards End*. New York, 1921.

Gladstone, Mary. *Mary Gladstone (Mrs. Drew) Her Diaries and Letters*. Ed. Lucy Masterman. London, 1930.

Gladstone, W.E. *Diaries of William Ewart Gladstone*. Vols 1–13. Oxford, 1994.

Gustafson, Axel. *The Foundation of Death: A Study of the Drink-Question*. London, 1884.

Hamilton, Sir Edward Walter. *Diaries of Sir Edward Walter Hamilton 1883–1885*. Ed. Dudley Bahlman. Oxford, 1972.
Hand, J.E. *Good Citizenship*. London, 1899.
Harcourt, Lewis. *Loulou: Selected Extracts from the Journals of Lewis Harcourt (1880–1895)*. Ed. Patrick Jackson. Danvers, Mass., 2006.
Hardie, Keir. *The Citizenship of Women*. London, 1906.
Haweis, Rev. H.R. *Music and Morals*. 3rd ed. London, 1873.
Hill, Octavia. *Letters to Fellow Workers, 1872–1911*. London, 2005.
Hodder, Edwin. *The Life of Samuel Morley*. London, 1887.
Jameson, Anna. *Communion of Labour*. London, 1859.
Jeune, Lady. *Ladies at Work*. London, 1893.
Kingsley, Charles. *Alton Locke*. Prefatory by Thomas Hughes. Edinburgh, 1881.
Klein, Hermann. *Great Women Singers of My Time*. London, 1931.
– *Thirty Years of Musical Life in London, 1870–1900*. New York, 1903.
A Lady. "Lady Councillors." *County Council Magazine* 1 (February–July 1889): 21.
Lansbury, George. *My Life*. London, 1931.
Liddell, Mrs Edward. *Work in Dark Places*. London, c. 1890.
Lonsdale, Sophia. *The Recollections of Sophia Lonsdale*. Ed. Violet Martineau. London, 1936.
– "Women's Work amongst the Poor." In Lady Jeune, *Ladies at Work*. London, 1893.
Lyttelton, Edith. *Alfred Lyttelton – An Account of His Life*. London, 1917.
Lyttelton, Kathleen. *Women and Their Work*. London. 1901.
Lyttelton, Lady. *Correspondence of Sarah Spencer*. London, 1912.
Mackinder, H.J. *University Extension: Has It a Future?* London, 1890.
Marshall, Florence. "Music and the People." *The Nineteenth Century* (February 1881).
Martineau, Caroline. *Aunt Rachel's Letters on Water and Air*. London, 1871.
– *Chapters on Sound*. London, 1875.
– *Earth, Air and Water; or, The World We Live in*. London, 1881.
Mason, Miss Bertha. "Good Citizenship." *White Ribbon* 7, no. 11 (September 1903): 173.
Maugham, W. Somerset. *Liza of Lambeth*. London, 1953.
Maurice, Frederick. *The Life of Frederick Denison Maurice, Chiefly Told in His Own Letters*. London, 1884.
Mearns, Andrew. *Bitter Cry of Outcast London*. London, 1883.
Meath, Countess of. *Diaries of Mary, Countess of Meath*. Ed. Reginald Brabazon. London, 1900.
Meath, Earl of. *Prosperity or Pauperism*. London, 1888.

Miss Emma Cons and Miss Jane Cobden Local Government. 1889.

More, Hannah. *Coelebs in Search of a Wife*. New York, 1810.

Morrison, Arthur. *Child of the Jago*. London, 1896.

– *Lizerunt*. London, 1894.

"Mrs. Sophie Bryant, D.Sc." *The Woman at Home*. 1897.

Notestein, Wallace. "Lady Frederick Cavendish." In *English Folk*. London, 1938.

Palmer, Roundell. *Memorials, Part I, Family and Personal 1766–1865*. London, 1896.

Pearce, C.E. *Sims Reeves – Fifty Years of Music in England*. London, 1924.

Phillips, Mrs Wynford. *An Appeal to Women*. Westminster Women's Liberal Association Leaflet, c. 1890, Women's Library, London Metropolitan University.

Romanes, George John. "Physiological Selection." *Nineteenth Century* 21 (1887): 59–80.

Ross, Ellen. *Slum Travellers: Ladies and London Poverty, 1860–1920*. Berkeley, 2002.

Schleswig-Holstein, Princess Marie Louise. *Memories of Six Reigns*. London, 1956.

Shore, Louisa. "The Citizenship of Women Socially Considered." *Westminster Review* (July 1874).

Tait, William Archibald. *Catherine and Craufurd Tait, Wife and Son of Archibald Campbell, Archbishop of Canterbury, a Memoir, edited at the Request of the Archbishop*, ed. William Benham. London, 1882.

Talbot, Caroline Jane Stuart. *Parochial Mission Women: Their Work, and Its Fruits* London, 1862.

Taylor, Samuel. "Literary and Musical Entertainments for the People." *Transactions of the National Association for the Promotion of Social Science, London 1858*. London, 1859.

Thompson, Rev. Gerald. "The Church of England Temperance Society's Homes for Inebriates." *British Journal of Inebriety* 10, no. 3 (January 1913): 141–4.

Tuke, Dr Hack. *A Dictionary of Psychological Medicine*. Philadelphia, 1892.

Twining, Louisa. *Recollections of Workhouse Visiting and Managing during Twenty-Five Years*. London, 1880.

– *Workhouses and Women's Work*. London, 1858.

Ward, Mary (Mrs Humphry). "An Appeal against Female Suffrage." *Nineteenth Century* 25 (June 1889): 781–8.

Watherston, Edward J. "A National Necessity." In *Prosperity or Pauperism*, ed. the Earl of Meath. London, 1888.

Webb, Beatrice. *The Diary of Beatrice Webb, Volume One 1873–1892*. Ed. Norman and Jeanne MacKenzie. London, 1982.
– *My Apprenticeship*. Cambridge, 1979.
– *Our Partnership*. Cambridge, 1975.
Williams, Harcourt. *The Old Vic Saga*. London, 1949.
"A Woman's Work on the County Council." *Pall Mall Gazette*, 14 February 1890.
"Women as Citizens." *Englishwoman's Review*, 16 October 1899, 283.
Wood, Vice-Chancellor William Page (Lord Hatherley). "Parochial Mission Women: A Paper Read at the Church Congress, 1863." London, 1864.
Woolf, Virginia. *Flight of the Mind: The Letters of Virginia Woolf, 1888–1912*. Ed. Nigel Nicolson. London, 1975.
– *Mrs. Dalloway*. New York, 2005. http://dx.doi.org/10.5117/9781904633242.

Newspapers and Periodicals

The Birmingham Daily Post
The Calcutta Liberal and New Dispensation
Church of England Temperance Chronicle
Coffee Public-House News and Temperance Hotel Journal
County Council Magazine
The Country Gentleman
The Court and High Life
Daily News
Donohoe's Magazine (Boston)
The Englishwoman's Review of Social and Industrial Questions
The Englishwoman's Year Book
The Era Almanack
Funny Folks
The Graphic
The Illustrated London News
John Bull
Journal du Grande Monde
Judy or the London Serio-Comic Journal
Man about Town
Moonshine
The Morning Post
The Musical Times
Newcastle Courant
The New York Times

The New Zealand Tablet
The Nineteenth Century
The Old Vic Magazine
Pall Mall Gazette
Penny Illustrated Paper
Punch
Review of Reviews
Royal Cornish Gazette and Falmouth Packet
Shafts: A Magazine for Progressive Thought
Sporting Times
The Sunday Circle
Sussex Daily News
Vanity Fair
Waverley
Westminster Gazette
The Woman at Home
The Woman's Signal
The Women's Penny Paper
Work and Leisure

Secondary Sources

Books

Anderson, Anne. "Bringing Beauty Home to the People." In *Women and the Making of Built Space in England 1870-1950*, ed. Elizabeth Darling. London, 2007.

Ariès, Philip. *Western Attitudes towards Death, The Hour of Our Death*. New York, 1981.

Askwith, Betty. *The Lytteltons: A Family Chronicle of the Nineteenth Century*. London, 1975.

Auchmuty, Rosemary. "By Their Friends We Shall Know Them: The Lives and Networks of Some Women in North Lambeth 1880–1940." In *Not a Passing Phase: Reclaiming Lesbians in History 1840–1985*, ed. Lesbian History Group. London, 1989.

Bailey, Peter. *Leisure and Class in Victorian England: Rational Recreation and the Contest for Control, 1830–1850*. London, 1987.

Battiscombe, Georgina. *Mrs. Gladstone*. London, 1957.

Beaven, Brad. *Leisure, Citizenship and Working-Class Men in Britain, 1850–1945*. Manchester, 2005.

Bell, E. Moberley. *Octavia Hill, A Biography*. London, 1942.

Bell, Quentin. *Virginia Woolf*. New York, 1972.

Benson, Edward White. *Phoebe, the Servant of the Church*. London, 1873.

Biagini, Eugenio. "Liberalism and Direct Democracy: J.S. Mill and the Model of Ancient Athens." In *Citizenship and Community: Liberals, Radicals and Collective Identities in the British Isles 1865–1931*. Princeton, 1996.

Blake, Catriona. *The Charge of the Parasols: Women's Entry into the Medical Profession*. London, 1990.

Blocker, Jack S., Jr, David M. Fahey, and Ian R. Tyrrell, eds. *Alcohol and Temperance: A Modern History: A Global Encyclopedia*. Santa Barbara, 2003.

Booth, John. *A Century of Theatrical History 1816–1916: The Old Vic*. London, 1917.

Boyd, Nancy. *Three Victorian Women Who Changed Their World: Josephine Butler, Octavia Hill, Florence Nightingale*. London, 1982.

Bradley, Katharine. *Poverty, Philanthropy and the State: Charities and the Working Classes in London, 1918–79*. Manchester, 2009.

Britain, Ian. *Fabianism and British Culture: A Study in British Socialism and the Arts*. Cambridge, 2005.

Brown, Callum. *The Death of Christian Britain: Understanding Secularization 1800–2000*. Abingdon, 2009.

Burman, Susan. *Fit Work for Women*. New York, 1977.

Bush, Julia. "The National Union of Women Workers and Women's Suffrage." In *Suffrage outside Suffragism*, ed. Myriam Boussahba-Bavard. Basingstoke, 2007.

– *Women against the Vote: Female Anti-Suffragism in Britain*. Oxford, 2007.

Cannadine, David. "War and Death: Grieving and Death in Modern Britain." In *Mirrors of Mortality: Studies in the Social History of Death*, ed. J. Whaley. London, 1981.

Chalus, Elaine. "That Epidemical Madness: Women and Electoral Politics in the Late Eighteenth Century." In Hannah Barker and Elaine Chalus, *Gender in Eighteenth-Century England: Roles, Representations and Responsibilities*. London and New York, 1997.

Clark, Anna. "Gender, Class and the Nation: Franchise Reform in England, 1832–1928." In *Re-reading the Constitution: New Narratives in the Political History of England's Long Nineteenth Century*, ed. James Vernon. Cambridge, 1996.

Cockram, Gill G. *Ruskin and Social Reform: Ethics and Economics in the Victorian Age*. London, 2007.

Colley, Linda. *Britons: Forging the Nation, 1707–1837*. New Haven, 1992.

Collini, Stefan. *Public Moralists: Political Thought and Intellectual Life in Britain 1850–1930*. Oxford, 1991.

Copelman, Dina. "The Gendered Metropolis." *Radical History Review* 60 (Fall 1994): 38–56.

– *London's Women Teachers: Gender, Class and Feminism 1870–1930*. New York, 1996.

Covert, James Thayne. *A Victorian Marriage: Mandell and Louise Creighton*. London, 2000.

Craig, David. *John Ruskin and the Ethics of Consumption*. Charlottesville, 2006.

Currie, Robert, Alan Gilbert, and Lee Horsley. *Churches and Churchgoers*. Oxford, 1977.

Daggers, Jenny, and Diana Neal, eds. *Sex, Gender, and Religion: Josephine Butler Revisited*. New York, 2006.

Darley, Gillian. *Octavia Hill*. London, 1990.

Daugherty, Beth Rigel. "Morley College and Virginia Woolf." In *Virginia Woolf and Her Influences*, ed. Laura Davis and Jeanette McVicker. London, 1998.

Davidoff, Lenore. *The Best Circles: Social Etiquette and the Season*. London, 1973.

– *Worlds Between: Historical Perspectives on Gender and Class*. New York, 1995.

Davidoff, Lenore, and Catherine Hall. *Family Fortunes*. Chicago, 1987.

Digby, Anne, and John Stewart, eds. *Gender, Health and Welfare*. London, 1996.

Englander, David, and Rosemary O'Day. *Retrieved Riches: Social Investigation in Britain, 1840–1914*.

Fieldhouse, Roger. *A History of Modern British Adult Education*. Leicester, 1996.

– *The Workers' Educational Association: Aims and Achievements, 1903–1977*. Syracuse, 1977.

Findlater, Richard. *Lilian Baylis: The Lady of the Old Vic*. London, 1975.

Finlayson, Geoffrey. *Citizenship, State and Social Welfare in Britain 1830–1990*. Oxford, 1994.

Fletcher, Ian. "Some Aspects of Aestheticism." In *Twilight of the Dawn: Studies in English Literature*, ed. O.M. Brack, Jr. Tucson, 1987.

Fletcher, Sheila. *Victorian Girls: Lord Lyttelton's Daughters*. London, 1997.

Foreman, Amanda. *Georgiana, Duchess of Devonshire*. London, 1998.

Frow, Ruth. *Political Women 1800–1850*. London, 1989.

Gilbert, Pamela K. *The Citizen's Body*. Cleveland, 2007.

Gillett, Paula. *Musical Women in England: Encroaching on All Man's Privileges*. New York, 2000.

Gleadle, Kathryn. *Borderline Citizens: Women, Gender and Political Culture in Britain 1815–1867*. Oxford, 2009.

– *British Women in the Nineteenth Century*. Basingstoke, 2001.

Gleadle, Kathryn, and Sarah Richardson, eds. *Women in British Politics 1760–1860: The Power of the Petticoat*. Basingstoke and New York, 2000.

Glick, Daphne. *The National Council of Women of Great Britain: The First One Hundred Years, 1895–1994*. Ipswich, 1995.
Goldman, Lawrence. *Dons and Workers: Oxford and Adult Education since 1850*. Oxford, 1994.
Gooddie, Sheila. *Mary Gladstone: Gentle Rebel*. London, 2003.
Gordon, Eleanor, and Gwyneth Nair. *Public Lives: Women, Family and Society in Victorian Britain*. New Haven, 2003.
Greenlee, Robert. *John Logie Baird, the Man Who Invented Television*. Bloomington, 2010.
Haig, Alan. *The Victorian Clergy*. London, 1984.
Hall, Catherine, Jane Rendall, and Keith McClelland. *Defining the Victorian Nation: Class, Race, Gender and the Second Reform Act of 1867*. Cambridge, 2000.
Hallet, Nicky. *Lesbian Lives: Identity and Autobiography in the Twentieth Century*. London, 1999.
Hamilton, Cicely, and Lilian Baylis. *The Old Vic*. London, 1926.
Harrison, Brian. *Separate Spheres: The Opposition to Women's Suffrage*. London, 1978.
Harrop, Sylvia. *Oxford and Working-Class Education*. Nottingham, 1987.
Heeney, Brian. *The Women's Movement in the Church of England 1850–1930*. Oxford, 1988.
Hilton, Boyd. *The Age of Atonement: The Influence of Evangelicalism on Social and Economic Thought 1795–1865*. Oxford, 1988.
Hollis, Patricia. *Ladies Elect: Women in Local English Government 1865–1914*. London, 1987.
Holst, Imogen. *Holst*. London, 1974.
– *The Music of Gustav Holst*. London, 1951.
Jackson, Patrick. *Harcourt and Son: A Political Biography of Sir William Harcourt, 1827–1904*. Cranbury, NJ, 2004.
Jalland, Pat. *Death in the Victorian Family*. New York, 1996.
– *Women, Marriage and Politics 1860–1914*. Oxford, 1986.
Keane, Melba Cuddy. *Virginia Woolf: The Intellectual and the Public Sphere*. Cambridge, 2003.
Keating, P.J. *Working-Class Stories of the 1890's*. London, 1971.
Kidd, Alan. *State, Society and the Poor in Nineteenth-Century England*. London, 1999.
King, Steven. *Women, Welfare and Local Politics 1880–1920*. Eastbourne, 2006.
Koven, Seth. *Slumming: Sexual and Social Politics in Victorian London*. Princeton, 2004.
– "The Whitechapel Picture Exhibitions and the Politics of Seeing." In *Museum Culture*, ed. D. Sherman and I. Rogoff. Minneapolis, 1994.
Kriegel, Lara. "The Yorkshire Ladies Council of Education." Unpublished MA thesis, University of Leeds.

Krishnamurthy, Aruna. *The Working-Class Intellectual in Eighteenth- and Nineteenth Century Britain*. Burlington, VT, 2009.

Lang, Michael. *Designing Utopia: John Ruskin's Urban Vision for Britain and America*. Montreal, 1999.

Levine, Philippa. *Feminist Lives in Victorian England: Private Roles and Public Commitment*. Oxford, 1991.

Lewis, Jane E. *Women and Social Action in Victorian and Edwardian England*. Stanford, 1991.

Livesey, Ruth. *Socialism, Sex and the Culture of Aestheticism*. London, 2006.

Maguire, G.E. *Conservative Women: A History of Women and the Conservative Party, 1874–1997*. London, 1998.

Maltz, Diana. *British Aestheticism and the Urban Working Classes 1870–1900: Beauty for the People*. Basingstoke, 2006.

– "Delicate Brains." In *Women and British Aestheticism*, ed. Talia Shaffer. Charlottesville, 1999.

Mandler, Peter. *Aristocratic Government in the Age of Reform: Whigs and Liberals 1830–1852*. Oxford, 1990.

Mandler, Peter, and Susan Pedersen. *After the Victorians: Private Conscience and Public Duty in Modern Britain*. London, 1994.

Maurice, C. Edmund. *Life of Octavia Hill as Told in Her Letters*. London, 1913.

Maurice, Emily S., ed. *Octavia Hill: Early Ideas, from Letters*. London, 1928.

Mayhall, Laura Nym. *The Militant Suffragette Movement*. New York, 2003.

McDonald, Deborah. *Clara Collet, 1860–1948: An Educated Working Woman*. London, 2004.

McKibbin, Ross. "Why Was There No Marxism in Great Britain?" In McKibbin, *The Ideologies of Class: Social Relations in Britain 1880–1950*, 1–41. Oxford, 1990.

McLeod, Hugh. *Class and Religion in the Late Victorian City*. London, 1974.

Meacham, Standish. *Toynbee Hall and Social Reform 1880–1914: The Search for Community*. New Haven, 1987.

Meller, Helen. *Leisure and the Changing City 1870–1914*. London, 1976.

Midgley, Clare. *Feminism and Empire: Women Activists in Imperial Britain 1790–1865*. Abingdon, 2007.

Morgan, Simon. *A Victorian Woman's Place: Public Culture in the Nineteenth Century*. London, 2007.

Murdoch, Lydia. *Imagined Orphans: Poor Families, Child Welfare and Contested Citizenship in London*. London, 2006.

Niessen, Olwen Claire. *Aristocracy, Temperance and Social Reform: The Life of Lady Henry Somerset*. London, 2007.

Nord, Deborah Epstein. *The Apprenticeship of Beatrice Webb*. Amherst, Mass., 1985.

Norman, Edward. *The Victorian Christian Socialists*. Cambridge, 2002.

Oddy, Derek, and Derek Miller. *The Making of the Modern British Diet*. London, 1976.

Olsen, Gerald Wayne. "Drink and the British Establishment." Unpublished manuscript, 2009.

Parker, Julia. *Citizenship, Work and Welfare: Searching for the Good Society*. Basingstoke, 1998.

– *Women and Welfare: Ten Victorian Women in Public Social Service*. London, 1989.

Pedersen, Susan. *Eleanor Rathbone and the Politics of Conscience*. New Haven, 2004.

Pennybacker, Susan. *A Vision for London 1889–1914: Labour, Everyday Life, and the LCC Experiment*. London, 1995.

Poovey, Mary. *Making a Social Body: Cultural Formation 1830–1864*. Chicago, 1995.

Pope, Barbara Corrado. "Angels in the Devil's Workshop: Leisured and Charitable Women in Nineteenth Century England and France." In *Becoming Visible: Women in European History*, ed. Renate Bridenthal and Claudia Koonz. Boston, 1977.

Prochaska, Frank. *Christianity and Social Service in Modern Britain: The Disinherited Spirit*. Oxford, 2006.

– *Schools of Citizenship: Charity and Civic Virtue*. London, 2002.

– *Women and Philanthropy in Nineteenth-Century England*. Oxford, 1980.

Pugh, Martin. *The March of the Women: A Revisionist Analysis of the Campaign for Women's Suffrage 1866–1914*. Oxford, 2000.

Purvis, June. *Hard Lessons: The Lives and Education of Working-Class Women in Nineteenth-Century England*. Cambridge, 1989.

Rendall, Jane. "Citizenship, Culture and Civilisation: The Languages of British Suffragists 1866–1874." In *Suffrage and Beyond: International Feminist Perspectives*, ed. Melanie Nolan and Caroline Daley. New York, 1994.

– "The Citizenship of Women and the Reform Act of 1867." In *Defining the Victorian Nation*, ed. Catherine Hall, Keith McClelland, and Jane Rendall. Cambridge, 2000.

– *Equal or Different: Women's Politics 1800–1914*. Oxford, 1987.

Reynolds, K.D. *Aristocratic Women and Political Society in Victorian England*. Oxford, 1998.

Reynolds, K.D., and Peter Mandler. "From Allmack's to Willis': Aristocratic Women and Politics 1815–1867." In *Women, Privilege and Power: British Politics 1750 to the Present*, ed. Amanda Vickery. London, 2001.

Richards, Denis. *Offspring of the Vic: A History of Morley College*. London, 1958.

Roberts, S.K. *A Ministry of Enthusiasm: Centenary Essay on the WEA*. London, 2003.

Rose, Jonathan. *The Edwardian Temperament 1895–1919*. Athens, Ohio, 1986.

– *The Intellectual Life of the British Working Classes*. New Haven, 2001.

Rowell, George. *The Old Vic Theatre: A History*. Cambridge, 1993.

Royle, Edward. *Victorian Infidels: The Origins of the British Secularist Movement 1791–1866*. Manchester, 1974.

Rubinstein, David. *A Different World for Women: The Life of Millicent Garrett Fawcett*. Brighton, 1991.

Schafer, Elizabeth. *Lilian Baylis: A Biography*. Hatfield, 2006.

Scotland, Nigel. *Squires in the Slums: Settlements and Missions in Late Victorian London*. London, 2007.

Shiman, Lillian. *Crusade against Drink in Victorian England*. London, 1988.

– *Women and Leadership in Nineteenth-Century England*. London, 1992.

Speaight, Robert. *William Poel and the Elizabethan Revival*. London, 1954.

Stansky, Peter. *Redesigning the World: William Morris, the 1880's and the Arts and Crafts*. Princeton, 1985.

Stedman Jones, Gareth. *Outcast London: A Study in the Relationship between Classes in Victorian Society*. London, 1984.

Summers, Anne. *Female Lives, Moral States: Women, Religion and Public Life in Britain, 1800–1930*. Newbury, 2000.

Sutherland, G. "The Movement for the Higher Education of Women: Its Social and Intellectual Context in England, 1840–1880." In *Politics and Social Change in Modern Britain: Essays Presented to A.F. Thompson*, ed. P.J. Waller. London, 1987.

Thane, Pat. "Late Victorian Women." In *Later Victorian Britain*, ed. Terry Gourvish and Alan O'Day. London, 1988.

Thompson, F.M.L. *The Rise of Respectable Society*. London, 1988.

Vernon, James. *Politics and the People*. Cambridge, 1993.

Vicinus, Martha. *Independent Women: Work and Community for Single Women 1850–1920*. Chicago, 1985.

– *Suffer and Be Still: Women in the Victorian Age*. Bloomington, 1972.

Vincent, David. *Bread, Knowledge and Freedom: A Study of Working Class Autobiography*. New York, 1982.

Wahrman, Dror. *Imagining the Middle Class: The Political Representation of Class in Britain, c. 1780–1840*. Cambridge, 1995.

Walker, Pamela. *Pulling the Devil's Kingdom Down: The Salvation Army in Victorian Britain*. London, 2001.

Walkowitz, Judith. *City of Dreadful Delight: Narratives of Sexual Danger in Late-Victorian London*. Chicago, 1992.

Ward, W.R. *Religion and Society in England 1790–1850*. London, 1972.

Waterfield, Giles. *Art for the People: Culture in the Slums of Late Victorian Britain*. Dulwich, 2000.

Waters, Chris. *British Socialists and the Politics of Popular Culture*. Palo Alto, 1990.

Weltman, Sharon Aronofsky. *Performing the Victorian: John Ruskin and Identity in Theater, Science, and Education*. Cleveland, 2007.

Wiener, Martin. *Between Two Worlds: The Political Thought of Graham Wallas*. Oxford, 1971.

Williams, S.C. *Religious Belief and Popular Culture in Southwark 1880–1939*. Oxford, 1999.

Wohl, Anthony. *Endangered Lives: Public Health in Victorian Britain*. London, 1984.

Zakreski, Patricia. *Representing Female Artistic Labour 1848–1890: Refining Work for the Middle-Class Woman*. Aldershot, 2006.

Articles

Anderson, Anne. "Octavia Hill's Fellow Workers: Lady Ducie and Lady Brabazon, Wealth, Power and Vocational Philanthropy." *Women's History Review*.

– "Queen Victoria's Daughters and the 'Tide of Fashionable Philanthropy.'" *Women's History Magazine* 41 (June 2002): 10–15.

Bird, Elizabeth. "To Cook or to Conjugate: Gender and Class in the Adult Curriculum 1865–1900." *Gender and Education* 3, no. 2 (1991): 183–97.

Budge, Geoffrey. "Poverty and the Picture Gallery: The Whitechapel Exhibitions and the Social Project of Ruskinian Aesthetics." *Visual Culture in Britain* 1 (2000): 43–56.

Dingle, A.E. "Drink and Working-Class Living Standards in Britain 1870–1914." *Economic History Review* 25, no. 4 (1972): 608–22.

Fowler, R. "On Not Knowing Greek." *Classical Journal* 78, no. 4 (April–May 1983): 337–49.

Gerard, Jessica. "Lady Bountiful: Women of the Landed Classes and Rural Philanthropy." *Victorian Studies* 30 (Winter 1987): 183–210.

Goldman, Lawrence. "Intellectuals and the English Working Class 1870–1945: The Case of Adult Education." *History of Education* 29, no. 4 (2000): 281–300.

Goodman, Joyce. "Constructing Contradiction: The Power and Powerlessness of Women in the Giving and Taking of Evidence in the Bryce Commission 1895." *History of Education* 26, no. 3 (1997): 287–306.

Harrison, Brian. "Oxford and the Labor Movement." *Twentieth Century British History* 3 (1991): 226–71.

– "Philanthropy and the Victorians." *Victorian Studies* 4 (1966): 353–74.

Hunt, G., J. Mellor, and J. Turner. "Wretched, Hatless and Miserable Clad: Women and the Inebriate Reformatories 1900–1913." *British Journal of Sociology* 40, no. 2 (1989): 244–70.

Kelly, Serena. "A Sisterhood of Service: The Records and Early History of the National Union of Women Workers." *Journal of the Society of Archivists* 14, no. 2 (1993): 167–74.

Levine, Philippa. "So Few Prizes and So Many Blanks: Marriage and Feminism in Later Nineteenth-Century England." *Journal of British Studies* 28, no. 2 (April 1989): 150–74.

Livesey, Ruth. "Reading for Character: Women Social Reformers and Narratives of the Urban Poor in Late Victorian and Edwardian London." *Journal of Victorian Culture* 9, no. 1 (Spring 2004): 43–68.

Morris, Jeremy. "The Strange Death of Christian Britain: Another Look at the Secularization Debate." *Historical Journal (Cambridge, England)* 46, no. 4 (December 2003): 963–76.

Mumm, Susan. "'Not Worse Than Other Girls': The Convent-Based Rehabilitation of Fallen Women in Victorian Britain." *Journal of Social History* 29, no. 3 (Spring 1996): 527–46.

Nord, Deborah Epstein. "'Neither Pairs nor Odd': Female Community in Late Nineteenth-Century London." *Signs* 15, no. 4 (Summer 1990): 733–54.

Pedersen, Susan. "Gender, Welfare, and Citizenship in Britain during the Great War." *American Historical Review* 95, no. 4 (October 1990): 983–1006.

Peterson, M.J. "No Angels in the House: The Victorian Myth and the Paget Women." *American Historical Review* 89, no. 3 (June 1984): 677–708.

Philips, Anne, and Tim Putnam. "Education for Emancipation: The movement for Independent Working Class Education 1908-1928." *Capital and Class* 4, no. 1 (Spring 1980): 18–42.

Purvis, June. "'Women's Life Is Essentially Domestic, Public Life Being Confined to Men' (Comte): Separate Spheres and Inequality in the Education of Working Class Women 1854–1900." *History of Education* 10, no. 4 (1981): 227–43.

– "Towards a History of Women's Education in Nineteenth Century Logical Analysis." *Westminster Studies in Education* 4, no. 1 (1981): 45–79.

– "Working-Class Women and Adult Education in Nineteenth-Century Britain." *History of Education* 9, no. 3 (1980): 193–212.

Reed, John. "Healthy Intercourse: The Beginnings of the Working Men's College." *Browning Institute Studies* 16, special issue on Victorian Learning (1988): 77–90.

Rendall, Jane. "Women and the Public Sphere." *Gender and History* 11, no. 3 (1999): 475–88.

Rose, Jonathan. "The Workers in the Workers' Educational Association, 1903–1950." *Albion* 21, no. 4 (Winter 1989): 591.

Rowbotham, Sheila. "Travellers in a Strange Country: Responses of Working-Class Students to the University Extension Movement – 1873–1910." *History Workshop Journal* 12, no. 1 (1981): 62–95.

Sawer, Marian. "Gender, Metaphor and the State." *Feminist Review* 52, no. 1 (1996): 118–34.

Schneer, Jonathan. "Politics and Feminism in 'Outcast London': George Lansbury and Jane Cobden's Campaign for the First London County Council." *Journal of British Studies* 30, no. 1 (January 1991): 63–82.

Vickery, Amanda. "Golden Age to Separate Spheres? A Review of the Categories and Chronology of English Women's History." *Historical Journal (Cambridge, England)* 36, no. 2 (1993): 383–414.

Woollacott, Angela. "From Moral to Professional Authority: Secularism, Social Work and Middle-Class Women's Self-Construction in WWI Britain." *Journal of Women's History* 10, no. 2 (Summer 1998): 85–111.

Index

www.ingramcontent.com/pod-product-compliance
Lightning Source LLC
LaVergne TN
LVHW090152080826
844660LV00013B/775/J

* 9 7 8 1 4 4 2 6 4 2 3 1 7 *